Lions, Donkeys and Dinosaurs

Lewis Page began his military career as a reservist pilot and ended up in the Navy, where he became a mine clearance diver and qualified as a commando. After eight years at sea, mostly in very bad weather, he was put in charge of the Plymouth diving and bomb disposal team and trawled the British coastline from Swanage to Liverpool. As such, he is one of the few in the British forces to have actually seen and dealt with 'weapons of mass destruction', although of British manufacture.

LIONS, DONKEYS AND DINOSAURS

Waste and Blundering in the Armed Forces

LEWIS PAGE

Preface by Harold Evans

WILLIAM HEINEMANN : LONDON

Published in the United Kingdom by William Heinemann, 2006

1 3 5 7 9 10 8 6 4 2

William Heinemann
The Random House Group Limited
20 Vauxhall Bridge Road, London, SW1V 2SA

Random House Australia (Pty) Limited
20 Alfred Street, Milsons Point, Sydney
New South Wales 2061, Australia

Random House New Zealand Limited
18 Poland Road, Glenfield
Auckland 10, New Zealand

Random House (Pty) Limited
Isle of Houghton, Corner of Boundary Road and Carse O'Gowrie
Houghton 2198, South Africa

The Random House Group Limited Reg. No. 954009

www.randomhouse.co.uk

A CIP catalogue record for this book
is available from the British Library

Papers used by Random House are natural, recyclable products made from wood grown in sustainable forests. The manufacturing processes conform to the environmental regulations of the country of origin

ISBN 0 434 01389 7

Typeset in Sabon by
Palimpsest Book Production Limited, Polmont, Stirlingshire

Printed and bound in Great Britain by
Clays Ltd, St Ives plc

Strength of my country whilst I bring to view
Such as are mis-called captains, and wrong you
And your high names, I do desire that thence
Be not put on you, nor take offence

from the poem 'To True Soldiers'
by Ben Jonson

Contents

Introduction   1

 1. Men with Guns   15

 2. Tanks   49

 3. Artillery   65

 4. Helicopters   79

 5. Fighters   103

 6. Bombers   127

 7. Logistics   165

 8. Warships   187

 9. Brass Hats and Rear Echelons   219

10. The British Defence Industry   243

11. Politics   271

12. Over To You   293

Table of Ranks   308

Glossary   309

Index   349

Preface

As a young officer in the Royal Navy, Lewis Page chose a specialism that is basically dangerous all the time, that of the mine-clearance diver. At Cambridge he was in both the Officer Training Corps and the Air Squadron. For light relief, he underwent the all-arms commando course run by the Royal Marines and is thus entitled to wear the green beret. As well as adrenalin, these activities stimulated thought – quite startling thought about the men and mechanisms charged with the defence of Britain. He is able to share his observations with the rest of us because he has terminated his military career; he could see it was destined to take him away from the sharp end of the business and further and further into uninspiring administration.

The first thing to say about his book is that it is not boring. In fact, it is riveting. This is a fairly important quality since the more people who read it and become restive, the better chance we and our children have of getting alive out of some nasty scenarios bound to be heading our way given the number of crazies in the world and the lethality of the instruments of death they can get their hands on. Yes, you have heard the one about weapons of mass destruction before, but our failure to find any in Iraq doesn't mean we have suddenly been rendered invulnerable. Whoever you want to blame for the hostility directed at citizens in the West from various obvious quarters and some less obvious, the fact remains that when civilised discourse is exhausted, we may have to fight for our lives – as we have already fought for the lives of innocents in the Balkans and should in all conscience have fought in Rwanda and Darfur.

Of course, the 'we' in that sentence is generic. We delegate our protection to the armed services and Page brilliantly documents two things: the few hundred thousand people in the real fighting units are brave and resourceful, and for the last two decades we have served them with dud rifles, poor boots, shoddy light machine guns, substandard fighter planes, and escort ships whose only real use is as venues for diplomatic cocktail parties. We citizens pay our taxes which pay for the warships, planes and army battalions, but that is about all we do. What Scotty Reston once said of Latin America is true of defence: we will do everything for defence except read about it. I had no idea until I read this book that so much money had been spent in recent decades to so little purpose, and is still being spent. The planet of bleak military acronyms is not one we are inclined to visit. It seems remote and bewildering; the authorities don't provide maps and the press can't sustain attention to detail, except on those occasions like the death from friendly fire of Sergeant Steve Roberts when it scents a political quarry. In the meantime, the real story escapes informed scrutiny.

Page pursues the real story with a genuine passion for the men (and very few women) who do the fighting. He has a gift for explication married to an unusual combination of tenacity and wit. He assembles the ranks, tells us what they do, how they are organised, and then describes how we fit them out, at what cost, and just why we do not get value for our 30 billion or so. The political priority for both Tory and Labour governments hasn't been the squaddie, it's been the industrial worker; it's not the fighter wing, it's the huge conglomerate called British Aerospace (BAE), the arms makers who make deals with the plenitude of military brass. Why on earth, Page asks, are we cutting back on our excellent infantrymen? The answer he gives is that we are squandering umpteen billions on other ventures, especially the 'Euro-collaborative mess' of the Eurofighter, which is not required in the numbers ordered, is very absurdly expensive, and very late. 'All that we have really bought is the continued existence of British Aerospace which is hardly very useful: as long as it continues to exist, we will probably have to keep giving it money.'

One of the most revealing accounts is how we acquired the fine Apache attack helicopter. We could have bought it fairly cheaply from the Americans who had already paid for its development and built 800. Instead, we set up an entire production line at Westlands to make just 67 Apaches. The cost of doing that was around £2.5 billion. Everyone likes the idea of doing our own thing, especially MPs of both parties with constituency interests, but it's an absurd way of providing welfare for British workers and deeply reckless and irresponsible when one consequence is to send sons and daughters into harm's way without the right equipment. The home-built Apaches cost us nearly £40 million each. That was triple the going rate; Israel got its Apaches for less than £12 million apiece. 'We could have bought the helos direct from Boeing,' he writes, 'then simply given the 755 jobless people a million pounds each – surely enough to set them up for life – and saved ourselves a billion.' It was the same story with the airborne early warning aircraft. We could have bought the American AWACS E-3 but spent a billion pounds developing the Nimrod. Its radar did not work and some bold uniformed people risked their necks saying so. When it was cancelled we had nothing to show for our billion.

What maddens Page, though he is a satirist rather than a shouter, is that a quarter of one of these lost billions could provide the front-line infantryman with a 50 per cent rise in his abysmal pay and give him really good boots and an excellent new rifle every year.

The misdirection Page analyses so well is deep seated. It is not the work of evil or consistently stupid men: some good decisions are made. It is systemic, a consequence of confusion about our role and our capacity, the risks endemic in long-term investment in the technology of arms, misplaced sentiment, service jealousies, expediency, greed, and muddled priorities – all important but all critically aggravated by habitual secrecy in government Ministries and corporations and, with very few exceptions, lamentably lax scrutiny from press and Parliament.

In 1958, as a young newspaper reporter I was dispatched to Germany to find out what I could about the readiness of the British Army of the Rhine. The battalions I stayed with were the common soldiers Page characterises as 'lions led by donkeys'. At the Ministry level I did not get very far, but on the ground officers and men surprised me by the frankness of their comments on the shortcomings of their equipment, the antique rifle and the radios that would only work if the signaller risked transmitting from the top of a haystack and could not transmit at all at night. The stories I wrote led to a little rumble in Parliament. Page's examination is much more wide-ranging and much more thorough – my RAF days are no comparison to his in the Navy – and ought to provoke a more sustained response. Achieving more rational defence procurement will need the best brains we have and a steely resolve. There are many vested interests, many careers and pensions at stake. Administrations come and go.

Perhaps it is too much to hope that this penetrating and patriotic analysis will rouse press and Parliament to perform their duties better over the next decades. I wouldn't count on it. Perhaps we would get some enlightenment from a probing Royal Commission with a sense of urgency. For now, we can just be glad that Lieutenant Page decided not to be a donkey.

Introduction

During World War I the British Army was famously described as 'lions led by donkeys'. The lions were the heroically brave and long-suffering common soldiers of the day – and perhaps their equally brave junior officers, who shared their men's dangers and many of their hardships. The donkeys were the commanding generals, who shared neither risk nor hardship, wasted their soldiers' lives with incredible profligacy, and condemned them to conditions which were literally hell on earth while failing all the while to achieve useful results.

The lions are still around. Today's front-line British servicemen and women are every bit the equal of the excellent regulars of 1914, though far fewer in number. The training, contrary to popular perception, is often harsher than it was then, and generally more relevant to the job in hand. The basic human material is the same or better; less inured to hardship than the young men of a century ago, the youth of today make up for this by being better educated and generally better nourished. (Despite many dire prognostications as to the diet of today's kids, it seems unlikely that it has sunk to the levels seen in the slums of the 1890s.) British sharp-end operators in combat for the last few decades – and there has been a fair bit of fighting – may not be unrivalled, but they can fairly be described as unsurpassed.

One might suppose the donkeys to have gone. On those rare occasions when British generals, admirals or air marshals command forces appropriate to their rank these days, they tend to perform at least adequately and occasionally brilliantly. The campaigns of the last four decades have all had successful outcomes, or at any rate acceptable ones, which in military terms is often the same thing. Casualties have tended to be low, almost miraculously low in some cases.

But this had also been the case in the decades before 1914. The mere fact that soldiers armed with repeating rifles, machine guns and artillery had been able to competently slaughter enemies with spears didn't, in the end, turn out to mean that the army was ready to face the Kaiser's men. Even the Boers were more of a handful than they really should have been, and they weren't the only ones to give us a bloody nose in the pre-1914 era.

Similarly, the mere fact that Britain was able to play a part in the shattering American blitzkrieg of 2003 against a hopelessly outclassed and mostly defeatist Iraqi military doesn't mean that all is well with our forces today. Even small numbers of guerillas can still give us a very hard time, as we have seen these thirty years in Northern Ireland. At least we have – painfully slowly – learned some valuable military lessons from the long troubles there. Two decades ago in the South Atlantic, Argentine aviators gave a seminar which was bloodier and costlier yet, and those lessons we have failed to learn, just as British officers at the turn of the last century often failed to learn when they had the chance. It seems that some donkeys may still be around.

In certain respects, too, our military establishment was actually much better and more efficient in 1914. British soldiers at least had good rifles, machine guns and artillery back then – the latest kit – even if their commanders often didn't know how to use such tools. British sailors went to sea in warships which were at least adequate to meet the threat they were facing. The big-gun dreadnoughts of the late 19th and early 20th centuries were perhaps the first of the great defence projects, engines of war so expensive that even the great powers struggled to afford handfuls of them. But older types of ship had no more chance against the dreadnoughts than spearmen have against machine guns; if a navy wanted to win – or even survive – a serious fight, it had to change the way it did business. Simply purchasing updated versions of what it already had would not do. The Royal Navy, in the run-up to 1914, made such a change: it shifted emphasis completely to the new technology, with an attendant restructuring of careers and personnel. It was able to face dangerous German opposition on tolerably equal terms.

The situation today is very different. British soldiers have spent most of the last two decades unhappy in the knowledge that their rifles and light machine guns were among the shoddiest in the world. Worse, Britain is pitifully weak in today's new tools of land warfare (most obviously, battlefield helicopters and close air support) and in the rare cases where these are available soldiers have little access to them. Unsurprisingly, British ground-forces commanders remain poorly acquainted with the use of such things, and tend to favour the methods of bygone years.

The navy's adaptability has gone, too. Our present admirals pour huge resources into combating the enemies of the past even though these have very largely disappeared. When they do consider the threats which are actually out there in today's world, they attempt to use the ineffectual methods which they grew up with rather than proven, practical ones which would involve some changes in the structure of the navy. No 21st-century hole is too round to be filled with the traditional 1970s square naval peg, expensive and damaging as the process of battering it in may be.

And let's not forget that today we are blessed with another huge, hidebound bureaucracy in the form of the Royal Air Force. Back when there was only the army and the navy, there could be only one zone of inter-service conflict. Now we have a minimum of three. The problem of interservice rivalry has thus at least tripled in magnitude, rather than having merely increased by 50%. It has become almost the primary factor in modern military thought – or what passes for military thought. Useful weapons and techniques are ignored or marginalised where they might lessen the prestige of a given service, or require close cooperation with a rival. Needlessly expensive, excessively destructive, sometimes useless and often downright dangerous methods are pursued with fanatical vigour if they seem to offer an advantage in budget or personnel terms. The inter-service warfare is waged with such fury that Britain is robbed of any real ability to change its defence posture: the available resources are always split three ways, no matter where the greatest threat may lie.

And the armed services themselves are by no means the only huge, ponderous critters in the modern British defence establishment. There are plenty more: the Defence Procurement Agency, the Defence Logistics Organisation and BAE Systems plc are only three of the biggest and least responsive. It takes immensely longer to get things done than it used to, despite the fact that events happen and knowledge spreads in the world outside faster than ever. Big, unwieldy monsters which fight terrible battles with each other and run a severe risk of collective disaster – due to changing conditions, better-adapted competitors or perhaps a sudden, cataclysmic event – tend to remind one of dinosaurs. This description fits most of our large, rear-echelon defence organisations very well.

So. We still have a few lions. We have an annoying number of donkeys, too. These latter – as was also sometimes the case in 1914 – may have had previous careers as lions, and may resemble lions at a casual glance, but they still bray like donkeys. Both of these groups, however, have dwindled in significance within our modern defence establishment. The majority of those who are paid from the defence budget work in the dinosaur sector – in huge, stupid, uncontrollable organisations and projects – often battling each other destructively. The lions whose lives are pledged in forfeit for ours deserve better support than this, and we, the taxpayers and voters, deserve better too. The money we spend on defence could easily buy us a powerful, flexible military with a truly global reach. At present, we have only a pale imitation of one. This really ought to change.

Perhaps you don't think so; perhaps you feel that Britain doesn't need any such military. You disapproved of the Iraq invasion of 2003, and the expulsion of Iraqi invaders from Kuwait in 1991 as well. Rather than use violence, you would have preferred to leave the Falkland Islanders under forced Argentine dominion in 1982. Nonetheless, the chances are that you often watch the news and find yourself thinking that *someone* should send troops. East Timor, Sierra Leone, Darfur, Kosovo, Bosnia-Hercegovina, Monrovia, Somalia. Rwanda, for God's sake. And if someone is to send troops, realistically it should be the richest nations of the earth a lot of the time. That puts Britain firmly in the frame.

So, you probably do want the UK to have capable, modern armed forces; certainly, if you pay UK taxes you are paying for such forces to exist. But you aren't getting your money's worth. This means that we need to see some major changes in the Ministry of Defence and the way it does its business.

Such changes are only likely given a serious, informed public debate. History suggests that the only other path to military reform, in Britain anyway, would be a prolonged war against tough opposition. (Even then, assuming a British victory, our military establishment would likely sink swiftly back into its old ways shortly afterwards.) An informed debate can only take place among a knowledgeable and engaged public; and that, sadly, no longer exists in the United Kingdom. The final generations of national servicemen, the last large group of British citizens with first-hand knowledge of their own forces or of military technology, are now retiring. Even second-hand acquaintance is scarce nowadays; today's armed services are so small, in personnel terms, that few modern Britons have serving friends or relatives any longer. The modern Royal Navy has fewer uniformed personnel than many police forces. One is more likely, on average, to know a Manchester police officer than one of Her Majesty's sailors or marines.

The British people support their servicemen and women in general – we are mostly proud of them – but normally we know almost nothing about them, the lives they lead or the jobs they do. In particular, we know very little about the many different tactics, weapons and units, each with its attached service and civilian communities, which compete for public money. Discussion of such matters is semi-open at best. Far more than most public-service professional groups, the British military is today allowed to settle its affairs in-house, without any real public scrutiny. This sort of trust is no longer accorded to doctors, teachers and many others, but the defence establishment is left largely alone. Occasional stories do make the daily news: major procurement decisions, for instance, get wide coverage – always as faits accomplis, however, and generally covered from the viewpoint of business and economics rather than defence. Only the most superficial, non-committal analysis is normally offered.

The quality press produces regular, in-depth supplements on health, education, social policy and so forth; entire mass-audience periodicals are also devoted to these subjects. Hours of broadcast time are similarly allocated, and apparently intelligent discussion of specifics in these fields is easily accessed. Wherever possible, performance and results in non-defence government departments are measured using harsh, cruel numbers and league tables by independent assessors, despite the protests of the professionals concerned. Journalists are relatively free from interference in these areas; anyone can walk into a hospital or a university, and most people in these fields are not muzzled by the relevant ministry to any great degree. The public – the customers, after all – may judge for themselves, and often do.

But what broadsheet produces a weekly defence supplement? Where may one read regular independent reports on the value for money provided by military organisations, as one can for schools and hospitals? True, there are occasional TV programmes, but once one has eliminated fiction and productions with an almost unwholesomely intense interest in the SAS, little is left but documentaries which might as well be ministry PR for all the serious information they contain. A century ago, the results achieved by ships in fleet gunnery trials were in the daily press; best-selling authors wrote serious discussions of current military affairs. Those days are long gone.

Such mainstream-media defence journalists and commentators as do exist tend to be at the MoD's mercy, in the same way that celebrity interviewers are often under the thumb of public-relations agents. Most defence journalists feel that they need access to the MoD in order to do their job: they need pictures, interviews and leaks, and in the most extreme cases, as in Iraq at present, they often need actual physical protection. Just as an interviewer who gives a celebrity a bad write-up will never get another interview, the defence hack who seriously criticises the MoD may be frozen out, unless he is a major media heavyweight.

This was made abundantly clear to me by a senior officer in the MoD media apparatus early in 2004. I was just leaving the navy then, and had written an article in the press critical of naval policy. This had resulted in an invitation to appear on BBC Radio's *Today* programme. The night before the broadcast, the said senior officer telephoned and enquired whether I had any ambitions towards a career as a defence commentator. He strongly suggested that I would find it difficult to stay in touch with matters military if I didn't moderate my line the following morning. In the event his threats and other inducements were largely irrelevant, as I was on air for barely thirty seconds.

To be fair, questions of defence policy are not usually completely simple. They can be difficult to cover in the space of a short article or broadcast. For a hundred years and more, the technology of violence has become more complicated (and so has the jargon that goes with it). To give a very basic example, army A has far fewer soldiers than army B; surely it must be the weaker of the two? But army A's soldiers have rifles and machine guns and army B is equipped almost entirely with spears. Army B may do a lot better than one might expect, as the Zulus and others have taught us; nonetheless, army A is the one to bet on. A modern defence pundit would say that it had more 'effects-based technology' than army B. Put rather better, army A may be expected to win because

> Whatever happens, we have got
> the Maxim Gun
> and they have not

as Hilaire Belloc said – the Maxim being the first proper machine gun much used by the British. That was the situation a hundred years ago. In the modern age, the British struggle to select a decent rifle or machine gun, and there are now also the helicopter, the armoured combat vehicle, night vision equipment, secure comms and dozens of other tools to think of. And all this is merely to consider the infantry aspect of land warfare.

Such complexities, the defence brain trust might argue, mean that nobody can usefully join the debate unless they have studied intensively in the field, preferably for years. Therefore, public interest in the armed forces is only useful if it takes the form of unqualified support; anything else is dangerous and not to be encouraged. Public interest, after all, can easily become public pressure, and this in turn often translates into political pressure (normally described in defence circles as 'political interference'), which sometimes – this being a democracy – has to be yielded to.

Such arguments are occasionally combined with that of 'national security', a much-abused concept within the Ministry of Defence and, some would argue, the government as a whole. Even

the most innocuous pieces of information about military operations and weapons are frequently claimed to be critical secrets,
usually on the grounds that they have appeared within classified
documents. The information may be widely available in the public
domain, but this doesn't matter. National secrets can only be
discussed by those with the appropriate clearances, a group which
of course does not include you and me.

This is all a bit like saying that only doctors can usefully discuss
the survival rates of patients at a given hospital, and only teachers
should know the exam results at schools. And claiming that things
are secrets once they are on the internet or in *Jane's Defence
Weekly* merely makes one look stupid. Or lazy, or even verging
on corrupt, as when bureaux of well-paid intelligence officers
spend comfortable careers collating and issuing highly classified
information, all or most of which is available at a fraction of the
cost in the public domain.

Over and above such obstruction is the problem of language.
Old-fashioned armed-forces types and military historians are bad
enough in this regard; their speeches and writings are sometimes
unintelligible even to their colleagues. But the military conservatives do have some respect for clear language. They may use recon-
dite vocabulary, but at least they string it together properly. Far
worse, usually, are the modernisers, typified by the American
Office of Force Transformation. This body was recently set up to
rearrange the US armed forces into something more suitable for
the 21st century, and transformationist doctrine is very popular
with some of our own military thinkers. But, splendid as the principle may be, it is usually impossible to work out what a transformation enthusiast is going on about. The director of force
transformation himself, Vice Admiral Cebrowski, attempting to
make things clearer, stated in November 2001:

> I've expanded somewhat . . . for my own working definition, and
> that is that transformation are [*sic*] those continuing processes and
> activities which create new sources of power and yield profound
> increases in military competitive advantage as a result of new, or
> the discovery of, fundamental shifts in the underlying rule sets.

Just so.

All this notwithstanding, while defence policy may occasionally involve rockets, it isn't rocket science. It may indeed be rather difficult to explain the ins and outs of a given issue within a column or two of newspaper text, but it can normally be done in no more than a few pages. In a book such as this one there is the scope to cover most of the basics, using fairly plain English and no mathematics more complicated than percentages.

I am trying to make several points.

Firstly, the combat personnel of the British armed forces are very deserving of reasonable rewards and solid support, and adequate funding for this is, in fact, provided. No major increase in defence expenditure will be advocated here. It may or may not be true, as a general principle, that giving government departments more money causes more waste. It is completely clear, however, that the Ministry of Defence in particular wastes much of what it gets now.

Secondly, combat personnel are actually a very small minority among Ministry of Defence employees. Perhaps more surprisingly, they are also a minority among the actual uniformed armed forces, even using a very wide definition of 'combat personnel'. The services are ridiculously top-heavy, with thousands of senior officers who have no military tasks to perform, and there are larger numbers yet of civil servants and contractors also living well off the defence budget. One can find fatter cats elsewhere, perhaps, more deserving of public bile; but a thousand medium-to-plump cats on £50,000+ per year and government pensions are actually more expensive than a handful of corporate mega-tabbies. In any case, we are paying for corporate-weight fat cats as well, among the arms manufacturers.

Thirdly, these many non-combat personnel, uniformed and civilian both, actually receive most of the rewards which the taxpayers would probably wish to go to the fighting people. Those who are genuinely likely to get into harm's way on our behalf are comparatively poorly looked after. The young soldiers (occasionally, young sailors) who actually risk life and limb, and the junior officers of all three services who are likely to be with them at the sharp end, can only dream of £50,000 salaries. The officers might reach such heights after a decade or two, if not the enlisted types, but in fact most will leave the services without ever doing so.

Fourthly, much of the money supplied for the fighting people's support – that, for instance, used to purchase their equipment – tends to be squandered outright. The priority is not to obtain good equipment, or even to get value for money. It is, always, to provide well-paid British civilian jobs. To a certain extent this is understandable, even laudable; all other things being equal, of course the money should go into the British economy. However, all other things are not equal. Everyone agrees that the buy-British (or buy-European) principle should be secondary to giving our fighting people equipment of reasonable quality and price. And yet one can say without exaggeration that British combat personnel get weapons and equipment which are always expensive, always late, generally faulty or completely useless on arrival, and which frequently stay that way for far too long. Some expensive items are *never* made to work properly. A civilian, whose car, television and mobile phone probably worked on the first try, simply cannot imagine how bad defence-procured equipment is. Even relatively trouble-prone civilian systems, such as personal computers, are models of reliability compared to their military equivalents.

Fifthly, and perhaps most tragically, much of the remaining wherewithal – the precious few people who are in combat positions, and the trickle of funding that makes it past the various procurement jobberies – is also wasted. Many existing front-line units are set up and equipped to fight enemies which do not and will not exist, or which could be better dealt with by other means. To a remarkable extent, the British order of battle is still designed to fight a suddenly-hot cold war, or even a small replay of World War II, despite much glossy paperwork and spin to the contrary. This means that the few units and people useful for the real world are often heavily overworked, when we could easily have more of them.

I want to make these things more widely believed for several reasons.

Most importantly, because nowadays I am a civilian. I – we – live in a dangerous world, full of evilly disposed governments and organisations. We Western civilians depend utterly on the potential of Western military forces for our safety; it therefore behoves us to take an interest in their efficiency.

I am also nowadays a British taxpayer – a real one, not a government employee the way I used to be. Every time any money passes through my bank account coming or going, the government takes its bite; and it ostensibly spends a lot of that money on my defence. Close on *thirty billion pounds* of all our money goes on defence every year, in fact, and much of it – most of it – is wasted or stolen or diverted to other purposes. It upsets me; it should upset you.

Finally, on a more personal level, I'm a huge fan of our forces – of the useful parts of them, anyway. I always was, from an early age. I never seriously considered any other career than the armed services. Doctor Samuel Johnson wrote, 'Every man thinks meanly of himself for not having been a soldier, or not having been at sea.' Perhaps he was right, in the 18th century. It doesn't seem to be generally true nowadays. But it's true of me: *I* would have thought meanly of myself if I hadn't ever worn a uniform. So I spent a good deal of time with and around the army in my late teens, and got quite far towards being an army officer at one stage. I was three years in the RAF too, as a member of the Cambridge University Air Squadron while an undergraduate – university air squadrons are a splendid deal where the RAF teaches you to fly, even pays you a small sum, and you need do nothing at all for them in return.

In the end, I actually became a Royal Naval officer, and spent eleven happy years in a variety of interesting employment. Most of this time was at sea in minehunting ships, or underwater as a mine-clearance diver. I was also able to qualify as a commando with the Royal Marines. I finished up in charge of the Plymouth diving team, which among other things functions as a bomb-disposal unit under army command. (Unlike most of the British armed forces, I have actually encountered and disposed of genuine 'weapons of mass destruction', albeit British ones rather than Iraqi.) Being a bomb-disposal operator was an excellent job.

I loved it in the forces – in the real, useful British armed forces. In my opinion there is no better work. But I had to leave in the end. Once you get to a certain point, particularly as an officer, you can no longer avoid becoming part of all the problems I have just described. In my case, you reach the stage of being forced into the non-useful part of the navy, as a prelude to decades of pointless desk work. No matter what kind of officer you are, if you stay in you will almost certainly spend the great bulk of your later career – say, two thirds of your working life – as a uniformed Ministry of Defence bureaucrat. You will become a donkey or a dinosaur, no matter how much of a lion you might originally have been. I chose to leave while my self-respect was still reasonably intact, but I can't say I'm happy about it.

So. Academic impartiality and distance is not a priority here. Dry, non-committal analysis of military matters is already available by the ream, and is one of the principal reasons why the subject is horribly boring to most people. This book is intended to combine accurate facts with personal assessment. It is meant to entertain and to inform: but most of all it is meant to start arguments, not finish them.

The mess in the British defence establishment is not the fault of any single individual, nor of any dozen individuals. It is the product, in the end, of weaknesses in the system. These persist because the whole area is not much subject to informed, critical scrutiny by outsiders. Names will be named occasionally in this book, but this is not to imply that the named individuals are worse public servants than others of their rank and position.

I know what I'm writing about. Having flown with the RAF, marched with the army and been to sea with the Royal Navy, I know the people. As an ordnance-disposal specialist, I know weapons and their effects; not just seagoing ones, but air, land and chemical munitions, and improvised terrorist devices too.

The right to include salty sea stories and other service anecdotes is reserved, but wherever a fact or figure is given it has been checked as rigorously as possible. The usual source of information is the Ministry of Defence itself, as this admits of only three possibilities:

1. The MoD information is accurate. If it makes them look like idiots, they probably *are* idiots.
2. The MoD have massaged the information in their own favour. If it still makes them look like idiots, they are doubly idiots, in that they can't even falsify information properly and the situation is even worse than described.

3. The men from the ministry have somehow got the information wrong in such a way as to make themselves look worse than they really are, in which unlikely case they are truly incompetent.

So you can trust the figures in this book. Furthermore, military doubletalk is eschewed or explained. The facts about what modern military technology in general, and the British forces in particular, can and cannot do are made clear. Some interesting tales are told. But all bathwater has been carefully checked for babies: if mistakes have been made nonetheless, they are honest ones.

CHAPTER

1

Men with Guns

That one may become eminent in learning, it costs him time, watchings, hunger, nakedness, headaches, rawness of stomach, and other such inconveniences . . . but that one may arrive by true terms to be a good soldier, it costs him all that it costs the student, in so exceeding a degree as admits no comparison . . .

Don Quixote, Miguel Cervantes

In matters of organised violence or war, or 'defence' if you prefer, sooner or later things come down to men with guns. By this is meant those, nearly always men rather than women, who carry personal weapons and whose main fighting function is the use of those personal weapons. In more advanced and well-financed militaries such as the British, these men will be very much in the minority; less than 10 per cent of our armed forces currently do this job. In paramilitary or shoestring forces, they may be nearly everyone. They are generally known as infantrymen by forces professionals, although this term actually includes a lot of people whose work is not the handling of personal weapons. Riflemen is a better military word, although it has other meanings in a British context.* The media often call such men ground troops, or boots on the ground. Those who do the same job for the other side are normally known, rather more plainly, as gunmen. There are many other terms: grunts, legs, foot-sloggers and so on.

---

* When British soldiers say 'riflemen' they often mean members of the Royal Green Jackets regiment, the modern decendants of various rifle-equipped, green-uniformed skirmisher units which made their names in the Napoleonic and American wars.

Infantry riflemen are the controllable element of force, as far as the well-capitalised militaries are concerned. Other arms such as the air force, navy and artillery have limited options for dealing with the enemy, or indeed anybody they encounter. All they can usually do is blow something up or leave it alone. It is possible, even likely, that neither of these actions will help us in our aim: generally, to convince everyone in a given area to comply with British policy.

British policy may be 'Do what the UN says' or 'Don't steal all the food and drugs from aid workers' or 'Stop shooting at each other.' Often it is nothing so clear-cut, which creates problems for everyone. It could even be something nasty like 'Knuckle under to the corrupt, despotic local government.' But, if you won't do whatever it is, the infantry can respond with measured degrees of violence rather than simply vaporising you straight away. They can talk to you, shout at you, grab you and lock you up . . . or kill you. Just you, on a good day; not you and several other people nearby. Not you and your family and maybe your whole block as well. This is the unique infantry capability.

Other arms of the service probably can't talk to you at all. Their first and gentlest way of interacting with you may be to blow up your house. This is a problem, both for you the target and for the promotion of British interests. As John Paul Vann, the legendary American counter-insurgency specialist, said of Vietnam, what is necessary is *selective* killing, 'and the worst thing for that is an airplane. The next worst thing is artillery. The only thing which may work is a rifle, when you know who you're killing.' Vann eventually changed his mind about indiscriminate bombardment, but by that point he had been under terrible stress for a long time and was no longer – in the idiom of the time – very tightly wrapped.

So, there will usually be a need for infantry, the selective killers, in any given situation. They may be all that is required, or only part of it, but they will be wanted at some stage. The infantry are the sine qua non of effective military action. Everyone in the armed forces knows this. Both the Royal Navy and the Royal Air Force maintain infantry forces of their own, separate from the army. Regardless of conceptual notions of sea and air power, they know what is really necessary.

Which leads us to take a look at the British infantryman. First of all, we see that he is still always a man. Women are now allowed to serve in many front-line positions: they can crew combat aircraft and ships, and they can be in various land units which may be well to the fore in battle. But there are still a lot of jobs they are barred from. Sometimes this is for supposedly practical reasons. For example, no women can serve in British submarines, as separate showers cannot be provided. (This is perhaps more of a cultural matter: the Dutch navy simply has mixed facilities, and anyway it isn't as though British submariners are known for taking a lot of showers.)

In the case of the army the objection is rather harder to pin down. Tank and infantry units do not accept women, no matter how fit and strong they may be, because it is feared that they would 'upset the fighting cohesion of the team'. The nice face of this argument is the suggestion that men would seek to protect women more than they would male comrades. In actual fact, the institutional fear is probably that women are too soft. What isn't often said plainly is that these are the up-close kill teams: groups – gangs, if you like – organised to shoot, stab, bludgeon or even burn people to death, or purposely run them over with heavy vehicles. In other words, to commit grievous bodily harm on a grand scale *and see what they are doing*. An attack pilot or a politician may do much bloodier deeds, but he or she will not be viscerally aware of doing them. Feminists might have to push the idea that women are just as vicious as men in order to gain them access to a job that very few would want. Unsurprisingly, this has not occurred. It may even be the case that women genuinely aren't as nasty.

In any case, for the present, the infantryman is still a man. He is generally quite young: most join at sixteen or seventeen years old,* a majority leave before they reach thirty, and almost nobody is allowed to serve in the real, active infantry past the age of forty. The teenage infantry recruit is unlikely to be very well educated: typically he will have no qualifications at all, and only very basic literacy and numeracy are required to begin with. Despite not

---

* Though they can't be sent to fight until they are eighteen. The forces would not wish to raise the recruitment threshold to eighteen, however: they get a very large number of young men by offering them jobs unconditionally before they have taken their exams.

having very high educational standards, a lot of infantry units, in common with some other parts of the forces, are struggling desperately to fill their ranks. Some have started to take recruits from as far afield as Fiji. (This has had the side-effect of enormously strengthening the army rugby team.)

Seeing Fijian faces in Scottish regiments is a modern phenomenon. One should recall, however, that there have always been entire units recruited abroad: the famous Gurkhas. The terrible men from Nepal will make up more than 5 per cent of the British army infantry after the current reductions are complete, and they don't have any recruiting problems at all, funnily enough. Like the NHS, the infantry may do well in future to seek many of its recruits overseas. At present, the great majority of them are still from the UK and Ireland as of old.

Once he has been recruited, the young infantryman must be trained. He will be deprived of sleep, and will learn to polish boots, clean buildings, perform ceremonial drill and do as he's told, like any other serviceman. He will then move on to do infantry training, which will be very much harder. There are two main unpleasantnesses to it, and it is these which account for most of the high wastage rate.

The first nasty bit is marching with kit, known as tabbing in the army and yomping in the marines. In the same way that Eskimos have many words for snow, foot soldiers have many words for marching with kit. Young infantrymen must learn to carry immense loads, sometimes well over a hundred pounds, for many miles over rough country, often at speed. Anybody who has done this will know how unbelievably painful and horrible it is. One does get used to it after a while, but it never really becomes pleasant. There are many different schools of marching, involving varying loads, different speeds and so on. Nowadays, as we shall see, there are some who feel it to be a rather obsolete skill. It is still the case, though, that performance in marching with kit is perhaps the best quick, handy measure of how good infantrymen are; or at any rate how committed they and their leadership are to being good.

The second really nasty thing about infantry training is exposure. Everyone else in the armed forces normally has some better option than simply sleeping in the open, just as they usually have better ways to get somewhere than walking. But the infantryman spends much of his time unshielded by vehicles, buildings or tents. Not many modern Brits realise just how deadly their native climate is, or how fast they would probably die if left exposed to it. Infantrymen learn early on.

And one shouldn't think, having perhaps been on a camping holiday, that one has really sampled infantry life. Bear in mind that the infantryman cannot wear waterproof clothing when marching, patrolling or fighting. It will sweat him literally to death on the march or in battle, and it is far too noisy to wear when sneaking about at night – this is what soldiers mean by patrolling, not walking a beat. Thus, he gets soaked whenever it rains. In any but the warmest conditions, as soon as he stops moving briskly about he will begin to die of the cold. And he can't warm up around a campfire or in a tent, because he is usually 'tactical', that is, trying not to be seen. There is no camp fire, nor any tent as such; just a minimal shelter which he has brought with him, largely open to the elements. There may be a chance to heat up a drink over a small burner, but that will be it. All this means that a good infantryman, in northern European or equivalent climes, packs his sleeping bag with religious care. Sooner or later he must stop moving and rest, and then, if his clothes are wet, he will die: unless he has a dry sleeping bag.

So our infantryman needs a good pair of boots in which to march. He also needs tough, breathable clothing for normal wear, and some lightweight, breathable waterproofs for when he isn't engaged in violent effort or asleep – ideally Gore-tex or some similar micropore material. He needs a good sleeping bag, covers to keep it dry, a backpack . . . the list goes on. And he will need different things in different climates, although some items will be in common.

Does he get all this? Well, things are better than they used to be. Infantrymen still tend to buy bits and pieces at camping shops, but it is a far cry from the days when the commandos were dubbed Millets' Marines because they had to buy much of their kit at a popular high-street chain. The standard combat boot isn't partic-ularly great, but one can manage; if you carry a lot of spare socks and spend plenty of time on foot maintenance, it will do until it wears out after a few months' field use. There are various better boots with which you may well be issued if you are in an infantry

unit and there are any left. A similar situation exists with waterproofs. The regular nylon ones are pretty poor, but quite adequate
Gore-tex is often available to those who can show a need. And
it goes on: the standard webbing and rucksack are pretty much
OK, the issue sleeping bag is warm but heavy, and so forth. One
may have difficulties actually getting it all, however; there is a
tendency for the best gear to be snaffled early, often by rear-
echelon types who don't really need it, leaving the front line short.
Provided you can actually get a full issue of kit, your clothes,
boots and harness will be perfectly adequate if not as good as
the latest stuff in the camping shops.

This might be said to represent a decent, if not sparkling, effort
by the Defence Clothing and Textiles Agency (DCTA). Most of
the kit is OK, and most of those that need it have most of what
they should have. Nonetheless, they really could do better.

Elsewhere, things aren't going nearly as well. Our infantryman
may survive to reach the battlefield in decent shape, but this is
no use unless he can fight and win. For this, he needs weapons.
First and foremost, he needs a decent personal small arm: a gun.

The standard personal weapon in the British forces is the SA80
rifle. SA80 stands for Small Arms 1980, indicating its genesis
decades ago as a project to replace several weapons of the day.
The SA80 system was to provide, primarily, a normal assault rifle
in 5.56mm NATO calibre. The rifle's proper name became the
L85A1, and it is officially known as an Individual Weapon rather
than a rifle, because that is how things are done in the Ministry
of Defence.

Apart from rifles, infantrymen carry various other weapons.
The basic infantry unit is the fire team, of four men. According
to doctrine, one of the four should have a more powerful weapon,
capable of delivering heavier volumes of fire than a rifle, but still
using the same ammunition: in other words a light machine gun.
The team should also be able to shoot grenades from a launcher.
Hand grenades have very limited range, and it is often difficult
to hurl them in such a way that the thrower himself isn't endangered. The standard method of using hand grenades, in fact, is
to 'post' them rather than throw them: that is, place them into
an enemy trench or bunker at arm's reach. In this way one can
be reasonably sure of not blowing oneself up.

Thus the SA80 programme also provided a slightly heavier version of the rifle, designed to deliver longer bursts of automatic fire. This was called the L86A1 Light Support Weapon, or LSW. Finally, a way to shoot grenades was required. It was clear that 40mm launched grenades were going to be the NATO standard, but these were not chosen as there was no British launcher available. Despite their obvious deficiencies, 'bullet-trap' grenades, launched by fitting them over a rifle muzzle and firing a bullet into them, were selected instead.

The basic SA80 rifle started life in 1985 with several glaring design flaws. The magazine catch stood proud of the weapon's side, so that if it bumped anything (such as the user's chest) all the bullets would fall out. Build quality was atrocious: plastic parts would melt when the gun got hot, metal bits would snap when it was stripped for cleaning. The safety catch was defective: the gun would fire when dropped, whether the catch was engaged or not. Often this was the only way you *could* get it to fire. One of Britain's pre-eminent small-arms experts, Ian Hogg, commented on the SA80 in 1990:

The first five years of this rifle's service have been disastrous . . . It will take some time for the poor reputation gained by the initial issue weapons to be overcome.

Some time indeed. The simpler flaws were eventually fixed, but the rifle remained flimsy and unreliable, and the machine-gun variant, the LSW, was even worse. Launching a grenade would cause the rifle to lose its zero – that is, the sights would become wildly inaccurate until carefully recalibrated on a range. The grenades were thus, sensibly, ignored for the most part and British infantry training continued to emphasise the use of hand grenades, or full-blown anti-tank rockets and mortars when more range was required.

The rumblings of complaint about the SA80 continued throughout the early 1990s, despite the various fixes. Trials and tests were held, but the results were whitewashed time and again. This was made easier by the fact that the SA80 weapons are outstandingly accurate. Indeed, the LSW, although useless as a light machine gun, functions well as a sort of low-powered sniper rifle – although why one would want a low-powered sniper rifle is difficult to fathom. However, accuracy beyond a certain level is irrelevant. The whole point of an assault rifle is that there is seldom any need to fire at a target beyond a few hundred metres, and machine guns are for delivering automatic fire, not aimed single shots. Having a very accurate weapon is nice, but it is better to have one that will reliably go bang when the trigger is pulled, and this the SA80 would not do.

So badly made, indeed, was the mechanism which locked cartridges into the breech that it became a standard drill to assume its failure. Users were taught, after releasing the bolt forward, to then slam it with the heel of their hand so that it would lock home. By doing this on every occasion, time would not be wasted in taking aim and then finding that the weapon would not shoot. This manoeuvre was actually in the manual, described as a 'forward assist'. It is not necessary with any other assault rifle in the world, and measurably slows down reloading in combat – particularly as the SA80 is clumsily designed, so that one has to reach over the weapon to get at the cocking handle. A classic Ministry of Defence solution: rather than admit to a problem and fix it, simply force the troops to make do.

Unsurprisingly, the SA80 gained a dreadful reputation. Anyone who had a choice of weapon – for example the SAS – carried something else. But the great mass of the infantry were forced to soldier on. Matters came to a head in the late 1990s, when the paratroops, deploying into expected combat in Kosovo, flatly refused to carry the abject Light Support Weapon. They obtained much heavier and bulkier 7.62mm medium machine guns, not intended for use at fire-team level, preferring to carry extra weight rather than have inadequate firepower.

After years of stonewalling, the Ministry of Defence bowed to the inevitable. Even then, however, a face-saving solution was found. In 1997 it was finally admitted that the SA80 had reliability problems, but only in 'extremes of temperature'. It remained a 'good weapon'. However, it would be modified, ostensibly for greater reliability in the desert – many of the complaints had arisen from the rifle's shocking performance in the 1991 Gulf War. The modified version would be known as the L85A2. The cost of the modifications would, of course, be borne by the taxpayer rather

than the manufacturers of the defective goods; this was an enhance-
ment to an already good system, remember, not the fixing up of
a shoddy piece of rubbish. In any case, the factories which produced
the SA80 had been government owned when it was designed.

When this announcement was made, I was a trainee on the All
Arms Commando Course, most of which involves extremely
vigorous infantry work with the SA80 rifle. The course takes place
in Devon, not the desert or the arctic. But our SA80 rifles and
LSWs still didn't work. Pieces fell off; most of us fastened them
together with tape while in the field. Many weapons, especially
the LSWs, required a 'forward assist' after every shot, not just
when reloading; they were thus slower to fire than World War I
bolt-action rifles. They required endless maintenance to keep them
in a condition where they would shoot at all.

I had carried the previous service rifle, the 7.62mm SLR, under
similar conditions some years before. The contrast was unbelievable. The SLR, a Belgian design, was solid and robust. It worked
without forward assists, you could operate the cocking handle
easily, it remained in one piece even when subjected to violent
impacts, it had less protrusions to snag on things and required
only twenty minutes of maintenance each day to keep it shooting.

It wasn't just me who thought badly of the A1 SA80. Every
single instructor on the commando course, from the course officer
down to the corporals, acknowledged that it was awful. Many
of them were platoon-weapons experts with wide experience of
other rifles. These extremely forceful men nevertheless still insisted
that we wring the best results from our SA80s. This required
hours of work, and – ideally – an illicit extra bolt group.

The bland assurance from on high that the L85A1 was a 'good
weapon' was rather annoying.

In any case, the modification programme got under way at a
cost of £92 million to sort out the 200,000 rifles and LSWs in
stock: that is, £460 for each gun. The ministry asserted that this
was cost-effective, as purchasing new ones would cost, apparently, £500 million, a staggering £2,500 per weapon. This is totally
untrue. The American M16, as preferred by the SAS, can be
bought *retail* for well under £400. This whopper was necessary
as replacing the defective guns with new ones would have been
to admit that they were defective. Which they weren't, of course,

officially speaking; they simply had problems in extreme conditions. (Outdoors, for example.)

The modified L85A2 rifle and L86A2 machine gun duly appeared, and it seemed that most of the problems had finally been ironed out. The much relieved ministry trumpeted positive comments on the A2s from the troops, such as this from Sergeant Jamie Miles, a marine weapons instructor: 'The SA80 A2 was introduced to us at 45 Commando last November . . . initial reaction to that was "OK, this weapon looks the same [as the A1] but it is actually performing extremely well."'

So much for the A1 having been a good weapon.

Front-line troops took the A2 rifle to Afghanistan and Iraq. Apparently it finally does work tolerably, nineteen years after the SA80 appeared, although it has been an uphill battle to get the soldiers to believe it. As for the LSW, it continues in service, also modified, as the L86A2. But the ministry has also quietly purchased a new light machine gun, the FN Minimi. This is a Belgian design, has been in service with other armies for years, and it can actually deliver useful automatic fire, which the LSW still cannot do despite the modifications.

Similarly, the bullet-trap grenades have been retired, in favour of a normal 40mm grenade launcher designed to mount under the barrel of an A2 rifle. The launcher is German manufactured and works well. There was no admission of problems with the old grenades; the army just woke up one morning and decided to switch to 40mm on a whim, it seems. One member of each fire team now has this combination weapon. Other countries have had such systems for decades, but the MoD still finds grounds for self-congratulation in its introduction despite the fact that only a few arrived in time for the Iraq invasion.

All these systems are due to be replaced in 2020, according to the ministry: probably sooner in reality.

So, to sum up. The rifles have at last been rebuilt so that they work acceptably, at the same cost as buying new ones. The grenades have had to be replaced. The machine guns have also been expensively modified, and then replacement machine guns have been purchased anyway. The taxpayers have had to pay twice – in the case of the machine guns three times over – and the troops have had to struggle with shoddy, defective weapons for over fifteen years. Plenty of people will have completed their entire service without once being issued a reliable weapon. The A2 variants will only be around for a further fifteen years anyway, so these weapons have been defective for half their service lives despite having now cost several times what is reasonable. This has to be a catastrophic tale of bungling and malfeasance, whichever way you slice it.

But no, apparently not. Actually, it is all just one of those things, old boy: nothing to get worked up about. The press, the only thing that the Ministry fears, is quiescent, seemingly satisfied that everything is now OK. Not one former or serving official or senior officer will be disciplined or have his pension taken away. Not a single minister or ex-minister will even be questioned for obediently spouting bureaucrats' lies.

There is a reason why defence commentators tend to react apathetically, if at all, to the SA80 fiasco Unbelievably, by Ministry of Defence standards, it is quite a minor cock-up, as we shall see. For now, back to the infantrymen.

So, our infantry fire team have undergone lengthy, arduous training, a minimum of seven months' worth. If they're lucky and good at scrounging, they have decent boots and kit. Certainly if they are somewhere dangerous like Iraq, they carry A2-pattern rifles, one with grenade launcher, and one of them has a Minimi machine gun instead. If they are merely walking the streets of Northern Ireland, they still have A1s, at the time of writing.

Two fire teams make up a section, in British usage. The section leader will be a corporal in his twenties; he will probably be a fairly hardbitten individual who has been through testing leadership training on being promoted. He will take charge of one fire team directly, and the other will be led by the next most experienced man in the section, usually a lance-corporal by rank. The remaining six are private soldiers; in many British infantry units, however, this rank has some other title than Private, such as Guardsman, Marine or Rifleman. Their starting annual pay is just over £13,000, rising to a bit over £22,000 for the corporal: in other words, everyone in the rifle section earns less than the national average.*
The Ministry of Defence would make the point here that these men

---

* Just under £25,000 p.a. in 2004, according to the Office for National Statistics.

have greatly reduced living costs compared to civilians. In fact, however, this only applies in a seriously useful way to married personnel. Indeed, this may have been a factor in some of these young men getting married very early, to the probable detriment of their future happiness; but most will still be single.

Three eight-man sections are the basic units of a platoon (a troop in the marines). A platoon has a commander, who is a junior officer, generally a brand-new, fresh-from-training second lieutenant. This young officer has a sergeant to assist him. British infantry sergeants have been privates, lance-corporals and corporals, and have gone through even more intensive training on top. If corporals are tough eggs, sergeants are usually downright scary. The platoon sergeant will probably be in his late twenties or early thirties and will have immense natural authority; unlike his nominal superior the young lieutenant, who is still effectively on probation. The two of them will be the only ones in the platoon getting decent pay – around the national average wage for both – although the sergeant, probably married, may be getting a somewhat better deal overall. (Provided he isn't divorced, of course; this is even more likely for him than most thirty-something Brits. He may be on his second or even third marriage.)

Apart from all these people, there is a radio operator who keeps the platoon commander in touch with his superiors. Every man in the platoon has a headset radio, or will soon, but these only have enough range for them to talk to each other. Furthermore, the platoon has an extra corporal in charge of a manoeuvre-support section. This is typically two teams of two men equipped with general purpose machine guns, or GPMGs. These are larger, medium machine guns firing powerful 7.62mm bullets as opposed to the 5.56mm of the SA80s and Minimis. So, from a maximum platoon strength of thirty-two men, twenty-four are actually in rifle sections and available to do things like kicking in doors.

Three platoons together make up what is normally known as a rifle company. This will be under the command of a major in his early thirties, with a company sergeant-major* to back him

---

* Sergeant-major is a job rather than a rank, in the British forces. Company sergeant-majors are Warrant-Officers 2nd class in rank: regimental sergeant-majors are WO1s.

up. There is also a company second in command, an officer of captain's rank. Once upon a time, captains commanded companies, but the increasing number of majors and decreasing number of companies long ago put an end to this. Such processes are termed 'rank inflation', and are very common throughout the armed services.

The unit above a company is generally known as a battalion, but may, of course, go by other names. Normally it will have three ordinary or rifle companies, a manoeuvre support company and a headquarters company. These latter two companies provide a wide range of heavy weaponry and various support services. The battalion has its own artillery in the form of mortars, its own radio operators, its own combat engineers and its own reconnaissance unit. It can act as a pocket army in its own right, although this seldom happens. It will exceed 600 men at full combat strength. Of these, a mere 216 are in rifle sections, and thus are actually classic men with guns who can really do John Paul Vann's 'selective killing'.* We are beginning to see why it takes so many troops to control even small areas effectively. (The situation is not quite as bad as it seems at battalion level, though: all 600-plus are infantrymen who probably started their career in an ordinary rifle platoon. At least 400 of them could be made available to carry out basic tasks if necessary.)

The battalion is the basic home unit of the British infantry; it lives together much of the time, and, until 2004, infantrymen would spend their entire operational careers with their original battalion. The commanding officer is a lieutenant-colonel who will have started off as a platoon commander in the same battalion perhaps fifteen years earlier. He has done well to be promoted from major, and better yet to get a command. He now has an excellent chance of promotion to even higher rank, provided he doesn't make any serious mistakes.

Battalion CO is the first level at which a commander is provided with a staff: a group of officers who are not commanders or seconds in command of units. Their job is to advise the commander and help him plan and direct the battle. There is also

---

* Or even less. Sometimes the ninth rifle platoon doesn't exist, having been reassigned to one of the non-rifle companies.

a truly fearsome regimental sergeant-major, the top enlisted man of the battalion: he started out as a young private in the same unit or one of its ancestors around twenty years ago. Having become RSM, he is exceptionally highly regarded; rather than being hurled out into the cold wind of civvy street when he turns forty, like most long-service enlisted men, he will probably be given a 'long engagement' officer's commission. He will then be assigned to a nice comfortable desk job, perhaps as families officer (in charge of liaison with the battalion's wives and children) while his pension builds up to something he can live on.

Infantry battalions are grouped into regiments. However, with the reduction in numbers over the centuries, most infantry regiments in 2004 had only one battalion left (of full-time regulars, anyway; there are normally part-time reservists as well). Each infantry regiment has its own beret, its own cap badge and its own traditions. These often include unusual rank titles, certain toasts in the mess and some very outlandish ceremonial uniforms – kilts, bearskins, etc. As many regiments have been formed by amalgamating several units, there is often an amazing amount of hoary custom to be kept up. Even where a regiment has two or three regular battalions (for example, there are three in the Parachute Regiment) the regiment itself is not a combat formation; more of a clique within the infantry. Its battalions will be assigned to different commands as required, and seldom operate together.

This whole business with the special hats and so forth is held to promote terrific esprit de corps, although this might be said even more to come from building an entire career around the same unit. The set-up is known as the regimental system, despite being mainly concerned with single battalions, and is unique among modern armies. As one might expect, it is a personnel manager's nightmare, and in reality it isn't uncommon for under-strength battalions to be reinforced from other units when going operational.

Naturally, just to make things more complicated, the closely knit battalion typically doesn't fight together as a unit even when at full strength, despite all the rhetoric about regimental bonding. Particularly in high-intensity warfare, the British front line will be made up of temporary battle groups rather than battalions.

These are bossed by a lieutenant-colonel and his staff, but the units under his command will normally be a mixture of rifle companies and other things such as tank squadrons, as appropriate to the task in hand. Thus, in combat, the companies of any given battalion may be far apart and not working for their own CO.

Battle groups are arranged into brigades, under the control of a brigadier and his staff; the rank of full colonel offers no chance to command anything, in British service. Two or more brigades make up a division, commanded by a major-general*, this is pretty much the largest land force that Britain would expect to send to any given war, nowadays. Only two real combat division set-ups actually exist in the British army, despite the fact that there are over forty major-generals on the payroll. Even two divisions may be a trifle optimistic; the army often needs a bit of a rest after deploying just one division into a serious scrap, as the aftermath of Iraq has shown.

In theory several divisions constitute an army corps, and several of those a field army, commanded by a lieutenant-general and a full general respectively. We have nearly twenty of these senior generals, but there is no longer any real suggestion that they might command such formations, unless perhaps in an allied scenario. The entire full-time British army, assuming that one could somehow muster it into one formation (not feasible) would barely make up a large corps. Remarkably, there is a rank above full general, that of field marshal. Even the armed forces have been made to feel that this is overdoing the number of senior ranks a bit, though, and officially nobody gets promoted this high any more.

Just as a battalion has various bits and pieces apart from rifle companies, or a platoon has extra personnel apart from its rifle sections, brigades and divisions have many things other than infantry: but we'll get to those later.

As a further complicating factor, army infantry battalions are assigned a 'role'. Boiled down, the role designates what transport

---

* There are no minor-generals, disappointingly. And a lieutenant-general is indeed senior to a major-general; this is because major-generals were once sergeant-major-generals.

the battalion will use to move into battle, which will in turn affect how it operates and what you can do with it. Also, importantly, how expensive it is. Until lately, most battalions would change role every few years, on a system called the infantry arms plot. This was seen as necessary under the system of soldiers spending their whole careers in a single unit, in order for infantrymen to gain experience in all the different roles and for everyone to get a chance at the fun jobs. However, it does also mean that at any one time a number of battalions are unavailable for use, due to being in the process of changing roles. This system is being shaken up as this book is written.

The first role is that of armoured infantry. Armoured infantry are meant to fight a full-on, money-no-object, Hollywood-high concept sort of war, in which both sides will be using heavy artillery and tanks and the terrain is suitable for this. In other words, only gentle hills, and not too overgrown or swampy. No mountains or jungles, thank you. We also take it largely as read that neither side has achieved total air dominance over the battlefield. This kind of scenario is fairly hard to dream up nowadays, but formerly the tank and artillery obsessives of the Red Army, backed up by the massive air strength of the Voyska PVO* and Frontal Aviation, provided an obvious opponent. One might describe this type of fighting as the lessons of World War II, selectively learned.

Conventional army wisdom holds that in such a war both sides will roar across the battlefield at high speed, off-road, and the high explosive will fall like hail. Thus, our armoured infantrymen must ride in a vehicle which can go fast cross-country (usually this means tracks rather than wheels). To survive the expected storm of shot and shell without having to stop and hide all the time, the vehicle should be well armoured. And it would clearly be a crying shame if it didn't mount some heavy weapons too. By now, we are talking about something not unlike a tank, except that it carries a bunch of infantrymen ready to jump out and

---

* The Soviet air defence force, which was separate from the main air force. Voyska PVO provided fighter cover for the strike aircraft of Frontal Aviation, in addition to defending the airspace of the USSR. 'Voyska' means 'Troops', or 'Force'. PVO stands for Protivo-Vozdushnaya Oborona, or Anti Air Defence.

scrap on foot – this is what is meant by 'dismounted close combat' – and it lacks the brutal armour-smashing main gun of the tank proper. This beast is getting to be nearly as expensive as a tank, though: and there's the rub. These armoured infantry fighting vehicles (the British version is called Warrior) cost a fortune. The British army only has enough of them to kit out nine battalions.

This brings us on to the next role, that of mechanised infantry. In British service, 'mechanised' nowadays means economy-class armoured. A further six infantry battalions are equipped with the Saxon vehicle, which is the poor man's Warrior. It is wheeled rather than tracked, uses mainly truck parts, and is lightly armoured and armed. This makes it vastly cheaper to buy and operate than a Warrior, but it would have great difficulty keeping up with the armoured juggernaut in a blitzkrieg operation and wouldn't survive long against first-division opposition. More importantly in the modern world, it is easily taken out by a gunman armed with a simple anti-armour rocket. Every third or fourth terrorist or insurgent in the world has one of these nowadays, so the Saxon is seldom the vehicle of choice. However, it shrugs off AK47 bullets and mortar shrapnel well enough, and it beats walking.

Armoured/mechanised warfare is the reason why some argue that the traditional infantry obsession with burdened marching is now out of place. An armoured infantryman can leave his rucksack (bergen, he calls it) in the Warrior when he dismounts. When it comes time to move a long distance, he gets back in and rides. Surely there is no great need for him to be fit and strong enough to go for miles with eighty or a hundred pounds on his back?

The trouble with this is that there are always dozens of new pieces of kit waiting in the wings which people would like to hang on our infantryman. They have only been prevented from doing so until now because he was already staggering under the maximum practical load. As soon as he seems likely not to need any given thing, a swarm of boffins will rush out and load him right up again. The moment our man manages to get rid of his bergen, he will be given a much heavier bulletproof jacket, more and better night-vision equipment, a better radio, satellite navigation and so on. Even if none of this is available, he can always usefully carry more weapons and ammo, and probably will. Thus, movement on foot with a heavy load remains a prime infantry skill, now and probably for ever. In any case, armoured/mechanised vehicles are far from universal in the British service.

In fact, we've got 9 armoured and 6 mechanised battalions. The remaining twenty-plus army infantry units are 'light'. This means that the only transports they possess are four-ton trucks, which need reasonably good roads and are not really battle-worthy. Even a good squirt from a machine gun will probably take out a four-tonner and most of the men inside. Thus, a light infantry battalion is going to have to get out of its trucks and foot it whenever the enemy are about in strength. These men must then carry all their kit and weapons on their backs, barring a few Land Rovers and suchlike. Light infantry are actually extremely heavily burdened on the march.

One should note, as an aside, that there actually is an infantry regiment called the Light Infantry. If you have just thought, 'I bet they aren't light infantry', you are getting the hang of the British army. The First Battalion, the Light Infantry is, indeed, currently roled as armoured – that is, heavy – infantry. The regiment is known as the Light Infantry for what it did during the Napoleonic wars.

Light infantry are often thought to be a cheap and feeble sort of unit, compared to the expensive heavy types. They move very slowly in the presence of the enemy or the absence of decent roads, and it is generally predicted that heavy armoured forces will roll right over them in a battle. Famously, the light US troops who deployed to the Saudi border in 1990, to forestall a possible invasion by Saddam Hussein's armour, cheerily referred to themselves as 'speed bumps'. However, light troops do have weapons which can damage or destroy armoured vehicles. A couple of men in each fire team often carry one-shot shoulder-fired anti-tank rockets (even more weight) and there is a group of longer-range anti-tank missiles at battalion level. Furthermore, many parts of the world are difficult for armour to move through: jungle and mountains, for example. Light infantry may be slow, but in these environments the armoured lads often can't move at all. Apart from all this, any opposing armoured force will struggle to survive for long in the presence of modern air power. So even in big, proper wars, light infantry may well have a part to play; they were there in strength for the Iraq invasion of 2003.

Anyway, proper, capital-intensive wars are getting scarce. But business is booming in the field of improper, cheap, labour-intensive, nasty war: and for this, light infantrymen are very useful indeed. When the enemy must be hunted down deep in the jungle or high in the mountains, you need light infantry. When you want to actually control a city rather than smash it to dust or drive through it occasionally in a tank, you need light infantry, and lots of them. Armoured infantry can do much of the same work, of course – they need only dismount from their vehicles to become as light as you could wish – but they are far more expensive. One should note that the British brigade remaining on the ground in Iraq in 2005, in addition to its normal complement of three armoured battle groups, has a further three light infantry battalions attached. As ever, the light infantry turn out to be required in rather greater numbers than one might think.

It is this latter type of fighting that the British Army and marines have mainly been doing since the end of World War II. Barring the very brief armoured opening assaults of Gulf I and II, we have mainly been engaged in lower-intensity campaigns. This is why, historically, the army has kept so many light infantry battalions, even though they weren't thought to be of much use against the expected swarms of commie tanks, should the cold war ever have turned hot.

Naturally, as it finally becomes clear even to the Ministry of Defence that the cold war really is over and that we will probably be involved in as many low-intensity wars as ever – if not more – we are cutting down on light infantry. As this book is written, four light battalions are being selected for the chop. However, this is not a matter of considered policy, much as defence minister Geoff Hoon has lately tied himself in knots trying to say that it is: it is the consequence of administrative bungling, as we shall see.

There is, formally, another infantry role: air assault infantry, often considered a subset of the light variety. Here, the idea is that the soldiers ride in and out of battle in helicopters. A helicopter is every bit as vulnerable to enemy fire as a four-ton truck, of course:

more so, in some circumstances. However, it can fly too high or too fast to be easily shot up, and it laughs at tough country, fixed defences and other obstacles. Anyone who has ever really dealt with problems of ground and movement can see why soldiers tend to love helicopters. Even so, military helicopters must try to avoid actually landing and taking off under enemy fire, which means that heli-borne soldiers may expect to march a good bit more than armoured ones.

Three British light battalions are assigned specifically to the air assault mission, although in fact there is nothing magical about it, and other infantrymen often ride in helicopters too. Two of these units are from the Parachute Regiment, and the other is a normal army infantry battalion – currently the Argyll and Sutherland Highlanders, a fearsome crowd of cut-throats who could only be considered 'normal' when compared to the Paras or commandos. One would expect an air assault unit to be even more expensive than an armoured one, helicopters being expensive things: but Britain has implemented this idea on the cheap, for various reasons. Unlike an air assault unit in the US or other armies, a British air assault formation does not possess any troop-carrying helicopters. On occasion it will be lent some, but the aircraft in question belong to someone else, usually the air force, and aren't always available. In most ways, a British air assault battalion is just another light infantry one, and indeed is used as such much of the time.

So, the main types of British infantry may be said to be armoured, mechanised, air assault light and plain-vanilla light. But there are some further anomalies and sub-divisions.

One of these is the Parachute Regiment, the legendary Paras, who are something of a special case. The three battalions of the Parachute Regiment are trained to jump into combat by parachute, which would seem to mean that there is another entire role here. As recently as 1998, Britain maintained a full parachute brigade organisation, 5 Airborne Brigade. As well as the three Para battalions, this had parachute artillery(!), headquarters, signals and everything, all complete.

There were a few problems with this, however. Even before helicopters came on the scene, mass parachute operations had, at best, a mixed record: there was a strong tendency for them to

turn into heroic disasters. Since the advent of troop-carrying helicopters in the 1960s, very few significant drops have been made;
the last time British Paras made a combat jump was into Suez,
in 1956. Essentially, the only reason that large numbers of troops
would nowadays go in by parachute would be if the target were
beyond helicopter range. The trouble with this is that our men
would then be far ahead of our own front lines, with no way of
getting out again – unless a serviceable runway could be captured
and the surrounding five kilometres-plus cleared of hostile fellows
with surface-to-air missiles. This risky grab-an-airport caper is
the main thinking behind modern-day parachute capability: the
seizure of an 'airhead' to permit more troops and equipment to
be flown in, or to extract a parachute raiding force.

However, as we shall see later on, Britain is so weak in transport aircraft that such an operation would be marginal at best.
The ability of the RAF to deliver the airhead brigade* in any
reasonable amount of time was always extremely doubtful, let
alone the idea of then flying in even more troops afterwards, plus
vehicles and supplies enough for them to be mobile and able to
fight. During the Strategic Defence Review of 1998 this was
(finally) noted. The army would henceforth restrict itself to
'battalion-level parachute operations'.

One might have thought that this would result in Britain maintaining only a battalion-sized force of paratroops. In fact 5
Airborne Brigade itself did close down, but none of its component parts went away, or even stopped being parachutists. All
three Para infantry battalions remain jump trained, as does a regiment of light artillery, an engineer unit, signals and so forth. Most
of these things, including two of the Para battalions, became part
of the newly reorganised, notionally helicopter-borne, 16 Air
Assault Brigade in 1998; but they kept their jump wings and red
berets, and they still like to spin scenarios which would involve
them getting to make a combat drop. Apart from the Argylls and
its helicopters – when it has any – 16 Air Assault Brigade closely
resembles the old 5 Airborne. The remaining Para battalion went
off to do other things. In 2004 this unit, the First Battalion, the
Parachute Regiment – 1 Para to its friends – was removed from

---

* Sorry, that should be *airborne* brigade, of course.

the normal infantry altogether and disappeared into the secretive Directorate of Special Forces. The plan is for it to become a so-called 'ranger' battalion.

So the British Army has an awful lot of paratroops considering that it is supposedly limiting itself to single-battalion drops (and not many of those, if it has any sense). One reason for this may be that paratroopers are not just ordinary soldiers who have been trained to parachute jump. After all, parachuting is no longer a dangerous thing calling for brave men, as it was in 1940; it is a popular leisure pursuit. But a British Para, quite apart from the pleasant recreation of jump school, has been through an especially gruelling and severe selection and training programme, particular to the airborne forces. This is called P Company.

P Company is far more difficult than the parachutist course, and confers the hard-earned right to wear the red beret. (Actually maroon, in the British airborne. Should you ever encounter a British soldier with a bright scarlet beret, he or she is actually a military policeman, a very different beast.) This extra-harsh regime makes the Paras an elite among the infantry, as they have been through longer and tougher training than the rest. The maroon beret thus possesses a certain credibility which the bearskin, for example, might be said to lack. And the undeniable glamour of the airborne tends to attract the keenest and most aggressive young soldiers. The teenage hardcases of Britain have heard of the paratroops, and would quite often like to be part of the airborne legend; they are less impressed with how well a regiment may have done at Waterloo.

The resulting special edge tends to make the Paras an obvious choice when the British government needs some muscle: they have been involved in most of the action since World War II. It was their status as the army's toughest, most aggressive and most in-demand soldiers that kept the Paras at three-battalion strength, not the parachute. And it is as light or perhaps helicopter-borne infantry that they can realistically expect to be deployed, rather than as a drop force, although the new 'ranger' unit may get up to all sorts of larks.

The parachute, then, is slowly becoming a regimental totem rather than a real tool, at least as far as line infantry are concerned, but the Paras will live on because they are good soldiers: just as

the Fusiliers and the Lancers do, despite the passing of the musket
and the lance.

That's the army infantry covered: some forty battalions, in the
process of coming down to thirty-six. But these cuts are not a
simple matter. The problem is that the arms plot mechanism, the
system of changes in role every few years, was already struggling
to provide enough ready-for-duty battalions to do all the current
tasks at any given time. Most units were being rotated through
the cycle of leave, training and deployment much faster than was
good for them. For this reason, in addition to deleting four battalions from the list, the whole infantry is supposedly to be reorganised into regiments of at least two battalions and the arms
plot is to stop. The head of the army, General Sir Mike Jackson,
has made this very clear:

> The ending of the Arms Plot means that the **current existence of
> single battalion regiments has run its course** [General Jackson's
> emphasis]. The whole Infantry must now move to a large
> Regimental structure. It is significant that this was the intent of
> previous Army Boards in 1961/62, 1966/67 and to some extent
> in 1992. This Board has had the opportunity to grasp the nettle.
> *Press statement by General Sir Mike Jackson,*
> *Chief of the General Staff, December 2004.*

The plan is that soldiers will now move about within the new
large regiments during their careers. Every battalion can be given
a permanent role and base location, and men will be able to gain
wider experience by changing battalions within their regiment.
The end of the arms plot, and effectively the end of the famed
regimental system – for much of the infantry, anyway – will free
up those units which were formerly unavailable for duty due to
being in the process of changing role. This will allow thirty-six
battalions to do the work of forty.

Sounds good; nobody really liked the arms plot. But there are
a lot of problems here. British infantrymen are primarily loyal to
their regiment and their country, probably in that order for many
of them. Concepts such as the good of the army as a whole, or
even the infantry as a whole, are well down the list. And the

large-regiment plan will see a lot of famous names disappear. There will be a great deal of pain and grief. As an example, soldiers will no longer be able to make a career as members of the Black Watch, or the Argyll and Sutherland Highlanders, or any other of the legendary Scots infantry units. From now on, all Scottish infantrymen are one. They will serve in the Royal Regiment of Scotland, which will have only one badge, one tartan and one choice of crazy Scottish headgear and ceremonial weaponry.

Furthermore, the pain is not being evenly distributed. The Paras were ring-fenced from the outset; so, more controversially, were the Gurkhas. There are understandable reasons for both of these, however, and much though it sticks in the craw of the rest they can just about swallow this. But the five Guards battalions were not merely ring-fenced; they were also permitted to maintain their status as individual regiments. This, for a lot of the line infantry, is the final straw. The Guards famously spend significant amounts of time on public ceremony in London – the Changing of the Guard at Buckingham Palace and the Trooping of the Colour are only the two best-known of the various shows that the Guards put on. With the best will in the world, it is difficult to see how they can be as good at real soldiering as their colleagues who do not have this extra burden. And yet they are the ones left untouched.

There was much talk of national identity in the justification for the Guards' preferential treatment, but in fact only three of the five Household battalions have such an identity – the Scots, Irish and Welsh Guards. If national identity were really the issue, surely the Coldstream and Grenadier Guards could have amalgamated to become the de facto English Guards, whatever you chose to call them. It is fairly clear that the real reason the Guards have been exempted from the changes is because they have a lot of pull and public visibility. This particular nettle was evidently a bit too painful to grasp.

And there is more. The large-regiment concept is not to be uniformly applied. Perhaps a trifle embarrassed by the fact that he himself is a Para and is presiding over the preservation intact of his own regiment while others go to the wall, General Jackson has delegated the detailed reorganisation to several lower-level headquarters. (This is General Sir Mike Jackson of Kosovo fame – or Bloody Sunday fame, if you prefer – who has not so far seemed an irresolute man, but this sort of thing requires a different kind of resolution.*) This means that some of the new regiments will be truly large, with five battalions like the planned Scottish super-regiment, allowing an infantryman some genuine career scope. Some, though, where the priority was to save names and hats, will have only two battalions; there are going to be several such. Indeed, the Royal Irish Regiment and the Guards units will still be single-battalion, despite what General Jackson thinks of that idea. This can hardly be described as consistent or sensible; the nettle hasn't really been grasped at all.

And the scope for inter-regimental hair-pulling is wider yet: the handing out of the permanent roles and locations will surely be the occasion for some fierce infighting. Not many will want to be mechanised rather than proper armoured infantry, for example, and some flavours of light will be a lot more prestigious than others. One can't help but notice that the Guards have already bagged one of the scarce armoured slots. So one may be sure that there are dark mutterings and plottings afoot in the infantry messes and clubs

---

* See Chapter 6 for General Jackson's role in the Kosovo intervention. As a junior officer in 1972 he was also present during the infamous Bloody Sunday episode in (London) Derry, when the Paras shot dead thirteen people during street protests. Then-Captain Jackson shot no one himself, on this occasion at least, and seems to have been involved only peripherally. The Paras have always claimed that they were fired on first, although none of them were hit and no solid evidence of hostile fire has ever been found. Independent observers tend to assess the whole thing as a tragic mistake, though both republicans and paratroopers claim that the other side caused it on purpose. It is certainly true that the Paras of the early 1970s were dangerous men, not ones it would ever be wise to throw bricks at. It is also true that the Provisional IRA are quite cunning and ruthless enough to fire a few rounds in a situation like that and then melt away, leaving the Paras to discredit themselves and the British government. Those who condemn the Paras unreservedly and with them the British state should perhaps recall that the British security forces have lost over a thousand dead in the current Troubles: they have killed fewer than 400 themselves. Restraint of this sort is quite uncommon when powerful armies battle insurgency. By contrast, US forces fighting at the time of Bloody Sunday eventually left between ten and twenty Vietnamese bodies behind them for every American lost.

up and down the land at the moment. The army infantry will be a very different organisation in which to live and serve from now on. This round of cuts is not exceptionally deep, but it has precipitated a much more radical change than those which went before.

It would be nice to think that all this was for a good reason, but of course it isn't. It is simply the best way that General Jackson and his colleagues can think of to cut four battalions, minimise the outcry from the better-connected regiments' powerful friends, and avoid working the remaining thirty-six to death. The start point was a cut in numbers; why this was thought necessary, we shall see later.

But we aren't done yet: the army, perhaps curiously, is not the only outfit in the men-with-guns business. Britain actually possesses something like a further five battalions' worth. Soon, one in every eight infantrymen will not be in the army at all.

The best known non-army foot soldiers are the Royal Marine Commandos, the navy's land-combat force. Once upon a time the Royal Marines were employed in small detachments aboard warships, providing boarding and landing parties and, being disciplined volunteers, assistance to the ship's officers in controlling their unruly press-ganged sailors. Those days are long gone, however.

Nowadays, the main operational units of the British marines are three lightish infantry battalions.* A marine recruit undergoes especially long and arduous training, much as paratroopers do; this qualifies him as a commando, and wins him the right to wear a green beret. The words 'marine' and 'commando' have a useful resonance like that attaching to 'paratrooper' or 'airborne'. The marines likewise possess an appeal in the public mind, and despite a good deal of rivalry, occasionally violent, are very similar in outlook and attributes to the Paras. They too have been something of a standby for the British government since World War II; famously, there is said only to have been one year since 1945 when Royal Marines were not under fire somewhere.

The marine commandos are focused on amphibious warfare

---

* Confusingly to the uninitiated, these units are called 'Commandos' rather than 'battalions'. The word refers to the unit as well as to the troops themselves.

rather than airborne operations but, like the Paras, are employed more as extra-tough light or helicopter-mobile infantry than in their specialist role. However, amphibious landings being rather more practical than parachute ones in most circumstances, such operations have taken place in living memory: Iraq 2003, Falklands 1982.

The other noteworthy thing about the commandos, apart from their elite status and amphibious flavour, is that they are currently trialling a new set-up for light infantry, known as Commando 21. Rather than three rifle companies, an HQ company and a manoeuvre-support company, a Commando nowadays is made up of two close combat companies, two stand-off combat companies plus logistics and command companies. They are also re-equipping with a small, lightly armoured tracked vehicle called Viking. The stand-off companies are able to deploy various kinds of heavy weaponry, such as heavy machine guns and mortars, which would formerly have been under battalion control.

It is nice to see someone having a think about the traditional battalion structure, which has been much the same for a long time. But one can't help noticing that a Commando 21 unit will muster only 192 men in rifle sections, as compared to 216 in a normal battalion; it has lost a rifle troop, despite the overall strength going up from 682 to 692. Funnily enough, as we lose indians we gain chiefs. There are significantly more boss jobs under Commando 21, and it should noticeably improve promotion chances in the marines. Thus, it will probably be very popular. We may well see the idea spreading.

So the navy has its own private army, although in fact it is on pretty much permanent loan to the normal army as the basis of an elite light brigade. This could be viewed as jolly sporting of the navy, paying for an extra land-force brigade, and indeed the navy itself formerly tended to think so: the marines' survival was occasionally in doubt back during the cold war. Nowadays, the navy is only too glad to have something so visibly useful, given the sparseness of serious maritime opposition. Great care is taken to emphasise the marines in naval publicity material.

Interestingly, the air force is also in the infantry game. The Royal Air Force Regiment – known as the 'rock-apes' after the Barbary apes of Gibraltar, for some reason – is partly an organisation of chemical-defence specialists. But the RAF Regiment also has six of what it calls field squadrons, which are basically light infantry rifle companies: potentially two battalions' worth. They have pretty much the same equipment and training as ordinary light infantry. Unlike the marines, RAF infantry are employed entirely under their parent organisation's control, assigned to 'ground defence'. UK air bases are pretty well secured by civilian agencies and police, so one must presume the field squadron role to be that of security for RAF units deployed abroad. However, this might well be the responsibility of the host nation, or could be undertaken by the deployed units themselves – all RAF personnel are trained in defensive ground combat, and a typical aircraft squadron contains hundreds of people. All in all, airfield defence seems like rather a narrow focus for around 5 per cent of the UK's future infantry strength. Indeed, the rock-apes themselves seem to have notions of some higher purpose than merely being heavily armed security guards. For example, one of the field squadrons is parachute-trained. Why this is required for an airfield security unit is something of a poser: but there it is.

If the RAF Regiment infantry are to survive, they will probably need to become more flexible and join in with the army, as the marines have done. Mind you, many observers suggested as much before the Strategic Defence Review of 1998, and the RAF Regiment sailed through unscathed, mad parachute unit and all. So perhaps not.

There is one further group in the British armed forces which consists primarily of men with guns; indeed, they are perhaps the quintessential form. These are the men of the Special Air Service and the Special Boat Service, the SAS and the SBS. They are commonly referred to as comprising the whole of the UK special forces, though in fact the director of special forces also has other, less well known formations reporting to him. The SAS and SBS are his gunmen, however. Just where 1 Para will fit in remains to be seen.

The special forces proper, formally speaking 22 Special Air Service Regiment of the British Army and the Special Boat Service of the Royal Marines, are both small battalion-equivalents, with the SAS the larger of the two. Nowadays they work together as a national asset, and their training is largely in common: there isn't all that much to choose between an SBS swimmer-canoeist and an SAS trooper in general terms.

They are, essentially, the ultimate light infantrymen. (Always men, still: women can join the other, shadowier UKSF organisations, but not the fighting teams.) The SAS and SBS are the infantrymen you would create if resources were no object. Only proven servicemen are recruited, theoretically from all arms and branches. Actually, however, SAS/SBS selection and training heavily favours former infantrymen, and most who pass have such a background, often in the Paras or commandos. The training alone is immensely profligate of manpower: it lasts a full year, much of it overseas, and has a 90 per cent failure rate. In other words, it costs the armed forces up to ten years' worth of fully trained serviceman time to get a single SF operator. This is not even to include the time of the training staff, who will themselves already have gone through this process. Nor does it include the lavish further training our man receives after finally struggling out of the end of the basic pipeline.

Once you have actually managed to obtain one of these million-dollar super-troopers, then, it makes sense to equip him properly. And this is the true beauty of being in the SAS or SBS. The Ministry of Defence has somehow managed to buffalo the media into accepting that *absolutely everything* about the SF is a secret.

Brilliantly, this leaves the SF free to buy whatever kit they like, within reason. Nobody knows that they aren't buying British – needless to say, they mostly aren't – so it doesn't matter. Their choice cannot be used, for example, to criticise the awful British-made rubbish that is often inflicted on the regular forces.

For example, in 2001, when the controversy over the SA80 A2 modification programme was at its almost-unnoticed height, the MoD issued a press-briefing question and answer sheet regarding the matter. Here is a direct quote:

Q: Do the UK's special forces use the SA80 weapon system?
A: I am sure you will understand that the MOD cannot divulge details of the weapons used by the SF as this

would assist potential adversaries in countering or neutralising UKSF capabilities.

Oh really. A more forthright version, in a dream MoD briefing, might have gone like this:

Q: Do the UK's special forces use the SA80 weapon system?

A: No, of course they don't [mordant, incredulous laugh]. They're the premier experts on small arms in the world, for goodness' sake, and they have their choice of equipment! The only people anywhere who carry the SA80 are those who don't have any alternative – regular British troops. Oh, and the Mozambique army use it, apparently, but they didn't have a choice either. They got the SA80 as part of a British aid package.

Q: What do the special forces use, then?

A: When they want a 5.56mm rifle they normally use the American M16; when they want a 5.56mm light machine gun they use the Belgian-designed Minimi, again like the Americans. All the Americans, that is, not just special ops people. Both of those guns were available very cheaply when we bought the SA80. Proven designs. We could have thrown the unions a bone by making them under licence here.

Q: Well, why didn't you?

A: God knows. No, seriously, the fact is we were in the process of privatising Royal Ordnance just then – that is, selling off the government rifle plant, among other things. They were the ones who came up with the SA80. The Royal Small Arms Factory wouldn't have been worth tuppence if it hadn't had the order for the new rifle, would it? And a foreign make under licence wouldn't have been any good; there were all the design bods to think of. Why would the private sector buy a design bureau that couldn't sell its designs? Lot of chaps would have had to be let go if we hadn't gone with the SA80: and then somebody might have asked why we'd had them on the government payroll all those years, given that they didn't design the previous rifle either. Come to think of it, that plant hadn't actually brought out a new rifle of its own since the Lee-Enfield, and that was in the 1890s. No wonder the SA80 turned out to be a mess. The buyers actually shut the Enfield plant down straight away and shifted production elsewhere.

Q: Who bought Royal Ordnance, then?

A: British Aerospace. We had to guarantee them the second tranche of SA80 production, naturally. Even then they only gave us £190 million for the whole shooting match, the rifle plant and a lot of other things besides, and they stiffed us on the pension fund to boot. You'll be hearing their name again.

Q: When?

A: Well, later on after we had a whole bunch of duff SA80s, some made by us and some by BAe, we decided to get the guns fixed once and for all. We paid £92 million for that, to Heckler and Koch, who are a good, reputable firm and seem to have done a decent job.

Q: Phew. At least we had the sense to go to someone else, eh?

A: Well, not really. Can you guess who owned Heckler and Koch just then?

Q: Not British Aerospace?

A: Now you're getting the idea. We order dud guns from ourselves, in order to sell our gun factories to BAe for a knock-down price. We then order even more dud guns from BAe. But the guns are no good, so years later we have to give BAe a lot of the money back to finally fix the bloody things once and for all. They sold H and K not long after they got the A2 upgrade contract, you know. I wonder how much that made for them? And another thing—

[*Suddenly a group of ministry PR staff burst in. After a struggle, A is subdued and stuffed into a sack. The ministry guys wrestle him from the room.*]

Sadly, Ministry of Defence briefings aren't like that. Getting back to the UK special forces, at least the veil of notional secrecy – it *is* pretty notional, at least regarding equipment – allows the SF to buy proper kit. This goes further than just rifles, boots and so on; the SAS has been known to use American-made Stinger anti-aircraft missiles, for example, rather than the British issue. Regrettably perhaps, that's about where it stops – it isn't possible, for example, to get the special forces to buy aircraft and warships.

We have finally seen all the men with guns in the British military. There are two battalion-equivalents of special forces super-troopers, six of elite paratroops and commandos, and thirty-five-odd of line infantry or equivalent. As things stand, despite the fact that their equipment tends to be none of the best, these men are the jewel in the British defence crown. They are some of the toughest, most professional, most experienced soldiers anywhere in the world. A few groups, such as the French Foreign Legion or the special ops forces of various nations, might match or exceed some of them: but nobody else can field forty-plus battalions of comparable quality.

Much of this is due to circumstance rather than institutional brilliance on the part of the British forces, or any national virtues that might be said to exist. The British infantry are fortunate in long having been all-volunteer and relatively long-serving. They are also the right size to have gained a lot of experience from the many wars ('trouble spots', 'conflicts', etc) that they have been to. The sergeant-majors serving as this book is written may just have joined up in time for the Falklands; they will then have spent much of the 1980s in pre-ceasefire Northern Ireland, had a trip to the Gulf in '91, done some tours in the Balkans, perhaps Sierra Leone and now back to the Gulf again. They *ought* to be good, with only forty-odd battalions doing all that.

Many of the other rich nations who might be expected to have similar troops have been handicapped by conscription (France) or been averse to expeditionary action, or both (Japan, Germany). American infantry are nowadays volunteers, and America does get about a bit, especially lately. But a lot of American riflemen leave after a mere two years' service, even in the elite formations; Brits aren't even *allowed* to leave until they've done four years, and most stay longer. Furthermore, even the longer-serving US soldiers and marines have tended to see less action per head – again, until lately – as the US maintains no fewer than fourteen divisions, compared to Britain with less than that number of brigades.

So the British infantry are probably the best there is. But cracks are starting to appear. Already, a noticeable proportion of these excellent men are not British at all, at least by origin, and there are plenty of vacant places; it is getting difficult to find Brits willing to sign up. One might suggest, as many of the older guard among the infantry themselves do, that the Nintendo generation lacks the grit for the work. This may be true. It might also be true, however, that plenty of young British blokes would be willing to swap their trainers for combat boots, pick up a rifle and walk the streets of Basra or Kabul. Only the boots aren't great, the rifle may not work, and they'll have to go through some very severe training before running a real, serious risk of death or rough handling overseas. Then, during their brief spells at home, they'll find themselves being massively out-earned by famously low-paid groups such as nurses and firemen, both of whom work easier shifts, go home every twenty-four hours and run negligible risks. Perhaps they aren't as slow as some might think, the Nintendo generation.

And yet, an extra £10,000 a year per front-line infantryman – enough for a 50 per cent increase in the abysmal pay, and to buy really good boots, good equipment and an excellent new rifle *every year* – would only be a matter of £250 million or so. That is, less than 1 per cent of the defence budget.

What on earth is going on? Whatever can be so important, and so outrageously expensive, that we are actually cutting back on our splendid, useful, hard-bought infantrymen, rather than sorting out their problems – given that it would cost us almost nothing to do so?

Let's find out.

CHAPTER

2

Tanks

What is the role of cavalry in battle?
To lend tone to what would otherwise be a vulgar brawl.

Cartoon caption, *Punch*, 1892

It is often said that the navy and air force man their equipment, whereas the army equips its men. However, this is only really true for army infantry; the armoured corps are all about manning equipment – or they should be. It behoves us, then, to examine the tank.

Like the infantry, tank units in the British army have always had the Regimental System. Unlike the infantry, the tank men seem likely to keep it. The army has a thing called the Royal Armoured Corps, which one might suppose to be the administrative umbrella for all British tank units: but of course, this being the British Army, it isn't that simple. The Household Cavalry, the sovereign's personal horse guards, would no more stand for being lumped in with the rest than the Foot Guards would admit to being line infantry. Thus, if one wants to refer to all British tank units, one should formally say the 'Household Cavalry and Royal Armoured Corps'. I shall just say armoured corps, to save ink.

Once upon a time, the word 'tank' referred to pretty much any armoured tracked fighting vehicle, regardless of its actual use. Classic fighting tanks would be modified as mine-clearance vehicles, infantry carriers or whatever, but they were all still tanks. Nowadays these vehicles have other names, usually mad portmanteau ones such as the Armoured Infantry Fighting Vehicle of the last chapter. The serious tank, designed not to carry infantry but to fight in its own right, is referred to as a Main Battle Tank.

Like most other military systems, it has grown in complexity over the decades.

A modern Main Battle Tank, such as the British Challenger II, is a big brute, weighing a bit over sixty tons. It is also expensive: the whole Challenger II project is reckoned to have cost the government £2.2 billion for 386 fighting tanks, putting an individual Challenger at nearly £6 million in early-90s money. This is only a quarter of the price of an older strike jet, and a tiny fraction of the cost of a new one, but it isn't peanuts.

The tank carries four men: the tank commander, who directs its activities; the gunner, who fires its turret weapons; a loader for the main gun, who also doubles as radio operator; and the driver. The crew is seen by the army as being roughly equivalent to a rifle section, so a tank may be commanded by a corporal. The purpose of the Main Battle Tank, boiled down, is to carry its main gun onto the battlefield and use it. Other vehicles have all-terrain speed, armour plating and machine guns; the distinguishing feature of the tank is its main armament.

A tank cannon is a highly specialist piece of equipment, not found anywhere else. Unlike nearly every other type of modern gun, it is a smoothbore, having no rifling in its barrel. This is because it is not primarily intended to fire exploding shells, but rather big darts made of ultra-hard heavy metal. These metal darts have fins, and so do not need the spin from rifling to make them fly straight. They ride down the gun barrel on plugs, or sabots, which confine the propelling gases behind them and then fall off once the dart is flying free. All this allows the dart penetrator to be shot from a long-barrelled tank gun at an insanely high velocity, achieving terrific armour-piercing power. Such projectiles are formally known as Armour Piercing Fin Stabilised Discarding Sabot ammunition, or APFSDS.

All this high-tech, expensive effort into getting the highest possible velocity and hardest, pointiest projectile is devoted to but one end: knocking out very heavily armoured moving targets. Tanks, that is. If the target wasn't moving, you would use artillery; if it wasn't armoured, you wouldn't need a penetrator round. This, then, is the purpose of the Main Battle Tank: to fight its own kind.

To be sure, tanks can be used for other things. In Iraq recently they were used to reconnoitre cities ahead of foot troops. A Challenger mounts two machine guns as well as its monstrous tin opener; it can use these against infantry, or simply run them over – called grunt-crunching by the tankers. The main gun can also fire an exploding shell instead of a dart. But a tank is a mind-bogglingly expensive and difficult way to put a couple of protected machine gunners into battle, and used as a conventional cannon its main gun isn't especially effective. Designed as it is to shoot its rounds on very flat trajectories, it cannot be elevated high enough to get useful artillery range. As for probing dangerous cities, an armoured infantry carrier is a better choice. Indeed, shanks's pony may be better yet, if you are really serious about a good result in the long run.

A tank isn't just pricey; it is also monumentally difficult to deploy. Moving Main Battle Tanks around the world is one of the biggest headaches any modern army has to face. You don't want to drive the brutes anywhere under their own power: they are incredibly destructive. Tanks must not be driven at speed on a road you want to use again afterwards, and it is very bad for the tank as well as the road surface. You don't really want to drive them off-road, either, through friendly country – it won't stay friendly for long, not with its crops destroyed, fences flattened, small buildings knocked down, etc. Tanks are moved overland by rail, or, failing that, on tank-transporting road vehicles; and god forbid you should ever have to fly one anywhere.

Really, then, we're only going to all this trouble and expense if we think there will be enemy tanks for our tank to fight. The trouble with tank killing as a reason to have tanks is that there are now many other ways to do it. The best way is from the air, with a guided weapon released from a safe altitude, high up. If you don't have such things, a lower-flying airman can do the job with rockets or cannon, or by using a cluster-bomb. He will run some risk from ground anti-aircraft fire, but he is in no danger from the tank itself. One can also chop up enemy armour effectively using certain kinds of artillery and ground-launched missiles of various types. Again, these methods don't involve any danger. The tank has no chance to fight back, and that's how we like it.

If all this fails, you will have to work within the range of the enemy tank's weapons. You could use a tank yourself. This might well be seen as playing to the enemy's strengths, as his own tank is also designed as a tank killer. Fighting tanks with tanks, in the modern day; is a bit like killing dogs by getting down on all fours yourself and biting them to death. You *could* do it that way, but it's needlessly dangerous and difficult.

Alternatively, you could prepare an infantry ambush with anti-tank weapons, but this means that you must let the enemy come to you, and the army hate that. The best defence is usually seen as being a good hard offence. It must be tank versus tank, then, if we aren't to rely on air power or artillery. The modern tanks of the Western democracies are much better than any likely opposition, especially in their ability to see the enemy and shoot first when operating at night. Even so, using tanks to fight tanks is dangerous, and extremely troublesome logistically.

Despite all this, the army likes tanks. Institutionally, it has no faith in help from the skies. It doesn't believe that artillery can reliably hit moving armour, and this is, indeed, not a simple thing. Most of all, it doesn't like to sit still. Generals want to be able to move forward and smash the enemy without assistance. Until the end of the cold war this whole mindset was more reasonable: there was no guarantee whatsoever that the skies over the Central Front would have been ours, and the airmen hadn't yet acquired their current abilities against ground armour.

Three or four tanks make up a troop, the armoured unit equivalent to an infantry platoon. The troop commander, a young lieutenant as in the infantry, commands one tank; his sergeant commands another, and corporals the rest. Several troops' worth of tanks make up a squadron rather than a company, in British usage. Tank squadrons form regiments, equivalent to infantry battalions. A regimental CO and his staff will form the nucleus of a mixed battle group in combat, just as infantry lieutenant-colonels do. Such a regiment, equipped with Challenger II, will field up to fifty-eight tanks with 232 crewmen and will have between 500 and 600 total personnel. As in the infantry, there will be all sorts of stuff other than actual tanks attached at various levels.

Most of the soldiers in a cavalry regiment, despite the usual army insistence that every cap badge is worn by a unique breed, are pretty similar to the men in the infantry battalions. Teenage troopers, hardcase corporals, tough-as-nails sergeants and genuinely fearsome sergeant-majors; many of the cavalry units have non-standard ranks, customs and so forth, just as the infantry do, but the men themselves are of a similar sort.

Cavalry officers are genuinely somewhat different. They are noticeably more upper class. This is a tradition of long standing in the British army, going back to the days when officers' commissions were bought and sold, and a cavalry commission was always worth more than an infantry one. Indeed, it goes back a lot further than that. Ever since men started taking horses to war, it has been the toffs who rode while the less well-circumstanced walked, right back through medieval knights to the Roman equestrian class. It is no coincidence that in many languages modern words for aristocrat or gentleman or knight translate literally as 'horseman' or 'rider'. (Spanish *caballero*, French *chevalier*, German *ritter*.) In English we have 'cavalier', which once meant the same thing. Nowadays it suggests a quality of being offhand and snooty, perhaps, but in a swashbuckling and stylish way – a good word, then, for modern cavalry officers. The infantry have their socially elite regiments too, of course. Some Guards battalions, and certain others, are just as exquisite as the cavalry. Generally, though, if you're looking for a truly exclusive officers' mess, the cavalry is the place to be; and this goes beyond a mere public-school education and pukka drawl. The cavalry still really prefer that young officers know how to ride a horse. Some skill at polo is an advantage, too.

I first encountered the cav mindset during my basic naval training, when we had a cavalryman as the army exchange officer at Dartmouth. Unsurprisingly, he was in charge of the riding club. The rule at Dartmouth was that you had a certain number of 'free' periods, but these were to be filled with some approved sportsmanlike activity. The various clubs and societies would thus make a pitch to attract the new cadets each term, and I can still remember the one delivered by the dashing major on behalf of the riding club.

'Now then,' he said. 'You are all young men and women. At the moment you are just starting out at the college here, but soon you will get some leave. You will meet a lovely young person of the opposite sex, and you will hit it off, because all the nice girls love a sailor, and so of course do all the *nice boys*.'

Pause for polite chuckle from the crowd.

'After a while, this person will invite you to come and stay at their family home. You will get up in the morning and you will go down to breakfast, and everything will be super.

'But then,' the major went on, 'something terrible will happen to most of you naval officers.'

We all wondered what it could be.

'You will just be having your breakfast and wondering whether to enjoy a little tennis later on, or perhaps go for a walk in the grounds.'

(Needless to say, I never met a girl from this sort of home. I don't think many of us did, actually; but the major was off in his own happy Noel Coward world by now.)

'But then – horror – someone will say that it's a lovely day for a ride. Everyone will agree, and the horses will be brought round. But most of you *naval* officers will have to bow out, because you *will not be able to ride*. And someone else will cut you out, and your girlfriend or boyfriend will dump you and break your heart, and it will be *very sad*.

'Unless, that is, you join the riding club. Thank you.'

More than swagger and horsemanship is necessary to become a cavalry officer. One also generally needs some money. Some regiments still make it quite plain to aspiring officers that they will require an income beyond their salary. For example, it is very normal in all British messes to be 'fined' occasionally for minor misbehaviour: that is, to be made to buy drinks for the others, usually for some heinous crime like bringing your headgear into the mess, or leaving the table before the loyal toast. There is also often a rule that if the mess president fails to spot your error within a given time, it is he who must pay. In a normal mess such fines are seldom seriously expensive: a bottle of wine, or a round of port, say. A cavalry fine, by contrast, might easily run to a case of vintage champagne. This sort of environment is only for those in receipt of a comfortable supplementary income.

The cavalry are very nice about this, however. Since most of them were forced to swap their horses for tanks, there has been a regrettable necessity to have a fair number of mechanics attached to each regiment. These people are not cavalry troopers; they are craftsmen and women of the Corps of Royal Electrical and

Mechanical Engineers, the REME. (Not at all the same outfit as the Royal Engineers, the Sappers, who are much grander than the lowly REME, though not as grand as the cavalry. Sappers will deign to perform only civil engineering.) The mechanics are not the problem, however: with them comes a technical-corps officer, and he or she needs to be a member of the cavalry officers' mess. REME officers are required to hold an engineering degree* and are not usually from the same level of society as the cavalrymen. They will only rarely possess any inherited wealth.

According to army people I have met, a fairly civilised process has been developed for getting round this. The mess president simply sits the new technical officer down upon joining, and has a friendly chat, something along these lines:

Mess president: Well, well. Sit down, sit down, won't you. Welcome to the regiment. Splendid. Tea? Splendid. Here we are. [*Serves tea, with great ceremony. Probably has his with a slice of lemon. Wipes moustache with a silk handkerchief he keeps in his sleeve.*]
New REME officer: Thank you, sir. [*Sits down, fiddles with spectacles nervously. Takes tea. In all likelihood does something utterly frightful with the milk, revealing lowly origins.*]
MP: [*Winces slightly at the milk blunder.*] Now then. Whenever we get a new REME officer, I always like to have a little chat about mess life, you know, make sure we all get along swimmingly as part of one big happy family. [*Quotes some regimental slogan or motto at this point.*] There is one thing which occasionally used to cause the odd bit of bother, you see: our mess bills generally run at about [*names an outrageous sum*]. D'you think you'll have any difficulty with that?
NRO: [*Chokes.*] But, sir, that's more than my pay!
MP: Oh, ah, yes. Well, I quite see your point there, of course. Cheese and nuts and so forth are shockingly

---

* Unlike Sapper officers, which may explain why the Sappers prefer to avoid any activity much more technical than digging a big hole, or perhaps building a bridge.

expensive these days. What sort of bill do you normally pay?

NRO: Er, well, about thirty or forty pounds a month, sir.

MP: Well, well, shall we say thirty-five pounds a month, then? Splendid. I very much look forward to having you with us.

[*For the rest of the REME officer's time with the regiment, he receives a bill for precisely thirty-five pounds every month.*]

So the cavalry really are different; the officers, anyway.

Getting back to equipping these colourful men, we can see that the British army only possesses enough Challengers for six regiments, and indeed this is all the Main Battle Tank regiments we have. There are, however, a further six armoured-corps regiments on the books.

Four of these are designated 'formation reconnaissance' units. Rather than mighty Challengers, these lads ride Scimitar light tanks.* The Scimitar is old and weakly armed, mounting only a 30mm cannon like that on a Warrior infantry vehicle. This may be enough to see off other light tanks and infantry carriers, but if a Scimitar ever runs into a real tank it will almost certainly come off worst. Scimitars are supposed to operate ahead of the main British line in a reconnaissance role, finding the enemy for the main force to deal with.

The reconnaissance platoons within the armoured-infantry battalions and Challenger regiments also have Scimitars for just this purpose, so one might wonder where 'formation recce' comes in. The book answer is that a formation recce regiment will operate even further forward, under the control of a higher-level headquarters. Formerly, this would have been a division HQ, but this didn't add up. With only two fighting divisions, which is the most the British Army can field, one would realistically require only two

---

* The cavalry themselves dislike the term 'light tank', preferring 'armoured fighting vehicle' (or even 'armoured car' among the older generation). However, everybody else – including most of the army – says 'light tank', and this is not a book for cavalrymen so I shall use the more common phrase.

light-tank regiments. Some cavalrymen, in that case, would be out of work. But that's not a problem; books can easily be altered. The plan is now for all armoured and mechanised brigades to have a Recce regiment. Indeed, one of the Challenger units is soon to mothball its heavy tanks in favour of Scimitar for just this reason.

So, six heavyweight tank regiments and four light recce ones, soon to be five and five. But there are twelve armoured-corps regiments. What are the other two doing?

Perhaps strangely, one of them is doing nuclear-biological-chemical defence. A unit exists called the Joint Nuclear, Biological and Chemical Defence Regiment, which is equipped with decontamination pumps, gas-proof detector vehicles and so forth. Its creation was recommended in the 1998 defence review, which immediately created a panic in which everybody struggled to avoid being handed such an obvious lemon. Decontamination and so on are all very worthy, of course, but not many soldiers genuinely want to be spraying things down with decon hoses and peering at chems meters when they could be letting off big guns or roaring about in tanks.

But, as we have seen, the Main Battle Tank is starting to look like a lot more trouble than it is usually worth and the army already has more light-tank regiments than it knows what to do with. The armoured corps, then, was looking distinctly vulnerable by 1998. Another organisation which was backed up against the chopping block was the RAF Regiment, which we met in the last chapter. It was thus the armoured corps and the rock-apes who were left without chairs when the NBC music stopped, and it is they who provide the manpower for the Joint NBC Regiment – an oddball pairing if ever there was one. In days of old such a task would surely have been handed to the logistics corps, or the REME, or someone like that, but by 1998 such people were already horribly overworked in our many ongoing modern wars and commitments – unlike the tank men and the rock-apes.

Characteristically for the British cavalry, the armoured corps outfit that was made to go and scrub chemicals with the horrid RAF was the Royal Tank Regiment – the so-called 'poor man's cav'. This regiment was formed during World War I to operate the new tanks which had just been invented. At that stage the proper cavalry were still hoping to get some horsey combat and weren't interested. Later on, the horsed regiments – slowly and reluctantly – changed over to tanks (most of them did, that is). They remained, however, far more swanky than the RTR. To this day, if you really want to be a tank officer but didn't attend a decent public school and can't ride a horse, your best bet is the Royal Tanks.

To be fair, the RTR might not have been lumbered with clean-up duty if it hadn't been a two-battalion regiment: the RTR is an exception to the rule of no battalions for tanks (of course there's an exception!) The 1st RTR are now chemical scrubbers; the 2nd RTR are still happily driving Challengers. A small niche thus remains for the ordinary middle classes to be tank officers. But one suspects that the public schoolboys of the pukka cavalry would never have found themselves commanding chemical clean-up crews no matter what. They have certainly escaped scatheless from the 2004 cuts.

While on the subject of the Royal Tank Regiment in recent times, it is hard to ignore the 'body armour' controversy which sprang up following the death of Sergeant Steve Roberts of the 2nd RTR, five days into the Iraq invasion of 2003. Sergeant Roberts was killed by a bullet which hit him in the chest while he was dismounted from his tank. The army admitted to his widow that had he been wearing the latest Enhanced Combat Body Armour (ECBA) he would have lived. This was especially galling as Sergeant Roberts had earlier been issued with ECBA, but it had then been taken away in order that it could be given to another soldier.

All this led to considerable uproar. It was felt by some that the ECBA issue exposed monstrous failings in the MoD supply system. There were calls for the defence minister, Geoff Hoon, to resign. The body armour issue became a mainstream media story, and was debated in Parliament.

There are in all truth many things wrong with the military procurement and supply system. The ECBA issue, however, is one on which Whitehall is pretty well clean: sadly, it was seized upon with such enthusiasm as to obscure all else. The ECBA 'story' and similar non-starters are about all that the MoD has lately been called to account for in the public domain. Given the endless succession of real blunders at the ministry, its officials must be glad to spend their time on such safe ground.

The clue regarding ECBA is in the name: enhanced. Until 2002 standard British combat body armour was a lightweight ballistic vest, quite incapable of stopping a bullet. Reasonably enough: in the high-intensity wars of the past it was rare for soldiers to be hit by bullets. Most wounds were caused by shrapnel from weapons such as artillery shells or mortar bombs. Light, flexible armour can protect against these threats, but to stop bullets, especially high-powered ones, heavy rigid plates are required. The considerable extra weight was not thought worthwhile. Modern infantry already carry huge loads in the field, so much so that it is sometimes necessary to dispense with even lightweight armour if troops must march on foot.

But high-intensity, full-on wars have been rare for some time now, even as a threat. Long foot marches with full kit are also, nowadays, unlikely during real operations. In low-intensity conflicts like Northern Ireland heavy body armour has always been more appropriate. In this sort of campaign a foot soldier can leave his bergen at a secure location, and he doesn't carry rockets, mortars, grenades and other heavy items. He can manage the weight of a bulletproof flak jacket; and the enemy are much more likely to shoot him using small arms, having few heavy weapons. Heavier body armour has often been worn in Northern Ireland and similar situations.

Then came Iraq. Our troops were supposedly facing a high-intensity battle; the Iraqi army was large and theoretically had a lot of heavy weaponry. Our soldiers would need to carry a full range of ordnance, and might expect to be hit by fragments and shrapnel more often than bullets. Conventional wisdom would have dictated only light body armour.

Fortunately – and most uncharacteristically for the MoD – conventional wisdom was ignored. It was spotted that few of the troops bound for Iraq would need to change base on foot; most had some sort of transport. They would not be required to make long marches humping all their personal equipment, and as a result could manage heavier body armour. This would be worthwhile, firstly because a good deal of urban fighting against lightly equipped militia was expected; secondly, because these days even one casualty is one too many. There was not much heavy personal armour in stock at the time; but, within weeks, tens of thousands of extra sets were obtained. Naturally, the priority was to get them to infantrymen deployed in Iraq, rather than tank crews. Very sadly, for this reason Sergeant Roberts didn't get to keep his ECBA, but one can't say that he was given no protection. He had a tank, after all, and modern Main Battle Tanks mount the best and toughest armour in the world.

On ECBA, then, the MoD deserves some very mild congratulation. An opportunity to improve matters was seen in advance, a fairly good effort was made to do something about it fast, and there is no doubt that many British lives were saved. It might have been done sooner, but it was probably only the imminence of war which provided funds. In normal times ECBA might not have been in widespread service for years; too often, such initiatives have waited until many good people are dead. For once, Whitehall was ahead of the curve.

So why did the Roberts case cause such a flap?

The first part of the problem was the MoD's instinctive response whenever something goes wrong. Whenever a mistake is made, the men from the ministry always strive furiously to suppress the facts, hoping that time will pass and indignation will die down before anything becomes public. And Sergeant Roberts' death had, in fact, been the result of an unfortunate mistake; it just wasn't really anything to do with body armour.

What had actually occurred was a friendly-fire incident. Rather than being shot by an Iraqi, Sergeant Roberts was hit by machine-gun fire from one of the RTR's own tanks. This was perfectly well known in the MoD, and should have been quite obvious to outside observers. To begin with, the only reason Mrs Roberts even knew that ECBA would have saved her husband's life was that a forensic pathologist, having carried out a post-mortem on the sergeant's body, had said so in an MoD report. This had been almost the only document released to Mrs Roberts by the MoD. It isn't normal to carry out a full forensic autopsy on battle casualties. The MoD was clearly investigating this particular death with unusual thoroughness, and the only likely reason for this to occur would be suspicion of friendly fire. Furthermore, the pathologist specified that the fatal bullet had been a 7.62mm *tracer* round, giving a strong indication that it had come from a British weapon rather than an Iraqi one.* As if this wasn't enough, Sergeant Roberts' commanding officer, in the customary letter to Mrs Roberts, had all but stated that the sergeant had been accidentally shot by another of his men. The letter said that another RTR soldier had opened fire in support of Sergeant Roberts, killing an Iraqi, but 'tragically, Steve was also hit'.

So, everyone should have been well aware that the sergeant had been shot by one of his comrades, although nobody seems to have been willing to tell Mrs Roberts so in plain language. This is normal; the MoD always tries to cover up friendly-fire cases, usually claiming that this is to spare the bereaved families anguish. What it is actually hoping, of course, is that it will avoid being called to account for having killed its own people. In one now well-known case during the Falklands War, a Royal Navy destroyer shot down a British Army helicopter due to a failure of communication between army and navy HQs – that is, due to bad staff work. Various fabricated stories were given to the families of the dead soldiers in that case, and the truth didn't come out for years. Similarly, Mrs Roberts was denied any proper account of her husband's death for well over a year.

None of this was made clear in the British press, though the facts were plain enough to anyone with even a little military knowledge. (I submitted an article to one well-known journal in an attempt to clarify matters, but it was rejected. 'No justification after all for national witch-hunt in Roberts case' wouldn't have made a good headline, I suppose.) Instead, Opposition press and politicians worked themselves into a frothing lather and repeatedly called for Geoffrey Hoon's resignation on the obviously spurious grounds that he had failed to get ECBA to tank crews. Mr Hoon was at that point mired up to his eyebrows in

---

* The machine guns of the Challenger II tank, as operated by Sergeant Roberts' unit, fire NATO 7.62mm bullets. The ex-Soviet AK47 assault rifle, the weapon most commonly used by Iraqis, also uses 7.62mm ammunition, but of Soviet pattern. It is very normal to use tracer ammunition in machine guns, much less so in rifles. The pathologist who wrote the MoD report almost certainly knew whether the sergeant had been killed by NATO or Soviet ammunition – the bullets are quite different despite being the same calibre. It would be interesting to know whether he was encouraged to omit this information from Mrs Roberts' report.

a colossal financial crisis which he was utterly failing to sort out (see Chapter 11). He must have been hugely relieved that his enemies were so enthusiastically yelping along on such a false scent.

The glacial MoD investigation eventually wound its slow course, and everybody finally began to realise that nothing more lay behind the ministry's shiftiness in the Roberts case than a fairly open-and-shut friendly-fire killing. There was no real villain in the case, no blundering senior officer or inefficient bureaucrat, far less any ministerial malfeasance: just an unfortunate soldier who made a tragic mistake in a high-pressure situation and shot one of his mates. Such deaths are no new thing. They happen every so often even in quietest peacetime, and in wartime the chances of such an accident inevitably rise. Sergeant Roberts goes in the very best of company: thousands of other British heroes have died accidentally at the hands of their brothers in arms, all the way back through all the wars Britain has ever fought. In the end, the armed forces are in the industry of death and violence. They are always going to suffer more industrial accidents than other employers do, simply because their machinery is intrinsically more dangerous, *by design*. If the MoD had felt able to be honest just for once and tell Mrs Roberts this at the outset, it might have saved itself a lot of trouble.

It would also have been nice if the nation's press hadn't felt it necessary to form up into a baying pack and chase off after a single industrial accident. It would have been nice if Geoff Hoon had been required to answer for the many serious errors he had actually committed – of which, more later – rather than for something which was obviously not his fault. But then, as I pointed out in the introduction to this book, there is very little informed outsider scrutiny of defence matters in this country. Nobody knows about things like tracer bullets and tank weapons; nobody pays attention to the detail. Nobody except you, of course, reading this.

Getting back to that sort of detail, in this case the make-up of the armoured corps, we have now seen ten regiments of tanks and one of chemical scrubbers. That leaves just one regiment of the twelve unaccounted for. What could they possibly be doing?

Anyone acquainted with the British cavalry will not find it hard to guess the answer. The twelfth unit, formally titled the Household Cavalry Mounted Regiment, still rides horses at work, rather than just in their spare time. This work is entirely ceremonial, of course; even the British cavalry aren't – quite – mad enough to actually use horses in combat any more. The riders are real army cavalry troopers, though. They spend perhaps half their careers in the other Household Cavalry regiment, one of the formation recce light-tank units, and half performing mounted ceremonial. The basic riding course alone is twelve weeks long, longer than the commando course or bomb-disposal school. The Household Cavalry are the fellows you see in Whitehall sitting on their horses, wearing gleaming breastplates and polished helmets with plumes. It is they who provide the outriders when the Queen goes for a spin in her carriage.

Remarkable stuff, this. One in every six British tank men actually spends much of his career as a ceremonial horseman. The Household units like to emphasise the fact that they also do real military work, and of course this is true. No one doubts that the Household Cavalry are as good at modern soldiering as they could possibly be, while also being probably the world's best at ceremonial horsemanship and funny hats. But, unless they are all somehow much more able men than the rest of the army, there is no way they can be up to the standard of the others.

So, that's the armoured corps.

First, heavy Challenger Main Battle Tanks, which are essentially a terrifically cumbersome and needlessly risky method of attacking enemy tanks. Even the army admits this, and is mothballing some of them. Not many people outside the tank community really think that the Challenger will be replaced when it wears out.

Then, light Scimitar tanks, which are a reconnaissance system, competing for business with many others. These vehicles are actually also operated by infantry as appropriate: a further five regiments of cavalry-manned Scimitars seems frankly excessive, especially when you consider that other infantry vehicles such as the Warrior and Viking can also do the Scimitar's work perfectly well.

And, of course, we still – absurdly – have a mounted regiment. None of this equipment looks particularly impressive or valuable, particularly the horses and shiny breastplates, but not a single one of the twelve armoured-corps regiments is to go. These are *very good* regiments, of course – that is, very well-connected ones. It appears that they will even retain the hallowed Regimental System, which the infantry have mostly lost – apart from the Guards, of course, who have as many powerful friends as the cavalry. Really, General Jackson and his fellow members of the Army Board might have considered a few cuts here, rather than confining the pain to the infantry. The mounted regiment would seem especially ripe for the chop. But it appears the old saw about equipping the man rather than manning the equipment may be true. The army, it seems, prefers first to keep certain men – certain regiments, that is – and only then consider their equipment.

Still, whatever one thinks of the relative merits of the cavalry, we have only seen 6,000 or so tank-and-horse soldiers to add to our 20,000-odd gunmen. There are a good 200,000 people in the armed forces, and another 100,000 civilians on the MoD payroll. It seems likely that the cavalry will turn out to be more useful than some of these. What's everyone else doing? Where's our £30 billion a year going? The whole Challenger buy, remember, was less than 10 per cent of one year's spending. Whatever our money is going on, it's not men with guns. Mostly it isn't tanks either, it would seem. So what else is there?

CHAPTER

3

Artillery

Spend our resentment, cannon, – yea, disburse
Our gold in shapes of flame . . .

'On Seeing a Piece of Our Heavy Artillery
Brought Into Action', Wilfred Owen

In days of old, the artilleryman was very much an up-close killer.
He would fire his cannon at someone he could personally see, no
more than a few thousand metres off. Such work is called direct
fire. The infantry and cavalry do this for themselves nowadays,
and the artillery are seldom involved. The gunners are still very
much around, however, just further away. The range of the big
guns has increased immensely. Even the lightest pieces of the Royal
Artillery today can throw their shells nine or ten miles. It is rare
for gun crews to be able to see the place which they are
bombarding; they shoot at a set of map coordinates. After the
first shells have fallen, usually fairly close to where they are
wanted, corrections are passed back to the battery and the aim
is adjusted to bring the next salvoes precisely on target. This is
indirect fire, and it is what modern artillery is all about. A division's artillery can pour thousands of tons of shells into a small
area in a matter of hours, delivering destructive power comparable to that of a small nuclear weapon.

Such shattering, long-range bombardment first really hit the
battlefield during World War I. A common perception exists that
the awful slaughter of the trench fighting was a matter of machine
guns: in fact, far more soldiers were slain and injured by shell-
fire than by bullets, in all the mass wars of the 20th century.

During World War II the artillery made up fully a quarter of the British Army, and a similar expansion had taken place in other countries. The big, long-range gun had truly become the 'God of War', as Stalin said in 1944. (The Red Army were perhaps the greatest exponents of its use, then and later.)

Like the infantry, artillery had to learn how to keep up with tanks. The Second World War saw the first serious use of self-propelled guns, artillery pieces built into tracked chassis to accompany armoured forces. Nowadays these are the traditional, mainstream form of artillery, forming the third part of the armoured juggernaut along with the infantry combat vehicle and the tank itself. Today's British version is the AS90 (this stands for Artillery System of the 1990s, although it might better be described as a system for the 1980s). The AS90 is a NATO-standard 155mm gun with a range of fifteen miles or so if unmodernised, mounted in an armoured tracked vehicle. Like the Warrior, the AS90 closely resembles a tank to the untutored eye, but it is actually quite different.

As well as actual guns and gun crews, to hit anything at normal artillery ranges you need someone who can see the enemy and the shells falling, to talk the guns onto target. This might be somebody from another part of the army altogether, as when an infantryman or cavalryman requests artillery fire support. The Royal Artillery, however, prefer to be directed by one of their own if possible. Their Forward Observer Officers, one of whom is normally attached to a rifle company or tank squadron, are actually senior to the officers left behind in charge of the guns. This makes sense, as the FOO has a more stressful and difficult task, and is in charge of what the guns are actually doing even though he or she isn't anywhere near them. Since the advent of satellite navigation and laser rangefinding, a competent FOO and Observation Party (OP, the FOO's accompanying team) can often call down the first salvo right on top of the target, without the need to adjust. It should be borne in mind, though, that this is still done by working out the map coordinates to be hit and passing them to the guns. If the target moves out of the way before the shells arrive, they will still miss.

It should also be remembered that 'right on top' is a flexible term when it comes to artillery. A dumb artillery shell may strike anywhere within the gun battery's 'beaten zone', which is normally to be measured in scores of metres. The beaten zone itself is only centred as accurately as the navigation systems of the gun and the OP, probably thirty metres or so from where the FOO actually wanted it. In a traditional military context this hardly matters. The target is something big, like a group of vehicles or a bunker complex. We actually *want* to smash up a wide area, and so we plaster hundreds of shells all over the place. It doesn't matter that we can't be very precise. All we really want is more range and more destructive power, to reach ahead of our own speedy tanks or, conversely, to give us time to engage the enemy tanks before they roll over us.

This sort of thinking, carried to its ultimate, has resulted in the rocket cluster-bomb systems which some modern armies have for 'depth fire' capability. The British Multiple Launch Rocket System, also in American service, is a prime example. This is a pod of twelve big rockets on a tracked vehicle. These rockets can fly twenty miles or more, significantly further than a shell from an unmodernised gun, and each one scatters 644 explosive armour-piercing bomblets. The rockets are even less accurate than shells, but that isn't a problem because the bomblets cover such a large area. An MLRS vehicle will normally loose off its dozen rockets in less than a minute, putting a majority of their *eight thousand* bomblets into a box downrange 500 metres square. Everything in the box – some sixty acres – will be blasted utterly to hell. Even armoured vehicles will be wrecked within this area, and immense amounts of damage will be done all around it. This is not even to mention that at least 400 of the bomblets will fail to detonate and remain scattered through the pulverised rubble. Each one is as dangerous as a hand grenade with the pin half pulled, and far more difficult to clear up. (Hand grenades are easily made safe or bulldozed out of the way. Not so the armour-piercing cluster bomblet, which will destroy any vehicle which touches it and is not readily rendered safe.) Every time you fire an MLRS rocket, you are sowing a field of landmines.

This kind of murderous splatter weapon made sense against the Red Army in the 1980s. Presumably the West Germans would have been so grateful not to have been nuked or communist-occupied that they would have put up with huge sections of their country being turned into uninhabitable moonscape. Even so, rocket artillery never became as widespread as self-propelled guns.

The traditional set-up in the British army is for gun regiments at brigade level and rockets at division. Thus an armoured or mechanised brigade has a regiment of AS90 self-propelled guns attached, and when brigades combine to form a division the divisional artillery boss will also have a further regiment of MLRS at his disposal. Britain's two combat divisions thus formerly called for six gun regiments and two rocket ones, all ready for the blitzkrieg on the Central Front.

We still seem to prefer the blitzkrieg set-up. We still send tanks and heavy guns to our bigger wars. In 1991, for Gulf War I, we also sent rockets. As time went by, however, the negative PR implications of cluster weapons started to become noticeable. It also became apparent just how difficult and dangerous it was to clear up after them. (Several deaths have occurred in British ordnance-disposal teams during the last decade while clearing 'friendly' cluster submunitions, albeit mostly air-dropped ones rather than artillery-fired. Not a single British ordnance-disposal operator has been lost to terrorist devices over the same period.) In 2003, despite having put a full division on the ground for the invasion of Iraq, Britain chose not to deploy MLRS due to concerns over its destructiveness.* This was clearly a disappointment for the divisional artillery commander:

> A number of highly desirable capabilities were omitted . . . These included . . . most critically from an [artillery] perspective, any multiple-launch rocket systems . . . analysis indicated that the extensive spread of oil infrastructure in our likely area of operations would significantly curtail the firing of weapons systems with a large beaten zone
>
> Brigadier Andrew Gregory, Commander of
> Royal Artillery in Iraq 2003, writing for the
> US Army's Field Artillery Journal.

---

* There was no concern over the use of cluster-submunition weapons, however. There is a conventional artillery shell which scatters 88 bomblets just like those from an MLRS. The British artillery fired 2,000 of these shells in 2003, which will have left 900-odd lethal duds scattered about.

Artillerymen like Brigadier Gregory see the big guns and rockets as a way of life: in a very real sense, as their work and home and self-image and club all rolled into one, the way infantry and cavalry see their regiments. The British artillery, in fact, is properly speaking just one regiment, the Royal Regiment of Artillery, with a history as long and glorious as any in the army. Confusingly, this one regiment has many sub-regiments. It ought to be called a corps, really, but it isn't. Trying to make sense out of the British Army will eventually send you bonkers.

Taxpayers, though, and perhaps genuinely impartial staff officers – rare beasts – should see the artillery as a way of putting explosives where we want them put, rather than as a tribal culture. The AS90 or the MLRS should not be looked at in isolation. The weapon is merely the penultimate link in a long chain along which the munitions move from the factory to the place where they go off. There are many ways to blow things up. The significant factors are how many people we must put into danger to do it, how much it costs, how fast the weapon system can be deployed, and how accurately and efficiently the good news is eventually delivered; never forgetting to consider, as we recall from John Paul Vann, whether explosives are really the answer to the question.

In this sense, most of the artillery doesn't come out well. A battery of guns, usually six in number but eight when mobilised for war, is quite cheap, true – well under the price of current strike jets. But the guns and the forty-odd men and women in their crews are the least of it. Each battery normally provides forward observer teams to the battle group it is accompanying, and there are many other personnel attached. A battery is actually a major's command, like a rifle company: it contains a lot of people. Three batteries make up a full regiment, equivalent in numbers to an infantry battalion. If the artillery regiment is attached to a 'square brigade', with four battle groups rather than three, it gets bigger in proportion. The Third Regiment Royal Horse Artillery, in just this situation for the Iraq war, took the field at a strength of 1,000: one gunner for every nine shells it fired. All these people must go up into the vicinity of the front lines, well into danger.

Then, once you've got them all assembled, the artillery are potentially an even greater logistical headache than the tank men.

A hulking, armoured, tracked AS90 weighs forty-five tons. It is every bit as troublesome as a tank, and every bit as difficult to deliver to the battlefield. Once there, its terrible hunger for ammunition may strain even the strongest of supply chains. During World War II, a division's artillery might easily fire thousands of tons of shells in just one day. Nothing even close to these amounts got fired in Iraq, but there is little point in sending the guns if you don't give them the option of doing this. Many, many logistics-corps truck drivers are needed to move such massive loads of high explosives. These men and women are often seen as having rear echelon jobs, but, in an environment where the only enemy troops keen to fight are the stay-behind militias and other irregulars, this is hardly the case. Driving a truckload of high explosives to a gun battery in Iraq has to be a very worrying job, perhaps more worrying than actually being a gunner.

An artillery shell, then, is not just something which is fired out of a cannon. It is something which must first be shipped to the theatre of war, like all ammunition including aircraft bombs or missiles or what have you. At that point, air weapons can often be put straight into their launchers. This will happen somewhere quite safe like Kuwait, or aboard a carrier offshore. Only a couple of flyboys need risk their arses from here in order to deliver air weapons right to the enemy, and provided the flyboys are sensible, as we shall see, even their risk is tiny. The shells, by contrast, must normally be driven across hundreds of miles of perhaps inadequately pacified country, at some effort and likely some risk to hundreds of our people. Then we require many hundreds more artillery soldiers, who must get within a few tens of miles of the target on the ground, to actually carry out final delivery. These soldiers and their very heavy equipment were none too easy to get there in the first place – compared to the strike jets – and have the same massive requirements for fuel, water, food and other supplies as their infantry and cavalry colleagues.

In the old days, this comparison would have been unfair. Our flyboys couldn't operate at night or in bad weather, might have been defeated by the bad flyboys, and anyway didn't want to help. Even if it was a lovely day and they were winning, they'd rather be hundreds of miles into enemy airspace, blowing up targets of their own choosing, rather than actually helping the ground forces. Perhaps worst of all, the old-time flyboys had almost no real ability to accurately hit anything – certainly not without flying so low that they'd very likely get shot down. All of these things have now been fixed except the unwillingness to help, and to some extent this is the army's own fault. Artillerymen have seen their centuries-old way of life threatened by air support for a long time now, and they are a very influential army community. Even when the air force or the flying parts of the army try to make friends, the mainstream army is often unreceptive until the war actually starts.

But the writing is really starting to appear on the wall, and the artillery can certainly read it. A hugely troublesome and manpower-intensive capability to hosepipe explosives indiscriminately across the landscape, no more than a few miles beyond the lead combat units, is not going to keep the Royal Regiment in business for long. The buzz phrase of the day is 'depth fire' in the gunner messes; it has been for some time. The artillery are desperate to get at that further-off place, well ahead of the lead ground units, where the good targets are still to be found – before the bloody air force nails them all.

They need to hurry. Part of Brigadier Gregory's account from 2003 is especially telling:

> It was hoped many Iraqi formations would indicate a desire to surrender, avoiding combat and potentially allowing them to form a nucleus of a new Iraqi army. However, a lack of feedback forced us to revert to kinetic targeting of assessed positions. The only alternative to kinetic targeting would have been to expose Coalition Forces to potential danger, something that was clearly unacceptable. This issue, in part, resulted in the significant expenditure of artillery ammunition.

'Kinetic targeting' means blowing people away. In plain English, then, the advancing Coalition knew where all the Iraqi units were, and could easily have bombed them off the map. Instead, they chose to scatter leaflets and make broadcasts suggesting surrender. Most humane. But the Iraqis just sat there, failing to give any 'feedback', and by now our lead units were getting to where the Iraqis might be able to harm them. Also, crucially from the brigadier's point of view, our artillery could now reach the enemy formations. Funnily enough it was at this point that the decision was taken that the Iraqis had missed their chance to throw in the towel, and the artillery duly got some rounds off. The interesting thing is that it was only the possibility of their surrender that let the Iraqis survive long enough to be killed by artillery. If they had been thought to be resolute, the brigadier implies, very few artillery shells would have been fired at all. The Iraqis would have been bombed as soon as they were found, and the artillery would have largely sat idle.

Even *with* these engagements, the Royal Artillery didn't do much in Iraq, certainly nothing like enough to justify having them there in such strength. The massively swollen Third RHA and its associated supply chain has to be one of the most difficult, slow-to-deploy and manpower-intensive ways one can think of to put nine thousand shells' worth of destruction into Iraq.

In other words, the artillery really need to get some serious 'depth fire' capability, or they may not be invited to the party in future.

The only means of doing depth fire used to be rockets, but in recent years the big guns have made a comeback. Barrels can be lengthened, allowing the shells to achieve higher muzzle velocities and so fly further. Modernised, long-barrelled AS90s, known as Bravehearts for some reason, are coming into service at the moment. One can also fiddle with the shells. Modern 155mm rounds may have rocket motors, allowing them to fly much further. A simpler ploy is 'base bleed' ammunition, which releases gas from its back end not to provide thrust, but simply to reduce air drag on the shell. Guns may soon be able to reach as far as fifty miles, or even more.* They can certainly shoot further than

---

* Not that this is new. The German Pariskanonen ('Paris guns') of 1918 bombarded the French capital from a range of seventy-nine miles. These were not practical weapons, however: they required a railway line to move or traverse, and burned out their bores after seventy shots even when firing slowly. In building these guns, the Germans merely wanted to make the point that they had managed to get within artillery range of Paris. In those days it was possible to build insane artillery pieces and railway lines for them faster than one could move the front line fifty miles. The fifty-mile-plus artillery of today and tomorrow is mobile, handy and robust – in this context.

the current MLRS. There are also smart, target-seeking 155mm shells already available which could strike mobile targets, as well as getting away from the messy cluster-munitions approach.

Depth fire, then, is doing better and better, although even the most ambitious artillery projects seem unlikely to confer a range much greater than 100 or 200 miles. This is perhaps by design. Remember, if the range becomes too great, there is no need for anything really resembling an artillery regiment. The gunners could become as wimpy and rear-echelon as air force ground crew, or might find their new weapons being mounted on a ship out at sea. This is not what they want *at all*. Such factors suggest that the artillery are probably mistaken to see depth fire as their salvation, in the long run. As soon as depth fire becomes truly deep it is unlikely any longer to be recognisable as artillery, and the Royal Regiment will cease to be the obvious unit to operate it. A cruise missile, for instance, is a good example of a truly deep-fire weapon; and cruise missiles are always in the air force or navy.

There is another problem with depth fire. Once you have the ability to hit things miles and miles into enemy-held ground, you need to know where to aim. An observation party embedded with a lead rifle company or tank squadron is no use here. The artillery need to find targets way beyond these people. Their term for this new activity is 'Surveillance and Target Acquisition', or STA. It is a buzz phrase with the rest of the army nowadays, particularly as it might justify the large numbers of surplus recce cavalry. They can now be employed as 'STA assets', even in the absence of heavy forces for which they might reconnoitre. Rather than roving ahead of Main Battle Tanks, they will direct the strikes of depth-fire artillery.

However, as with normal artillery support, the Royal Regiment prefers its depth fire to be directed by its own people. The Gunners may find the light-tank men all too willing to pass targets to other shooters, especially if they get beyond artillery range, as dashing cavalrymen tend to. Certainly the gunners can't afford to rely solely on the cavalry if depth fire is to really flex its muscles.

Thus we find a lot of interesting people in the Royal Artillery's own STA regiments. Some, like the sound-ranging and radar teams, have been around for ever. These units locate enemy artillery by the sound of their guns firing or the radar tracks of their shells. Rather old hat nowadays, really. Waiting until the other side's guns are actually firing does give them a chance of hitting us, which is scarcely ideal. In any case, there is a terrible risk that some air force blighter will nab them first if we hang about that long. And we still need to find all the non-artillery opposition, too, which the counter-battery detectors will never help with.

A better idea altogether is the gunners' own pocket special forces organisation, which is to normal obervation parties as the special forces are to normal infantry. The elite artillery spotters of the Special OPs, like the SAS and SBS, advertise for volunteers from across the armed forces. This is necessary because of their arduous training, which only the toughest and most motivated will pass. These men are supposed to be inserted covertly, probably by air, far beyond our own front lines. Then they sneak about secretly, calling in depth-fire artillery on things they may find. One could rely on the normal Special Forces to do this, but they would be all too likely to let the air force in on the fun. The gunners need their own men out there.

Another idea, probably more practical given the speed of advance these days, is the use of drone reconnaissance aircraft, UAVs (Unmanned Aerial Vehicles). These were originally developed by and for artillerymen – largely American artillerymen, but the principle holds good. Conventional flying organisations such as the air force and army aviation are run by pilots, and pilots understandably were not interested in unmanned aircraft. But the gunners were, and the Royal Artillery has an entire regiment devoted to operating the Phoenix drone. Unfortunately from the gunners' viewpoint, the air arms have now also grasped that unmanned aircraft are an excellent way of generating business:

'I love UAVs!'
> US Air Force Lieutenant-General T. Michael Moseley,
> Coalition air commander, briefing reporters during the
> Iraq war of 2003.

The UAV will now be top of the RAF's Christmas list as well, if they have any sense, presenting the possibility that yet another of the gunners' many aerial spotting organisations may ultimately be lost to their control. The artillery were instrumental in the formation first of the RAF's ancestors and then of the Army Air Corps, both of which subsequently became hated competitors. For the moment, though, in British service, the artillerymen have a monopoly on recce drones. They will fight hard to keep them, as Brigadier Gregory makes very clear:

> 'The British Phoenix UAV . . . operates from within the divisional area, an important factor in guaranteeing the essential requirement that UAVs . . . remain under the full command of the land commander.'

The requirement is essential to artillerymen, not anyone else. If the joint commander, or worse yet the air commander gained control of UAVs, the drones might start finding targets before they were in artillery range.

The gunners aren't going down tamely, that's for sure. And they do have better to offer than lead-footed AS90 dinosaurs or carpet-destruction cluster-rockets, neither of which have ever seen much action. The busiest gunners in the army since the end of World War II, actually, have been the light artillery. These are attached to the always-in-demand elite light infantry. The marines of 3 Commando Brigade have a light artillery regiment attached rather than one of AS90s, and so does the mostly-Para 16 Air Assault Brigade. (The Para gunners have a magnificently absurd name: 7 Parachute Regiment, Royal Horse Artillery. This conjures up a truly amazing mental picture. In fact, however, they eschew the horse, and while they are maroon-bereted and jump-trained, they have never parachuted their guns into combat: nor are they likely to.)

Light artillery are equipped with 105mm guns, which can't move under their own power. However, they are easily towed behind various vehicles, can be lifted about swiftly by helicopter as well, and they are a dream to deploy worldwide compared to AS90 or MLRS. They have less range and firepower than 155mm pieces, of course, but their deployability has won them a lot of business which heavier artillery has been denied. The light 105mm was the only land artillery which could be used in the Falklands, for example. Even in the supposedly high-intensity Iraq operation light guns deployed in similar numbers to AS90s, and actually fired significantly more shells: 13,000 as compared to 9,000. Light artillery are much harder to argue against than heavy AS90s and MLRS.

The final major Royal Artillery subculture is the air-defence units, or 'cloud-punchers' as their fellow gunners call them. They will soon be the only ground anti-aircraft teams in the forces, the RAF having just retired from this game. The army has three air-defence regiments, equipped with a mixture of Rapier and Starstreak missiles. One regiment is attached to each of the two combat divisions, and there is a third in case of a need to protect something else – London, perhaps; this unit is home-based less than ten miles from the capital.

This all seems sensible enough, but the cloud-punchers have punched no clouds in anger since the Falklands, and seem unlikely to get much excitement in future. British forces will only find themselves under air attack these days if something has gone horribly wrong, and ground-based missiles are a last-ditch, emergency defence. Fighter planes are much better, as we shall see in Chapter 5.

So, the cloud-punchers can hardly be the posting of choice for keen young gunners in today's world, and the shoulder-launched Starstreak scarcely seems to call for artillerymen to operate it. Even the comparatively complex Rapier was formerly handled by RAF rock-apes, at least half infantrymen by trade. It might make more sense to simply let anyone use anti-aircraft missiles who had a need, rather than keeping this work as a gunner preserve. The special forces and the marines already do this, not being subject to the army's union rules.

There is one last unit to mention in the Royal Regiment, one which handles the key military task of wearing spiffy 19th-century uniforms and riding horses. The King's Troop, Royal Horse Artillery – actually a battery-sized unit – is different from the Household Cavalry Mounted Regiment in that most of its soldiers stay with it for their entire careers. The shining-breastplated cavalryman in Whitehall may have spent time in the recce tank squadrons attached to the commandos or the Paras, and can claim to be a serious soldier. The equally gorgeous horsey cannoneers firing ceremonial salutes in Hyde Park have normally done nothing else and can make no such claim – apart from their officers, who are visitors from the real artillery.

The army and the Royal Regiment, however, should probably not be blamed for the costly and irrelevant existence of the horse gunners. They had actually mechanised their last horsed artillery unit in 1939, and left to themselves seem unlikely to have looked back. The King's Troop, rather than being tremendously old as one might think, was formed after World War II at the personal command of the sovereign. Just to clear up any confusion, one should note that several other artillery units have 'Horse' in their titles too, but this is for purely historical and class reasons; they have no horses. Once upon a time, the horse artillery was much more prestigious than the normal artillery whose gunners had to march, just as the cavalry was swankier than the infantry. The mounted gunners were willing to accept motor vehicles, but not to have the same unit titles as their social inferiors. Within living memory it was still felt that a background in 'horse artillery' units had a bit more cachet, but this attitude is slowly passing.

Anyway, forget about horses. Let's get back to the combat artillery. There are two light-gun regiments, six of AS90s, one of MLRS, three of air-defence and two of STA spotters and plotters. This is overwhelmingly a cold-war tank-cataclysm sort of mix, heavy of hand as artillery should be but mostly heavy of foot as well. The army *has* noted this. The artillery has been affected by the events of 2004 like everyone else, just not very much. Some regular gunners are now swapping back to MLRS again – no doubt with a certain amount of muttering about people making up their minds – on the grounds that the MLRS vehicle (at twenty-five tons) is a bit easier to get into action than an AS90 – and to hell with any lettuce-eating moaners who don't like its effects. Some more AS90 batteries will mothball their big hogs to form a third light-gun regiment, in support of the soon-to-appear third light brigade. This is all sensible enough, but it is hardly a comprehensive reorientation. No gun batteries will actually shut down, and the Royal Artillery will remain essentially a rather heavy, old-fashioned organisation for the inefficient tube delivery of explosives.

As John Paul Vann so astutely reminded us in Chapter 1, many

– perhaps most – military problems can't be solved even by the most correct and accurate application of high explosives, disappointing as that may be. Perhaps the best thing about the Royal Regiment of Artillery is its traditional readiness to be used as infantry where required. Many, many British gunners in the post-World War II era have heard the sound of enemy fire, but it has normally been in the infantry role with rifles in their hands rather than while serving their guns. They may want to focus on that sort of operation even more in future, especially as there will be less infantrymen around.

General Jackson certainly isn't a light-forces radical, then, not by any stretch of the imagination. He isn't acting like a general whose budget has increased, either, depite the fact that defence spending has indeed gone up. The 2004 army plans seem more those of a conservative cold war armour general required to save some money. The cavalry and artillery survive unscathed as to manpower and with only incremental shifts in organisation, while the infantry are decimated and their survivors given the biggest shake-up since Cromwell. Of course, it's possible that what we are actually seeing is a single light-infantry radical desperately struggling against the forces of conservatism, but the results are the same.

Meanwhile, we still haven't found anything that could really account for where all our money and manpower is going. Another dozen regiments-plus of artillerymen and women, with quite reasonably priced equipment – the whole original AS90 buy was only 1 per cent of a single year's defence spending – that's it, in the artillery. Whatever one might think of their relevance and the difficulties and expense of *using* them, they certainly aren't expensive to *have*. The men with guns, armoured corps and artillery taken together – the vast majority of the land forces' actual fighting department – represent only a small fraction of our available effort: perhaps 10 per cent of the MoD's people, all of whose kit could have been bought with less than 20 per cent of one year's budget. Whatever our defence establishment thinks its job is, it isn't fighting our enemies on the ground.

CHAPTER
4

Helicopters

The helicopter approaches closer than any other vehicle to fulfillment of mankind's ancient dreams of the flying horse and the magic carpet.

Igor Sikorsky, helicopter designer

If something hasn't broken on your helicopter, it's about to.

Helicopter pilot saying

Helicopters are a very, very emotive subject in the British armed forces, and generally in the forces of all nations rich enough to operate them seriously. Some people like them; some people don't. Among those who do like them, there is fierce argument as to how they should be used. Once you have some helicopters, there is bitter inter-service wrangling over who should own and operate them.

To begin with, it may help to take a brisk look at what a helicopter actually is, and some of the facts of life regarding them.

A modern helicopter is powered by one or more gas turbines, that is, by jet engines which are optimised to turn a drive shaft rather than to generate thrust by blasting gas out of their back ends. An ordinary piston engine like the one in a car could be used, but it isn't powerful enough: such a helicopter will struggle merely to lift itself into the air, and would not be able to carry any significant load. The gas turbine is what makes the helicopter a practical proposition. However, the turbine does rotate its drive shaft extremely fast, and a gearbox is necessary to bring the speed down. This gearbox is large, complex, heavy and under terrific mechanical stress.

The gearbox transmits the power to the main rotors, which

seem fairly simple. On the face of it, they are just a big propellor, pointing upwards to pull the helicopter into the sky. However, if that was all they were, there would be no way to control the helicopter in flight. In fact, the rotors can be fiddled with in various cunning ways by the pilot, enabling the helicopter to move in any direction, hover, or go up and down. This ability to twiddle the rotors while they are spinning and supporting the whole aircraft means that the rotor hub is an extremely complex piece of kit; it too is under enormous stress, as are the blades themselves.

Finally, without some form of intervention, a helicopter with only a main rotor will spin round and round madly in the opposite direction to the blades as soon as it gets off the ground. There are various solutions: a small tail rotor to provide a counterthrust, two main rotors which counteract each other, or the exhaust of the turbine can be vented in such a way as to hold the aircraft still. All of these have been employed successfully. None is as simple as it sounds.

So, everything in the helicopter is mechanically complex. Worse, it is all whirling and spinning very fast, usually under terrific stress and often in opposition to something else close by. If you whirl something round and round, for example a weight on a string, its natural tendency is to snap and fly off violently. This is also true of most parts of a helicopter. By making all these things out of very tough materials, maintaining them very carefully and replacing them frequently, one may be fairly sure that a helicopter will work as advertised. It is still a dangerous way to fly.

These are the basics of a helicopter: turbines, gearbox, rotors. Apart from that, a flimsy aluminium fuselage is usually included, to streamline the beast and protect its passengers and machinery. So far, you have a flying box; you will also need to purchase navigation and communications equipment as a minimum, and probably expensive night and bad-weather instrumentation too, for military use. Then, if you want the helicopter to do anything other than just carry people and stuff about, you will need to buy 'mission systems': weapons and/or sensors to find and strike your enemy. These might be quite cheap and simple, as when the US Army made the first dedicated attack helicopters by attaching off-the-shelf guns and rockets to Huey transports. That was the exception to the rule, though. Nowadays, mission systems typically cost more than the basic helicopter does, often by a very large margin. Today's ground-attack and submarine-hunting helicopters are extremely complex and expensive, to the point of insanity in some cases.

Once you have got your helicopter into the air, you may be disappointed. It can't go as fast as other aircraft, nor as high, nor as far without refuelling, and it can't carry as much stuff. All this means that if there are any hostile fighters in the sky, your helicopter will not last long. Also, if you want to take your helicopter far afield – say, beyond Europe – you don't really want to fly it there under its own power. It will take days, and will probably need maintenance on arrival.

As one might imagine, a helicopter is troublesome to maintain, and expensive to buy and operate, even by the standards of military jets. It is never really safe, far less so when it is being pushed hard and people are shooting at it. And it guzzles fuel at a furious rate. As an example, a late-model Chinook burns three *tons* of fuel to fly a couple of hundred miles, and it can only lift nine or ten tons of payload while doing so.

However, all this trouble and expense does get you a pretty amazing capability. The helicopter is, as its father Igor Sikorsky said, the nearest thing to a magic carpet yet devised. Anyone who has travelled by commercial jet knows how extremely inconvenient the need for runways can be – the journeys to and from the airport are typically the most difficult part of the trip. The helicopter doesn't need a runway: just a small pad or open flat area, if it is to actually set down. Often it doesn't require even this. People and things can get on or off hovering or slow-flying helicopters just about anywhere, using a variety of ropes and winches or simply by jumping.

And while a helicopter may be slow for an aircraft, it is fast compared to anything else. Military helicopters generally cruise at around 150 mph. This can translate into something of a miracle: soldiers and equipment can move miles in minutes, taking no notice of inconvenient hills, valleys, rivers, built-up areas, swamps or whatever. The helicopter can also ignore most enemies beneath its flight path, unless for some reason it is compelled to fly low. The only exception is serious, heavy anti-aircraft missiles.

Used in the right way, this is clearly a tool of great military potential. Furthermore, while they can't generally fly direct to global trouble spots themselves, helicopters – the smaller ones, anyway – are relatively easy to air freight.

All this means that helicopters, or 'helos'* as forces types tend to call them, are used extensively in the military. Armies find them very useful, although various army communities dislike them. For navies unable to afford gigantic aircraft carriers – almost all navies – the helicopter is usually the only flying option. Air forces, curiously, do not find helicopters nearly as attractive; left to themselves, they would really only use them for retrieving airmen shot down in hostile territory. However, for reasons of turf and status, the air force generally likes to stay in the game.

In land fighting, the helicopter can do a number of things. The first is moving soldiers and equipment about. Helos are excellent for this, though limited as to weight. They can move infantrymen or small, light vehicles and artillery pieces, but not usually anything bigger. If the helicopters are properly equipped and the pilots properly trained, they can operate at night without difficulty, and, with some effort, even in bad weather and low visibility. The big downside of helicopters, apart from their expense, maintenance burden and thirst, is their extreme vulnerability to ground fire when flying low, particularly when hovering, landing or taking off. There is a very tight limit on how much armour you can hang on something that has to be able to fly. If, like a transport helicopter, it is quite large and needs to carry heavy loads, you can't really protect it at all. Given the helicopter's natural tendency to come apart violently even when left to itself, one doesn't normally need to hit it very hard to cause some kind of catastrophic failure. If a helicopter is unfortunate enough to slow down when in range of a hostile machine-gunner or rocket-propelled-grenadier, there is a very good chance that it will be destroyed, probably taking all on board with it. If the black hat has a proper shoulder-launched anti-aircraft missile, the only way for the helicopter to be safe at all is to stay high up or far away.

What this means is that helicopters must make serious efforts

---

* Pronounced he-lo, like J-Lo.

not to land or take off close to the enemy, or they will take heavy losses. When military transport helicopters were first used extensively in combat, by the Americans in Vietnam, this rule was often ignored. Lots of US Army and Marine aviators, showing tremendous bravery, flew in and out of so-called 'hot LZs' in those days (a landing zone is hot when it is under enemy fire). Even against Viet Cong and People's Army of Vietnam troops generally lacking in heavy weapons, this practice took a fearsome toll. Such operations have never been the norm for British forces, who seldom have enough helicopters and are much more sparing of them.

Since Vietnam, some guerillas have made a speciality of ambushing helicopters. This isn't nearly as easy as ambushing ground vehicles, but it can be done if you have a good idea where the helicopter will land, or where it will fly low and slow. The mujahedin of the long Afghan war against the Russians got very good at this. Of course, they had effective anti-aircraft missiles furnished by the Americans, which helped a lot. And it is well known that the Americans are now losing a steady trickle of helicopters to ground fire in Iraq – perhaps, on occasion, ground fire from the very same men that they armed back in the 1980s, or their sons and nephews anyhow.

But it doesn't have to be this way. A contrasting example to Vietnam is British use of helicopters in Northern Ireland, prior to the Provisional IRA (PIRA) ceasefire. Throughout most of the present Troubles, the roads of South Armagh, a small, overwhelmingly republican region on the border, the so-called 'bandit country' of Northern Ireland, were extremely dangerous for British forces. Mines, ambushes and so forth meant that road travel was usually a very bad option, especially as the use of heavy armour could not be countenanced. (Tanks versus rebels seldom turns out well in the long run, as the Russians and Chinese have found in the past, and the Coalition may yet find in Iraq.) Yet there was still a need for the security forces to be able to respond to incidents in South Armagh, to mount patrols, and to move personnel and supplies to and from the heavily fortified bases in Crossmaglen, Bessbrook and elsewhere. The helicopter was the answer: the heliport at Bessbrook barracks became one of the busiest in the world.

PIRA, despite all this activity, never succeeded in ambushing a

British helicopter, although two were wrecked during 'barrack-buster' mortar attacks on British bases. This failure was not due to incompetence or lack of effort on the guerillas' part. PIRA is an extremely expert organisation, and for many years was a world leader in developing new terrorist/freedom-fighter techniques. Bringing down British helicopters was a high priority of theirs; they even attempted to develop home-made anti-aircraft missiles. This may sound crazy, and indeed it never panned out, but one should reflect that PIRA did achieve a good deal of success with home-made anti-armour weapons and mortars. Nevertheless, missiles aside, PIRA already had weapons which the Viet Cong had found quite sufficient to shoot down American helicopters: rifles, rocket-propelled grenades and machine guns.

It is fair to say that PIRA never had as many of these things as the Americans' various adversaries did. The other big difference was in the operating methods of the British forces. For instance, a common occurrence was a report of a terrorist bomb being discovered – an improvised explosive device, or IED. This might well be a genuine device, emplaced perhaps by one of the warring paramilitary groups to kill or terrorise supporters of the other side. Not uncommonly, though, its real purpose was to draw British forces out of their secure bases and onto ground of PIRA's choosing. For this reason, it is a standard drill for a British bomb-disposal team, on setting up to deal with an IED, to first check the vicinity of its own command post for a second bomb.

Similarly, British forces responding to incidents in South Armagh had always to bear in mind that the real root of the matter might well be a desire to draw their helicopter into an ambush. Consequently, the helicopter would seldom go straight to the actual incident. A common tactic, in the case of an IED, was to sling the bomb-disposal team's vehicle and equipment under the helicopter and deliver it to some random location nearby. In this way the team could avoid making a dangerous road journey through bandit country. They had only a short drive of a mile or so from a completely unpredictable direction, usually off-road, to reach the incident, and would get there much faster than if they had driven all the way. And the valuable, vulnerable helicopter was never exposed to danger, as it would have been had they simply flown straight there.

This is the way to use helicopters, then. Exploit their speed and their safety when at height, but avoid placing them close to danger when flying low and slow. It will often mean a lot of walking for those who go by helicopter. Not everybody is going to be able to take a vehicle, unless you have a truly amazing number of helos. A bit of footslogging is a lot better than getting shot down, though.

So, the transport helicopter is a top piece of kit, especially if used right. However, land-battle helicopters are also used for other things: specifically, for reconnaissance and to attack enemy ground forces. Recce helicopters seem to have pretty much had their day. If you have unmanned recon drones, it is hard to see why you would send a helo. The copter is much bigger and more easily noticed; costs a lot more; can't go as far; can't stay up nearly as long and is unlikely to get you any more information. It also means a chance of losing people to enemy action, unlike the drone. The US Army, tellingly, has recently cancelled its Comanche recce helo, despite having already spent approximately $8 billion on it. The small Gazelle helicopters currently used by the British in this role will probably be limited to 'liaison' duties in future – flying senior officers or other 'small packages' about, generally behind friendly lines. They seem unlikely to be replaced.

This leaves us with the dedicated attack helicopter, known as the gunship in Vietnam. An attack helicopter proper is specifically designed to carry weapons and strike the enemy itself. The British army is in the process of introducing the American Apache in this role.

One might think: how refreshing. Rather than some decades-long Euro-collaborative mess or a vastly expensive reinvention of the wheel by Britain alone, we are simply buying American. Decent up to date-ish kit, and since the Americans have already paid the development and set-up costs, presumably cheap as well. After all, the US already has over 800 Apaches in service. They should be down to quite a reasonable price by now.

One would be completely wrong in thinking such a thing. *Of course* we didn't just buy the helicopters from America. Rather, an entire new production line was set up here in Britain by Westland, in order to make a grand total of sixty-seven helos. In fact, the first eight were made in America anyway, so the British line produced just fifty-nine aircraft. The rough overall price of this programme was £2.5 billion. In other words, each bird cost the British taxpayer nearly £40 million. Israel ordered twenty-four Apaches direct from America in 1999, paying less than £12 million per helo.

Brilliant. We paid more than triple the going rate for our Apaches, throwing the best part of *two billion pounds* down the drain, all in the name of providing employment for British workers. Even if you think that this is what the defence budget is for – many people seemingly do – Apache yielded strikingly poor results, considered as a welfare scheme. The lead contractor and the MoD, both of whom have every reason to exaggerate, estimate that around 34,000 man-years of work was delivered to the British population as a result of the Apache buy. Assuming a human working life of forty-five years, that equates to 755 people saved from the dole. We could have bought the helos direct from Boeing, then simply given 755 jobless people a million pounds each – surely enough to set them up for life – and still saved ourselves a billion. Just to round things off, the helicopters had to be put into storage for two years after they were built, because the training simulators – again, we didn't just buy these from Boeing – didn't work and so the army didn't have any pilots ready to fly the Apache. This was the only aspect of the mess that made any headlines, although it is a comparatively unimportant one.

All in all, it seems mildly amazing that angry taxpayers didn't stone the minister for defence procurement in the street over this huge rip-off, or at least pelt him with rotten eggs or something. The Right Honourable James Arbuthnot MP was the guilty man, in case you're wondering: a Tory. Jobs for British boys no matter the cost is a genuinely cross-party principle, unfortunately. The honourable gentleman later became opposition spokesman for trade and industry – perhaps a more appropriate portfolio for one with his evident priorities. Unfortunately, since the 2005 election he is once more in a position to affect Defence matters, as chairman of the Commons Defence Committee.

Sadly, frustratingly, embitteringly, this is still a comparatively good MoD project. We may have been viciously ripped-off by our own government and defence industry, but at least we got a small number of working helicopters at the end. The MoD is quite capable of throwing away that sort of cash on things which are completely pointless or don't work, even in many cases ending up with nothing at all; and it often takes much longer to do it.

Anyway, back to attack helicopters in general. The thing about an attack helicopter is that it is, effectively, a close-support strike aircraft. One could just as well use a jet such as a Harrier or a Tornado to do what the Apache does. The friends of the attack helo point out that it can operate from improvised forward bases without runways; their opposition point out that the Harrier can do this nearly as well. Attack helo advocates point out the helicopter's ability to fly 'nap-of-the-earth' – using hills, buildings and so forth to hide from enemy radar and even visual observation. In particular, the rotor-heads would cite a famous raid undertaken by a force of US Apaches in 1991. American aviators were able to fly in undetected, nap-of-the-earth, and destroy a key Iraqi air-defence radar station. This created a big hole in Saddam's air defences, and allowed the Allied air forces to pour through and bomb the dickens out of everything, which air forces at least believe to be a vital precursor to any sort of serious operation.

The trouble with this argument is that while nap-of-the-earth helicopters may be safe from big air-defence radars, they are well within range of shoulder-launched missiles and often of machine-gun or rifle fire. It is generally much safer to fly high up for most of any flight over enemy territory. The last thing you want to do is get too close to enemy ground troops in any kind of aircraft. If you can't fly high because of enemy radars and heavy missiles, there are lots of ways to deal with them.

At around this point in the debate, the artillery generally stick their oar in and suggest that some lovely big guns with terminally guided shells would be far better than either jets or helicopters; then the armoured corps point out that this is all highly dishonourable, and the only pukka way to deal with enemy ground units is to set about them with a tank. And so the weary day winds on. Moreover, a key point to remember is that all of these people are competing, in the end, for the job of blasting enemy tanks and armoured vehicles. This seems foolish, as the majority of our adversaries haven't got any.

Whatever you think of such wider issues, the need for aviators to stand off from enemy ground units is now well recognised. The latest Apaches, including ours, mount targeting radars and use homing missiles. This allows them to engage ground targets from high up and miles away, as is sensible. That does tend to make them look even more like strike jets, of course. Indeed, a British Tornado doing this job uses a version of the very same missile. Which is the better way to deliver it, air force jet or army helicopter?

As a matter of technology the answer is simple. The jet can carry much more, much further, much faster. The only technical reason ever to use helicopters for anything is their magical ability to hover and so to do without runways. When delivering missiles or rockets or gunfire to the enemy, we are not using this ability – not if we have any sense, anyway.* We gain only the marginal advantage of being able to operate from quickly improvised forward bases, at least as far as land fighting is concerned. This is really a case of making a virtue out of necessity, given the helicopter's limited range, and it will not win you a vote of thanks from your logistics people, who must now move immense amounts of fuel and munitions much further forward. If for some reason you truly need to operate strike aircraft from ad hoc bases, a jump-jet such as the Harrier makes more sense than a helicopter does. From an engineering and numbers point of view, it is really hard to see why anyone ever decided to build helicopters dedicated purely to ground attack.

But let's look at the question more closely: Which is the better way to deliver the same missile, air force jet or army helicopter? The key words, of course, are not 'jet' or 'helicopter' but 'army' and 'air force'. Much of the proliferation in ways to hunt the increasingly rare and endangered enemy tank springs from the eternal struggle between different branches of the armed forces, rather than from any real need to have so many ways of doing it. One can make a very credible argument that the specialist attack helicopter only exists due to inter-service conflict in America.

---

* The US Army's attack helos initially took a nasty drubbing over Iraq in 2003, as they had thought that the Apache's armour would allow them to hover low over enemy forces and pick their targets at leisure. They had to swiftly relearn the Vietnam-era skills of 'running fire' – delivering strikes while at speed.

This is because the US Army can have any helicopters it likes, but it isn't generally allowed to operate fixed-wing planes. As the army hates relying on the air force for support, the creation of strike helicopters was inevitable, whether they are as good as jets or not. In fact, they almost certainly aren't as good as jets, but the army, within broad limits, doesn't really care as long as they work to some degree. The key thing is that they are flown by soldiers, not air force pukes.

Naughty US Army, you might be thinking; why can't they just play nicely with the other children? But they might have a point. The air force really doesn't like placing its planes under the direction of ground troops. Close air support has generally been a poor relation in all air forces. The USAF can be made to assign aircraft to help the army on a temporary basis, but you will never see a squadron of F-16 strike jets permanently under the command of an army ground formation. On the other hand, every US Cavalry colonel has his own squadron of Apaches. When an Apache blows something up, then, it is likely that the ground forces wanted it done. That can be quite important, as we shall see. Even if F-16s *are* better than Apaches – more efficient at destroying things, that is – it's important that they destroy only things which really need destroying. Perhaps the best indicator of something genuinely needing to be blasted is when some poor grunt on the ground says it does.

In Britain, by trying really hard, we have managed to achieve an even stupider inter-service result. Back in the early 1950s the situation was similar to that across the pond: the army wanted helicopters, and the RAF, initially disdainful of such Heath-Robinson whirly things, agreed that the soldiery could operate them. (The first British military helicopters were typically unprepossessing in appearance. Legend tells of a pilot landing one at an American base. As he got out, a welcoming American is said to have asked, 'Gee, buddy, did you make it yourself?') The Army Air Corps thus began to take shape.*

However, fairly soon it became clear that helicopters were going

* Unlike most of the army's corps, it is not 'Royal'. Nor will it be while the RAF maintains any influence.

to be important things. In 1956 Egypt's President Nasser nation-alised the Suez Canal Company, after a disagreement with Britain and America over the financing of the Aswan Dam. Britain, the majority shareholder in the company, had lately withdrawn its troops from the canal zone under the terms of its treaty with Egypt. Now the British prime minister, Anthony Eden, decided to seize the zone once more. The French were happy on this occa-sion to support Britain (it was clear that an Anglo-French seizure of the canal would annoy America, although the French did have other reasons).

Seeking a pretext for military intervention, the French and British secretly arranged for an Israeli attack on the Sinai, the part of Egypt lying between the canal and Israel. The Israelis were more than happy with the idea of smashing up Nasser's forces and gaining an Anglo-French canal zone between them and central Egypt to boot. They would do their part – seeming to threaten a damaging war which might close the canal to international trade – and the British and French could then step in 'to restore stability to the region'.

Like many fiendishly cunning plans, the whole thing came badly unstuck. The Israelis attacked the Sinai with their customary effi-ciency, comprehensively defeating four Egyptian divisions. They had jumped the gun, however, leaving the British and French scrambling to get ready, and there was now an embarrassing delay during which stability briefly returned to the canal zone. Only then did the Anglo-French force attack, rather making a nonsense of the idea that they were doing so in order to calm things down.

For our purposes, the most interesting thing about the Suez operation was that it saw some of the earliest serious use of heli-copters in combat roles. (The US had already used lighter helos in Korea, but mainly for casualty evacuation.) Helicopters flying from ships in the Mediterranean carried Royal Marine Commandos ashore at Port Said, in the first ever amphibious heli-borne assault. The primitive helos of the day could lift only small loads and had to make many trips, but even so 415 men and twenty-three tons of materiel were landed in just eighty-three minutes. The way of the future was plain.

It can be no coincidence that the Suez operation also saw the last ever combat drop by British paratroopers. The jump into El

Gamil airfield by 3 Para is still remembered wistfully in airborne circles. It was a textbook success, with the aggressive Paras scattering more heavily armed Egyptian defenders before them. El Gamil, however, is on the Mediterranean shore. Helicopters from the ships were delivering supplies to the paratroops within forty-five minutes of the drop. Another battalion of paratroops, indeed, arrived the next day by landing craft. Nowadays it would be hard to see the point of using parachutes in such an operation, although the Paras themselves would remain the ideal men for the job.

The marines and the paras, together with French forces, secured Port Said within two days and began advancing rapidly down the canal, sweeping the Egyptians aside. But the motives behind the operation were quite plain to the rest of the world. The Americans were furious, the Russians were rattling their sabres and the UN secretary-general was livid. A ceasefire was imposed, and the British and French forced to withdraw. Subsequently the secret deal with the Israelis came out, causing a massive stink, and the whole business went down in history as one of the worst ideas ever.

Militarily, though, it had been a tremendous success (apart from the unfortunate initial delays in getting ready). In particular, the use of helicopters aroused tremendous interest. All round the world military people began to see the helicopter as the next big thing. Clearly, a good deal of money was going to be spent on helicopters in future, and quite large numbers of people would be involved in maintaining and flying them. As any good bureaucrat knows, money + people = high-ranking jobs = we want some of that. The RAF and the army, as the Suez crisis played out, were engaged in a protracted bureaucratic struggle over who would control what aircraft. The RAF was now thoroughly determined to cut itself as big a slice of helicopter pie as possible.

In the end, a rule was agreed. Any helicopter with an all-up weight over 4,000 pounds and operating from a land base would be air force, not army. As helicopters grew in size, this swiftly became a dead letter; but the end result, as we see today, was to give the army control of attack helicopters and very small utility/cargo jobs, while the RAF ended up in charge of proper troop carriers.

Brilliant. The army winds up doing close air support, which is

at least formally speaking an RAF task, and battlefield transport
– an army job if ever there was one – winds up in the RAF. A
classic MoD result: we begin to see why the British 'air assault'
infantry brigade does not own any helicopter capable of lifting
more than half a dozen soldiers off the ground. This is because
the only helicopters the brigade's CO actually has command of
are the Army Air Corps ones: soon to be two Apache regiments
each with a squadron of utility Lynxes in addition. Each Lynx
can carry six equipped soldiers at most, so these sixteen aircraft
will be able to lift fewer than a hundred combat troops, not even
one rifle company. The Apaches can carry nothing but their crews
and weapons. If the air assault brigadier should ever want to
make an air assault, he must ask for RAF assistance.

And it gets more confusing yet. The Royal Navy and marines
had been first with helicopter mobility for ground troops in 1956,
and they weren't bound by the 4,000-pound rule. In the 1950s
anything that flew from a ship was guaranteed to have NAVY
written on it, no matter what it weighed. Memories were still
fresh of the 1930s, when the RAF had owned the Fleet Air Arm.
Life at sea not being much to the air force taste, seagoing aviation was shockingly neglected. The Fleet Air Arm thus had the
unenviable distinction of being one of the few air forces still
equipped with biplanes at the start of World War II. The navy
took it over as a result, and an embarrassed RAF left them alone
for several decades.

The absence of the weight rule for naval helicopters meant that
for a very long time the only really expert British helicopter troops
were the marine commandos. The navy provided troop-carrying
helos for the marines' use (their crews were – still are – known
as 'Junglies', from their early combat operations in Borneo). The
Junglies, until the mid-90s when their helicopters began to wear
out, were typically the first choice of anyone in the army or navy
trying to get a helicopter ride. RAF helicopter pilots were not
popular, on the grounds that normally they have failed to be
selected both for fast jets and heavy transports before being
assigned to helos – not the case with navy or army aviators.
Furthermore, until lately, their effectiveness was badly handicapped by the notion that 'We aren't a bloody taxi service for
the army, you know.' (This is a first-hand quote from an RAF

squadron-leader in the Support Helicopter force, in 1990. I am still puzzled as to what he thought he *was* doing in life.) Army pilots had a better attitude, but having spent their time training for anti-tank work were less expert at moving troops. In any case, as we have seen, the army has no proper lift helicopters, only small anti-tank Lynxes with some room in the back, and most of these will soon be replaced by the Apache.

So, we arrive in recent times with a right old mess. All three services are operating helicopters for the purpose of moving people and kit about: the RAF with Pumas, Chinooks and utility Merlins; the army with small utility-roled Lynxes; and the navy's Junglies with utility Sea Kings.* When all three services are doing something, it generally means that it is a very necessary and useful thing, as we have seen with the infantry. Utility/transport helicopters, then, are clearly important: also, clearly, wildly disorganised. Operating five types of helicopter at once to do basically the same job is scarcely efficient. On top of this, there is a severe 'fleets within fleets' problem, meaning that we are effectively operating many more than five types. This is because transport helicopters, being so very useful, are always being modified in small batches and terrific haste for whatever operation is next on the dance card. Thus, any given British Chinook, for example, may be very different from another British Chinook. It may or may not be desertised, may or may not have defensive aids and countermeasures, may or may not be equipped for night operations, and so on.

There are further problems: the Puma and the Sea King are both now so aged – they were introduced in the 1970s – that they really aren't a great deal of use. They can still get into the air fairly reliably in cold weather, if not with very heavy loads and not to any great height, but hot climates or high altitudes – the places where many of our enemies might be found – are beyond them. All helicopters lose power in hot and high conditions, and thus must be pushed harder to operate. As a helicopter

---

* 'Utility' here refers to a helicopter which was actually designed to do something else, like attack or anti-submarine work. The utility version comes without all the mission-systems gubbins, giving you a nice cargo/personnel carrier if all goes well.

gets older, the red line on the dial is reached more and more easily. The wise pilot doesn't like pushing past the red line, not in a machine which is all too prone to problems even when treated well.

Both of these rickety old cabs could be replaced with utility Merlins, but the utility Merlin, despite theoretically having been in front-line RAF service since 2000, does not seem to have really won the trust of the British forces. The RAF's twenty-two shiny new utility Merlins did not go to Afghanistan, nor to the Iraq invasion. When asked in Parliament why this might be, the ministry replied that it was because 'The Merlin HC3 has yet to achieve the required level of operational capability for it to be deployed to the Gulf region.' This, three years after its delivery to the front line. Helos normally only last twenty-five years or so; the Merlin HC3 has already passed the first 10 per cent of its service life without being useable.

Tired old Pumas and Sea Kings did go to the Gulf in 2003, but in fact most of the lifting was done by the only really good, really useful transport helicopter in the British inventory – the American-made Chinook. It is perhaps especially fortunate that the Iraq invasion was not delayed until summer, as the worn-out Jungly Sea Kings can no longer safely take off at all, even empty at low level, on hot summer days in Iraq. At the moment, then, the RAF's thirty-four Chinooks are the helicopters of choice for the British. The special forces, indeed, have several assigned just for their use, always the mark of a good system.

In another superb bit of procurement lunacy, the MoD recently bought eight new Chinooks for special forces use, to be designated HC3s, at a cost of £30 million each. Boeing delivered them in 2001, but the helicopters cannot be proven to satisfy UK airworthiness standards for anything but perfect weather. The MoD-written contract did not specify this. Boeing have done exactly what was asked of them – they are completely in the clear on this one – but the helicopters are effectively useless. The cost of getting the HC3s cleared for use was originally estimated at a further £15 million each, adding fully 50 per cent to the cost and delaying their entry into service by nine years. We are now told that it may not be possible to fix the problems at any price. As a result of this amazing cock-up, several of the existing Chinook

HC2s have had to be given expensive crash upgrades for special-forces use in the interim. The whole affair was, understandably, described by the chairman of the investigating Parliamentary committee as 'the most incompetent procurement of all time'. Sadly, he was wrong; cretinously managed as the Chinook HC3 purchase was, it is nowhere near being the worst of all time. It doesn't even qualify as the worst British helicopter procurement.

So, the whole transport helicopter situation is basically a dreadful, chaotic pile of steaming dung. Britain operates a grand total of 112 purpose-built transport helicopters plus 110 small attack Lynxes which can operate in a light utility role, soon mostly to be replaced by Apaches which can't. Of all these, only the more upgraded of the thirty-four Chinooks are really much good; the rest are either too small, clapped-out, non-functional, lacking vital equipment or all of the above. Just to give an idea of how pathetic this is, a single American *cavalry brigade** possesses eighty-two helicopters at standard establishment, and there are swarms more at higher levels of command. The US armed forces operate well over 3,000 modern, effective, useful transport helicopters. One expects America to have ten times our capacity, but not a hundred times. Even the Israelis, despite spending about a quarter of what we do on defence, possess more capability than us in this area: Israel fields 196 good, modern transport helos. *They* know what's important.

Now we see the other part of the reason that 16 Air Assault doesn't have any helicopters to ride in. It isn't merely that RAF pilots hate being a taxi service for the army. Even if the air force wanted to help, it hasn't got enough helicopters to do so. Having snatched the army's transports in the 1950s, the RAF has systematically neglected them ever since, just as it did for seagoing aviation when it owned the Fleet Air Arm.

The navy doesn't come out of this looking brilliant, either.

---

* The Americans would call such a formation an armored cavalry regiment, but it is a brigade-sized unit in British terms. This regiment is of several squadrons, as in Britain, but each US Cavalry squadron has nine troops arranged into three companies, rather than simply three troops. 'Cavalry' in the American army is not the same as 'Armor', which is the term for more conventional tank units. The US Army is sometimes just as confusing as the British one.

Finding itself with the best and most credible British airmobile force, in the form of the excellent Jungly–marine combination, it has shamefully failed to maintain it. The aircrews and the commandos are as good as ever, but their creaky old utility Sea Kings had their day long ago. Rather than replacing these, which have probably seen more combat action than any other aircraft in British service, the navy chose first to renew its anti-submarine helicopters. These, by contrast, have engaged one, solitary enemy submarine in their whole career. (During the Falklands War. The Argentine sub was on the surface at the time so it wasn't really an anti-submarine engagement as such. I merely mention it for accuracy's sake.)

In the navy's defence, this decision was actually taken in the late 1970s. Back then, nearly thirty years ago, the Soviet Red Banner Northern Fleet – perhaps the single most powerful submarine force in the world – was very much open for business. The Junglies may have been – definitely were – seeing more real action than the 'pingers' in the sub-hunter squadrons, but there was no ignoring the commie submarine threat back then. Not when the freedom of Western Europe was likely to depend on the Atlantic sea lanes being kept open. And helicopters are very useful for hunting submarines. Not only can they fly from any ship with a pad, rather than needing a monster aircraft carrier, their ability to hover means that they can lower a detecting sonar into the sea. Combine this with a search radar, sonar buoys and homing torpedoes, add the speed of the helo and the fact that it cannot be torpedoed itself, and you have the ideal anti-submarine tool. The navy possessed perfectly good Sea Kings for all this but it wanted to move on, and so the Merlin helicopter was born. The idea was that this new helo would be in service by the late 1980s, and then the navy could think about replacing the Junglies' aircraft.

Nothing of the sort took place. The anti-submarine Merlin project was a colossal, stupendous fiasco, easily outstripping anything we have seen so far. Sub-hunting Merlins finally began to reach the fleet in 2001, more than *twenty years* after the project commenced, with the almost unbelievable price tag of *one hundred and five million pounds per helicopter*, approximately five times as much as the original estimate. (It was a European collabora-

tive project, one need hardly say.) All through the 1980s and early
'90s, the programme had struggled with technical setbacks,
involving several prototypes crashing. Many of these snags were
related to the Merlin's triple-engined design, which was supposed
to allow the helo to keep flying even after an engine failure. In
the end, though, the extra power was gobbled up by the increasingly heavy and complex mission systems, and the helicopter
cannot really be said to be a huge success in performance terms.
Embarrassingly for such a new and expensive aircraft, a fully
armed and fuelled Merlin cannot actually hover in still air, even
with all three engines at full power; its ability to stay airborne
after an engine failure is correspondingly dubious in many situations.* The anti-submarine Merlin, like the utility version, is still
not really combat-ready as I write. Dire rumours continue to
circulate regarding the date at which it might achieve real-world
operational capability.

To give these insane figures a frame of reference, the Royal
Navy's forty-four Merlin Mark 1s have thus cost nearly as much
as NASA thinks it will need to send a manned mission to Mars.
And it gets worse: during the incredibly protracted process of
making the Merlin, its enemy disappeared. The Soviet submarine
fleet has closed up shop, leaving the helicopters with nothing to
do. The navy, having beggared itself buying the now rather pointless anti-submarine Merlin, has no further money to spend on
aircraft for a while. The venerable Jungly Sea Kings will keep

---

* Any helicopter achieves more lift for the same power when it is moving
forward through the air. Thus, a fully loaded Merlin can achieve a hover over
a point on the ground or sea if there is a wind blowing, as it must drive forward
into wind to stay still. In calm conditions, however, its rotors are beating air
which they have already churned up, meaning that they need more power to
get the same lift – power which the Merlin does not possess. This isn't quite
the crippling defect it might seem: a Merlin can still get airborne with a full
fuel and weapons load, even in a calm. Ashore it can taxi rapidly forward to
take off, and at sea its host ship can provide a wind over the deck by increasing
speed. Hopefully by the time the Merlin reaches its hunting grounds it will
have burned enough fuel to hover even without a wind, and so employ its
dipping sonar; if not it can always jettison some. Even so, considering the
immense, expensive efforts that were made to give the Merlin a good margin
of power, this is an unimpressive result.

flying for some years yet, therefore, much though this will become an increasingly pointless exercise as the airframes lose the last of their vestigial lifting capability.

So, chaos everywhere. This smelly tri-service helicopter situation became so bad in the late 1990s that the government was forced to take official notice of it; the Strategic Defence Review of 1998 was clearly going to have to recommend a solution. Furthermore, the review was just as clearly going to tell the army to finally shift emphasis from parachute to heli-borne operations. A real, serious heli-borne brigade was to be formed. This would clearly necessitate a shake-up in rotary-wing organisation. Some people were expecting to see radical reform. There were hopes that the new air assault brigade might actually possess some air transport, or even that Britain might go out and buy an appropriate number of functional helicopters for its armed forces.

Naturally, none of this happened. The only way to really integrate lift helicopters into the air assault formation would have been to take them away from the RAF. This would have been bitterly contested by the air marshals and only the most resolute of politicians could have done it. Furthermore, backing from the army would have been lukewarm. As we have seen, several influential army communities dislike helicopters, seeing them as a foolish distraction from proper meat-and-potatoes armour and artillery, and the army tends to lump useful troop-moving helos in with the more questionable attack birds. George Robertson, defence minister at the time, was quite resolute as politicians go, but not resolute enough for this sort of situation.

As for buying more helicopters, that would have called for some money. There was actually plenty available, but it had already been spent on various Cold War legacy projects like the Merlin. Besides, the defence budget has to be divided equally between the services. This isn't officially the case, but it always coincidentally works out that way somehow: which avoids ministers having to actually make decisions, or take charge of their uniformed subordinates in any serious way. It would have been difficult enough to wrench the lift helos from the RAF's always-vicelike grip in the first place. Giving the army extra money on top to get more would have had the air marshals incandescent with rage. Similarly, leaving the aircraft in the RAF and giving *them* the cash to improve matters would have had the admirals and generals up in arms. Plus, knowing the RAF, once they had the money they would have found some way to spend it on something more to their taste, like great big bombers.

Instead of any actual serious reform, then, it was decided to do the one thing that the armed services can always agree on: a new Joint headquarters was set up. All forces officers love these as they result in the miraculous creation of lots of high-ranking jobs out of nothing. Even better, senior posts in an HQ have few or no juniors beneath them. Thus the ratio of senior officers to junior officers rises, and everybody's chances of promotion get better. A new two-star slot and lots of other prime jobs were now up for grabs, without the appearance of so much as a single new helicopter.*

Another classic MoD result. We don't have enough helicopters, and the ones we do have are knackered. On the other hand, we have a wild superfluity of senior officers; indeed, their bickering and hair-pulling is what has led to the problem. Of *course* the solution must be to hire more senior officers, and do nothing about the helicopters!

The Joint Helicopter Command duly formed up, and took over all the transport, attack and recce helicopters in the British forces. Madly, the JHC also took command of 16 Air Assault Brigade. Rather than the brigade getting control of its helicopters, the helicopter people took control of the brigade! It's as though the logistics corps had taken over the light infantry, on the basis that they ride in lorries.

Looking to the future, there is an MoD project team thinking about getting some more troop-carrying helicopters one of these fine days. (There is also a space warfare think tank. That doesn't mean we'll be getting spaceships any time soon.) Naturally, this project is being run by the RAF and the navy, despite the fact that the army is the main customer. Also naturally, it hasn't even made up its mind what aircraft to buy, despite the urgency of the

---

* That is, a job for a rear-admiral, major-general or air-vice-marshal. A two-star officer is paid around £95,000 p.a. plus quietly magnificent pension, housing and travel package.

matter. We can be reasonably certain, having considered Merlin, Chinook HC3 and Apache, that whatever eventually happens it will cost a lot, take a long time, and quite possibly not work.

That's the British helicopter situation: and now we are starting to see some serious money being spent. At first glance it would seem that helicopters are more expensive than armour and artillery, and a lot more expensive than infantrymen. But let's set aside debatable helicopters like the attack and anti-submarine ones for a moment. Let's focus on the useful stuff.

Absolutely everybody agrees that utility/transport helos are very useful indeed. Like infantry, they are involved in almost every operation, and they are always in urgent demand. Tellingly, like infantry, all three services have them. They are useful for every type of military activity from humanitarian disaster relief up to full-bore, high-intensity conflict. Utility/cargo helicopters are, indeed, almost as basic a capability as infantry in the modern age. They are one of the few really good, really flexible, really useful things that the military has.

And actually, as opposed to aircraft crammed full of dubious whizz-bleep mission systems, utility helicopters can be quite reasonably priced. The US Army, to give an example, paid £3.3 million per helo in early-1990s money for its UH-60L Black Hawk troop carriers, about half the price of a Challenger II tank. The utility Merlin, able to carry a similar number of troops – whenever it becomes operational – cost us almost ten times as much, at £34 million per helo in late 1990s money. Looking at the US example, perhaps useful helicopters needn't be expensive after all.

Of course, one would still need to buy some. Britain largely hasn't bothered: £1.2 billion has been spent purchasing lift helicopters in the last twenty-five years, a third of which was on the idiotically bungled Chinook HC3 buy and the rest on the utility Merlin. This equates to a fraction of a single percentage point of what was available over that period. The Ministry of Defence could easily afford to have a big, useful fleet of modern transport helicopters, just as it could easily afford to properly fund its magnificent infantrymen.

It has failed to do either. Instead, it has spent twice this sum on an ill-judged job creation scheme involving a few attack helicopters (Apache) and four times as much on a similar effort to produce an even smaller number of sub-hunter helicopters which now have very little to do (Merlin). The amount of money spent seems to go up as the usefulness goes down. However, overall spending on helicopters, even including these ill-fated projects, has still been very small considered against the resources available.

Basically, the MoD doesn't really focus on providing helicopters any more than it does on infantry, tanks or artillery. Most of the resources we lavish on the MoD – the £30 billion a year and the 300,000 people – remain unaccounted for. What little has been spent on helicopters has largely been pissed away.

CHAPTER

5

Fighters

*If you don't know who the greatest fighter pilot in the world is
. . . it isn't you.*

Fighter pilot saying

Nowadays, whenever the British Army or navy go anywhere to
fight, they pretty much insist that the skies above should be under
friendly control, or under the control of the RAF anyway. The
idea that surface units can operate for long under serious enemy
air attack was largely put to rest during World War II, then given
the coup de grâce in the Falklands. There are a few exceptions
to the no-operations-under-hostile-skies rule: for instance, nuclear-
powered submarines need not be overly worried about the air
forces of our likely enemies. In general, though, if the opposition
control the skies, most of our land and naval forces can only go
there at a terrible price.

Air superiority, then, is a very important thing. This means that
we need a working system of fighter jets. Some would disagree;
historically it has often been thought that missiles might make
the fighter obsolete. In fact, a British government white paper of
1957 stated that the Lightnings then in production would be the
last manned fighters in the British forces. Given that the Lightning
was replaced by the Phantom, which in turn was replaced by the
Tornado F3, and the Eurofighter is on the way, the demise of the
manned interceptor was clearly not quite as imminent as Defence
Minister Duncan Sandys thought.

This is not surprising. There are various problems with using
surface-based systems to control airspace, mostly arising from one
simple fact: the world is round, not flat. This means that when

you are low down, say at sea level, you cannot see very far. The horizon will be only a few miles away. If your enemy is flying low, you will not see him until he is very close.

This is just as true when using radar, the method which all longer-range missile systems use to see and track their targets. (Occasionally radar beams bend over the horizon to detect objects beyond it, but this doesn't occur with anything like enough predictability or accuracy to be useful.) A ground radar has a straight line of sight to an aircraft 210 miles away if it is 30,000 feet up, but a jet or cruise missile flying at 500 feet can only be seen if it comes within thirty miles. These figures are approximate, taking no account of variable factors such as antenna height and terrain features, but they are a good guideline. Flying low isn't necessarily a brilliant idea for attacking aircraft, but it is an option. One would need a very large number of ground radars to create a barrier against such attacks.

This has led to the development of airborne radars. At first they couldn't pick out low-flying aircraft against the background of the earth, but this problem has long been solved. An airborne radar can go as high as its carrying aircraft can fly, easily 30,000 feet in the jet age. It can see an enemy flying at 500 feet nearly 240 miles off. A single airborne radar can thus watch as much border or front line as eight ground stations, and this ratio gets larger if our enemies fly lower and our radars fly higher, as they most likely can and will. The airborne radar can look deep into enemy territory as well, and it can move about much more easily.

Very well, the radar should definitely be up in the sky. But why can't we then shoot missiles from the surface at the targets we detect? Why do we need fighters?

The answer comes in several parts.

Firstly, the missile itself generally needs to see the target before it can be launched; this is normally done with a specialised targeting radar in the launcher. The targeting radar is different from the search radar which finds the target in the first place. Both are necessary and they can't usually be combined effectively. If the missile is fired from the ground, we find ourselves back where we started: regardless of the range of the missile, we need a large number of ground launchers if we are to see, and thus shoot at, any given low-level target. Launchers high in the sky –

that is, fighters – can see much further with their targeting radars, and so are better.

Secondly, our enemy aircraft are likely to be travelling fast, at high subsonic speeds – say 600 mph. The only exceptions are helicopters – fish in a barrel for any airborne defence net. A fighter jet can make a short sprint at better than Mach 2, usually; some even faster. This means that a single patrolling fighter can zoom into range of even fast-moving enemies over a wide area. Surface launchers will never be able to do this.

Thirdly, until relatively recently it has been very important to remember one critical fact about missile systems: they don't work very well. All missiles, that is, not just ground-based ones. The first generation, which appeared in the years following Sandys' 1957 white paper, were amazingly ineffectual, so much so that ordinary guns and cannons gained a new lease of life. Most air forces began re-emphasising dogfighting skills for fighter pilots, and it became common practice once again to include cannon in the basic design of a fighter. By the 1980s more effective missiles were beginning to appear, but one still generally needed to manoeuvre into an advantageous position to get an air-to-air missile kill: to dogfight. Only today are guided weapons beginning to fulfil the promise they seemed to hold out fifty years ago, in British service at least. And the world is still round, so the radars and launchers still need to be up in the sky.

For all these reasons, fighters and airborne radar aircraft are the best way to dominate and control airspace, whether one's own for defensive purposes or someone else's for offensive ones. However, as usual, the dead hand of the cold war still reaches out of the grave to exert a choking stranglehold on our policy. Also, the buy-British-and-damn-the-consequences rule remains very much in force.

First, let's take a look at the chequered history of British fighter procurement.

Back in the 1960s Sandys' white paper was getting a deservedly stiff ignoring. The British Lightning fighters then in service with the RAF were becoming obsolescent very quickly; they could only carry two missiles, and despite many improvements were never really able to stay airborne for long. They began to be replaced by American Phantoms in 1970, although the RAF loved the Lightning so much that some remained operational until 1985, to be finally replaced by the Phantom's successor, the Tornado F3.

The Phantom was a choice forced on the RAF by the navy, which at that point still had big aircraft carriers, left over from World War II procurements and able to operate regular fighter jets. The navy wanted the Phantom because it could fly from carriers. In any event it turned out well: the American-built Phantom was a sound fighter, and was also very useful for ground attack. This was all too good to last. The by-now struggling British aerospace industry, then being consolidated into one monster company, urgently needed more cash. This company was called British Aerospace, or BAe for short. (The government did the consolidating, and indeed owned it for a time. Theoretically, it is no longer an arm of the government but a private-sector corporation: we'll look at that some more later on.) Furthermore, the Phantom, being rather more useful than the Lightning – if not as lovely – was being worn out at a furious rate. A new fighter was going to be needed.

Unfortunately for British defence workers, no credible European or British fighter design existed. The RAF, to its credit, pointed this out and asked for special permission to buy American again, but was overridden. The navy was by now out of the conventional fighter game, having been told it couldn't have any new aircraft carriers. British Aerospace management, meanwhile, were eyeing the proposed fighter spend hungrily. They didn't have a suitable jet to hand, but they wanted that money: and the government wanted to give it to them, regardless of the RAF.

Britain had already combined with West Germany and Italy to build the Tornado low-level deep-penetration bomber. BAe twiddled the design a bit and, hey presto, it was somehow a fighter. The Tornado Air Defence Variant, later to be called the F3, was born. Everybody breathed a big sigh of relief. The government could give BAe yet another big wedge of cash, but it wouldn't be a controversial outright subsidy. This wouldn't just keep domestic military production afloat; at that time, the remaining British civil aircraft industry was only being kept going by the defence side of BAe.

The only people not chuffed to bits were the fighter pilots of the RAF, who had been given a truly awful jet to fly. The original Tornado bomber had been intended to carry out one mission, and one mission only: fly as low as possible, as fast as possible, deep into defended airspace to deliver big loads of dropped ordnance. At this, it remains supremely good. (It turns out to have been a suicidally stupid thing to do, but we'll get to that later). The Tornado Air Defence Variant was still basically the same jet, no matter what BAe said, and it showed. This was a severe problem. The whole point of a fighter is that it can go high up in the sky; it isn't supposed to hug the ground. To this day the Tornado F3 struggles to reach 30,000 feet, making it something of a joke to the pilots of other military jets. Apparently, it isn't uncommon to tease F3 crews by gratuitously reporting one's own – much greater – altitude whenever they are on the same radio frequency.

One of the few changes which BAe was compelled to make in order to notionally turn bomber into interceptor was to fit a fighter-style targeting radar, rather than the bomber's terrain-following set. This was another fearful mess: the planes were ready for delivery in 1985, but the radar was not serviceable until the early 1990s. While all this was happening, the navy had introduced two such radars aboard their Sea Harrier jump-jet:* Blue Fox in 1980, and its replacement, Blue Vixen, in 1990. The RAF's Tornados, meanwhile, were flying about with concrete ballast in their nose cones for lack of a radar. This was known with the usual black Service humour as Blue Circle radar, after the well-known cement firm. The delays to the F3 were so severe that the RAF had to obtain extra Phantoms to fill the gap: second-hand ex-US Navy aircraft were provided by the Americans.

Even once it had a radar, the Tornado F3 continued to be pretty much a laughing-stock. I can remember taking a ride in an RAF tanker in 2000 to a rendezvous just south of the Iraqi border. Back then, British and American fighters enforcing the no-fly zones above Iraq would meet tankers here to top up before going over hostile territory. On this particular day a brace of Tornado F3s were to fill their tanks from the aircraft I was riding in. The

---

* See Chapter 7 for a discussion of this remarkable machine.

tanker flew to the rendezvous at about 30,000 feet, the same as an airliner's cruising height. Proper jet planes fly up there because the thin air gives them the optimum balance of thrust, fuel economy and drag, allowing them to achieve the best speeds and the longest endurance. Imagine my surprise when, as we approached the rendezvous, the tanker began descending rapidly.

When I enquired why we were doing this, the tanker captain explained that the Tornados could only get up to his cruising height by using maximum power: in which case they would be burning fuel much faster than he could give it to them, making the whole exercise rather pointless. A fighter which needs full thrust merely to get up to 30,000 feet can scarcely have much power in hand for combat manoeuvres. Even a basic peacetime task like checking out a suspicious airliner is effectively impossible for an F3, unless the suspect's pilot chooses to cooperate. Indeed, whenever any realistic opposition has seemed to be in the offing, as in Gulf Wars I and II, nobody has cared to send F3s into combat. In both these conflicts F3s deployed to the war zone: both times they were relegated to patrolling safe areas, well away from even the slender threat of the Iraqi air force, while other nations' fighters went into harm's way.

It seemed to me something of a betrayal back in 2000 to be sending our airmen over the territory of a hostile, murderous dictator in planes which were clearly not combat-worthy. It still does. Needless to say, the fighter pilots found it an occasion for a cheerful rude gesture as they departed, rather than any signs of worry. But then you won't last long in the British forces if depending for your life on duff kit really bothers you.

Sadly, air combat is one of those fields where even the most competent people will still be beaten if their equipment is second rate. The excellent British infantryman has generally been able to overcome his rubbishy rifle and other kit problems to get good results in combat anyway. Our equally excellent Tornado fighter crews, fortunately, have never fought in an air-to-air battle. Judging by what happens to them in exercises against other air forces, this is just as well.

And our fighter crews *are* very good. The RAF sends its best student pilots into fast combat jets, the runners-up into tankers and transport aeroplanes, and the remainder into helicopters.

Within the fast jets there is another hierarchy of merit: fighter pilots are at the bottom, below the various kinds of bombers, but they are still fast jet material and not to be sniffed at. Indeed, no RAF pilot is actually bad. The training system rejects a lot of people completely, and it takes only very strong candidates to begin with. There is no shortage of well-educated, keen, able young people wanting to be pilots. Even the lowly, downtrodden RAF helicopter driver must possess solid ability, despite what his fast-jet oppressors may say in the bar.

RAF aircrew aren't just carefully selected; their training is second to none, too. It takes years even when things are going well. If, as is usual, there are delays, making a fast jet pilot can take the better part of a decade, and it costs £6 million for each one.* Pilots are thus even more expensive and difficult to obtain than special forces types. The chaps in the back seats of fast jets, called Navigators in the RAF (although in fact they spend more time operating weapons and sensors than navigating) go through a similarly intense process.

The lengthening of the training pipeline and the shift to graduate officers has led to a change in the nature of these jet aviators. Long ago, the majority would be swaggering young bloods in their early twenties, aggressively single and quite happy to go and spend a few months flying from some faraway airbase. Nowadays rather a lot of them seem to be older, steadier, married fathers. (There are women doing these jobs now, but very few: fourteen out of around 400 pilots in 2004. Many squadrons will still be all male, at least in aircrew.)

While on the subject of the people behind the machines, an RAF fast jet squadron should have twelve to sixteen air crews, the same number as it has jets. These people will all be officers, a mixture of flight-lieutenants and squadron-leaders by rank, corresponding to army captains and majors. The airmen will have passed through the junior ranks of pilot-officer and flying-officer, equivalent to army lieutenants, while still under training. They are rather better paid than most army officers, however: they

---

* The average time to train a new pilot reached six years in the late 1990s, according to the National Audit Office. Or in other words, 50 per cent were taking longer than 6 years.

receive substantial flying pay on top of their basic salaries. A newly qualified rookie pilot, almost certainly already a flight-lieutenant, will be paid around £36,000 p.a. in total; as a seasoned squadron-leader a few years later he will get between £45,000 and £55,000. In other words, roughly the same money as an army lieutenant-colonel, who may command a battle group of 700 men.

The commanding officer of an RAF squadron is not, as one might have thought, a squadron-leader; rank inflation has taken place since the RAF was set up, and the most that a squadron-leader can now hope to command is a flight, typically three or four aircraft. Flight-lieutenants, who would once have done this, can no longer really expect to command anything, except in ground branches. RAF aircraft squadrons, meanwhile, are nowadays bossed by wing-commanders, the same rank as an army lieutenant-colonel.

As an aside, one notes that navy and army aviation squadrons are still normally commanded by officers equivalent to squadron-leaders: lieutenant-commanders and majors respectively.* If the RAF had stuck to such a policy it would have very few jobs at wing-commander which could be described as command posts, and that would never do. Holding some sort of command at this rank is a necessary part of an air marshal's career portfolio, and it is taken as a given that the nation requires plenty of air marshals – forty of them at the moment, in fact, to run an air force with about that number of combat squadrons.

Despite the fact that aircrew pay is generous in service terms there is constant difficulty hanging on to trained pilots. The money is nothing special compared to that earned by an airline pilot, and an airline pilot's life is much more pleasant. This isn't just a question of in-flight beverage-cart service, still sadly lacking in even the latest fighters: the airline man spends less time away from home, in much smaller chunks, on a much more predictable

---

* Except in the case of navy Harrier squadrons, which are now integrated with the RAF ones as Joint Force Harrier. The naval Harrier COs have been bumped up to commander to match their RAF colleagues, which has in its turn caused a certain amount of bitterness both among other navy squadron commanders and the RAF ones, who normally command a larger number of jets and many more people.

schedule. Now that the average front-line aviator is married and quite likely has children, this is more important than formerly. Furthermore, wives nowadays tend to have jobs and lives apart from the service, and people are less willing to put their children into boarding school, despite the fact the the MoD will pay for this. This all tends to mean that time deployed overseas, especially at short notice, causes far more pain and grief than once it did.

There are other important differences in the manpower situations of army colonels and jet pilots. The army has over 1,700 lieutenant-colonels, and can field perhaps forty battle groups at its uttermost stretch – more like thirty, really. Even though many, perhaps most, of the swarming colonels are not suitable to command such units, at least a few hundred of them could do the job perfectly well. We need never fear having to send out a battle group lacking a CO. (Indeed, theoretically we could make up an extra battle group or two just from surplus colonels. That would be a truly entertaining thing to do.) By contrast, the RAF wishes to have 500-odd current, useful pilots, even though it has no plans ever to use its many mothballed aeroplanes. It is short of this figure by nearly a hundred, despite the fact that it has almost 3,500 aircrew officers wearing wings on their chests. Some of these people are navigators, of course; but an awful lot of them are pilots who are in desk jobs or who are too senior to fly combat. Not many will ever be useful fighting airmen again, although they will continue to draw flying pay, of course.

The knock-on effect is that the few useful pilots get worked harder, spending more time away from their families and so getting more and more tempted by the airlines. Their lives are still immensely pleasant, of course, compared to – for example – those of infantrymen. The time away they find so hard is generally spent in a relatively comfortable mess or quite often a luxury hotel, not a grim, fortified camp under frequent rocket or mortar attack. It is most unlikely that any enemy will ever really threaten them: they will never have to walk the baking streets of Basra in the gunsights of enemy snipers. There are honourable exceptions – the RAF Harrier force, for example, faces grittier conditions than most – but is hard to feel a lot of sympathy for the fast jet men in this context. The sweating, dusty foot soldier, however, doesn't have a well-paid and glamorous job waiting for him in civvy

street. Nor does the navigator in the back seat of the jet, in fact.
Nor, for that matter, do the army's swarming colonels. But the
pilot does, and he can't be held against his will after his initial
return-of-service period expires.

This situation has lately led to a number of financial retention
initiatives of late years, in which pilots are offered sometimes
quite large amounts of money – on top of flying pay – with the
aim of holding on to them for a while. Given that training a
replacement will cost millions and take years, this makes sense.
The navy, desperately short of combat-ready pilots for its Sea
Harrier jump-jets, has lately offered the remaining ones £50,000
lump sums to sign up for five more years. The authorities have
even bowed to the inevitable and offered help in eventually getting
an airline pilot's licence to those who will first fly naval aircraft
for a few more years. It causes a lot of grumbling and resentment in the rest of the navy, but – as they say in the Service –
that's life in a blue suit. Even if this kind of thing does cause
other personnel to depart the navy in a huff, they can be replaced
comparatively cheaply and quickly.

The RAF's approach has been rather different: it has chosen to
give payments to navigators as well, even though they are much
less likely to leave, having no very saleable skills other than those
which any ex-forces officer might be said to possess. Also, the
initial RAF retention payment was set up in such a way that
nobody under the age of thirty-seven got any money at all; it was
strictly for the very long-serving. Combat aircrew are older than
they used to be, but they mostly aren't *that* old. On our typical
fast jet squadron, the only one really likely to get any money
would be the CO and, frankly, keeping *him* in the service isn't
the problem. He has been a lifer for a long time or he wouldn't
have got where he is, and anyway his usefulness as a pilot is
nearly over. This is lunacy; it is the way one would expect the
money to be shared out if a group of senior, desk-bound pilots
and navigators had made the decision with their own financial
well-being and that of their contemporaries as the prime concern.
Funnily enough, senior, desk-bound pilots and navigators run the
RAF. As for their priorities, only they can know.

Other more reasonable schemes followed, and money began to
reach the relevant people. Efforts were made to speed up the

training process. Perhaps most significantly, the RAF revised the number of aircraft it expected to operate in future – downwards, naturally. The latest forecasts predict an overmanning in aircrew. The next step will almost certainly be some bright spark identifying spare capacity in the training pipeline, a resultant shortage of new pilots, and the whole merry-go-round will start all over again. No matter what the manpower figures, a lot of money has flowed and will continue to flow into the wrong hands. Non-flying officers continue to draw substantial flying pay, and in no few cases have pocketed large sums on top. There may be an incentive to stay in the RAF; there isn't much of one to keep flying, other than the love of it.

Now let's return to the front line: to our jet squadron. Apart from the aircrew, from twelve to thirty in number, there are also between two and three hundred ground personnel, mostly non-commissioned ranks but including a number of non-flying officers. This is about the minimum number of people the RAF feels it needs to operate a group of aircraft – somewhat more than the other services seem to, but in all fairness not wildly more. Military aircraft need a lot of cosseting to maintain even barely acceptable availability rates. Stint too much on technical manpower, and they stop working entirely.

It is relatively rare for an entire squadron to deploy anywhere as a unit; more normally, jets and people will be taken from several. The numbers of personnel per deployed aircraft will tend to remain high, however: a detachment of eight aircraft will often be accompanied by well over 200 ground staff, and a single plane based overseas may result in foreign placements for fifty-odd. These figures definitely represent some feather-bedding; a single naval aircraft, for example, often goes to sea for months accompanied by less than ten people. However, given that the RAF has the people (and it does) they may as well get their knees brown.

In fact, it more than has the people. Those in operational, deployable flying squadrons will typically be only a minority at an RAF station, and a lot of RAF stations have no aircraft at all. In addition to any flying squadrons, an RAF base will have several non-flying 'wings', usually an Admin Wing, Engineering Wing and Operations Wing. Each of these has hundreds of uniformed RAF personnel who are not required or expected to deploy to war with the squadrons. The technicians of the engineering wings, as distinct from those in the flying squadrons, are generally responsible for second- or third-line maintenance for which an aircraft would normally return home to the UK. The ops wing is made up of people such as the base's air traffic controllers – and there is a separate, deployable air-traffic/radar unit for operations overseas.

The RAF sees the whole station as a fighting unit, hence the very large uniformed strength and the fact that the job of station commander in the UK is often described as 'flying' or even 'front-line'. The airmen developed this viewpoint during World War II, when bases frequently had to keep operating their planes while under attack from enemy bombers. The other services have always found this curious – the naval dockyards, for example, which were hammered every bit as severely by the Luftwaffe, have always been mostly civilian manned. The army and navy would argue that a large proportion of the RAF's uniformed posts at UK stations are actually civilian in nature or unnecessary, especially nowadays with the likelihood of a military attack on the UK extremely low. A full general in the army was quoted unattributably on the subject a few years ago:

> I . . . do not hold to the view . . . that the RAF should be disbanded and that their aircraft should be flown by the Army and RN. What I advocate most strongly is that they are outrageously overmanned for what they do and deliver. Some of what they do now could be sensibly privatised . . . I consider that the RAF must be forced to identify their core business.

As a full general in the army, of course, this officer is living in something of a glass house when it comes to overmanning – it is hard to see why the army needs any officers at full general rank at all – but he does have a point in that the RAF's personnel-to-aircraft ratio is very high, at around 150 uniformed people per deployable combat aircraft, as of late 2004. This contrasts sharply with the Fleet Air Arm figure of just over thirty, or the Army Air

Corps at approximately twenty.* Or even with the Israeli air force, probably a fairer comparison. Its aircraft inventory is actually larger and more sophisticated than the RAF's but it operates with around sixty people per useful combat airframe. One must remember that many air force systems are more complex and manpower-intensive than those of the army and navy. Nonetheless, the RAF would seem to be wildly overstaffed, even by the not-very-rigorous standards of the other services.

Attempts to control this RAF feather-bedding have so far been unsuccessful. A civilian aeroplane-servicing centre was set up in Wales by the Defence Aviation Repair Agency. This facility, known as Project Red Dragon, was to run along the lines of the civilian maintenance yard long operated in Portsmouth by the army and navy for their helicopters. (This use of cheap civilians to carry out UK-based, third-line work is one reason why the sailors and soldiers manage with relatively few uniforms per bird.) However, when it came to the crunch – when the Welsh project's existence seemed likely to actually lead to a significant fall in RAF uniformed strength – it was brushed aside. The RAF awarded its maintenance work to itself, preserving its own uniformed personnel, and it now appears that the Welsh facility may have to shed employees or even shut down for lack of work. Meanwhile, the RAF will continue to have very large personnel numbers relative to its strength in the air.

These numerous RAF ground staff, or blunties as the aircrew call them – they don't work at the sharp end – are much envied by the other services, which may account for some of the carping. Their foreign deployments are seldom, short, safe and pleasant. Their conditions of service are relatively excellent. Pay at any given rank is no better than that in the army or navy: but, crucially, the RAF does not throw out its enlisted men and women at the age of forty, as the other services do. This allows airmen and women to build up very pleasing pensions. Of hard lying, seasickness and other army or navy unpleasantness, there is almost none. And when it comes to fighting, as the old saw has it, an RAF enlisted rank is the cleverest thing to be. Army officers, apart

---

* This includes technicians of the Corps of Royal Electrical and Mechanical Engineers, who handle maintenance.

from the most junior, send their soldiers forward into battle. Navy officers take their sailors with them. But in an air force squadron, uniquely, the enlisted airmen and women send the officers out to fight, and stay behind themselves.

All this keeps the people of the RAF pretty happy, if you ignore the cheesed-off combat pilots – less than 1 per cent of the strength. Personnel turnover, unsurprisingly, is significantly less than in the army and navy. The only downside is the inevitably slow promotion resulting from long service and high retention, so air force corporals and sergeants tend to be quite old compared to their counterparts in the other services. What all this tells us, really, is that there is no personnel weakness in the RAF barring a certain shortage of pilots, and even this could probably be fixed quite easily by simply offering the cocky little sods massive salaries.* It would cost very little in the great scheme of things, particularly if you restricted the money to useful pilots rather than dishing it out to anyone wearing wings. In the end, the aircrew are an elite and have trained long and hard; the maintenance crews are lavishly manned, well treated, well looked after and thoroughly experienced. The actual aircraft, unfortunately, are not worthy of their users nor the excellent care they receive.

Which brings us back to the Tornado fighter. The non-flying upper echelons of the RAF would loyally defend the F3 on the grounds that, despite its inability to dogfight, it is a perfectly acceptable supersonic missile launcher. They have lately spent £140 million plus refitting it with some rather more effective missiles than those originally supplied, in fact. As one might expect, there were severe problems in doing this, due to the ever-troublesome F3 radar, and there has been some question as to whether any real extra capability was achieved. The air marshals nowadays like to claim that the F3 was never intended to be a dogfighting aircraft, which does rather raise the question of why – if that isn't just a complete lie – it was designed with a built-in cannon.

---

* They do tend to be cocky. With reason, I would say. Their tendency to be short is said to be a matter of fitting into ejection seats, or tolerance for G forces. Or perhaps it is just that only someone with a certain amount of small-person syndrome can ever make a really good fast jet pilot.

Nobody is really convinced by this argument. Only two nations ever bought the Tornado F3: Britain and Saudi Arabia. The most reasonable explanation for the Saudi F3 purchase would seem to lie in the ongoing scandal regarding lavish BAe entertainment of Saudi princes. One notes that the House of Saud also ordered American F-15s for actual use, as opposed to the F3s which they seem to have bought for the accompanying free gifts. And it gets worse: the RAF could find no use for all the Tornados that were forced upon it. Of 170 fighters originally procured by the UK, just sixty-eight are in operational service as I write. The rest are mainly in mothballs. Some were lent to Italy for a while, before being rejected by the disgusted Italians in favour of American planes.

All in all, the Tornado F3 is to fighters what the SA80 is to rifles. It is an industrial subsidy poorly disguised as a weapon system, to the very great hazard of our front-line service people and the very great detriment of our military capability and credibility. The RAF, as a result of having the F3 crammed down its throat, has not possessed any decent fighters for over a decade. This is rather a basic capability for a supposedly first-rank air force to be lacking. However, during the long and depressing Tornado F3 saga, the world picture has changed significantly.

Back in the 1980s, when the F3 was supposed to enter service, the air forces of the West were facing the mighty Voyska PVO and their regiments of highly capable MiGs and Sukhois. Missiles were coming along, but they still required the steely fighter jockey to dogfight against his adversary to be sure of a kill, and it wasn't uncommon to find oneself doing the job with guns as of old. Nowadays, our likeliest adversaries are terrorist and paramilitary organisations, or the warlords of the world's failed and failing states, and they do not possess fighters at all. There are also a few distinctly naughty governments around who might conceivably need to be disciplined or even removed, and some of these possess small air forces with a few fighters. If they do, the aircraft will generally be aged ex-Soviet birds, probably crippled by shoddy maintenance and flown by crews in a poor state of training and morale. It is always a mistake to write off an enemy just because he isn't first division, as courageous and expert Argentine pilots showed in 1982 (and, no doubt, British F3 crews would have done had they ever been put to the test). Nonetheless, the enemy fighter threat is a shadow of what it once was.

Furthermore, air-to-air missiles are starting to become what they were always supposed to be. They still need to be fired from supersonic, high-flying aircraft, because the world is still round, but the long-heralded demise of the dogfight may finally be at hand. In fact, if the Tornado F3 could fly at a decent height, its new missile fit might almost be said to have made it into an effective fighter. (It can't, however, and the missile fit seems highly dubious. Anyway, the F3 is on the point of going out of service. In fact, the first squadron has gone without being replaced, as part of Mr Hoon's mad scramble to balance his budget.)

What all this means is that the day of the cold war-style ultra-specialised air-to-air fighter is over. Monstrously over-powered, brilliantly agile, lightweight super-fighters like the American F-15 are no longer really needed. They see more use, nowadays, converted to ground-attack missions. In the unlikely event that some fantastically brave opponent came against them in his rusting second-hand MiG, rather than intelligently fleeing or giving up as the Iraqis have tended to, F-15 pilots would not use their amazing manoeuvring powers to blow him away with cannon fire or a tail-chasing infrared missile as of old. They would launch a long-ranging advanced missile from afar, never getting close enough to see the poor fool die.

So there really isn't much requirement for any further generation of super-fighters. What Britain needs is a nice multi-purpose jet, able to deliver smart ground-attack munitions as its main work, but also capable of mounting a good modern air-to-air missile and making a supersonic intercept should anyone contest our mastery of the air. Contrary to the official line on the Tornado F3, it does need to be able to fly high, but this isn't actually difficult for competent designers to achieve, especially as low-level bombing will not be necessary or sensible. This plane should also be able to operate from our proposed new aircraft carriers, which will – under current plans – not be able to handle normal jets. Thus it needs to be a jump-jet like the Harrier, able to descend vertically supported by jet thrust.

Amazingly perhaps, Britain is at work on just such a project, jointly with the US for a change rather than in some disputatious, unworkable European alliance. Needless to say, this programme – called variously the Joint Strike Fighter, Joint Combat Aircraft or F-35 – is having technical problems. These arise in large part from the jump-jet requirement, which we could probably avoid if we were sensible. Naturally, we aren't being sensible (see the discussion of aircraft carriers in Chapters 7 and 8) but it seems very likely that the snags will be fixed over time and that the F-35 will be just what Britain requires for pretty much all its realistic future combat jet needs.

Good lord. So everything's pretty much on track, then? How odd. Surely this isn't British defence procurement?

No, of course it isn't. Way back before the MoD got involved with the F-35 in 1996 it had mired us in a disputatious, unworkable European alliance for the purpose of building a monstrously over-powered, brilliantly agile, lightweight super-fighter. This project, as is normal, has had many names over its decades-long gestation; the MoD nowadays likes to call it Typhoon. It is better known, however, as the Eurofighter. It was called Eurofighter 2000 at one stage, in an attempt to disguise the fact that the plane was originally meant to arrive by 1995. This ploy backfired badly: the year 2000 came and went without the arrival of any jets, causing some red faces at BAe and the procurement agency.

The Eurofighter project was formally begun in 1985 (perhaps a good indication of just what the RAF really thought of the F3s which were then arriving). It swiftly became a dreadful, unkillable vampire, draining the defence budget year after year with ever-increasing costs and seemingly interminable delays. Nothing could drive a stake through its heart; it seemed to be eternal, lurching on unstoppably no matter what happened. The cold war ended, and Voyska PVO, its enemy, went out of business. European partners cut their orders massively, raising the unit costs for everyone. The clearly much more sensible F-35 project began. Generations of service people came and went. The Eurofighter carried on.

There was some talk, occasionally, of giving up on it, and this would still have been possible until quite recently. By the mid-90s, the Eurofighter was so late that it was obviously time to simply cancel it and let the F-35 take its place. Indeed, this nearly happened at one point. But the armed services, as ever, did not stand united. The F-35, as far as Britain was concerned, had begun as a navy project to replace the Sea Harrier. The RAF didn't want some navy cast-off like the Phantom – though the Phantom had been its last effective fighter – it wanted a proper land-bases-only super-jet. And shutting down the Eurofighter would have required a lot of BAe people to go and find honest work. Only unanimous effort from all the forces could have killed it, despite its horrifying cost and time overruns.

There was no such consensus. The undead cold war corpse that was the Eurofighter continued to hold the taxpayers helpless in its ghastly, blood-sucking embrace.

At last the aircraft are here. The RAF has actually had some since 2003, but naturally this does not mean they are anywhere near being ready to use. Current expectation is for 'initial operating capability' – working to some degree but not yet as advertised – in '2006/2007'.* By that point it will have been at least twenty-one years since the programme kicked off. The MoD estimate of the eventual total cost is *twenty billion pounds* based on Britain buying 232 Eurofighters, putting each plane at *eighty-six million*. Just to round things off, it seems that the one thing which was good about the F3 – its ability to go quite a long way and then hang about for a fairly long time without refuelling – will not be an attribute of the Eurofighter. Every jet will need its own tanker, probably, if it is ever to patrol skies other than those immediately above its base.

Furthermore, nobody really believes that the RAF needs – or even wants – 232 of these things. Defence commentators** believe that the RAF's eventual intention is to form seven Typhoon squadrons, which makes sense as it matches the number of Tornado fighter and Jaguar ground-attack units, the types the Eurofighter is officially nominated to replace. It also fits with the RAF's stated plans for pilot numbers. But that would stack up at about 115 jets once we include a few spares, not 232. Indeed, Britain has only actually committed to buy 144 at the moment: already more than we require.

The trouble is, of course, that most of our £20 billion is already spent: on development and setting up. Reducing the number of

---

* RAF official website.
** Charles Heyman, editor of Armed Forces of the United Kingdom, for example.

jets would reduce the overall expenditure, but not by anything like £86 million per aircraft. Every time the total order is reduced, the price per plane goes up. Furthermore, it is going to cost a lot more on top to make the beast useful for ground attack; and this will have to be done or it will see very little real duty. One should note that it is already being described as a replacement for the Jaguar – the Jaguar is a useful ground-attack plane, but the Eurofighter most certainly isn't.

A more accurate way to describe the cost of a single Eurofighter, then, is eighty-six million pounds *and rising fast*. It will be a miracle if it doesn't leave the £100 million-per-aircraft mark far behind. The Eurofighter would then have the dubious distinction of having beaten the anti-submarine Merlin to become the all-time most expensive and pointless British military aircraft, for a few years at least. (See Chapter 10 for a discussion of the aircraft which is likely to take this title away.)

It begins to become clear, then, why the MoD is clinging so desperately to the figure of 232 Eurofighters, for public consumption anyway. A realistic assessment of the bottom line on this grossly bloated disaster would cause an outcry. Indeed, it is even conceivable that the RAF will be forced to actually take delivery of the full number, just to save MoD face and fill BAe coffers; the excess aircraft can always be mothballed, as was done with the Tornado F3. This would keep the headline price of each plane below £100 million. This is almost unbelievable. We buy eight- or nine-figure aeroplanes, and put them straight into storage. Forget about the butter mountain, it's the fast-jet mountain we should be worried about. Given that the programme will probably cost fully £20 billion – or even more with ground-attack conversion – and no more than 120 jets will actually fly no matter how many are bought, we might say that the real cost per Eurofighter is *one hundred and seventy million pounds per plane*.

Yes, this seems more like British defence procurement.

But wait. Interminable, expensive and pointless as the Eurofighter programme has been, it is still not the worst part of the air-to-air story. We will get, in the end, some jets. It may have cost us an absurd amount, and taken for ever, but they will be there; and if we somehow fall through a time warp back to the late 1980s, they will be very useful.

Fighters are not the whole package, though. We also require dedicated radar aircraft, to detect the enemy and loose the fighters onto their quarry. The most well known, most widely used aircraft of this type is the American Boeing E-3 Sentry, also known as the AWACS, for Airborne Warning and Command System. It is a 707 airliner with a great big rotating radar stuck on top; in the large fuselage is a crew of around twenty. These people and their many expensive computers keep track of all the aircraft in hundreds of miles of sky, acting as air-traffic controllers for friendly forces as much as they direct fighters to intercept enemy ones. In the intensely congested airspace of modern war, even the vast capacity of the AWACS occasionally gets overtaxed. For example, an American E-3 mistakenly unleashed F-15s against a brace of US Army helicopters over northern Iraq a few years ago. The fighter pilots never set eyes on the targets they had been ordered to destroy; the kills were made by missile from afar. Other errors have occurred. But they were human, administrative cock-ups; the AWACS itself works pretty well.

Of course, we didn't simply buy the AWACS, which came into US service in 1977 and was jointly adopted by every other full member of NATO except Britain the following year. (Well, actually we did buy the AWACS, but much later on.) By 1977 we were already engaged upon building our own version. The RAF had eleven mint-condition maritime-patrol Nimrod aeroplanes standing about doing nothing. These planes had been mothballed for the same reason that the extra Tornados would soon be, and excess Eurofighters may yet be – British industry's need for money had dictated their purchase rather than any military requirement. The Nimrods were based on the long-defunct Comet jetliner of the 1950s, but they were still bandbox fresh in the mid-1970s. It was decided that these could be turned into radar aircraft and the General Electric Corporation (GEC) – now part of British Aerospace – got the job.

Ten years later, in 1986, several prototypes were flying, but their radars still didn't work and there didn't seem to be any great likelihood that they ever would. Amazingly, the uniformed testing and assessment personnel actually stated this clearly, rather than being bribed or browbeaten into silence as is usual – their careers no doubt suffered. The Nimrod AEW project was finally axed, and Britain decided to get E-3s like everyone else. Despite the fact that the carrying airframes for the Nimrod-AEW had been furnished up front by the government, and so hadn't – for this purpose – cost anything, over a billion pounds had been spent. A billion pounds, to obtain *absolutely nothing*. Indeed, less than nothing – several potentially usable aircraft had been converted into junk. And a billion pounds was real money back then; it would have bought around what £2 billion does today.* This, then, might be a realistic contender for most incompetent procurement of all time; it makes the Chinook HC3 buy, desperately stupid as it was, look positively brilliant.

So we eventually wound up with Boeing E-3s, a decade after everyone else and having wasted prodigious amounts of money before even buying them. Yes, that sounds like British defence procurement.

This is all the sadder because, like infantrymen and transport helicopters, fighters and airborne radar fall into the definitely useful category. They aren't debatable in the way that tanks, much of the artillery and attack helicopters are. But, unlike infantry, tanks, artillery or helicopters, we have really spent some major money on fighters and radar planes. The Eurofighter alone is going to wind up costing us most of an entire year's defence budget; or, to put it another way, about three times as much as a manned mission to Mars – it really has come to something when one is routinely measuring wasted money in Mars missions.

We don't get much in return for the huge sums we fork out. Our current fighters are distinctly substandard even after expensive upgrades, and were completely useless for much of their service. We only achieved proper airborne radar capability very late, after wasting ridiculous amounts. The replacement fighters will be ideally suited to fight the wars of yesterday, not those of tomorrow, and they are so outrageously costly that we are currently involved in a mad scramble of economies, forced upon us largely by the need to pay for them.

There was absolutely no need for us to have been so comprehensively, repeatedly ripped off. As opposed to the £86-million-and-counting Eurofighters, we could have bought F-15s from the

---

* Inflation calculations courtesy of the Economic History Association.

US to replace the abject F3 – or, better, to replace the Phantom in the first place. The Saudis recently obtained seventy-two of them, with matching accessories, for $371 million, less than £3 million per jet. We could thus replace our entire fighter force with F-15s for the headline price of two or three Eurofighters. And the F-15 would be really very adequate; it is the best fighter in the world, in fact, and is already available in a ground-attack-capable version.*

All in all, it might be more accurate to say that we have only ostensibly put massive resources into fighters. In reality, successive governments – both Labour and Tory – have spent decades diverting vast amounts of defence money into shoring up our domestic aircraft industry, as represented by BAe. As a result, we barely have any fighter capability at all now, we will have far too much of completely the wrong kind in future, and the Ministry of Defence has empty pockets – despite substantial funding – just as it comes under the most intense operational strain. All that we have really bought is the continued existence of BAe, which is hardly very useful: as long as BAe continues to exist, based on past experience, we will probably have to keep giving it money.

In fact, if you want a short answer to the question posed at the end of Chapter 1 (Why on earth are we cutting back on our excellent infantrymen?) it would be: To pay for the Eurofighter. Not to pay for 'network enabled capability', as Mr Hoon would have us believe; not, indeed, to pay for anything relevant to the future at all. We are cutting because the Eurofighter bills need settling.

No more Eurofighters should be bought. The 144 we have

---

* The US Air Force is now trying to say that it isn't that good after all, in order to justify having bought an even more super-duper ultra-fighter, with added Stealth features, to replace it. This is the stupefyingly expensive F-22 Raptor, now just arriving, which may end up costing more per aircraft than the headline price of a Eurofighter. The USAF is suspected in some quarters of having deliberately lost a recent air-combat exercise against Indian MiGs in an attempt to push the case for the F-22. Even so, they have yet to really explain who or what it is meant to fight – rather like the RAF with its Eurofighters. In fact, the only scenario in which either plane seems genuinely useful is that of war between the US and one or more of the Eurofighter nations. The French not having participated in Eurofighter, this seems unlikely.

regrettably already ordered will be far more than we need against the air opposition we are going to meet. These can be converted for strike use – ideally by someone other than their rapacious builders – at some future date. We have plenty of bombers for a while, as we shall see in the next chapter.

If this pushes the cost per Eurofighter through the roof, so what – it still makes more sense than buying hundreds and then moth-balling most of them, as we have done too often already. The titanic total bill would be significantly reduced, and that's what counts.

Indeed, if the Eurofighter winds up costing £120 million plus per plane, as it probably would if we only took a sensible number, we might finally see some real house-cleaning at the MoD. Maybe a few of the people who have been in charge of this colossal disaster over the decades will actually be held to account – some ex-ministers roasted, some civil servants and/or senior officers stripped of their pensions, just for once. (I know, I'm a dreamer – but what a lovely dream.) Maybe, dream of dreams, BAe might be allowed to sink or swim, rather than being able to count on massive UK defence contracts no matter what junk it produces.

If they all – ministry bigwigs and arms makers together – wind up on the dole queue, or even begging in the streets, that's no worse than what happens to a lot of ex-servicemen.* Unlike ministry bigwigs and arms manufacturers, low-ranking forces people have often done something useful while they were employed by the government. If ex-rankers can beg their bread and sleep in the gutter despite having served us well, there seems no reason why those who let us down shouldn't join them.

Even if none of this excellent stuff happens, there would surely be at least one concrete benefit from slashing our Eurofighter order. Our European partners would be so angry with us for driving the price per plane up – even though we are the only country that hasn't yet done this – that they would probably never collaborate with us again. That alone would save us a fortune over the next few decades.

---

* The charity Crisis estimates that 'up to three in ten homeless people are ex-Forces personnel'. Some 22 per cent of rough sleepers surveyed on one winter's night in London had an armed-services background.

So, when you've finished this book, write a stiff letter to your MP demanding fewer Eurofighters and more government scalps, with copies to all your favourite newspapers and broadcasters. Before you do that, though, there's plenty more you should know.

CHAPTER
6
Bombers

. . . the Royal Air Force is a force for good in the world. It contributes to society in many different ways.

What do you know about the RAF?
Ministry of Defence fact sheet

The quote above is quite correct. As we have seen, the RAF has often possessed some sort of fighter force. It provides a small number of helicopters, too, and a couple of battalions' worth of infantry. It also has some transport and tanker aircraft, a remarkably large police and dog-handling organisation, three full time professional bands, swarms of meteorologists, air traffic controllers . . . many things. The RAF truly does contribute to society in many different ways, but all of the above – even the fighters – are distractions, sideshows to the main event. Bombing is what the RAF was created to do, and what it institutionally likes to do. Its main contribution to society is to drop explosives from the sky.

This has always been the case. The RAF only came into existence as a separate force, towards the end of World War I, because of a perceived need to carry out long-range, strategic bombing raids. These don't seem to have achieved anything much, as one would expect with 1918 aviation technology, but then neither did the contemporary German attacks on London. Regrettably, however, the idea caught on. Despite endless examples proving the contrary, many people to this day believe that wreaking explosive destruction in the enemy's urban centres is a good way of bending him to your will. The air forces of the West are very slowly moving away from the idea, but the whole barbaric notion has such a hold now among other people that we may be living with it for some time yet.

With the outbreak of World War II, the long-anticipated war of the bombers began. Many thought that the new aircraft, much more capable than the primitive biplanes and zeppelins of the Great War, would be able to shatter the morale of nations. So terrible would be the hammer from the skies that one side or the other would be forced to sue for peace within months from the rubble of its civilisation. The only policy that made sense was to grit one's teeth, hit first, hit hardest and keep on hitting until the enemy gave up. Attempting a defence was pointless. The bomber, according to the wisdom of the day, would always get through.

In the event, this proved wrong on several counts. The Blitz was terrible indeed, as our parents and grandparents remember – terrible beyond the conception of those who are nowadays so easily panicked by a single truck bomb. But, as our parents and grandparents also remember, it would have taken a lot more than the Blitz to break the British in the 1940s. The same was true of the Germans. Despite subsequently suffering even more shattering aerial bombardments, Germany did not give up until Allied soldiers met on the Elbe. Indeed, it turned out to be very difficult to subdue anybody by any sort of bombing, no matter how savage. In the Far East the Americans delivered super-blitzes which made Coventry or even Dresden look mild. The almost unbelievably murderous 'fire storm' effect, which nowadays we would expect to see only in the aftermath of a nuclear explosion, was achieved by using kilotons of incendiary bombs on the highly combustible cities of Japan.* But the Japanese did not surrender.

Only with the arrival of the nuclear weapon did the bomber men finally deliver on their promise to break nations from the air. Fortunately the nuke was born into a world sick of mass warfare, so it has seen little use to date. One shudders to think

---

* 'Fire Storm: violent convection caused by a continuous area of intense fire and characterised by destructively violent surface indrafts. Sometimes it is accompanied by tornado-like whirls that develop as hot air from the burning fuel rises. Such a fire is beyond human intervention and subsides only upon the consumption of everything combustible in the locality.' *Encyclopaedia Britannica*.

what the gung-ho bomber advocates of the 1930s might have done to Europe if they had been armed with nukes in 1939.

Speculation aside, other fallacies in the strategic bombing scheme had been exposed. The bomber did *not* always get through; far from it. The bomber crews of the Luftwaffe, the RAF and later the US Army inflicted frightful slaughter on the burning cities of Europe, but proportionally speaking it was nothing to the casualties they suffered themselves. It may not have been much consolation to the bomb-wracked civilians below, but at least they could be sure that the airman hammering them was far less likely to survive the war than they were. Indeed, he was less likely to survive than just about anyone. Casualty rates of over 90 per cent during initial tours in bombers were not uncommon.

Such a shocking waste of expensive aeroplanes and highly trained, heroically brave airmen might be justifiable. Military machines and military men, after all, are there to be used: used up, if necessary. Even the slaughter of innocents can perhaps be excused, if it is a mistake or occurs as a regrettable side effect of a genuinely worthwhile military mission. Attempts were made to target enemy military bases or industrial production. Destroying the submarine pens of the Atlantic coast, for example, or shutting down German steel, would have been well worth the loss of a few hundred RAF bombers. If German or French civilians got blown up in the process, well, the getting of omelettes is known to require the breaking of eggs.

So we broke a lot of eggs; but omelettes came there none. Despite five years of the most savage pounding, German industry continued to be, if not its usual matchless self, startlingly capable. In the final year of the European war the Germans developed the first ever assault rifles, jet fighters, cruise missiles and ballistic missiles and put all of them into mass production. And the submarine pens continued to send out their wolf packs. The tanks continued to roll off the production lines, with new models introduced right into 1944. Both panzers and U-boats had to be dealt with the old-fashioned way – by meeting them on the battlefield and out at sea. The magnificent, superb bravery of the bomber crews had been in vain.

The problem was that bombers back then had no real ability to hit their targets at all. On a bad day they could easily wind

up dropping their whole load completely at random in the coun-
tryside. On a good day the airmen would find their target city,
but even then the bombs would typically fall far away from the
aiming point. Various efforts were made to improve accuracy, but
the error was still to be measured in kilometres rather than metres.
As any good modern-day terrorist or bomb-disposal man will tell
you, even a very big bomb needs to go off within twenty metres
or so of its target or there is little chance of any effect beyond
broken windows. High explosives aren't magic.

So the great bomber offensives of World War II failed. Forget
about the moral issues; the heavy bomber had failed as a weapon
system. But the heavy bomber was not the whole story, far from
it. Air power had also offered something much better.

During the closing campaigns of the war Allied fighters had
won control of the skies over all the contested seas, and over the
battle fronts in every theatre of war. It was here, above the struggling surface forces, that the airmen found the chance to be really
useful. At first with modified fighter planes, and later on with
specifically designed attack aircraft, low-flying pilots could find
and strike the enemy very effectively. No need to drop a gigantic
bomb load from miles up, trying to achieve the impossible feat
of hitting a ball-bearing factory or whatever, in the vain hope
that this would mean a few less tanks produced in the year ahead.
Instead, swoop down on an actual tank and blast it with a well-
placed bomb from a few hundred feet. Or, even better, use a more
easily aimed, more accurate weapon, such as a rocket or a cannon.

By 1945 every Allied army had a 'tactical air force' attached,
delivering just this kind of assistance. Every Allied fleet or convoy
at sea had an aircraft carrier. Close air support could be said to
have been born. (Actually, a similar situation had developed in
the later stages of World War I, at least ashore. There's nothing
like real war to make armed forces efficient.) Air support for
surface units had been demonstrably, brilliantly useful. But tactical
air over land was essentially a matter of working for the army,
while the maritime equivalent of battlefield tactical air actually
was part of the navy, formally as well as practically. Not many
jobs for air marshals there; not much justification for an independent air force.

Unsurprisingly, then, the air forces of the victor nations tended to cling to the long-range, deep-strike strategic bombing mission as their great white hope. Depressingly, America – which had managed to avoid having an independent air force almost until the end of the war – had caved in to its own bomber generals and allowed them to split off from the US Army, with promotions all round. With the arrival of the nuke, which seemed to make accuracy irrelevant, the air forces were all set to get the bomber through once more. Radar and fighters, which had so mauled the heavy aircraft of the late war, would soon be overcome. Bigger, higher-flying, faster bombers would be built. There would still be a chief of air staff in every country, to rank with the heads of the army and navy. Great days were ahead.

And, indeed, a start was made on all this. In America, the mighty eight-engined B-52 Stratofortress was built. In Britain, the great V-bombers appeared. These big planes were intended to fly high and deep into Soviet airspace, and deliver the knockout nuclear strikes that would win the postulated war of the future. However, a subsonic bomber 30,000 feet up could be seen coming on radar hundreds of miles off. There was ample time for the defences to act. A big missile or a patrolling jet fighter could fairly easily make an interception. Something new was needed: something higher and faster still.

The ultimate answer to this problem was the Inter-Continental Ballistic Missile, the ICBM. An ICBM is basically a space rocket. After blasting off, its multiple stages launch the payload – the nukes, that is – into space, to complete most of their journey outside the atmosphere at terrific speed. Arriving over the target region, the warhead, the spent rocket stages having been left behind, descends to re-entry hypersonically – many times faster than sound. Shooting it down is still, despite many *Star Wars*-type attempts to develop countermeasures, just about impossible – especially as each missile may well carry many warheads, perhaps mixed with decoys, which re-enter the atmosphere separately and attack multiple targets (these are called Multiple Independent Re-entry Vehicles, or MIRVs). History proves that the bomber often doesn't get through, but the MIRV'd ICBM almost certainly will. For now, anyway. Probably for a long time, actually, no matter how much money the Americans spend on counter-missile systems.

ICBMs, then, had made the strategic bomber obsolete, certainly for the purpose of delivering nukes. The next stage in heavy bomber development, the supersonic, super-high-altitude bomber, was sensibly binned. The USAF actually got quite far along with its B-1 programme before it was closed down. This had the pleasing effect of completely wrong-footing Voyska PVO, whose ultra-specialised MiG-25 super-high-altitude fighter was produced with vast effort and at great expense just to stop the B-1 – which then never turned up.

The bomber men were now on the ropes. They had nothing in particular to offer that couldn't be done better with an ICBM, and they were having increasing trouble convincing even themselves that they could get through serious air defences. In America, with money comparatively plentiful, the USAF embarked on several high-tech methods of penetrating the radar and fighter screens they expected to face. The long quest for Stealth was begun in great secrecy, and, while that was being sorted out, the USAF began to take on enemy air defences directly. If radars and missile launchers couldn't be flown over, they would by god be blasted out of the way.

This latter notion grew into today's SEAD: Suppression of Enemy Air Defences. The USAF began pioneering it in the skies of North Vietnam, where the aircraft involved were known as wild weasels. These specialised planes would fly over Ho Chi Minh's Soviet-supplied defence networks, not to deliver bombs against factories or bases, but to destroy the air defences themselves. This was especially convenient for the USAF as it was proving quite difficult, against the low-tech North Vietnamese forces, to find any other worthwhile targets. Wild weasel aircraft could detect enemy radars – after all, a radar is just a big radio beacon, in effect – and bomb them, or jam their frequencies. Later they acquired the ability to launch missiles which would home in on the radars' emissions.

But Stealth and wild weasel programmes were shockingly expensive, quite beyond the means of the RAF, along with most other NATO air forces. The European bomber men turned to a rather simpler solution. They could never fly as high and fast as an ICBM. They couldn't afford to become radar-invisible. They couldn't afford to blast their way through the enemy radars and missiles. Instead, they would simply fly low.

As we saw in the last chapter, this can be a very effective tactic when the main worry is enemy ground radars and surface-to-air missiles. Defenders need lots of ground radars to even get a glimpse of a fast, low-flying attacker, and then they have little time in which to engage him before he is gone from their screens. Indeed, if the attacker flies really low, right down in the valleys, they may never see him at all. They won't even be able to loose fighters onto him. All this is rather to ignore the fact that our low-level bomber man is bound to be noticed once he starts dropping his bombs, and in all likelihood there will be some air defences in the vicinity of his target if it is worth bombing at all. These will have a good chance of bringing him down. Also, if one is up against a first-division team, with fighters and airborne radar which can look down, the whole concept becomes entirely untenable. A certain selectiveness of vision, however, often occurs in military circles. The aim of the European bomber men was not, one must remember, really to fight the commies. It was to find a way of having some bombers.

This low-level scheme led to the Tornado strike jet, which was developed cooperatively in Europe. The Tornado came into RAF service in the deep-strike role in 1980, and it will be with us for some time yet. The Americans were welcome to go head-to-head with the commies; the Western Europeans would cunningly slip through under the radars, flying deep into Warsaw Pact territory. Here they could deliver nukes, if required – but missiles could do that. The bomber men, however, would also be be able to drop conventional weapons, thus giving NATO some options other than immediately going nuclear.

There was some question as to what these conventional bombs might usefully hit. By now, nobody was pushing the idea of smashing enemy industry. In a cold-war-turned-hot scenario, this would have been entirely pointless. The task was to stop the vast Soviet tank armies already in the field, not to prevent more from being built. But of course one didn't want to just attack tanks; this would be merely to work for the army. A certain amount of that, by all means, but a proper air force must look to strike deep into enemy territory. The RAF's Tornados, then, expected to hit such things as key bridges, railway junctions or what have you, supposedly disrupting the enemy's supplies and impeding his movements. Best of all, they would make war against the Soviet air forces. Not in the air – too expensive, and no requirement for lovely bombers – but by attacking their bases.

The low altitudes at which our bombers would fly meant that such pinpoint targets as bridges and runways could perhaps be hit, despite the fact that the accuracy of aircraft bombs was still pretty much as bad as ever. This role was known at the time as Interdictor Strike, or IDS. Nowadays it is called Air Interdiction. Both these phrases are meant to imply bombing which is best directed separately from ground tactics, at a higher level, thus justifying the existence of a separate command structure.

By the late 1980s the operational bomber crews of the RAF had become the best high-speed, low-level flyers in the world. Piloting a jet through hills and valleys at 600 mph is desperate, hair-raising stuff, even without people shooting at you. The Tornado crews had paid a grim price in training accidents to get this good. Even the remaining V-bombers, before they finally disappeared, had converted to the low-level penetration role. If anybody could have flown those missions for real against the Soviets, the late-1980s RAF would have been the men.

Luckily, the question never came up. In 1991 the Soviets were closing up shop. But the low-level penetration concept nonetheless had a trial that year – against Saddam Hussein.

Saddam, back then, had a small but potentially annoying air force. He also had an air-defence network, with radars and SAMs all complete. It was evident that the might of the Coalition air forces – for which read the USAF – would soon clear most of the air defences away: but in the opening days of the air campaign there was scope for low-flying raids to penetrate the still-up-and-running Iraqi defences and hit their airbases. The RAF's Tornado men had spent their whole lives training for this, and they were duly sent in. The particular trick of the Western Europeans – led by the RAF – was 'runway denial'. Having flown in at high speed and low level, hopefully undetected, one would then be aiming to put an enemy airbase out of commission. Proper air force war, you see: air power fighting air power, not merely acting as an adjunct to grubby foot soldiers.

The best way to put an airbase out of business at a stroke is to smash up its runway and then prevent it from being mended.

Hence, runway denial. However, this isn't entirely simple. Firstly, a runway, being narrow, is devilishly difficult to hit with free-falling ordnance. Even landing an aircraft on one is highly skilled work, and an aircraft is powered and guided constantly all the way to touchdown. Secondly, if one merely makes a hole in a runway, some tiresome fellow with a bulldozer and a load of quick-setting concrete will probably have it serviceable again in a brace of shakes. To deal with this the Tornado forces of several nations had developed special runway-denial munitions. The RAF version was known as the JP233. The idea was that the attacking Tornado would fly low and slow along the enemy runway, with the JP233 canister spewing out hundreds of different submunitions. Several of these would be heavy cratering charges, which would make a line of big holes. The rest would be a mix of time-delay and booby-trap mines, which would make the wrecked paving so dangerous that rebuilding it would take a very long time.

Fiendish, eh? That would show the Iraqis who was boss. The RAF duly began flying low-level strikes against Iraqi airfields, using a mix of JP233 and ordinary bombs. Within seven days they had lost five Tornado bombers from a force of forty-five, all to ground anti-aircraft fire in the vicinity of their targets. Low-level flight was indeed an excellent way to avoid the radars and big missiles on the way in, but it was a bloody dangerous method of attacking a point-defended target. Flying low over even primitively equipped enemies had, as ever, turned out to be risky work.

The RAF's Tornados had thus taken 10 per cent casualties in a week; they had literally been decimated. By contrast, the overall Coalition casualty rate was 0.05 per cent per combat sortie, much of which was due to the Tornado losses. The low-level mission was clearly unsustainable. Fortunately, by this point, the USAF's wild weasels and Stealth bombers had largely cleared up the Iraqi radar network and most of the heavier SAMs. It was now safe to fly higher up, and the Tornados gratefully did so. Only one further aircraft was lost.

The RAF management levels still contend that the low-level phase in Iraq was necessary and useful, and that all the years, lives and money thrown into deep-penetration low-level attack were not a dreadful, wasteful error. They say that the low-flying strikes of '91 were highly successful in closing down the Iraqi runways. Given that nearly all of the surviving Iraqi air force managed to successfully take to the air during the same period and flee to Iran, one must surely take this with a pinch of salt. The fact is, however, that even if it had worked the whole concept had been shown to be almost suicidal. If relatively feeble Iraqi point defences alone could shoot down more than one in ten of the Tornados operating against them, one can only imagine what the bristling land-air weaponry of Soviet Central Front would have done.

But there was no need for this to become an issue, and indeed it never really has. Almost without breaking step, the deep-bombing advocates changed their ideas. It was obvious idiocy to make deep raids at low level. Bluster aside, even the air marshals realised this quite fast as soon as they began losing Tornados. The trouble was, the best bomber crew in the world can't put a free-fall dumb bomb anywhere near their aiming point from high up. Even the RAF had been forced to acknowledge this, after nearly eighty years of trying.

Fortunately, there now seemed to be a solution: the famous 'smart bomb'. As is usual in weapons development these days, the Americans had come up with these. The earliest smart bombs had been dropped on North Vietnam at around the time the Tornado's design was being sorted out. These used a fairly basic idea. One takes a regular, dumb bomb and attaches guidance fins to it. The fins are controlled by a simple seeker head. The seeker head can be simple because it isn't trying to do something technically difficult like pick out a tank or a ship; all it is looking for is a bright light of a very specific colour. As the bomb plummets down through the air, the fins steer it so as to hit the bright light.

The bright light is supplied by shining a laser beam where you want the bomb to hit. Like the laser pointer in a presentation, this creates a bright dot. Provided you can hold the laser steady on target, and the bomb can see the dot, it will probably hit within a few tens of metres – no matter how high up it may have been released. The laser can be in the bomber, in another aircraft, or even in the hands of a soldier down on the ground – usually a special forces type, as the chances are this is all taking place deep in enemy territory.

The especially clever thing about the smart bomb, from an air force point of view, is that it is quite cheap compared to other guided weapon systems. One can thus afford enough for one's jets to keep flying missions for a good while without running out of things to carry. This is important, in order to justify having plenty of jets. Of course, one then needs to find lots of things to blow up.

With the introduction of smart weapons, then, the bomber men seemed to have found the holy grail they had been seeking for so long. They could fairly reliably hit difficult targets like runways, bridges, railways and so on, which had always tended to elude them before, and they didn't have to fly dangerously low to do it. The RAF rushed smart-bomb equipment to the Gulf, and finished up the 1991 air campaign operating relatively safely from on high.

The air marshals now knew that their whole low-level plan had been lunacy. They still refuse to admit anything of the sort – a couple more decades must pass first – but the facts speak for themselves. The JP233 suicide weapon has been quietly binned, and the Tornado has been extensively re-equipped with new ordnance, designed to be released from higher altitudes. Furthermore, while the RAF still can't afford Stealth, they are making an effort to develop SEAD wild weasel capability. Nobody really wants to try going in fast and low for real ever again, although training for it is quite good fun if one is that sort of person, as RAF fast-jet crews always are.

So it would seem that effective bombing is finally here. In the age of the smart bomb and the wild weasel, one can blast the enemy's air defences out of the way and fly through, safely high up, to deliver pinpoint attacks which will swiftly bring him to his knees. No more messy Blitzes. No more desperate, hell-for-leather suicide missions, down within the range of even the cheapest anti-aircraft weapons. And, especially, no need to go and work for the army. Indeed, with luck the soldiery will be relegated to pottering about afterwards taking the bad guys' surrender.

Many people feel that this view of modern war was confirmed during the air campaign of 1999, against the Serb rump of Yugoslavia. During this offensive a force of over 500 NATO bombers, supported by 600 other aircraft, flew strike missions against the Milošević government for eleven weeks. The operation was code-named ALLIED FORCE; the aim was to compel the withdrawal of Serb ethnic cleansers from the province of Kosovo, where they were genocidally oppressing the ethnic-Albanian majority. The Serb forces did eventually withdraw, and NATO ground troops were, indeed, confined to a peacekeeping and humanitarian role in the aftermath. Bomber men the world over rejoiced. At last an air war had been fought and won, with no serious involvement by pesky ground troops.

A few people were sceptical, however. For a start, the bombers, again, had experienced a lot of difficulty in delivering accurate strikes. Heavy cloud cover over Serbia meant that smart-bomb lasers could seldom be reliably held on their targets, and nobody was fool enough to go in below the clouds, get shot down by the Serbs' plentiful low-level weaponry, and allow Slobodan Milošević to parade captured airmen on TV. All too often the NATO jets were reduced to dumping their vast loads of ordnance into the clouds at satellite-navigation coordinates. In many cases they were actually compelled to jettison their bombs into the Adriatic. It is actually quite common for a jet not to have fuel enough to haul its weapons home again if the target cannot be hit, so they must then be got rid of somewhere. This is sometimes known as the miracle of the bombs and the fishes. So many tons of munitions went unarmed into the sea, in fact, that a small fleet of NATO mine-clearance ships had to spend weeks clearing them up afterwards, lest the local trawlermen start getting nasty surprises. This clear-up after ALLIED FORCE was code-named ALLIED HARVEST, no doubt by some wag in NATO's naval staffs.

Despite these difficulties, most targets were eventually struck. However, the big problem, which had begun to appear as long ago as Vietnam, was a lack of worthwhile things to strike. Simply massacring civilians has gone out of fashion since World War II. Even back then there was a lot of doubt about how effective such a policy might be, quite apart from whether it was morally acceptable. Operations such as the London or Tokyo blitzes would nowadays never even be proposed.

Still, if one isn't out simply to kill civilians, what is one to bomb, in a country like Serbia? They don't make their own tanks or even their own rifles. There therefore isn't any military industry which can usefully be smashed up. You could try to hunt down the tanks they already have and pick them off, but this is only really feasible when those tanks are moving about, so that you can find them. Why ever would they move about, unless our troops were on the ground and facing them? Furthermore, the Yugoslav Army, under Milošević's control, only had 800-odd tanks. This is quite a few, but such a campaign is hardly going to provide enough work for 500 NATO bombers flying day and night. Anyway, ethnic cleansing isn't done using tanks. Even if you actually do nail all 800, slaughtering a few thousand inoffensive conscripts in the process, the Serb 'special police' and freelance murder squads will still be at their filthy work.

The bombers did spend a lot of time trying to pick off the Yugoslav Army's armour, for want of anything better to do, but it was a difficult task. In the absence of any ground opposition the Serbs' heavy equipment could be dispersed and elaborately hidden, and simple decoys made of wood were in widespread use. The bomber staffs claimed 300-plus armoured vehicles and 400-plus artillery pieces destroyed in Kosovo alone. However, after the Serb withdrawal, a NATO investigating team made up of US Air Force personnel spent some time checking all the sites where the bombers had struck. They found the remains of only twenty-six vehicles, twenty guns and a lot of smashed-up wooden decoys. The team said there was no evidence of any surreptitious removal of wreckage by the Serbs, although this was strongly suggested by the bomber bosses.

Much of the time, unable to find even wooden tanks to hit, NATO was reduced to blowing up bridges, power stations, 'headquarters buildings' in Belgrade (one of which, famously, turned out to be the Chinese embassy) and so forth. This was justified as inconveniencing the Yugoslav/Serb Army's movements, as well as those of the murder squads. Such bluster was unconvincing, as the Serbs already had all the forces they needed in Kosovo, and they weren't dependent on a big supply effort to do what they were doing. The infrastructure hits were also said to be putting pressure on the Serb civilian population, who would supposedly turn against Milošević because of the power cuts and cancelled trains he had brought upon them. Never mind that the

Germans had stuck by Hitler under far worse punishment, and the Japanese had stubbornly continued to follow the emperor's orders after the fire storms and even the nukes.

In actual fact, of course, General Wesley Clark, the military boss of NATO, had to bomb these things because there was nothing else to bomb. He had been given 500 bombers to use – only 500 bombers, no other forces – and this was all he could do.

Surely, though, this is just carping. After all, Milošević did give in. Inexplicably, on the face of it. The air campaign wasn't impeding his operations in Kosovo significantly, and it certainly wasn't convincing the Serb people that they were in the wrong. A lot of soldiers, though, as distinct from airmen, find a possible explanation for Milošević's capitulation by looking at an atlas. (Bless them; pongoes* do so love their maps.) When the Kosovo troubles first started to get world attention in mid-1998, the Serbs had no need to fear intervention on the ground. The only access to the province of Kosovo, other than from central Serbia, is across some very nasty mountain ranges. An international land force wishing to drive the Serb military out would have to enter via one of two narrow valleys: that of the Beli Drim river, from Albania, or by the Kačanik route from Macedonia. Narrowing NATO options still further, the Macedonians were unwilling to act as a base for a forcible entry into Kosovo, although they were quite happy to host NATO troops (largely in the hope of preventing ethnic-Albanian gunmen from taking over parts of Macedonia, something they still occasionally have a crack at). Even if Macedonia had been available as an invasion base, the supply lines of the NATO ground forces in Macedonia would have run though Greece, which was adamantly opposed to an invasion.

No such problems would have existed with the Beli Drim route, of course; the Albanians would have been only too happy to host an army intending to aid their ethnic brothers. But Albania's weak transport infrastructure would have struggled to cope with forces

---

* The other parts of the British forces refer to the army as pongoes. This is generally held to be because 'Where the army goes, the pong goes.' It is an article of faith in the other services that soldiers are strongly averse to soap and water. The name isn't commonly used in the soldiers' hearing, however, they being prone to violence.

sufficient to overcome those of Serbia. For this reason, most of
the heavy NATO troops were in Macedonia, although there was
a contingent in Albania. Even if an invasion army could have
been assembled on the Beli Drim, that army would have had to
make a costly assault through a single heavily defended mountain valley, known to have been mined by the Serbs, where all
the advantages would have been with the defenders. And the one
road running through the valley would have to be rebuilt into a
major highway if it were to act as the sole supply route for an
army and a big relief operation. Such an invasion, quite apart
from probably being a bloodbath and costing an immense sum,
would have taken many months if not years to implement. Major
roads are not quickly built. Not an option, then, that any of the
NATO governments were really up for.

So Milošević probably felt pretty safe, even when the bombs
started to fall in March 1999. The air campaign was making him
look good, or anyway less bad than he had been looking. He was
able to drive the remaining ethnic-Albanian civilians out of
Kosovo, in fact, and claim that they were fleeing NATO air strikes.
(This was rightly dismissed as rubbish in all quarters. Still, he
must have been pleased to have the fig leaf.)

But in March 1999, as well as the start of the impotent bombing
campaign, something rather more significant took place: Hungary
joined NATO. At first it was not clear just what this meant.
NATO is, formally speaking, a defensive alliance; member states
are not obliged to act with the others unless one of them is
attacked. But, the following month, the NATO heads of government held a summit meeting in Washington DC. Kosovo was top
of the agenda, and the assembled leaders were unanimous.
Milošević *would* do what NATO told him to, and the alliance
would use force as required to achieve this. NATO isn't the UN:
when it says such a thing, it just possibly means it. Prime Minister
Tony Blair in particular was strongly in favour of a ground operation. US President Clinton was not, but many in the US government were, and even Clinton stated that NATO would 'persist
until we prevail'.

Going back to the atlas, things now looked worrying for
Milošević, very different from the previous year. The Hungarian
border with Serbia lies just a hundred miles north of Belgrade, the

Serb capital. Good road and rail links run back from there, now through NATO territory, to Germany. And Germany is home to the Allied Command Europe Rapid Reaction Corps. ACE RRC is the hard fist of NATO, with two heavy armoured divisions which were now potentially becoming available for use against Serbia: one British, pretty much the whole of the British Army's proper armour, and one American. In fact, most of NATO's serious land-combat power is still based around there. Germany, remember, was where NATO had expected to fight the Red Army. The commander of the Rapid Reaction Corps was General Mike Jackson, late of the Parachute Regiment, whom we met in Chapter 1. At this point, he and his staff were actually in Macedonia, in charge of the NATO contingent there. Parts of the British armoured force from Germany were also there, among others, but their hands were tied by Greek and Macedonian control of their supply lines.

Suddenly the scenario didn't look good for Slobodan. The intervention force no longer had to embark its heavy equipment, sail to Albania, spend weeks disembarking at inadequate harbours, struggle with rickety Albanian transport links, and then build a major road through a mountain range while fighting all the way. It could simply entrain – much the easiest way to move heavy equipment – and deploy straightforwardly on the Hungarian border, where it had several short, strong, safe supply lines back to its home bases. From here, a couple of days' blitzkrieg across nice open country, no horrid mountain valleys, would see the lead Warriors outside President Milošević's front door. The Yugoslav Army would no more have been able to resist such an attack than the Iraqis were in 1991 or 2003.

Speculation along these lines immediately appeared in the more knowledgeable bits of the press following the NATO summit. Just to ram things home, the G8 nations endorsed NATO's demands a week later, making it quite clear that America and Britain were now willing to use ground troops against Milošević, and that Russia – despite being Serbia's closest and most powerful friend – was going to let them do it. With Hungary on board, it was clear that they actually could get the job done, quickly, fairly cheaply and without suffering any serious losses.

Unsurprisingly, Milošević threw in the towel at the next opportunity. He hadn't had an attack of conscience and bizarrely caved in to an air campaign that was doing him no harm; he had seen a route suddenly open up between him and the most powerful army in Europe, and a consensus developing which would see that force used. It also seems that he and the Russians had a quiet chat, during which the Russians assured him that Serb interests in Kosovo would be looked after if he agreed to pull out.

As the Serbs left Kosovo, the NATO contingents in Macedonia and Albania prepared to move in, under General Jackson's command. They would form K-FOR, the Kosovo Force, which would control the province until the UN could get a viable autonomous government set up. (K-FOR is still there.) But suddenly, before Jackson's forces could move, a small Russian detachment seized the airport at Priština, Kosovo's provincial capital. These men had been a few hours' drive away in Bosnia as part of S FOR (Stabilisation Force), the NATO-run international peacekeepers controlling Bosnia-Hercegovina. They had abandoned their post in Bosnia, crossed central Serbia – without interference, as one might expect – entered Kosovo and taken over Priština airport. Meanwhile, Russian airborne forces prepared to fly in. Russia's aim in negotiations thus far had always been to obtain a sector of Kosovo under its sole control. This had been rejected by NATO, but now it appeared that the Russians might impose a plan of their own.

US General Clark, the supreme military boss of NATO, wasn't having this. He ordered Jackson's K-FOR to confront the Russians in Priština and prevent any airborne reinforcements from landing. There was a certain irony here as the Russians were – officially, anyway – also under Clark's command, as part of S-FOR. The spectacle of two different groups of NATO peacekeepers fighting each other over who was going to keep the peace would have been an interesting one.

General Jackson, whose troops, led by two British brigades, would actually have to do the confronting, was in a less aggressive mood – less aggressive towards the Russians, anyway. This might seem odd in a member of the Parachute Regiment, but less so perhaps in the case of a former intelligence officer with a degree in Russian Studies, both of which are correct descriptions of the general. Some extremely frank discussions are said to have taken place between him and General Clark during which Jackson famously refused 'to start World War III' for Clark despite being under his command. Clark must have felt rather frustrated during his NATO tenure; none of his subordinates had carried out his orders. The bombers had failed to destroy the Yugoslav Army; part of S-FOR had invaded Kosovo when they were supposed to be in Bosnia; and then K-FOR had refused to stop them. NATO may not be the UN, but it isn't exactly the Wehrmacht, either.*

Eventually, after a good deal of tense negotiation all round, helped along by various countries refusing to let Russian airborne troops overfly them, it was agreed that the Russians would be substantially involved in K-FOR. They would not, however, get their own sector to run. This saved Russian face but prevented them from creating a Serb territory within Kosovo. Jackson's forces moved in and took over without casualties or World War III. Relative calm eventually returned, and perhaps one day international troops will be able to withdraw and leave the Kosovars to themselves, although it may not be wise to hold one's breath.

So, in fact, the liberation of Kosovo didn't herald a new age of aerial war. Rather, it seems to have emphasised the importance of politics and diplomacy – and secret back-room deals. In the military sphere, surface logistic factors such as mountains, roads and harbours were the keys to the matter. These have been the framework of war for millennia, and it seems they still are.

Since Serbia, the deep-target bomber men have been in action again, blasting the bejeezus out of both Afghanistan and Iraq. They have made further efforts to refine the smart bomb. The latest weapons now have onboard satellite navigation (GPS)** so

---

* Wehrmacht: the German armed forces of World War II. Famously deadly, well organised and obedient to orders, they were only defeated in the end by crushing weight of numbers. The Wehrmacht is still, in many ways, something of a model for other military forces. Of course, the Wehrmacht was so obedient to orders that it was perfectly happy to start a world war and attack Russia, unlike General Jackson. NATO is already a longer-lived and more successful organisation, funnily enough.
** Global Positioning System. An American military satellite constellation which allows a small portable receiver to locate itself easily and cheaply. It is used by civilians worldwide and indeed by enemies of America, as well as almost universally in US and Allied forces.

that if the laser fails due to bad weather, smoke, dust or shaky hands, the bomb will still fall somewhere near the target coordinates. The problem is that GPS is only accurate to about thirty metres, rather than the near-perfect location of a laser dot when working well. Add the error radius of the bomb seeker and we are now unable once again to reliably hit roads, bridges, runways or even quite large buildings. It's better than nothing, but it won't really do – especially where there may be civilians nearby, as in any urban centre. And GPS can be fairly easily jammed over a small area, too.

In any case, the underlying problem of modern strategic bombing campaigns is nothing to do with hitting the target. The real difficulty, as we have seen, is a lack of sensible targets to hit. In countries such as Iraq there isn't a great deal which can usefully be bombed, other than existing enemy ground forces. This latter often has to be done at the behest of our own ground forces. Too much of that, and the air force upper echelons would be out of a job, although their subordinates mostly wouldn't. Thus it is that we see, once again, electrical power and water being knocked out, television stations flattened, bridges down and so on – despite many protestations that infrastructure was not being targeted. And of course the 'headquarters buildings' downtown are hit hard, with inevitable 'collateral damage' all around.

It is really hard to see how this advances the cause of Western democracy. The military in such a country as Saddam's Iraq doesn't especially care if power goes out and roads are blocked. If anybody has generators and off-road vehicles, it is them. They will all be slaughtered if they stand and fight whether they have a working infrastructure or not, so depriving them of one can hardly be an important thing to do. However, you can thoroughly upset the civilian populace by such means. And attacking TV and radio stations merely gives the local government's propaganda credibility it wouldn't otherwise have had. It doesn't work, anyway. People will still be able to receive broadcasts from all kinds of sources. You will never control the media by bombing.

As for headquarters buildings, well, even if you have identified them correctly how on earth does blowing them up help? Would it paralyse Coalition military operations if you blew up the Pentagon, or MoD Main Building? Most of us who have served in the British forces believe that they would actually become more efficient without MoD Main Building. Certainly, nobody noticed the US military grinding to a halt when Al Qaeda successfully crashed an airliner into the Pentagon in 2001. The only thing left in the Baghdad HQ of any Saddam-era agency, if they had any sense, would have been a GPS jammer, thus ensuring that plenty of bombs would hit surrounding civilians instead. Actually, you don't even need a GPS jammer for that. There is an old bomb-disposal rule of thumb about munitions: 10 per cent will fail to function as designed. In other words, for every ten smart weapons you drop, one will be a rogue, striking at random; this is actually admitted by the air force. The percentage of misses will be much higher with dumb ordnance, and even in 2003 the Coalition dropped 9,344 dumb weapons into Iraq. The day of the all-smart war is still far off.

There has been much concern during the present Iraq conflict as to whether Coalition foot soldiers have abused or even occasionally wrongfully shot Iraqis. None whatsoever has been shown as to the wilful mass murder committed by air planners for dubious gains. Nothing in Iraq has compared with the Blitz or Dresden or Tokyo, but the men in the air planning staffs and the commanders who authorised them have killed and maimed noncombatants by the dozen for every one hurt by ground troops, without anybody once suggesting that they might have done wrong.*

A nineteen-year-old soldier, living in hellish conditions and constant fear, makes a mistake under pressure and shoots an

---

* A team of researchers from Johns Hopkins University in the US, in an article published in the Lancet, recently estimated a total of 100,000 Iraqi deaths as a result of the invasion. This was extrapolated from quite limited data using techniques more commonly employed in public health surveys; it is much higher than most other estimates. A more interesting statistic from the study data, however, was that of fifty-eight randomly selected violent deaths, only three were the result of fire from Coalition ground troops. All the rest were attributed to aerial weaponry. Both Iraqis and researchers were much struck by the fact that in two of the three shootings an apology was later given and compensation paid, in stark contrast to the cases of those slain from above.

unarmed man. Perhaps he doesn't even take a life; he merely roughs someone up or humiliates him and – unbelievably foolishly – takes photos. The soldier may well, correctly, be court-martialled. Such cases, quite apart from being crimes in their own right, do our cause incalculable harm. By contrast, a much older, more educated, better-trained senior officer working in a safe and relatively comfortable HQ decides to slaughter – not just strip and photograph, but *kill* and *cripple* – scores of innocents, including mothers, children and the elderly. (One should be quite clear that every time you order more than half a dozen air weapons delivered into an urban area, that is just what you are doing.) This much more serious, more criminal error, unjustified by any danger threatening the perpetrator or usually any measurably good results from his decision, goes *completely unremarked*. And all the staff officer's victims will have surviving young male relatives, who are now gunning for our nineteen-year-old foot soldier. The dictator was no friend of theirs in all likelihood but, by god, we aren't their friends any more either.

Why were we dropping all those bombs into Baghdad? To hit the pesky HQ buildings, of course. They'll be empty, but we've got the bombs so they must be dropped. Also, one recalls, the bombing was to achieve 'shock and awe'. That sounds suspiciously like the old 1930s doctrine, come to think of it: bomb them hard enough and they'll surrender. Every bit as wrong now as it was then. After all, you simply can't beat the 9/11 outrages for shock-and-awe value. Did America surrender? Did it hell. It strapped on its guns and went looking for someone to kill, just as some residents of Sadr City and Mosul and Al Fallujah are now doing. Some would say that just as the angry Iraqis, shooting up Coalition soldiers, are attacking the wrong targets, perhaps so is the equally justifiably angry USA, but there you go. Enraged men seeking vengeance for murdered civilians don't always think too clearly; they have a strong tendency to attack the target easiest to reach.

Oh, but surely deep bombing makes things easier for our troops during the ground assault, doesn't it? And anything that saves a few casualties among our boys is fine, of course.

That argument, taken to its logical conclusion, would allow the use of nukes, remember. It has done in the past, although in fairness one has to say that in 1945 you weren't talking about just a few casualties among our men. But let's stop short of that, and look again at the argument that deep strikes are in some way helpful to an advancing army. It's going to be helpful to our lads as they charge across Iraq, is it, that the bridges are down? Destruction of bridges is usually a ploy of *retreating* armies, remember; indeed, the paratroops were originally set up to prevent it. It's going to make it easier for our supplies to get through, that the road networks have been smashed up and the runways wrecked? Our lads are going to be really chuffed, are they, to find thousands of grieving, vengeful sons and brothers and nephews waiting in every city with the sole thought of sending a few enemy soldiers to Shaitan before they join grandma or sister or baby in paradise?* This is going to *save* us casualties? Please. You really have to wonder whether the air force and the army are on the same side at all, when it comes to deep bombing.

Of course, none of that officially happened in Iraq. Infrastructure was not targeted at all, according to the Pentagon. Air Marshal Burridge, the British theatre commander, leaves room for doubt, however:

> 'we wanted very much to be using minimum force so as to leave the infrastructure of Iraq . . . intact; *so we only did the minimum we needed to*' [my emphasis]
>
> > *Commons Defence Select Committee*
> > *minutes of evidence, 11 June 2003.*

It doesn't matter whether one listens to the Pentagon or the more honest testimony of Air Marshal Burridge. The Coalition air strikes of 2003 certainly caused a lot of damage to the infrastructure of Iraq. This didn't help matters for Coalition ground troops. US Army combat engineers report as much:

---

* The issue of whether females go to paradise, or whether it is the same paradise as the one that men who have died fighting infidels go to, is one on which Muslims differ occasionally. It seems safe to say that some at least would expect to meet lost loved ones.

The Bayji bridges, 9 kilometers to the south, were destroyed during Operation Iraqi Freedom [*and now required repair*] . . . Charlie Company, 14th Engineer Battalion, undertook this project, which is only the first phase in repairing the causeway to full use . . . This causeway is also of vital interest to Task Force Iron Horse as it is one of the division's alternate supply routes . . .

The 14th Engineer Battalion is [*also*] repairing Iraqi Highway 1 . . . [*the highway had been*] narrowed to one lane around one 15-meter-wide hole and a smaller 5-meter-wide hole, the results of an aerial delivered bomb . . . This is the first of four such repairs . . . The remnants of an aerial delivered bomb complicated the second set of craters . . . Completion of this project removes a bottleneck and ensures that the primary V Corps north–south main supply route remains open . . .

Engineer – the Professional Bulletin of Army Engineers,
July–September 2003

These are only a selection.

Thanks a bunch, air force, is what I'd be thinking if I were a combat engineer or logistics officer in Iraq just now.

And that, really, is my first point in this chapter. The thousands, maybe tens of thousands* of Iraqi civilians who died under the flail of the smart bombs and cruise missiles did not perish as part of the war between the Coalition and Saddam. They were casualties of the eternal war between the armed services of every major power, for budget and prestige and influence. The British and American air forces, and sadly (for I'm a navy man as says it) to some extent the navies, rely on bombardment deep into enemy-held territory for their raison d'être. That being the case, we will always bomb if we can, whether it serves us or not.

One may not care about dead Iraqis. They and people under the heel of many another oppressive regime have been dying like

---

* I disagree with most of the higher estimates of Iraqi civilian casualties, in particular the Johns Hopkins figure of 100,000 or even 200,000. Only 30,000 air weapons were delivered in the 'major combat operations' phase in 2003, and few since, a number not much greater than in the Kosovo campaign. The Kosovo/Serbia bombardment surely killed a lot of people, just as the Iraq one did, but nobody suggests it killed 200,000.

flies for decades at the hands of their own forces, after all, and that didn't bother us – not enough to do anything about it, anyway. Just as a matter of our own workmanship, however, such a low ratio of actual-military-benefit omelettes to broken Iraqi eggs has to be a matter of concern. And one should also reflect that some significant proportion of our slain ground troops must have died as a result of the savage pounding from the air. Fewer bombs dropped would have meant fewer bitter, bereaved young men willing to drive truckloads of explosive into checkpoints, fewer snipers, fewer rocketeers, fewer mortar teams. The air force's struggle with the army is indirectly killing our soldiers and marines, as well as foreign civilians. Sometimes it even kills them directly, as in the case of British bomb-disposal men who have died clearing up NATO or Coalition cluster-bombs. And, as the US Army engineers make quite clear, getting military supplies through a country which has been worked over by 'friendly' air forces is no simple matter.

It's especially ironic that the very same taxpayers who coughed up such immense prices for the jets, cruise missiles and explosives to wreck Serbia and Iraq are then mulcted all over again to repair the damage. We pay tens upon tens of millions for a Tornado GR4 bomber and its crew and maintenance team, plus a load of Paveway smart bombs or Storm Shadow air-launched cruise missiles – in order to blow up a bridge, let us say. This seriously inconveniences our own troops, as well as possibly killing a number of Iraqi civilians. We then pay another fortune to build a new bridge, and the engineers we send to do it are kidnapped and murdered as they work.

This isn't strategy; it's madness. Invade, by all means. There is absolutely nothing wrong with toppling evil dictators, even if they don't have any secret super-weapons and they had nothing to do with 9/11. But don't, for goodness' sake, blast the whole place to dust and ashes beforehand just because you can. Be very, very suspicious when somebody whose career depends on it tells you that this is necessary. That includes almost all air force officers above the rank of squadron-leader, and a smaller proportion of navy and army people. The Royal Navy, remember, is already in the business of attacking shore targets, and it would like to do more of this. As for the army, there are some influential ground-force communities who are quite pleased to have the strike jets well away from the land battlefield. Deep bombing is as good a way as any to stop the flyboys taking work from the artillery and cavalry.

Even the top brains of the air staff have noticed that they are causing damage which the British and American taxpayer will get the bill for. The director of Defence Studies (Royal Air Force), writing in the *RAF Air Power Review* the year after the bombing of Serbia, had this to say:

'If one wishes to close down a power station, a weapon delivered into the control room would have the same effect as demolishing the entire plant, but with less collateral damage (and less to repair when conflict moves into a peacekeeping situation).'

Sadly, this highly qualified senior officer (Group-Captain Peter Gray), employed at the time as an official government deep thinker on air power, seems not to have made the further mental leap to ask why on earth we would want to close down a power station. This is normal, of course, for any senior military officer when the given mental leap would call into question the independence of his own branch of service. Even more annoyingly, the control room is one of the most expensive parts of a power station, and, more importantly, the only place guaranteed to have people in it. There is almost certainly a different bit of the power plant you could hit that would cut off the juice just as certainly, be less expensive to fix later, and the demolition of which would probably not involve killing anyone. The transmission substation springs to mind. In the end, though, we would still have spent a lot of money in order to cause a power cut, and a lot more to fix the problem we had caused. It is hard to see how this benefits us. If some foreigners cut off *my* electrical power, it would not incline me to the view that they should have a greater say in my government's affairs.

Now we can see the sort of thinking which will have driven the selection of targets in the Iraqi strikes of 2003. Any British officers involved in planning those raids – and the MoD claims to have had substantial input, trying to give the impression of subtle, clever Brits impressing unsophisticated Yanks – will have been using doctrine drafted by Group-Captain Gray and will have been readers of the *Air Power Review*. (In sharp contrast to the actual air crews, unless their tastes have changed since I knew them.)

QED. Bombing deep into enemy territory is largely a waste of time, and usually does *us* more harm than good. Then, as if that wasn't enough, we have to pay for the damage.

There are exceptions, of course. Very occasionally one will find a spot, deep within an enemy air defence network, where a half-ton or so of high explosive will genuinely advance our cause. Most often, such targets are actually parts of the air defence network in question, which we wish to remove. In this case, a proper cruise missile such as the Tomahawk will do the job just fine. A cruise missile, as distinct from the horribly expensive space-rocket ICBM, is basically a one-shot robot jet plane, which approaches its target much as a low-level Tornado used to. It is comparatively cheap, at around £300,000 a pop for the ones now in service. (That's what the Americans pay; they, sensibly, buy Tomahawks in thousands. Britain initially purchased only sixty-five, paying £3 million each. However, a further batch of twenty-two cost only £1 million each, and after a while we will be getting the wholesale price. The Americans have also given us some for free.) Tomahawk carries a warhead equivalent to a smart bomb, is normally launched from a ship or submarine, and then navigates its way up to a thousand miles to its target ashore. It does this by GPS, although it has a back-up terrain-matching radar to deal with jamming and reduce the final error for a precise hit. The next version, the Tactical Tomahawk, will actually be controllable while in flight, with an on-board TV camera.

Three hundred grand is a lot to blow up one target, but the alternative is a jet with smart bombs or – for tougher, heavily defended things – a half-arsed, short-range air-launched cruise missile such as the RAF's Storm Shadow. One should note that each Storm Shadow, despite having a range of only 200 miles or so and thus requiring a Tornado to deliver it, reportedly costs £2 million, even though fully 500 have been ordered for the RAF and the French government is buying it also. This makes the Tomahawk look like much better value for money. (The makers of Storm Shadow? BAe, of course, in cooperation with France.)

The jet–Storm Shadow combo requires us to deploy a lot of expensive, potentially vulnerable support people to somewhere near the theatre of conflict, as well as an air crew who must actually go into harm's way. The Tomahawk requires nobody even to step ashore, far less fly over hostile territory, and it needs servicing only at long intervals, safely back in the UK.

Furthermore, the jet bomber requires us to have wild weasel capability, or it can be held off by a SAM network. The Tomahawk has no such difficulties: it flies too low for SAM radars, and if it gets shot down by other means as the low-flying Tornados did in 1991, so what? We don't lose tens of millions of pounds in kit and two irreplaceable airmen, we lose £300,000: 1 per cent of 1 per cent of a single year's defence spending. One also notes that nearly all the 1991 losses happened as the jets were *outbound* from their targets, which could scarcely have occurred with Tomahawks.

The Tomahawk is quite clearly the intelligent way to hit the very few deep targets we genuinely need to. The only advantage which the galactically expensive manned-bomber method gives you is that you can go on day after day hitting hundreds and hundreds more deep targets. This is not actually something we need to do.

RIP, deep-strike bombers, surely. Goodbye, air power? Perhaps.

But not, actually, goodbye strike aeroplanes. There is work yet for all our fast-jet aircrew and groundcrew, if not for all their bosses.

Remember the tactical air forces of World War II? Remember close air support? It was good stuff then, and it's good stuff now. Air strikes against enemy forces in the field are the big unheralded success story of modern military aviation. Forget about runways and bridges and power stations and 'headquarters buildings' and supposed chemical-weapons factories et ridiculous cetera. Actual enemy missile batteries, warships, tanks, armoured infantry carriers and artillery – that's what needs hitting, and correctly equipped strike planes are supremely good at it. Once those targets are gone, as they will be quite fast nowadays – if they were ever there to start with – you really *can* save a lot of ground troops' lives by putting close air support under their direction, acting as flying artillery. And, as we saw in Chapter 3, providing the ground troops with jets is a lot less troublesome than providing them with conventional artillery; or it would be, if not for intense opposition to this concept both from the air force and the gunners.

Battlefield air support can be quite a dangerous activity for the flyers involved, but there is no need for it to be. The light shoulder-fired anti-aircraft missile is out there, to be sure. It still doesn't threaten a high-flying aircraft, but it has made low-level work more tricky. Various responses are possible. The attack helicopter, for example: this is supposedly able to operate low over the battlefield where aeroplanes can't because it has some light armour, and also can use such ploys as hiding behind hills and popping up only briefly to make attacks. In fact, experience from Vietnam all the way to Iraq suggests that the helicopter is at least as dangerous a way to do ground attack as the aeroplane. The true reason for its continued presence above the battlefield, as we have seen, is probably that it is flown by soldiers who want to be there, rather than airmen who don't. Or whose bosses don't want them there, anyway, not too much of the time.

The US Air Force, alarmed by the fact that US Army aviation got much of the action in Vietnam, has made more serious efforts at air support than most. For example, it built the tough, armoured A-10 Thunderbolt attack plane, designed to fly low and slow in the teeth of ground fire and gut enemy tanks like fish. An extremely effective piece of kit in its day, if not much loved by its parent organisation, but the A-10's day is probably over. Why fly low and survive ground fire, when you can fly high and use smart weapons? Even attack helicopters are starting to operate more in this way.

Another Vietnam-era innovation was the side-firing gunship. Unlike a helicopter gunship, this is based on a transport aircraft, usually a C-130 Hercules. In the cargo bay is an array of guns, mounted to fire sideways out of the plane like the broadside of an old-time sailing ship. The gunship flies in big circles above its target area. From the viewpoint of the gunners, the ground at the centre of the circle sits still in their sights as the plane flies steadily round and round, too high for ground fire to reach. But the gunship's weapons are firing downhill, so to speak. Its shells and bullets can strike the target area without difficulty. The latest versions mount weapons up to 105mm calibre – small artillery pieces, able to reach miles. They can pick their targets just as if they were firing from a hilltop. With thermal-imaging sights, the gunners can see through darkness, cloud and smoke. They can generally tell if an individual on the ground has a weapon, even, and pick him off – or not – accordingly. Everything from a tank to an individual rifleman can be taken out, and nothing but an enemy fighter or heavy SAM can do anything about it.*

Despite its effectiveness and great popularity with the ground forces, the gunship is not popular in the USAF. It is a BUFF, a big ugly fat fucker, not a sleek and sexy jet. And there can be few more boring jobs for a pilot than endlessly flying round and round. The sort of person one finds with wings on his chest would always rather fly something a bit more dashing: a nice one- or two-man fast jet with a pointy nose, for choice. Much later, when he becomes a USAF general or RAF air marshal, he will still have the same preferences. The mighty USAF, with all its thousands of fast jets, possesses only twenty-one side-firing gunships. (They are mostly assigned to the Special Ops command. As ever, those lads get the stuff that actually works.) The RAF has never had any. All its money is reserved for the Eurofighter, and besides, Britain is so desperately short of transport aircraft that none can be converted for this sort of work.

The side-firing gunship is quite literally flying artillery and probably one of the best ways to deliver battlefield fire support from the air. Sadly, air forces being air forces, it will never be adopted

---

* Watching video taken from a gunship in action is a very sobering experience; you see individual figures being cut down unanswerably from the night sky, without ever seeing their enemy or knowing what hit them. Despite the discrimination possible, mistakes are still all too likely, especially where just about every adult male carries a weapon, as in rural Afghanistan. In one well-known case, a wedding was shot up by a cruising US gunship after the party-goers began firing into the air – the local equivalent of throwing rice or confetti. Footage from an AC-130 Spectre in action over Afghanistan is now circulating widely on the internet. Anyone who would like an understanding of this kind of warfare should watch it. Simply type 'ac-130 gunship video afghanistan' into any search engine.

in any great numbers. But this isn't too much of a problem. The fast jets which airmen love so much can also be very useful over the battlefield, assuming you can get them pulled away from the enemy's capital city. British Tornados and Harriers can carry Maverick or Brimstone missiles, which are released from high up to destroy enemy armoured vehicles or suchlike. (American pilots referred disparagingly to this work as 'tank-plinking' during the wars in the Gulf: they found it dull. Dull it may have been, but it was the main useful thing they accomplished.) The smart bomb, too, is an excellent tool for taking out enemies in the field. It has difficulty with moving targets, but military vehicles spend far more time sitting still than they do moving. An artillery position, or a bunker, or a tank regiment parked for the night, are all excellent smart-bomb targets. Strike jets are far better employed on this sort of work than knocking down bridges which our troops will need in a few days, or wrecking power stations which we'll only have to repair later.

In fairness to the USAF and the RAF, they are starting to realise this; 79 per cent of targets attacked in Gulf War II were Iraqi field forces. However, they still felt the need to hammer huge numbers of other things, including fully 163 VIP residences, party offices and similar completely non-military targets. The dream of 'regime decapitation' is still alive and well, although with Saddam now in custody and the Sunni insurgency – his former constituency – carrying on regardless, one hopes the notion may be losing credence.

So, a jet is better than a tank at doing a tank's job. It is probably better than artillery at doing the artillery's job, too. Jets can definitely destroy moving targets, a thing the artillery struggles to do, and they have other advantages in terms of area coverage and deployability. A forty-five-ton AS90 self-propelled gun is a nightmare to transport to the theatre of war, a worse nightmare to move up to the start line, and then remains a very serious logistic problem once in combat. Most of the kilotons of ammunition that heavy armoured forces use up are actually artillery shells.

By contrast, a jet flies itself to the theatre. It moves about within theatre with great ease. It uses similarly immense tonnages of fuel and munitions, but they have to be hauled only to the jet's operating base, not right up to the front line. In the past, armed forces which depended on jets to do what artillery had always done would often get into trouble; the Israelis burnt their fingers in this way decades ago. This was because the aircraft of the day couldn't really operate at night or in difficult weather conditions, and had to run severe risks in order to actually hit anything even in ideal circumstances.

Nowadays, things have changed. The long, long heralded all-weather, day or night, high-flying precision attack aircraft is genuinely to be had at last. The US Marine Corps, which is in the fortunate position of having its own strike jets with MARINES written on them, flown by marines and under the orders of marine ground commanders, doesn't bother with artillery to any great degree. Tellingly, despite having been pioneers in the use of attack helicopters, the jarheads* no longer prioritise these, either. Unlike the US Army, the marines are permitted to have jets, so they don't need attack helos. There are thus no jarhead Apaches, just Harriers and F-18s.

No such easy integration is possible in the other US services, far less in our own. The problem is that the air force doesn't want to work for the army, and the cavalry and the artillery don't want their jobs stolen by the air force, even if the airmen were willing to take them on. It isn't so much that officers in actual combat operations see an Iraqi tank and try to make sure that their own arm of service bags it. When things are for real, a commendable push to work together always occurs, with the army screaming for air support and the RAF furiously trying to deliver it. The problem is that they have not practised such things, not really, and their equipment is not suited to the job. During peace-time they seldom exercise together, working as they do for different bosses, and these different bosses prefer that they should train and be equipped for separate missions, not integrated ones, or someone might ask if perhaps we only need one boss – as in the US Marines.

This all became very clear in the 2003 Iraq invasion. The RAF had great difficulty striking battlefield targets. Here is Air-Vice-Marshal Torpy, the British air boss in Gulf II, admitting as much:

---

* The US Marines are so called due to their passion for extremely short haircuts, which has now been carried to the point where they seem to be wet-shaving the sides of their heads several times a day.

'One of the lessons that we have learned out of the campaign [is] that our targeting pods need longer range, better fidelity . . . positively identifying that a target is a military target.'

> *Commons Defence Select Committee*
> *third report, March 2004.*

In other words, RAF aircraft cannot tell an armoured vehicle from a pickup truck when at height. Furthermore, British land forces lacked the necessary forward air controllers and communications to get air support effectively integrated with the ground battle. (These had to be borrowed from the US Marines, funnily enough.) The House of Commons Defence Select Committee, examining the good air marshal and others including British generals, concluded:

'we feel that the shortcomings in the practice and training of close air support by the RAF and land forces which have emerged in recent operations must be urgently addressed'

> *Commons Defence Select Committee*
> *third report, March 2004.*

Their bold type, not mine.

The MPs of the committee, naturally, don't mean 'urgently addressed' in the sense of the forces being allowed to buy American targeting pods or weapons off the shelf. (I need hardly say that the current RAF targeting pod is made by a division of BAe.) They don't mean 'urgently addressed' in the sense of closing down artillery and cavalry units in favour of forward air controllers and placing jet squadrons under permanent army command. Really they don't mean 'urgently addressed' at all; they would just like everything sorted out, or not, with no political pain involved and some biggish defence orders placed here in Britain. The MoD knows this, of course, and ignores them. Later that year infantry units were the only ones closed down, and the only planes cut from the RAF were battlefield-strike ones; both of these measures taken so that we could afford the British-made Eurofighter, which cannot do air-to-ground at all.

Dropping ordnance is not all one can do from the sky; it is possible to do reconnaissance too. (This will also be unpopular. Remember how much of the British Army nowadays likes to call itself 'Surveillance and Target Acquisition'? All those light-tank cavalry aristocrats?) We aren't talking about flying over and taking a look these days, not even taking a look with thermal-imaging cameras as some of the RAF quite like doing. There is better on offer.

The USAF and US Army have a shared programme called JSTARS: Joint Surveillance and Target Acquisition Radar System. This is another 707 airliner like the air-scanning AWACS we saw in the last chapter; the difference is that the radar on the JSTARS plane is designed to sweep the ground, not the sky. It can pick out all the moving vehicles over hundreds of miles of country, and tell which ones are tracked rather than wheeled. All this information is revealed on computer maps in any US command post. The radar blips from JSTARS can then be checked out by any one of dozens of TV spy eyes in various aircraft, unmanned recon drones, satellites or whatever. There is now even a robot drone called Global Hawk with a mini-JSTARS-type radar in it.

What this means is that if you are an enemy of America, and you are stupid enough to get into any sort of tracked vehicle and drive it anywhere, you are a dead man. Just as you have been for decades, if you went flying in a no-fly zone. You can drive your armour in the dead of night, under heavy cloud, in a sandstorm; it doesn't matter. A JSTARS plane on patrol a hundred miles off, or a Global Hawk a bit nearer, will sniff you out. An unmanned drone, or a gunship, or a regular strike jet with a proper targeting pod will confirm that you have indeed done this incredibly foolish thing, seeing through the clouds with thermal vision. You are unlikely to realise that this is happening. And then you will die. A range of things might come for you: a homing anti-armour missile, or a smart bomb, or a gunship cannon shell, or perhaps a Tactical Tomahawk under operator control.

JSTARS and unmanned drones are clearly the intelligent way to do reconnaissance – rather better than light tanks or fast jets, anyway. Should you be lucky enough to have enemies who drive about in armoured vehicles, this is the way to find them. They will then almost certainly be best dealt with from the air before your infantry moves through. Without for a moment admitting any of this, the MoD would like to have a JSTARS-type system.

This gives us the chance to have a huge procurement cock-up: we seem to be seizing the opportunity.

We could simply buy the American JSTARS, which would cost in the region of £120 million per plane if we ordered it from Northrop Grumman and didn't attempt to buy British votes at the same time. Or we could let British Aerospace have a go, probably with disastrous and expensive results. On the face of it, the government still feels the dreadful shadow of the 1970s Nimrod fiasco, looming across the decades. It seems that nobody, not even the MoD, would be mad enough to let BAe handle a flying-radar project again. Nimrod, remember, was cocked up by GEC, which is now part of British Aerospace. We are thus buying our ground-scanning planes from Raytheon, a serious US defence contractor who should be able to do the job. The project is called ASTOR: Airborne Stand Off Radar. Raytheon got the contract because Raytheon has promised to spend most of the British government's money in Britain. Five planes will cost £800 million – £160 million per bird – significantly more than the Americans are paying for real, working JSTARS aircraft.

But this way cake is had, and eaten too. Raytheon will make the planes, not incompetent old BAe, but somehow it will still be done in Britain. Our high-tech manufacturing base will thus be sustained; surely that must be worth an extra £200 million. Or, to put it another way, the government gets some votes as well as some radar planes. (Never have quite seen how that works, myself. They take our money away, give it to some inefficient arms makers whom most of us don't know from Adam and wouldn't like if we did, and because the arms parasites happen to be British this makes us vote for more of the same. Well, not me. Not you either, if you've any sense.)

In this case, this isn't even happening. The devil is in the detail. Raytheon will not do the ASTOR work here; they will 'place work equivalent to 100% of the contract value with firms here'. This allows them to make the radars largely in the US, and simply buy call-centre time, financial services or other unskilled, Third World-type stuff to the same amount here in the UK. These things can then be sold on. There is no guarantee whatever that high-tech jobs or capability will accrue to the British economy under these terms.

Still, at least BAe won't be involved. At least they aren't getting any of our money, just this one time.

Of course they are. Realistically, if any of the tech at all was to be done in Britain, BAe would have to be involved. No matter that they scarcely have a glorious record in this area, BAe is almost the entire British defence sector. If you want to spend money on death-tech in Britain, and my word we seem to love to do that, you have to deal with BAe.

There is some other UK involvement, to be fair. This is principally from Shorts of Northern Ireland, who are part of the alliance producing the jets to carry the ASTOR electronics. The thing is, these are small business jets, costing in the neighbourhood of £15 million each, not 707 airliners like the JSTARS. As is normal in a modern military aircraft, most of the money will go on the mission system – radar and computers – not the airframe. As Shorts is only one of an international consortium making the Global Express business jets, the purchase of which will only represent 10 per cent of the ASTOR project cost anyway, one can't really say that this is a big thing for British industry. Much as the MoD would like to.

All in all, then, we seem to have managed to get the worst of all worlds. Most of the serious industrial investment will go abroad. What tech money is spent in Britain will go largely, as ever, to BAe, who have demonstrated that they don't deserve it. Despite not really having managed to benefit our economy at all, we have spent two hundred million pounds above what proper, working JSTARS planes would cost. And for this, we get a dodgy little half-arsed version which may or may not be any use. To give just one example of its limited capability, ASTOR will be able to stay airborne for nine hours, as opposed to twenty for the JSTARS. The latter's big 707 fuselage carries a double crew to relieve each other and so get more out of the equipment. Of course, if ASTOR doesn't work, a lot of people will be very happy, both in the army and the RAF.

So, the ASTOR project is being run in the way we have come to expect. Britain will have minimum capability at maximum cost.

To recap: the RAF has just over a hundred strike jets operational in the wake of the 2004 cuts. Fully sixty of these are Tornados, intended for the deep-strike mission, although they can perfectly well do useful work such as picking off tanks or other vehicles from on high, or delivering smart bombs to ground-war requirements. They could if they had decent targeting pods, that is. These could easily be bought in the States. They are snap-on equipment, and there would be no need for a big modification programme. The other forty planes are excellent Harrier jump-jets, the only dedicated close-support planes Britain has. The Harrier is especially handy as it can operate from small carriers – such as ours. There are also a few aged but reasonably effective Jaguars still operating, although probably not for long. All these hundred-plus jets really need is a pile of smart bombs, some proper battlefield targeting gear and lots of homing anti-armour weapons. They do not need the dubious Storm Shadow. Any time we really need to carry out a deep strike or close down enemy air defences we can use Tomahawk cruise missiles, which are cheaper, safer and better.

As the Tornados and Harriers wear out, we could simply buy F-35s (which we saw in the last chapter) to replace them. In a dream world all these aircraft would be placed under army management, living and operating much as the Harrier force does now, or they could be navy carrier planes. The relatively plush service conditions of the RAF and many of its cushy UK jobs would have to go by the board, but most would find it hard to weep for them. (One would need to stop the army selling all the planes and buying tanks and artillery with the money, of course. Likewise the navy would swap them for frigates unless prevented.)

It will never happen, sadly. The British government's ability to actually control its defence ministry is horribly limited; even reorganising the Guards has proved politically impossible. And the future doesn't look bright. The deep-strike bomber men are fighting hard for survival. Rather than simply having an open account with the US to buy more Tomahawks, the MoD has a project called Future Offensive Air System. This team is theoretically considering a range of alternatives, including cruise missiles and drones as well as manned aircraft. But one can't help noticing that the FOAS project team is in the Aircraft Cluster of the Defence Procurement Agency with the manned aircraft, not in the Weapons Cluster with the missiles. It is openly referred to as being the programme which will determine the Tornado's successor. Barring a miracle, FOAS will turn into another horrifyingly expensive manned aeroplane in addition to the F-35.

Thus, in the wars of the future, we will still be cursed with the ability to drop 500 tons of ordnance on deep targets twice a day, as the Tornado GR4 fleet can now do. This means that we will carry on doing so whenever we go to war, despite the fact that valid targets will almost certainly not exist – not in anything like sufficient numbers, anyway. The whole ghastly merry-go-round of shot-down airmen, slaughtered foreign civilians, beleaguered ground troops and costly reconstruction will go on, and we will continue to lack proper close air support. This means that we will continue to need vast amounts of heavy, troublesome artillery and armour, and thus that we will never have enough actual men with guns on the ground to get anything useful done.

Hopefully that letter to your MP is getting quite long now.

CHAPTER

7

Logistics

Amateurs talk about tactics, but professionals study logistics.

Attributed to General Robert H. Barrow (commandant
of the US Marine Corps), noted in 1980

Thus far we have looked at men with guns and at some of the many ways of finding enemies and throwing high explosives at them. In other words, we have been looking at tactics. Various service communities like to describe some of these things as strategies, for it is only at the strategic level that employment for the highest-ranking officers can credibly be found; they are tactics nonetheless.

And General Barrow is quite correct, if indeed it was he who came up with the old saw above: one can sit about discussing tactics, or even strategy, in any given situation as much as one likes, but chances are it will save a lot of time and hot air to talk logistics first. As we saw in the last chapter, until 1999 the Milošević regime was untouchable by ground forces for simple reasons of *logistics*, which limited NATO to the *tactic* of aerial bombing, much though this was unlikely to have any real *strategic* effect. Strategy, if you will, is what we would like to achieve. Tactics are ways of doing it. But logistics normally define what we actually can do in any given situation. We may have many tactics which would serve our strategy, but is it logistically feasible to employ them?

This is deadly boring stuff – counting up shipping tonnage and working out ways to move things about – not work which attracts the average young forces type. He would sooner be flying his jet, conning his ship or smearing green paint on his face and sneaking off into the woods to kill someone. The spectacle-wearing, pen-pushing, shiny-bottomed admin johnny whose business it is to find jet fuel, ammo, face paint or whatever for the steely combat hero, and get him to his place of business in the first place, is despised as a rear-echelon wimp if he does the job well, and actively hated if he does it less than well.

These logistics folk range from comparatively sharp-end types like the truck-driving marines of the Commando Logistic Regiment or their army counterparts in the 16,500-strong Royal Logistics Corps* right the way back to the Blighty-side desk wallahs of the Defence Logistics Organisation. The DLO employs nearly 30,000 people, almost all civil servants. However it is run by many senior forces officers. The boss is currently a four-star air chief marshal, the same rank as the heads of the armed forces. Even the chief of catering is a brigadier. These scores of thousands of supply people often seem a little excessive, given that there are fewer than 25,000 men with guns in the whole armed forces. There are continual efforts to control the numbers of bean counters; one is underway as this book is written.

But in fact the swarming blanket-stackers do have a sizeable job on their hands. Let's take a look at how bad it can get. Let's say, for the sake of argument, that Britain has decided to partic-ipate in a land war against a fairly serious country which has a largish army with lots of tanks and artillery – after all, it's happened twice in the last fifteen years, even if it was the same country. In this type of scenario, our army are probably going to want to send a heavy armoured division. (They will gaily say 'a British heavy armoured division', although 'the British heavy armoured division' is more accurate.) It is possible that our generals will be willing to take a bit less heavy metal in future, but only possible. Even after the reorganisation of 2004, which was supposed to make the forces radically lighter and more nimble to deploy, only two of the seven combat brigade set-ups existing in the British Army will be light; the rest will be one flavour or other of heavy. Anyway, lighter troops have their own logistical

---

* Aka the Rather Large Corps to the rest of the army; more soldiers wear the RLC cap badge than any other.

downsides. It is true, their helicopters or light(er) ground vehicles are much easier to handle and ship about than heavy tanks.
They *may* be more sparing of ammunition, having fewer heavy
guns to fire it from. But they make more use of gas-guzzling helicopters, so they will potentially burn as much fuel as the heavy
mob, and it will need to be comparatively troublesome aviation
fuel rather than diesel.

In any case, generals tend to get a very chilly feeling if the other
side has armour and big guns and they don't. Nobody wants to
be a speed bump for enemy tanks, much though this would be
unlikely in the presence of friendly up-to-date air support. Today's
generals don't really believe in air support, not deep down. They
all came up in the days when the enemy was just as likely to
control the skies as you were, and even if you had air support it
didn't work at night, or in bad weather, or sometimes for no
reason at all. (Only the last of these three problems remains to
be solved.) They know perfectly well that the Iraqi army was
mostly destroyed from the air rather than by tanks and artillery,
but they don't actually *believe* it. It will be a brave general who
agrees to go in light if there seems to be any real opposition. (Not
brave for himself, of course. His own personal arse will always
be quite safe, light or heavy. As our boys went into Iraq, their
theatre commander was sitting safely three countries away in
Qatar. Brave as regards his career prospects, is what I mean.)

Even if there isn't any seriously tooled-up opposition, the most
sensible and modern-minded of generals will still cling to some
heavy equipment. He may agree to leave his tanks and big guns
behind, but he will still hold out grimly for some sort of armoured
ride for his infantrymen, even in a lower-threat environment. And
one sees his point. It is a rare enemy who doesn't have lots of
shoulder-launched anti-armour rockets, such as the ubiquitous ex-
Soviet RPG* and only the most heavily protected vehicles can
credibly resist these at the moment. This means Warrior, for the
British Army. Theoretically one could save a lot of weight and
trouble by using the Saxon vehicle instead, but in the real world
Saxon is only ever going to war if we run out of Warriors. When

---

* Rocket Propelled Grenade, or Raketniy Protivotankoviy Granatomet ('Rocket
Anti-Tank Grenade Launcher') as the Russians would say.

every third enemy gunman has an RPG and every road may be mined with half a ton of explosives – as is pretty much the case nowadays – Saxon just isn't good enough. Nobody is going to have the guts to face the bereaved relatives of soldiers who have died in a blown up Saxon if the far tougher Warrior could have been sent instead. Saxon will probably never see deployed combat service again; it is a vehicle for training and for very-low-threat scenarios. The army has a project called Future Rapid Effects System, intended to get them some light, relatively easily deployed armoured vehicles which can resist RPGs at least. Judging by the hiccups the Americans are having with their equivalent Stryker programme, and the way in which even heavy Warriors in Iraq are still thought to need extra bolt-on RPG protection, it may be best not to hold one's breath.

So, we'll be stuck with the need to move massive armoured vehicles around the world a lot of the time. The only way the soldiery will perhaps agree to do without them is if they have a lot of helicopters instead, as in South Armagh, but, as we saw in Chapter 4, these bring with them vast requirements for fuel and maintenance, and anyway Britain doesn't have very many helicopters. In any case, our generals are likely to want more air support in proportion to their reduced requirements for heavy artillery and tanks, so the logistic needs will still be just as large, even if a lot of stuff no longer has to go as far into danger. What this adds up to is that most of the equipment and supplies are going to have to be sent by sea. It is going to take us weeks, not days, to get there: and we'll need a big harbour at the other end, in friendly hands, to use for offloading.

Eh? What on earth am I going on about? Surely this is the jet age. Everyone knows that soldiers go to war by airliner nowadays – they should be there in a few hours, not weeks. And what's all this about harbours? We've all seen pictures of mighty military transport aeroplanes with tanks driving off their ramps. (Well, I have, anyway.) Just send everything by air, for goodness' sake.

Fair enough. The soldiers themselves do indeed go to war by chartered airliner, usually. And there are several types of heavy military transport plane which can haul a fully armed and fuelled sixty-ton main battle tank round the world in a matter of hours. Amazing stuff. But the mathematics of going to war by air simply don't stack up – not at the moment, and probably not any time soon. The big problem is that our postulated single heavy division is quite capable, when fighting hard, of using up no fewer than *ten thousand tons* of supplies every single day. The bulk of this is fuel for its thousands of vehicles and ammunition for its hundreds of heavy weapons – fuel and ammo are the two prime logistic needs of modern armies. But our boys and girls also need grub, spare parts, medicine, mail, sunblock, loo roll and amazing numbers of other things. And, as we have seen, even lighter force options aren't likely to be all that light. The division includes a logistics brigade, which will collect and distribute all this stuff, but the supplies must first be delivered to somewhere reasonably handy so that the RLC chaps can get at them.

Just for a minute let's switch hats and imagine that we're the Americans. Let's say that those crazy Limeys have this division fighting hard somewhere, and us Yanks have nothing else to do but supply them using the USAF air transport fleet. Very well. America has a lot of very serious military airlift. We've got about 180 modern C-17 Globemasters and perhaps 120 ageing but even more enormous C-5 Galaxies. We also have fully 700 smaller Hercules C-130s, but these are quite slow, needing days rather than hours to make a long haul in most cases, and they can't lift much compared to the big boys; they aren't really suitable for long-distance work, and we Americans sensibly use them more for moving stuff around within theatre.

The Globemasters and Galaxies, though, can quite likely make a round trip to and from the war zone every day, and can theoretically carry 80 and 130 tons respectively at wartime maximum emergency loading. This would seem to mean that the whole fleet could shift an amazing 35,000 tons into theatre every day, easily keeping several divisions supplied.

In real life, though, this doesn't happen. During recent build-ups in the Gulf, the Galaxy has had an availability rate of only 70 per cent, although the more modern Globemaster has run at 85–90 per cent. Furthermore, one cannot expect to load planes to wartime emergency maximum repeatedly; one can't even expect to load them up to safe maximum when they are making back-to-back trips and turning round fast. Factors of bulk versus weight and operational constraints have meant that the average loads carried in recent operations have run at 54 tons for the Galaxy and 33 tons for the Globemaster.

Using these more realistic figures, and assuming that every serviceable aircraft is making a round trip to and from the war zone daily, we find that America can move approximately 10,000 tons of supplies per day. In other words, the entire US air transport fleet can barely support a single heavy division in combat. As for getting the division's thousands of armoured vehicles there in the first place, forget it. They're going surface freight.

Another point to bear in mind is that the Galaxy requires a proper paved runway to land on – an airport, then, or a military airbase, fairly undamaged and in friendly hands. The Globemaster can put down on shorter dirt or gravel strips, but this will reduce its availability rate. Furthermore, whatever the runway quality, we are assuming here that there is plenty of aviation fuel available at the delivery end, or our planes will carry even less.

Sometimes things aren't quite this difficult. Often, bulk vehicle fuel for the soldiers as well as jet juice for planes and choppers can be got locally, which saves a lot of hauling. By the way, we have taken it as read that there is plenty of clean water; there usually is. Perhaps the locals can't get any, but if you have lots of tanker trucks and purifying equipment, as a big military deployment does, you'll be fine in most places. The worst possible case is the one to plan for, though, and anyway, even without worrying about fuel and water, there will be immense amounts of stuff to move.

All this leads us to the reason why, in a book about the British armed forces, I have so far only mentioned the Americans' airlift capability. America, with its 300-odd heavy long-range transports, can, by making a supreme effort, deploy a division-sized light to medium-weight combat force, and supply it, by air; perhaps two unambiguously light divisions, in some circumstances. Even mighty America hasn't a hope of sending substantial, heavyweight units to war by air. Now let's look at our own situation.

The Royal Air Force currently has four – count them, *four* – large military transport planes, Globemasters originally leased from the US. They are the only ones in Europe. Mostly, when the British military needs something to go by air, it goes by charter freight or in one of the RAF's forty-five little Hercules C-130s.

British Hercules are of varying capacity, some being modernised and some not, but they average out at under twenty tons' realistic lift. The whole RAF fleet can haul no more than a thousand tons per trip. Since it is a turboprop rather than a jet proper, the Hercules travels slowly and doesn't have intercontinental range. Whenever it goes beyond Europe it has to make stopovers en route. The Hercules is an excellent workhorse for moving smaller cargoes around within a theatre of war, but it is a pretty feeble substitute for a proper long-haul transport.

What this adds up to is that Britain has almost no serious military air deployment capability at all. Clever planning using every aircraft we have would allow the UK to deploy a rather slim, very light but reasonably mobile brigade to an airhead no further off than Turkey. That is the uttermost limit of our reach, and remember that this would be a very clever plan, ie, one likely to go badly wrong in real life. Also, light but mobile means the soldiers wouldn't have to walk everywhere, but would only have ordinary Land Rovers and such to ride in, mostly – vehicles which can be taken out by anyone with a rifle. Some of the helicopters, too, would probably have to fly there under their own power, and the whole thing wouldn't exactly happen like lightning; it would take a week or so. If our lads got into a scrap, they would have to win without reinforcements as all our planes would be tied up simply keeping them supplied. We begin to see why the British parachute brigade was shut down, or ostensibly shut down. We had only the most marginal ability to fly it anywhere.

This leaves us Brits with surface freight, then, as the only option for almost every serious situation – that is, sea freight. Even in the early years of the 21st century this is still the way that nearly all things great and small move about, with the exception of people. Cars, fridges, TVs, oil, gas, grain, ores, tanks, guns, munitions; almost everything goes by ship. That's because it's nice and cheap. For most British military deployments, the MoD simply charters lots of merchant tonnage to move all the heavy gear to a harbour close to where it's wanted. Indeed, the ministry actually owns a small fleet of grey-painted merchant ships – among the very few merchant vessels left registered under the British flag – called the Royal Fleet Auxiliary. The RFA mainly provides fuel tankers and supply ships for the navy, but it includes a few support vessels for land forces. There is also a handful of such ships in the navy proper.

Provided the Egyptians are willing to let us use the Suez Canal, sea transport can get to most likely trouble spots in only a few weeks: but this isn't the sort of timescale most people are thinking of when the phrase 'rapid reaction' is used, as it often is in military circles. (Remember NATO's Rapid Reaction Corps? Made up mostly of heavy armour? It would take at least a couple of months to actually react to anything, other than an attack on its bases in Germany. And that, of course, is with instant agreement in NATO political councils. Ha ha!) Assuming a sea deployment, however, the fleet auxiliary and navy ships will not suffice for any serious force. Most of the tonnage will have to go in commercial freighters, as it did for both Iraq wars. Hence the requirement for a good modern harbour at the other end; only specialist amphibious shipping can unload without one.

Now it becomes clear why the Taliban were removed largely by fellow Afghans. The Americans would very much have liked to do it personally, but Afghanistan is far from the sea and surrounded by mountains, and all the airstrips were enemy held. Air support and special forces were pretty much all that America could get there, barring some sort of insanely ballsy seize-an-airport parachute lunacy.* Iraq, by contrast, has a nice flat land border with Kuwait, and the Kuwaitis, with reason, were more than happy to provide a build-up area for the Coalition.

Sea transport, then, is the limiting factor for the armies of the West. It makes them slow to arrive and usually dependent on some friendly local country to provide harbour facilities and infrastructure for offloading at the other end. Theoretically, one can make an amphibious landing without a harbour, but Britain would struggle to get serious heavy forces ashore that way, or keep them supplied. Realistically, such an amphibious force

---

* The Soviets did manage to take over Afghanistan during 1979 in an initially airborne coup de main, it is true, but their situation was very different from that of the US in 2002. The communists were in the fortunate position of having large numbers of military advisers and other forces already in key positions within Afghanistan, and in being able to send their main invasion force across the land border from the USSR to the north.

would have to capture a harbour, intact, pretty damn quickly if there was any serious opposition about. In the Falklands there wasn't, much, and the British campaign there was still a very gutsy move.

Such an amphibious assault is referred to in military staff jargon as forced theatre entry, as opposed to the usual method where some nice local chaps let us get our foot in the door without a fight. Theoretically, the other means of forced entry is a parachute landing, to grab an airport: but, as we have seen, this is realistic only for the Americans. Even they will think very hard before trying it. Amphibious forces can generally make a withdrawal if things go wrong; this is not the case with paratroops. Hence the US Joint Chiefs' very sensible reluctance to let the 82nd Airborne jump into Afghanistan, even to avenge 9/11.

So, logistics tells us what we can do: and it turns out to be a lot less than we might have thought, even for America. For Britain, with one of the more serious militaries outside the United States, it is enormously less than one might reasonably expect. Despite spending 8–10 per cent of what the Americans do on defence, we have at best 1 or 2 per cent of their airlift. Our sealift is largely reliant on charter shipping, quite likely flying flags of convenience and hardly dependable in a crunch situation. Heaven forfend that any large body of British troops should in the future have to make a fighting withdrawal by sea, as they have had to often enough in the past; doubly so, if it must be by air.

This is an unusually poor performance, even for the MoD. Why so little airlift? After all, heavyweight military airlift is another of those genuinely useful things that nobody can really argue against, like transport helicopters, or infantrymen, or close air support. Airlift is always vitally necessary, in every scenario from high-intensity war down to humanitarian disaster relief. It almost beggars belief that we have spent a billion pounds on dubious rubbish such as Storm Shadow, to give just one example, when this sum could get us another half-dozen infinitely more useful Globemaster C-17s.

In fact, we are amazingly fortunate to have the few we do.

Officially speaking, the RAF's Globemasters were leased as a 'short-term' measure to ameliorate our airlift situation while the proper solution was being sorted out. Actually, the leases have since been quietly bought out; now that the armed forces have managed to get some proper American planes past the conspiracy to keep BAe in business, they certainly aren't going to give them back. The Globemasters were never supposed to happen. After all, they are amazing beasts: powerful, capable heavy-lift aircraft, able to set down on rough strips after intercontinental flights. There isn't a manufacturer in Europe, much less the UK, which could produce anything like them, and it wasn't easy even for Boeing. (The US taxpayers were bled with even more than usual severity during the C-17's development.) Therefore, we weren't ever intended to have anything like them. Don't buy the best: buy what BAe has to sell. If they haven't got anything to sell, wait until they have. That's how we do things here.

Britain's utter lack of long-range airlift capability was officially noted as long ago as 1993: some giant brain at the MoD spotted – rather belatedly – that the cold war was over, and that we might need to operate beyond north-west Europe. Many of our continental NATO allies agreed, and a joint military requirement was drafted to the effect that some new aeroplanes would be needed to replace Europe's various pathetic little military air-transport fleets. With not one but several lame-duck aviation industries involved, it was very clear that the planes would be a collaborative Euro-project. Oh dear.

As one would expect after this sort of kick-off, bearing in mind the Merlin and the Eurofighter, pretty much nothing happened for the next five years while a desperate struggle went on to assemble a credible and politically feasible manufacturing consortium. This is an extremely difficult process. One cannot, for example, simply get the firm which is best at engines to do the engines, the best at wings to do them, and so on. The money value of contracts placed in each country has to be exactly in proportion to the number of planes it wants to order, almost regardless of whether that country can actually do that amount of work.

The MoD has stated categorically that this type of workshare arrangement has not occurred (in this case – they don't deny that it is normal practice). They say that all work will be dished out on a strictly commercial basis by the lead contractor, a genuine private-sector company called Airbus Military. It can only be a remarkable coincidence, then, that there is significant construction involvement by every nation ordering planes – even those noted aerospace giants, Turkey and Belgium – and very little by anyone else, other than some unavoidable American bits. (An aeroplane without US parts is no more likely than a computer without some US software in it.)

Indeed, rather contradicting the MoD's line, Airbus Military itself admits that 'strategic workshare . . . will be managed by the program's major European industrial participants: AIRBUS France, AIRBUS Germany, AIRBUS UK, EADS CASA, FLABEL and TAI'. In other words, it will be shared out by a committee of the purchasing countries' aerospace corporations. You can bet none of them will let a penny go elsewhere that they could hold onto, even if this means the customer (you and I) paying more. When you add this sort of thing to the natural complexity of a high-tech, multilingual, multinational engineering project, it becomes a miracle that such enterprises ever work at all. Often they don't, of course.

Finally the European contender was lashed together, in 1998. It was originally known as the Future Large Aircraft, or FLA. By now the reputation of such projects was extremely bad, however. Eurofighter and Merlin were ridiculously late and draining various European treasuries at a furious rate, and a Euro-frigate scheme was collapsing completely. Meanwhile, the Americans, spending vast sums, had seriously pushed back the boundaries of transport-aircraft technology with the C-17. They had also found ways to enhance old C-130 Hercules haulers to the point where they were almost new aircraft.

Britain now had a chance to buy C-17s and/or modernise its existing Hercules fleet. It wouldn't take long, and we would have vastly more lift and range, amounting to a serious worldwide reach if we got some C-17s. The Euro-transport FLA was only a bit better than an upgraded Hercules, but would cost vastly more. No more than an incremental improvement would be gained by going the Euro-route, at least as far as Britain was concerned. (FLA *is* significantly better than the teeny, aged twin-engined Transalls currently operated by the French and Germans. The two countries put together have even less airlift than Britain – and that's largely it, for continental Europe. This should perhaps be borne in mind when discussing an expeditionary role for the future Euro-army.)

The answer was so obvious that Lockheed and Boeing actually thought, just this once, that Britain might buy American rather than giving our money to BAe. As we've just seen, British money used to buy the FLA would accrue largely to British firms: to BAe, then, as Airbus UK is nothing more than BAe under another name. The American corporations actually went so far as to place adverts in the British national press, trying to inform the public that there was an alternative. They offered the usual sweeteners, as well: they would place work in Britain, and so forth. (And you can believe as much of that as you like, as with Raytheon and the ASTOR, but remember, defence money is for *defence*, not to support domestic industry; there's another government department for that.)

This produced enough visibility for some sort of covering for the government's back to become necessary if the Euro-plane was to be bought. And its purchase was very, very necessary from a political viewpoint. BAe would probably scale back its operation in Bristol if it was booted out of the FLA; and booted out it would certainly be, in the event that Britain didn't buy any. Well-paid British voters would be fired. Bristol's four MPs – all Labour, including a treasury minister and a cabinet parliamentary secretary – would be livid, and perhaps out of jobs at the next election. The French, Spanish, Turks, Belgians and Germans would be extremely testy, as the planes would then cost even more and there would have to be another lengthy pie-carving negotiation period. Set against all this was nothing more than the chance to gain a terrifically useful military and humanitarian tool. To give just one small example, a British decision in favour of the C-17 in 1998 would probably have saved some hundreds of lives in the wake of the 2004 Asian tsunami disaster. This perhaps puts lost UK jobs into their proper context. Nevertheless, Lockheed and Boeing were very naive to think they had a chance at all.

Sure enough, after a perfunctory competitive-tender process, the mediocre FLA somehow vanquished the hugely more capable C-17 and the much more economical Hercules upgrade. Nobody quite had the gall to keep calling it the Future *Large* Aircraft, however. This is unsurprising, given its puny size compared to real big transports like the C-17 or the ex-Soviet Antonovs which the MoD has often been compelled to charter. The FLA is now known as A400M. Catchy.

Just to round things off, FLA-A400M isn't expected to be with us until 2011 or so. Even if it turns up on time, the UK will be paying at least £100 million per plane: over half the price we pay for a C-17, then, to obtain roughly one third of a C-17's cargo capacity, with much less speed, much less range and not one single advantage. The A400M, if it is on time, will arrive eighteen years after we wanted it and will represent lamentable value for money. About par for the Euro-project course.

This massive delay has enabled a few people at MoD Main Building who remember what their job is to sneak in a few C-17s and Hercules upgrades, despite the Euro–BAe fix. These are characterised as 'temporary measures' pending the arrival of the A400M. In reality, they are vital parts of our future capability, rather more significant than FLA-A400M will be, despite its much greater cost. In the postulated British transport fleet of 2015, the twenty-five new A400Ms will have a maximum lift of 750 tons; the remaining, upgraded twenty-odd Hercules a further 400: and the soon-to-be-five Globemasters 400 more. The A400M, in other words, will provide less than half the future British lift. Unfortunately, total capability will still only be about half again what it is now – and even that totally insufficient increase will be due almost entirely to the 'short-term' procurement of our handful of Globemasters.

It is not merely the A400M that is the problem. The real reason that Britain has no airlift is because we simply don't seem to want any. Serious funds are not available, despite the crying need. Had we sensibly spent all the FLA-A400M money on C-17s instead, we could only have increased the UK fleet to twenty big birds at most. This would have represented a maximum total UK lift of 2,000 tons – still nothing like enough for sizeable deployments by air, although double what we have now. In a dream world we might also have spent our Eurofighter money on C-17s. That would give us over a hundred big lifters, enough to send serious forces anywhere on the planet within days, or to actually provide major humanitarian help, if we chose, rather than a mere token effort. The kind of muscle that our £30 billion-odd defence budget ought to buy us, in fact.

But that's a dream world. The Eurofighter money is mostly already gone, or at any rate the cheques are signed and can't be cancelled. Even if we hadn't already thrown that money away, we will never seriously prioritise airlift because the Service chiefs don't want to.

No, really. The head of the air force doesn't want an RAF full of bloody boring ugly transport planes working to army requirements. The navy would do their damnedest to stop him even if he did, because if sealift becomes less important then so do they. And the army would theoretically very much like some more airlift, but they certainly aren't willing to pay for it. The only way they might do so would be if the planes had ARMY written on them and were flown by soldiers, but of course the the RAF would never permit that.

Brilliant. So we're stuck with the Panamanian merchant fleet.

To be fair, not quite. Mildly embarrassed by our national reliance on rather dubious and unreliable international shipping, the MoD is modernising the Royal Fleet Auxiliary's transport flotilla. This is much cheaper than buying and operating Royal Navy vessels, and merchant seamen and ships can do this sort of work at least as well as the navy can. So far, so good: very cost-effective. It hardly represents much increase in capacity, however.

More cost-effectively still, the MoD is setting up permanent charter arrangements under which it gets first option on certain merchant cargo vessels operated by private shipping firms. This is to ensure that a sudden lack of capacity in the world charter market doesn't completely stymie some urgent future deployment. After all, what's to stop some tinpot dictatorship from chartering all the suitable ships, if they think we're going to invade them? Clever, but again distinctly economy class. There is now a third grade of British fighting sailor apart from navy and RFA, but these chaps, conveniently, won't appear on the civil service payroll at all.

Of course, all this merchant fleet involvement is not a new thing for British maritime strategy. Our merchant marine took the brunt of the casualties at sea in World War II, and the Falklands War couldn't have been fought without it. By 1991, though, British-flagged merchant shipping had pretty much disappeared,* and it was largely foreign-registered vessels which took the Desert Rats' heavy metal to the Gulf – both then and in 2003.

All this does make one sometimes wonder what the actual navy is for. There are two areas in particular where the line between combatant navy sailors and merchant seamen in support roles is far from clear.

Firstly there is the matter of operating aircraft from ships at sea. As we shall see in the next chapter, aircraft are usually the weapon of choice for actual maritime combat. But, more importantly right now, ships are an excellent way to carry aircraft to the theatre of operations and, even better, ships can make good operating bases for air operations overland. This simplifies logistics greatly: the immense amounts of aviation fuel, maintenance facilities and supplies, technicians, kitchens, food, accommodation and all the other paraphernalia required by military aircraft need never go ashore. They need no harbour, no land transport, no men with guns to guard them, and so on. As far as these aircraft are concerned, we need no friendly locals to provide airbases, harbours or anything else. Hurrah. One less headache for our beleaguered, if very numerous, bean counters.

Strangely, though, rather as in the case of airlift, Britain hasn't much capability on these lines. It's almost as if all the spiel about shifting focus to expeditionary warfare and away from the cold war was just waffle, with nothing to back it up. That said, Britain does possess a few vessels which are very useful for this sort of thing. The first three were ordered in the 1970s, designated as 'through-deck cruisers'. This odd name was merely a ploy to get round an insane government ruling of the time that the navy wasn't allowed aircraft carriers. Through-deck cruiser actually

---

* This is because it costs a fair bit to keep a ship up to code under British regulations. Also, shipowners are required to hire vaguely competent crews who will want to be paid some actual money. Why on earth would you do that, when you can operate dangerous rust buckets registered out of God knows where for pennies, and crew them with starving Third World nationals who can be paid with peanuts? Forget about call centres – outsourcing has been going on for a long, long time.

means pocket aircraft carrier. Then as now, the Service chiefs weren't in the habit of slavishly obeying every piffling order they got from their elected masters. The admirals' disobedience in this matter was extremely fortunate, as it was only the Harrier jump-jets aboard these ships which enabled the South Atlantic task force of 1982 to carry out its mission. (No significant land-based air support can reach the isolated Falklands – apart from planes based in Argentina, that is.)

Given the great usefulness of these ships in today's far-flung warfare – though they are small and feeble compared to real aircraft carriers – one would expect them to be a very high priority for the navy; indeed, a high priority for the armed forces jointly, if there were any such thing. These three ships would, one might think, be chock-full of useful aircraft and kept in a high state of readiness. Naturally, no such state of affairs exists.

Of Britain's three little carriers – since the Falklands, it has been officially OK to call them that – one is always laid up in mothballs, lacking a crew or any aircraft. The other two, until very recently, would normally carry a mix of Sea Harrier jump-jet fighters and Sea King or Merlin anti-submarine helicopters.

The trouble with the Sea Harrier is that it is of little use in hot climates. Jet engines lose power in such conditions, and the Harrier at sea is required to land vertically, supported entirely by jet thrust. Since the Falklands it has been upgraded with new, heavier missiles and in hot weather it can no longer land safely without dumping its weapons into the sea beforehand. Thus, routine patrols, the main job of a fighter, become impossibly expensive whenever the ship is anywhere hot – that is to say, nearly anywhere we might be having a spot of bother these days.* The Sea Harrier has duly been marked for the bin, and soon the only regular denizens of our two working carriers will be anti-submarine Sea Kings and Merlins.

These helicopters at least work properly – well, the Sea King

---

* The Sea Harrier's missile upgrade was intended for use against the Soviet Naval Air Forces above the freezing seas of the Iceland-Faeroes Gap, where it would have been perfectly practical. Unfortunately it wasn't actually delivered until 1993. A perfect example of the way Cold War thinking continues to hamstring us even today.

does, anyway; the Merlin no doubt will eventually. The trouble with them is that they aren't a lot of good for anything but hunting submarines. It is remotely possible that we might need to do that, but it is scarcely our carriers' likeliest mission. Whenever there is an actual fight, the anti-submarine chaps have to be hurriedly put ashore and useful aircraft, normally borrowed from the RAF, rushed aboard on an ad hoc basis. These are generally ground-attack Harriers, which don't suffer from the same problems as the Navy's fighter version.

So, only two of our aircraft carriers are actually kept ready to use, and those only get useful aircraft occasionally, when the RAF will lend some. Any sensible navy would have all three carriers up and running, crammed with useful fighters and strike jets. Given that the navy is not sensible and thus has no such planes, a sensible Joint command would insist that all three ships be put to work, and fill them largely with RAF aircraft. Sadly, there is no tri-service organisation with the authority to do that. The defence minister could theoretically make it happen, but he would meet with intense opposition. The navy would hate having the RAF aboard permanently – this would call the existence of the Fleet Air Arm into question. Also, other ships of which the navy is extremely fond might have to be laid up in order to crew the third carrier. Either that, or a few of the navy's many cushy shore postings might have to be axed.*

The RAF types would be even more upset. Life at sea is horrible compared to their usual environment, and there would be mass resignations among their comfortable old ground staff if sea service became too frequent. RAF equipment isn't designed for sea service, either; such operations require a lot of work and cause a lot of wear and tear. Anyway, the RAF barely has enough suitable aircraft for three carriers. One should note that pocket-size carriers like ours cannot operate normal planes, only jump-jets or helos.

Defence ministers with enough will and guts to sort out this sort of mess are not to be found. The taxpayers have been made to pay for three carriers, but they are only ever to have the use of two, for lack of useful aircraft. It isn't as though Britain couldn't

---

* Over half the Royal Navy's uniformed job slots are permanently ashore in the UK, rather than in ships or other deployable units.

afford the planes, either, or even make the Sea Harrier work in hot weather. For goodness' sake, there are scores of Tornado F3s – each at least as expensive as a Harrier, but sadly not usable at sea – also sitting in mothballs! This sort of thing is why one laughs so very hard when people say that the armed services cooperate with one another, or that there is such a beast as defence policy, although really tears would be more appropriate. Britain may not be a superpower, but we're a big enough economy to afford quite powerful armed forces. The only reason we don't have them is that our defences are almost unbelievably badly managed.

Anyway, to get on. Apart from two carriers proper (well, semi-proper) and one in storage, we have one other navy vessel which can support serious amounts of aviation. This is HMS *Ocean*, Britain's one and only helicopter assault ship. *Ocean* is a medium-sized job with a big flat top, strongly resembling a small aircraft carrier like the other three. The main differences are that she has no 'ski-jump' ramp for launching Harriers (and thus cannot operate them, only helicopters) and she has the facilities to carry hundreds of troops as well as her complement of aircraft.

As one might imagine, *Ocean* could fairly be regarded as the navy's single most useful ship. She has hardly stopped running from one crisis to another ever since she was launched; indeed, *Ocean* started work on her initial proving cruise, providing assistance to the victims of Hurricane Mitch in Central America. Since then she has been constantly busy. Interestingly, *Ocean* is quite a cheap ship for the navy to own and run. She was built using commercial techniques rather than the ridiculously expensive methods normally used to build warships, and her naval crew is unusually small for her size. So we'll be getting several more of these in a hurry, then?

I really must stop teasing. For all that *Ocean* is feverishly busy and a brilliant PR asset, the mainstream navy doesn't really like such ships. Who wants to be captain of a floating offshore helipad, watching the marines flying away to do the real work? Nobody, that's who. Besides, if there were more *Ocean*s, they would require more utility helicopters, which the navy hasn't got and isn't really that keen to have. At the moment it can barely scratch up enough tired, rickety old cargo-model Sea Kings for *Ocean*. These will be replaced – one fine day – by the new battlefield-support helicopter, as we saw in Chapter 4. At that point the navy could order loads more, enough to fill several more affordable *Ocean*s, but this is not likely, no more than the RAF is ever likely to acquire a big fleet of heavy transport planes. Just as the RAF would much rather have fast pointy jets, the navy would much rather have lovely sleek frigates and destroyers. Even supposing this sort of stupidity could be overcome, more than a couple of *Ocean*s would probably call for an expansion of the Royal Marines, or for letting the horrible army into the amphibious-assault club, and the navy doesn't much fancy either.

Of course, it is always possible for the navy to pass the distasteful offshore helipad work over to the merchant seamen of the Royal Fleet Auxiliary. They have already done a bit in this line. The Royal Fleet Auxiliary vessel *Argus* is, to all intents and purposes, another helicopter carrier just like the *Ocean*: a commercially built ship with a big flat deck whose main work is operating naval helicopters at sea. If her space below decks were full of marines and her crew all naval rather than partly RFA, she would actually be another *Ocean*. As it is, her designated war role is that of casualty-receiving ship,* and she only acts as a base for marines occasionally. Even so, the line between what is navy work and what is merchant-fleet support is becoming rather blurred. *Argus* does rather resemble a fifth carrier, despite not being in the navy at all. Naval helicopters also operate routinely from other RFA decks, rather more easily and much more economically than they do from navy ones.

The line between proper navy and merchant navy gets fuzzier yet with purpose-built amphibious-warfare ships, of which Britain has a handful. The modern ones have a small harbour built into their back ends, allowing beach-landing craft to offload vehicles and stores even in fairly choppy seas. There is usually a biggish helicopter deck, too, so that things can also be lifted off, but such ships aren't meant to host any helos themselves.

---

* A hospital ship, in other words. But a hospital ship is subject to various forms of international verification and inspection, and can never carry any combatant personnel – unless they are wounded or sick, of course. Inspections would be very annoying, and most of our current enemies would scarcely respect Geneva Convention rules about not attacking hospital ships anyway.

Britain will soon have six of these vessels: four will be cheap RFAs, but the two biggest, for no very explicable reason, are in the navy proper – at much greater cost. The stated reason for this is that these two will be able to carry an amphibious-assault command HQ, with all the associated communications and bigwigs, but there seems no real reason why all this couldn't ride on an RFA hull. Indeed, one would expect a command ship to be kept safer than an ordinary one; surely it is the RFA which should hold back in relative safety, rather than the navy? Perhaps the worry is the rather relaxed attitude of RFA sailors – compared to navy ones, that is – and the likely ill consequences of putting them anywhere near the top brass.

With *Ocean* and say four of the floating-dock ships – we won't be able to count on more than that, especially at short rapid reaction type notice – the navy and RFA together can transport about 2,500 troops and perhaps 400 light vehicles or artillery pieces, plus helicopters. The equipment on these ships will be all that can be moved ashore until we have a harbour. We might also employ one of the two remaining antique *Sir*-class RFA landing vessels, able to carry another few hundred troops and some equipment. These cranky old ships can only reliably disembark heavy kit by beaching themselves, a distinctly risky move, but they're OK for moving things about.* Sounds like a lot, doesn't it?

The problem is, 3 Commando Brigade alone, when mobilised for combat, musters well over 4,000 men – and potentially one woman. (At the time of writing, the first ever female has passed commando training and would thus be eligible to serve with the brigade, though not in one of the infantry formations.) Further shipping from outside the MoD would have to be found merely to transport the amphibious brigade, let alone any follow-on forces. *Argus* could be used, of course, or the one carrier that would be to hand – having only two manned and running means that just one is normally available to fight. However, this would

---

* There is no guarantee that the ship will be able to get off the beach again quickly, which would be particularly unfortunate if the land battle went badly, or – perhaps more likely – if bad weather should occur. A ship beached in big waves will swiftly be wrecked. The aged *Sir*-class vessels would probably crack up on beaching anyway, if anyone actually tried it this late in their careers.

involve having no provision for casualties, or doing without air support – neither really acceptable in an amphibious assault.

So we need to look beyond the navy and RFA merely to move our light amphibious brigade by sea. To carry out so much as a small commando assault on an enemy shore, we will be forced to rely at least partly on purely commercial ships and people. Any larger deployment will be almost entirely dependent on them. This naval willingness to comprehensively outsource quite essential and risky combatant work seems a little odd, especially since it isn't even done consistently. If the RFA can operate four of the floating docks, why not all six? If they can crew the *Argus*, why not the *Ocean*? Why not the carriers, for that matter? Speaking of ships which need to be kept safely out of danger, carriers are probably the ultimate example. Such was certainly the case in the Falklands, for instance.

Naval policy in this area is even more erratic overall. For example, Britain's hydrographic surveying and charting flotilla – a peacetime function if ever there was one – remains firmly in the proper navy. This is curious, given that we at least nominally expect RFA merchant skippers to actually pile their ships onto hostile beaches and certainly to do all kinds of other war work. We also expect other civilian seamen, quite possibly not even British citizens, to hang about not far away, primary targets for enemy attack, their ships loaded to the gunwales with our troops. And yet calm, safe surveying is seen as work for the real navy.

The hydrographic chaps – the 'droggies' as they are known to the rest of the navy – will tell you that they have key roles in naval mine clearance, or in surveying beaches ahead of amphibious assaults, or something dangerous like that. In fact, such jobs are almost always done by other ships and other people. Imagine sending a survey ship into a minefield ahead of the minesweepers. Imagine what the Special Boat Service, setting off to covertly recce and chart an assault beach, would say if you told them to take a bunch of bumbling hydrographers along. There is certainly no call for more than a small cadre of naval hydrographers for dangerous jobs. RFAs or – better – fully outsourced contractors could do the normal charting. What we have actually got, madly, is five sizeable navy ships and a substantial uniformed service community. The droggies are pretty safe, however, despite the fact that various rather more dangerous naval activities have been outsourced.

So, British seaborne logistics, our only real means of reaching round the globe, are distinctly chaotic. We are reliant on commercial shipping, only a little of which is in-house to any real degree. This is the case even for a brigade-strength amphibious assault, let alone any more serious commitment. The whole thing is run on a shoestring; commercial ships and commercial sailors, even when the government is buying, are quite cheap.

Strange, really. The navy could easily have a serious go at amphibious forced entry and general sealift, if it felt like it. One would have thought this to be in hand; naval staff gurus have been chuntering on about 'amphibiosity', 'deployed operations', 'littoral presence'* and 'far-flung power projection' ever since the early 1990s. Odd, then, that they have done so little about it. The last fifteen years have seen little more than a decades-overdue replacement of the inadequate amphibious ships we have had time out of mind, even far back into the cold war when forced entry and distant wars were not, officially, required. (They still happened, though.) What has the Senior Service actually been doing with its money?

We'll take a look at that next.

---

* Lurking off the coast of a war zone.

CHAPTER

8

Warships

It was the sinking Clampherdown
Heaved up her battered side –
And carried a million pounds in steel,
To the cod and the corpse-fed conger-eel,
And the scour of the Channel tide.

It was the crew of the Clampherdown
Stood out to sweep the sea,
On a cruiser won from an ancient foe,
As it was in the days of long ago,
And as it still shall be.

'The Ballad of the "Clampherdown"', Rudyard Kipling

A hundred years ago, in the decades preceding World War I, a revolution in warship design took place. It was led by the reformist First Sea Lord, Admiral Jackie Fisher. Various older types of ship were rendered obsolete by the appearance of the Dreadnought class of all-big-gun battleships. These mighty ships and their successors had tremendously thick armour plating; almost nothing could harm them except shells from the colossal guns of another dreadnought.* The battlewagons that developed from the original Dreadnought design were also some of the fastest things afloat. There was nothing they couldn't catch, and nothing they

---

* Such weapons eventually reached the astonishing calibre of 18 inches, in the Japanese super-battleships of World War II.

couldn't destroy once they'd caught it. A fleet of these ships could only be countered by another such fleet.

The catch, of course, was their enormous cost. In those far-off days, the Royal Navy was supposed to operate on a rather splendid principle called the two-power standard. This meant that the British fleet was to be kept at a size where it would be able to take on and beat the next two biggest navies in the world simultaneously. As the sole superpower of the day, Britain had – just about – been able to afford this. (Lest anybody think that such grandiose notions are gone from today's dull old world, the Pentagon's strategic plans strongly resemble a multi-power standard of sorts. Indeed, by any count of ships, the US Navy today appears to be operating on something not far off a ten-power standard.)

The dreadnought battleships put the two-power standard pretty much out of the window. Britain was hard put to outgun Germany alone, let alone Germany and France combined. Dreadnoughts cost so much that their adoption became a matter of heated national debate, especially as the Royal Navy was far from united in favouring them. Rudyard Kipling, despite having stated that only the navy had a right to an opinion on the subject, weighed in fairly heavily against the dreadnoughts. In 'The Ballad of the "Clampherdown"' he suggests that nimble cruisers would inevitably sink unwieldy dreadnoughts, and that the Royal Navy would find itself preferring captured enemy ships to its own – as it had during the Napoleonic wars. Incalculable sums of money would be wasted, according to Kipling, on 'Clampherdowns', as much as 'a million pounds in steel', if one could imagine so vast a sum.

In the end the tide of public opinion went against him, and against the navy's traditionalists. The slogan of the streets and the newspaper front pages was 'We want eight and we won't wait.' Fisher got his way, and the naval world changed for ever.

The great battleships make a good story, although a rather disappointing one in that they never saw all that much action. They were so valuable, and the results of losing them so potentially disastrous, that nations and admirals tended to be reluctant to risk them in combat. Meanwhile, time marched on, and the mighty dreadnought was rendered obsolete in its turn.

At the turn of the 20th century, then, almost everybody in the country had some idea of the facts regarding the latest warship designs. Big procurements were not merely business-section news-paper stories, reported after the fact, they were front-page head-lines before decisions were made. Best-selling authors were writing polemic verse about them, for goodness' sake. Unsurprisingly, with a debate as open as that, with the country so fully involved, the decision was made in the national interest. The citizens wanted their navy to have the best equipment it could, and the navy's conservatives, clinging grimly to old-fashioned ships and methods as they tend to do, were overruled. When war came and the big-gun fleets clashed, at Jutland in 1916, the Royal Navy held its own. If it hadn't modernised it would have been gutted, and the war would have been lost in an afternoon.

The situation is very different today. Not one British citizen in a hundred has any idea of the facts regarding modern warships. Reforming admirals such as Fisher are nowhere to be found: stick-in-the-mud conservatism is the guiding principle of the navy. Today's admirals are keen to pay lip service to the idea of change – they will happily buy new ships until the MoD is completely broke – but all they really want are shinier versions of what is already in service. They like what they are used to. We can see this from the fact that the Royal Navy's plans for itself have remained essentially the same for the last fifteen years and more, despite the vast and rapid changes that have taken place in the world around it and in the field of combat technology. Much of this period corresponds with my own career as a naval officer. I can tell this story first hand.

I joined the Royal Navy in 1993. The Soviet threat was already yesterday's news, and the echoes of the 1991 war with Iraq were still ringing around the world. In my naivety, I imagined that the navy would respond to the new geopolitical reality. Exciting times, I thought; big changes would be afoot. I was very green, back then.

At that time the defining scenario for everything was still that of a suddenly-hot cold war: a Warsaw Pact attack on the European NATO allies, using conventional weapons – at least initially. This had been fair enough, in the recent past. As late as 1989 the commies still maintained a hugely powerful striking force poised on the Iron Curtain, with five strong Soviet field armies in East Germany alone. (Remember, each field army is made up of several corps. The whole British Army is really no more than a corps in these terms, and it wasn't so very much larger back then. The Red Army was *big*.) The commies' spearhead unit was the ominously named Third Shock Army, composed almost entirely of tanks. One might reasonably entertain a certain scepticism about the purely defensive nature of all this hardware. Third Shock and its many supporting formations outnumbered the rather flimsy NATO opposition in place by a large margin. It was generally felt that in the event of a Soviet attack there were only two ways that we could retain any substantial foothold on the continent. The first was the use of tactical nukes – not seen as ideal, for obvious reasons – and the second was the speedy arrival in Europe of the entire US Army not already there.

Regrettably, the crafty Reds had this latter option covered. In their Arctic naval bases they maintained the Red Banner Northern Fleet, probably the mightiest single submarine force ever seen. These nuclear-powered submarines stood ready to swarm down through the icy seas of the Greenland–Iceland–UK Gap and cut off the sea lanes of the North Atlantic. Soviet Naval Air Forces, SNAF in cold war jargon, were also ready with regiments of long-range Bear bombers to shower heavy anti-shipping missiles from the sky. The US Army was not to make it across the Atlantic. Embattled Europe was not to receive any help.

The Royal Navy's plan in the event of war was to head north into the Gap and there die gloriously, hopefully staving off the waves of commie subs and aircraft long enough for the Americans to get across the pond. The soldiery could then get stuck into each other on a more even basis, and the evil hour when we had to go nuclear would be postponed.

Returning to my younger and pink-cheeked self in the navy of 1993, we had what appeared to be a reasonable fleet for the scenario. There were two pocket-sized aircraft carriers equipped with anti-submarine helicopters to fight the Red Banner submarines and Sea Harrier fighters which would try to hold off the SNAF. There were about fifteen attack submarines to fight their opposite numbers in the Russian fleet, and four nuclear-ICBM subs in case we were losing the game and decided to knock over the table. We had just over twenty frigates, whose primary purpose was again to hunt submarines, and a dozen destroyers: these could also hunt subs a bit, but their particular trick was air defence against the SNAF.

There were some other parts of the navy, less obviously necessary in the putative fight, but which had also carved themselves out niches in the cold war budget and were actually rather useful in real conflicts. We had the Royal Marines, basically a brigade of elite light infantry, and some rusty, cockroach-infested old amphibious shipping, though this was not enough to deliver them anywhere. The marines' ostensible job, in the event of the cold war turning hot, was to defend Norway. To be honest, though, if they hadn't been so useful in the Falklands, Northern Ireland and other real-world conflicts, the marines might well have been closed down and the Norgies left to do the best they could. There were also twenty minehunters. These little ships were supposedly provided in case the pesky Soviets were to mine the waters around north-west Europe, thus preventing our navy from getting to sea and the American reinforcements from reaching port. They had, however, actually seen rather more action in the Arabian Gulf during various spillovers from the Iran–Iraq wars of the 1980s, and then Gulf War I in 1991.

So: two carriers and a spare, just over thirty frigates and destroyers, a dozen or so attack submarines and four nuclear-missile ones, a brigade of marines and a score of minehunters. That was the cold war navy.

But change was afoot. The brass had checked under the bed, found no Reds, and realised that budgets were under threat. 'Amphibiosity' was the watchword now, it seemed; the navy would shift its focus towards 'power projection' in the 'littoral combat zone'. We would appear off the coast of rogue states, ready to launch air strikes, bombard the shore or land troops. No evil dictator would be able to sleep safe.

It sounded good. I went into the mine-warfare part of the navy, as it seemed obvious that the average world villain would find mines his best (or only) naval weapon. The Iraqis had heavily mined the northern Gulf in 1990 after they took Kuwait, and these mines had subsequently knocked out two major US warships – a pretty good score for a navy their size – and in the meantime there were still around half a million World War I and II mines left in British waters, which added a bit of zing to peacetime training. I didn't see much future in becoming a sub-hunter, that was for sure.

Ten years went by, and gradually it became clearer and clearer that the buzz words were not going to translate into any actual change. As the new millennium dawned, the plan for the Royal Navy of 2015 firmed up. We would have: two aircraft carriers, bigger than the current ones but still not able to operate normal jet aircraft; twenty frigates and a dozen destroyers; ten or so attack submarines and four nuclear-missile ones; a brigade of marines, with still-inadequate amphibious shipping, and twenty or so minehunters.

In other words, exactly the same navy I had joined at the beginning of the 1990s. There was to be no substantial change to the order of battle at all. It seemed like a rather startling coincidence that the mix of forces which had been judged the right one for the cold war also turned out to be just the ticket for the 21st century.

Meanwhile, on a more personal level, I had gone about as far as I could in the mine-clearing part of the navy. I had done every officer job aboard a minehunter except the captain's, and also been in charge of a team of mine-clearance divers. Unfortunately, such a career does not make one a contender to command a mine-hunter in the Royal Navy; indeed, no mine-warfare experience at all is necessary. What *is* required in a minehunter captain, oddly, is several years as a frigate/destroyer specialist. Just as it was the gunnery men who ruled the roost in Fisher's big-gun navy, frigate/destroyer officers run things in today's frigate-centric navy. It took World War II to get rid of the gunners. Nothing which might break the iron grip of the frigate and destroyer mafia is on the horizon at the moment.

The reason for this curious method of selecting minewarfare captains is that the minehunters need friends at the top. They would all quite likely have been got rid of long ago in favour of more frigates if frigate and destroyer men had no chance of a minehunter command. This is not so much the case with the other minority naval communities. Naval air squadrons are commanded by aviators, submarines by submariners, commandos by marines.

But the Fleet Air Arm has a two-star admiral to speak for it and so do the submariners, while the marines have their equivalent commandant-general. All these very senior officers spent their youth in the relevant branch of service and will struggle tooth and nail to preserve it, though the aviator admiral seems to be rather on the back foot at the moment. The minehunters have only a measly captain RN – equivalent to an army colonel – in charge of them, and he is often an outsider; he may not even care if they are all scrapped tomorrow. However, the policy of handing out minehunter commands as plums to high-flying officers early in their careers keeps the little ships fairly popular and ensures that a few admirals remember them fondly. This is probably a major reason for their survival, which is a good thing. Come a war, minehunters are almost always essential.

The navy would not admit for a second that this is what happens. The process is characterised instead as a way of training up relatively junior officers in command skills so that they will later make good senior officers. One does rather wonder what these senior officers might then do which is even half as important as the efficient functioning of the minehunter which was used to train them up. Only a small percentage of the RN's swarming senior officers command units of any sort, and only a few of those few are in charge of anything as relevant as a minehunter.

What is undeniable is the unfortunate side effect – that Royal Navy minehunter captains only rarely have any idea what they're doing. Fortunately, they are provided with trained officers to do it for them, so it isn't the end of the world, but it is usually difficult for the captain to provide any useful input. People often complain that minehunting operations make slow progress – that it takes a long time to clear a path through a minefield at sea. It took several days to open up the approaches to Umm Qasr recently, for example. I would submit that a fairly simple change to the way we select minehunter captains could yield some excellent results here, although that in turn might lead to the ships themselves disappearing even faster than they are doing at the moment.

Anyway, all that to one side, from my point of view it was pretty clear that I had nowhere to go but into the frigate/destroyer flotilla. To be fair, the navy had always made it very clear that it had no use for officers who were not at some stage prepared to make this move. It may happen early in one's career, or in a few cases, such as submariners, later on; but happen it will. Clearly, for me, the day had come. I decided to take a serious look at these ships, the supposed backbone of the navy's combat power and the backbone in all sober truth of its career structure. I had just spent ten years doing necessary work with equipment that could achieve the job; would that still be true aboard a frigate or a destroyer? (Not to spoil the surprise or anything, but here I am a civilian; so you can probably guess my answer. However, let me explain.)

Frigates and destroyers are collectively known as escorts; this is because their stated purpose in life is to accompany other ships and protect them from certain threats. These threats are generally broken down into three: the air threat, from things in the sky; the surface threat, from hostile ships; and the submarine threat. In fact, statistically our ships have generally been much more threatened by mines than any of these, but at least minefields don't follow you around, so you don't need an escort against them.

So, I thought, let's take these threats one by one.

Primus inter pares in the Royal Navy, even today, is the field of anti-submarine warfare (ASW). Until 1990 or so, this was fair enough. From the 1940s to the end of the cold war, the Royal Navy very reasonably expected to fight a terrible battle against enemy submarines, possibly for the very survival of the nation. Today, though, fifteen years on, the RN's continued obsession with hunting submarines is really starting to look odd. The Soviet Union has collapsed; the swarms of nuclear-powered and often nuclear-armed subs that used to lurk north-east of Iceland are rusting quietly in their bases. The submarine threat has, essentially, disappeared. How odd, then, that nearly all the new naval ships and aircraft delivered in the last decade have had ASW as their primary purpose. It's almost as though the navy and the defence procurement process had very little ability to respond to outside events.

The many anti-submarine specialists of the Royal Navy would disagree, naturally, as the moment we de-emphasise the submarine threat their careers are finished. They like to point up the subs possessed by a few of our potential rogue-nation adversaries. Iran, for example – just to pluck a name from the air – possesses three Russian-built diesel boats. Just a few such submarines, according to the ASW lobby, could suffice to deny us the use of the seas anywhere near our adversaries in any future conflict. This is quite a comedown from the Red Banner Northern Fleet. If twenty frigates was enough for those chaps, we can't need more than one or two for the Iranians. Not so, say the ASW lads.

If all this submarine-threat hyperbole were true, it would be serious news indeed for Britain and the other Western powers, and possibly the world in general. It would mean that the mighty industrial democracies could be easily prevented from deploying or sustaining military forces by any third-rate evil regime that felt like purchasing a few submarines. As we saw in the last chapter, the armies of the West still move almost entirely by sea.

However, this is fantasy. Even the most ardent anti-submarine specialist would admit that we're no longer talking about scores of nuclear submarines, as in the old days. We would be facing half a dozen subs at most, and – critically – these would have diesel engines, not nuclear reactors. They would, in fact, be rather similar to the German U-boats of World War II.

This is a very important difference, because a diesel submarine has to run on batteries whenever it is submerged. It cannot travel far like this, nor can it move at any speed, except for a single very short burst which it needs to save for getting away after making an attack. It is, in fact, more accurate to describe such vessels as very slow submersible torpedo boats than as submarines. This lack of submerged speed or range, back in the 1940s, meant that the U-boats had to run on the surface to get near Allied convoys. They very often launched their torpedoes while still on the surface, only diving once convoy escorts bent on retribution came near. The appearance of Allied radar and aircraft in the Atlantic made all this time on the surface very dangerous, even at night, and in the end most of the German submariners never came home. This is why serious modern navies employ nuclear-powered subs, despite the shocking expense and bureaucracy involved, and the constant safety panics: nuclear submarines can actually operate usefully under water. The diesel submariner may, it is true, recharge his batteries by extending a snorkel tube to the surface, allowing him to run his diesels while submerged. However, such a snorkel is quite easily detected by modern sensors and it restricts submerged speed to a crawl, so the method is of limited use.

And it gets worse for our rogue-state submarine driver: no end to his problems. Modern merchant shipping can travel twice or three times as fast as the convoys of World War II. (Even merchant ships are nowadays diesel-powered Motor Vessels. In 1940 that was quite advanced maritime technology, only used in specialist warship designs; freighters were simple Steam Ships, back then. Much slower.) More than ever, the submarine skipper has to be able to move fast and far to intercept his targets; he must run on the surface, unless he is nuclear powered. But aircraft with dedicated search radar can sweep vast stretches of ocean, day or night, and even standard anti-submarine helicopters have quite a bit of capability in this line. If we have either protecting our ships, the rogue-state diesel submariner will be forced underwater before he can get near, and thus left far behind.

So much for small numbers of enemy submarines causing havoc in our supply lines: a few aircraft will see them off, in the event that they can even find our convoys in the first place. The U-boats had to work with long-range reconnaissance aircraft in order to do so, something we could probably prevent. A Royal Fleet Auxiliary vessel makes an excellent base for anti-submarine helos, and it has long been common practice to use them in this way. Our RFAs will be shuttling back and forth to the war zone in any case; we need merely place the chartered merchant vessels in convoy with them, embark a few ASW helicopters, and what few enemy submarines may exist will be out of luck. The need for frigates to protect our supply lines – their main justification, nowadays – seems not to exist.

The slender potential of enemy diesel-sub forces was illustrated rather well in 1982. During the Falklands conflict the Argentines sent their four submarines to sea with a view to stopping our fleet approaching the islands – just such a scenario as the ASW boys nowadays like to spin. One of these boats was caught on the surface by our helicopters and badly damaged; it was later captured. Not a sign was ever seen of the other three – they certainly achieved nothing useful. In due course they trailed home with their tails between their legs, in sharp contrast to the tenacious and deadly Argentine aviators. At no time was any British frigate or destroyer in contact with an enemy sub, despite the huge anti-submarine circus which took place – rumour has it that quite a number of hapless whales were blown away by jumpy ASW operators.

It seems most unlikely that any possible rogue-state submarine flotilla would do better. In fact, the typical Third World navy is unlikely to be even this capable. At least the Argentines got all their boats out to sea; not many analysts think that Iran's submarine force could manage as much.

Of course, if you strain hard enough, there *are* various unlikely scenarios where one can imagine being worried by a Third World submarine force. (This is also true of invasion from space.) Perhaps in narrow straits or close inshore, well-handled enemy subs could manage to sneak into the vicinity of our ships, or there might be a few boats lurking submerged by luck in the very waters we wish to enter. Or, new types of conventional power technology *may* produce a much more capable non-nuclear submarine. Or let's go crazy and say that we're fighting the Chinese, who possess a few nuclear boats – and intercontinental nuclear missiles, so let's not really do that. Even if any of these unlikely things should come to pass, however, there would seem little point in using escort ships to solve the problem. Let's consider the case of a Type 23 frigate, our most modern anti-submarine ship, trying to find and attack a submarine.

The Type 23 can only find a quiet submerged boat, conventional or nuclear, by using active sonar: by 'pinging' sound pulses into the sea and detecting the echoes from the sub. (In case you are wondering, radar doesn't work underwater.) In order to listen for the echoes, the ship must be moving slowly, making itself an easy target. Worse, the pinging gives away the ship's position to the submarine well before it reveals the submarine to the ship. The enormous sums spent on making the Type 23 too quiet for submarines to hear are completely wasted. Despite it being our latest ship, having been supplied since the end of the cold war, it was designed in the 1970s to fight older types of Soviet nuclear sub. These were noisy and could be found without pinging, by simply listening: hence the expensive silencing. However, the Soviets' 1980s submarines were too quiet to be heard, so the central concept of the Type 23 was obsolete at that point, before the frigates were even built. The Type 23 became doubly obsolete with the disappearance of the Soviet threat in 1990 or so, just as the first ship joined the fleet. Why did we keep on buying Type 23s through the 1990s? Good question.

In the absence of helicopters or surveillance planes helping the frigate, the submariner will almost certainly be able to torpedo it before he is detected. So, the frigate is essentially at the submarine's mercy. Even if by some miracle our Type 23 manages to find a submarine without being sunk, the frigate will only be able to attack by sending its helicopter to drop a homing torpedo. Depth charges are old hat nowadays; they were used back in the world wars because they were the only thing available, but they basically didn't work. You have to be incredibly lucky to get explosives anywhere near a sub at depth by simply dropping them into the sea, as one did with depth charges. This didn't matter back then, as once the World War II submariner had been driven below periscope depth he could no longer launch torpedoes, and he would soon be left behind by the convoy.

The thing is, if a helicopter is a specialist anti-submarine job, it can actually find submarines on its own, as well as torpedo them. It doesn't need the frigate at all, and it becomes hard to see the point of having the frigate there, except as a helicopter pad. And, as we know, RFAs make better and cheaper helicopter pads. They can also do other useful things – unlike a frigate.

Anti-submarine helicopters have existed since before the Type 23 was even designed. One might ask why it ever got built. The answer is that the navy always starts with the idea of having frigates and destroyers, and only then considers what they might do. Both types of ship have had well over a hundred years of Royal Navy existence, during which they have changed jobs and designs several times. Like the RAF with its Tornado bomber, the navy was not serious about fighting the commies when it ordered the Type 23; it just wanted some frigates. A Tory defence minister of long ago, one John Nott, was wise to this. He attempted to limit the Type 23 to being a cheap helicopter pad with a listening sonar and nothing else, since that was what the navy had said it was for. He also planned to pretty much eliminate the useful navy as well, however: carriers, marines, minehunters and all. His agenda was to save money, not to stop the idiotic Type 23. After the navy's South Atlantic triumph in 1982 he was discredited and forced out of office. This saved the useful navy, but it also, regrettably, allowed the frigate mafia to turn the Type 23 into their idea of a proper warship, and to buy loads of them.

The utter uselessness of the Type 23 frigate in its only real role has – finally, at least twenty years after it was obvious – been noticed. From 2006 we will commence fitting six of these ships with a new pinging sonar (Sonar 2087) that may actually work to some degree, perhaps even allowing the frigate to detect a submarine before the sub sinks it. Even if this new kit works as advertised it will still reveal the frigate's presence and location to the sub before the sub is detected; it will still render the Type 23's expensive silencing completely useless; and there will still be lots of other pointless frigates without any useful capability at all except their helicopter pad. And, of course, the actual sorting out of the subs – in the unlikely event there are any to be found – will still have to be done by helicopter, so there will still be no good reason to risk frigates on this work. Sonar 2087 will cost nearly £30 million per frigate, and we will – at last – have got these absurd white elephants ready for the 1980s. The theme of throwing good money after bad is a common one in defence procurement.

So, the way to fight submarines is to stay well away from the dangerous brutes and let aircraft do it. Admittedly, each frigate or destroyer does carry a helicopter for just this purpose, but there are much cheaper and more flexible ways of getting these aircraft to sea. And sometimes the best way of all to hunt enemy submarines, better than using aircraft even, is to send in a nuclear-powered attack submarine of one's own. A diesel sub versus a modern nuclear-powered attack boat has the same chance as a pilchard does against a shark.

To sum up, then: the submarine threat has almost entirely disappeared. Even if it hadn't, escorts would be a very bad way of dealing with it. This has been true ever since effective ASW helos appeared in the 1970s. Aircraft and our own submarines would do a much, much better job. So why is the future Royal Navy to have twenty-five or thirty escorts, but only ten attack submarines and just two aircraft carriers? Carriers and nuclear-powered submarines are more expensive than frigates, but frigates aren't cheap. And some carriers, of the helicopters-only HMS *Ocean* and RFA *Argus* type, are just as cheap as – if not cheaper than – a frigate. They can perfectly well carry swarms of ASW choppers should the need arise, or cargo/utility jobs and marines in normal times.

As you may have gathered, it seemed pretty clear to me that going into frigates as an ASW practitioner was going to be a waste of my time and the taxpayers' money. (It was far too late for me to become a helicopter pilot.) I couldn't face spending the active part of my remaining career practising to defend the fleet against submarines that wouldn't be there, using equipment that couldn't stop them even if they did turn up. But cheer up, I told myself; the submarine threat is not the only one. Indeed, the others are rather more credible. Perhaps all is not lost. The chance to do something useful in my remaining naval career may still be there.

Our potential enemies often have some surface warships. These are much more common than submarines, in fact, being easier to operate and much easier to buy. Small, fast corvettes and attack craft are particular favourites. These will be armed with ship-killing, sea-skimming missiles such as the well-known Exocet, if obtainable, or possibly lighter stuff. Even a speedboat with soldiers aboard carrying shoulder-fired rockets can be disproportionately effective. Or, of course, a suicide vessel full of home-made explosives, as demonstrated upon the US destroyer *Cole* in 2001. The second stated role of frigates and destroyers is to defend our fleets and convoys from these attacks. This is Anti-Surface Warfare, or ASuW.

Again, however, we find that there are better ways of doing the job than using frigates and destroyers. Aircraft are the best way of dealing with surface targets: the attacking vessel is easily found from afar using airborne radar, and then it can be destroyed using missiles, or even simpler weapons if it has no anti-aircraft defences.

To give an example, the Iraqi surface navy, made up of attack craft, was largely wiped out in 1991 by Royal Navy missile-firing

helicopters shortly after leaving harbour. Like anti-submarine helicopters, these aircraft can be based on any ship, including RFAs;
pity the enemy fast-attack vessel which tangles with a few missile-
armed helos. The army's new Apaches could also be pressed into
service in this role, equipped as they are with long-ranging missiles.
Better still are strike jets, but they require land bases or aircraft
carriers. A big deck full of jets, or even a small RFA deck full of
helos, once again offers far more capability and flexibility than
a squadron of frigates.

But perhaps you can't use aircraft; maybe you don't have air
superiority*, or maybe none of your aircraft can reach the enemy
ships. In this case, submarines are an excellent answer. The sinking
of the *General Belgrano* in 1982 scotched the surface threat
against the Falklands task force once and for all; the Argentine
surface navy, sensibly, did not put to sea again.

If you don't have any aircraft at all, or submarines, the enemy
attack vessels may get through to your ships. In this case, you
will be forced to rely on escorts to detect the enemy and destroy
them before the attack can get home, and sadly you may well be
disappointed. It will be largely a toss-up between escorts and
attack craft as to who sinks whom, in the absence of any aircraft.
Even if the escort wins, it has only sunk a small, cheap vessel;
the enemy can afford several missile-attack craft for the price of
a frigate, and at least a dozen for the price of a destroyer. One
will get lucky sooner or later.

Attackers without missiles are much easier to deal with.
However, such boats are so cheap that you could sink them all
day and they might keep coming, and some of them are devilishly difficult to detect. If just one gets to close range it is quite
capable of crippling a warship worth hundreds of millions of
pounds, or the ships the warship is supposed to be protecting.
This goes double if it is crewed by a suicide party. And the situation gets worse if our ships are operating inshore; here there is
less time to see and destroy the attacker. Once again, the only
really useful thing that the escort warship brings to the party is
its helicopter. It appears that anti-surface warfare, like anti-
submarine warfare, is a pretty poor reason for having frigates

---

* Although in that case you're going to get creamed, as we found out in 1982.

and destroyers. Or the officers they carry, sadly for my naval career.

Drat. So what else can the escort warship do?

Well, there is another way for the evil dictator or military junta to attack our fleet: we have arrived at the air threat. The best has been saved for last. As may already be apparent, aircraft are the best way to sink ships. Quite apart from maritime combat, strike aircraft are always a better buy than either ships or submarines for evil dictators and military juntas. This is because they can be used for everyday business such as dealing with the domestic opposition, as well as the fairly unusual task (they hope) of driving off the forces of Western democracy. So the average opposition is going to possess some attack aircraft. Some may be capable of firing Exocet-type ship-killing missiles, but simple bombs and guns can be quite troublesome enough. Our fleet needs to defend itself from these various flying engines of death. No doubt the frigates and destroyers have a role here?

Well, we'll see.

According to conventional naval wisdom, the way to effectively defend a group of ships from air attack is a triple-layered defence. The outer layer should consist of fighter jets, which will hopefully intercept and shoot down the incoming enemy strike missions. Fighters require an aircraft carrier, at the very least a half-arsed jump-jet carrier like ours, though a proper conventional-jet-capable ship is better. The planes can also be based ashore, but relying on shore-based planes is risky. It is a sad fact that the Royal Air Force has not possessed a decent air-to-air fighter for many years now, as we saw in Chapter 5. The Eurofighter is finally approaching squadron service, but despite its astronomical expense, it has a few shortcomings. One of these is that, lacking range, it will have great difficulty covering a fleet at sea. Anyway, even if we had some useful land-based fighters, there may not be any available land bases – as was the case in the Falklands. There is also, from the naval point of view, a motivational issue with land-based aviators: they will no doubt have a decent stab at defending a fleet at sea, but they probably won't try as hard as pilots who need the ships to land on when they run out of fuel. As for carrier fighters, all we have is the Sea Harrier, and as we saw in the last chapter, that isn't likely to be of much use. Essentially, then, we don't have a fleet fighter screen; haven't had for years.

The brass would say that they have this covered. The F-35, now under development, will offer a pretty decent fighter capability. This plane will be able to fly from the future carriers, if they ever turn up, as it is to be available in a jump-jet version like the Harrier, but it won't suffer from the Harrier's problems – probably. So the fleet will be without a fighter screen for only a short further period. Well, another seven years at an absolute minimum: most likely much longer.

There is a further point here: to be effective, fighters need to be directed by a controller who can see the hostiles, using a powerful air-search radar. The controller may be aboard a destroyer, which has such a radar, but this isn't really good enough. If the enemy pilots know their business, they will be flying low on their run in, and a radar mounted in a ship will not be able to see them until they appear above the horizon. By then it will too late for fighters to intercept.

The correct solution is to put the search radar in a high-flying aircraft, where it can see the attack coming from far away. This method also avoids broadcasting the location of your fleet – a long-range radar acts as a massive radio beacon to the enemy. With a flying scanner, only the radar aircraft's location is revealed, rather than that of your ships. The Royal Navy has an improvised solution here: its airborne search radar is mounted in a helicopter, which can achieve medium altitudes and worthwhile performance, and is able to fly from our teeny carriers. This was rushed into service as an emergency measure in 1982, arriving just too late for the Falklands conflict – which cost us dearly. If these helicopters had been around during the fighting, Britain would most likely not have lost a single ship and our casualties would have been a fraction of what they were.

We will probably still have to use helicopter-borne radar with the new carriers, as they won't be able to operate conventional planes. I say probably, as this essential capability is very much on the back-burner at the moment. The navy isn't even sure about the carriers themselves, so it certainly isn't going to bestir itself to sort out seagoing radar aircraft in any definitive way. Why don't we get proper carriers? Then we wouldn't need to struggle with tricky jump-jet designs and inefficient radar helicopters. In essence, we aren't getting proper carriers because we feel we can't afford to, just as we also feel we can't afford proper amphibious shipping, or new Jungly helicopters. The navy can't afford these things, bottom line, because it insists on having ridiculously large numbers of escort warships.

So, frigates and destroyers have nothing to contribute to the fighter screen. But some enemy planes or missiles may get through this, the more so as there is no fighter screen at the moment and there may not be one for some time.

The next layer of defence, according to the navy recipe book, should be provided by long-range ship-to-air missiles that can shoot down any surviving attackers before they get close, or at least shoot down the ship-killer missiles they may now have fired at us. Escort ships which have these heavyweight anti-air missile systems are called destroyers, distinguishing them from frigates which do not. These systems are very expensive – hence, so are destroyers. In the Royal Navy we have the Type 42 destroyer and its Sea Dart missiles.

At last, you may be thinking, a job that needs doing, and one of these pesky escort ships can actually do it. There's a worthwhile job for a naval officer!

Regrettably, the Type 42 and the Sea Dart are very old indeed, almost museum pieces. The original missile-system designs date from the 1950s, and they were intended to deal with the Soviet Naval Air Forces of that day. Those old-time commies, sportsmen that they were, could be relied upon to fly in high, broadcasting their presence, and launch massive long-range missiles on high trajectories. They could be detected by a ship while still far away, owing to being so high up in the sky. By the time of the Falklands War, thirty years later, the state of the art had moved on a bit. The ship-killer missile was now fired by an attacker who had flown in low, hiding from his prey's radars below the horizon. He could pop up, launch his missiles, drop down into hiding again and run away like the dickens. Argentine Super-Etendard jets armed with Exocet missiles, able to deliver just such an attack, were a terrible threat to the Task Force in 1982. Radars at surface level, in a destroyer for example, cannot detect such attacks until they are far too close to do anything about them.

The only answer to the Exocet threat was to place destroyers between the main fleet and the enemy, turn their radars on to make them obvious targets, and hope that they would be hit, rather than the vital carriers and troopships. This didn't always work, despite the loss of the destroyer *Sheffield* while doing this job. The *Atlantic Conveyor*, a chartered merchant vessel carrying important stores and equipment, was sunk by an Exocet strike which came from an unexpected direction (fiendishly cunning, those Argies). The loss of her cargo severely handicapped our troops ashore, and another such sinking would probably have finished the campaign altogether. Fortunately, the Argentines ran out of Exocets.

Worse yet, it wasn't even necessary to use sea-skimming missiles to defeat the Type 42. A low-flying jet armed with simple bombs and guns could bounce over the horizon and be chopping up our ships well before a Sea Dart could be launched. Once again, the only tactic possible was to use our frigates and destroyers as sacrificial shields, at a grim cost in men and ships. Four RN escorts were sunk during the Falklands War, all by Argentine air attack, and many more damaged. Among the ships which never came back was the frigate *Ardent*, captained by an officer named Alan West. He survived, and is now Admiral Sir Alan, first sea lord – the head of the navy. Despite the great bravery of the escort crews, strikes got through: most famously in the case of the *Sir Galahad*, an RFA landing ship hit while unloading at Bluff Cove. The Welsh Guards, who were in the process of disembarking, took a severe mauling. British losses would have been much worse, probably catastrophically worse, if not for the fact that most Argentine bombs failed to go off.

So, even in 1982, the then-quite-new Type 42 destroyer was so obsolete as to be pretty much useless. Sea Dart missiles from 42s did shoot down a number of targets (notably a British army helicopter). However, *none* of the Sea Dart's victims was a missile, only one was a low-flying fast jet, and the jet in question was not coming at the destroyer which shot it down – luckily for the destroyer, or it probably wouldn't have survived long enough to get its shot off. The shoddiness of the 42 was evidently well known at the time, as we had already sold several of these ships to Argentina!

Depressingly, almost a quarter-century later, the 42 is still with us. Its replacement, the Type 45, is finally on the way. The first Type 45 should be with the fleet in 2007. Much of the endless delay in replacing the abject 42 was due to the navy's insistence on continuing to purchase useless Type 23 frigates beyond all sense or reason, right into the 21st century. The destroyer replacements were also slowed down by the existence of – you guessed it – a European cooperative project, called various things in its time but perhaps best known as the Common New Generation Frigate, or CNGF. This eventually came apart in the late 1990s, at some little cost to the various taxpayers, and Britain is now proceeding alone with the Type 45. Provided it works as advertised, the navy will finally have some proper AA missile capability.

However, that's a big proviso. The essential problem which prevents the old Type 42 from working effectively is simply the curvature of the earth, not a matter of technology. Sea-skimming ship-killer missiles – or attack jets, for that matter – can fly within metres of the wave tops and will not be seen by a radar mounted in a ship until they are well inside twenty miles. The whole design of the new Type 45 has been devoted to getting its fire-control radar as high above the sea as possible, in order to see further, but even so it is only thirty metres up. Such a radar is a heavy object, and putting a heavy object high up in a ship tends to make it capsize.

Assuming a missile flying low above the waves at 600 mph, the Type 45's Sampson radar will detect the sea-skimmer a little over a minute before it hits the ship. The ship-killers of the future may be supersonic, in which case there would be even less warning than this, just a few tens of seconds.* An Aster counter-missile must then be automatically launched and achieve hypersonic speed incredibly fast – we will need to routinely switch human operators out of the loop, which will probably lead to some nasty

---

* The good old commies were kind enough to build just such a weapon, the Moskit (Mosquito), NATO code name SUNBURN. This is now apparently available for export sale, at least in ship-launched versions, and is said to be in Chinese and Indian hands already. It would certainly be a much more intelligent buy for those fearing Western intervention than diesel submarines, especially if fitted in aircraft or shore-based launchers.

mistakes, but you do what you've got to. The Aster must then make a head-on interception, with both missiles moving at several times the speed of sound – the most difficult manoeuvre one can easily think of – and pulverise its target thoroughly enough for nothing to smash into its parent ship. There will be no time for a second try. It must be one Vampire*, one kill, every single time; or we lose a ship.

What will probably happen in reality is that at least two Asters will need to be fired against each ship-killer, so as to be reasonably sure of nailing it. Unfortunately the destroyer can only control a certain number of Asters in flight at once. ('More than ten', says the MoD, coyly. Not more than twenty, then.) It is therefore feasible, perhaps, to overload the computer with a massed simultaneous attack, much though this is supposed to be impossible. One also notes that each ship only has forty-eight Asters aboard: and these are of two types, one of which can't be used against sea-skimmers, being intended for targets further off and higher up. Let's suppose, for the sake of argument, that the ship is carrying only twenty-four of the short-range speedy Asters (as seems reasonable) and that nervous air-defence officers choose to launch three against each incoming ship-killer (also very reasonable). The Type 45 will then be able to shoot down only eight sea-skimmers before its silos are empty. Any enemy who can muster, say, twenty of these weapons has to be in with an excellent chance of eviscerating our future fleet, if it has nothing more than Type 45 destroyers to defend it.

That's speculation. What is stone cold certain is that all this surface-based hypersonic counter-missile business adds up to a very, very difficult technical challenge. The makers of the Sampson–Aster combo (aka the Principal Anti-Air Missile System, or PAAMS) reckon they're up to the job. PAAMS is a surviving piece of the ill-fated CNGF Euro-frigate and is itself a joint venture between the UK, Italy and France. Given the unimpressive tales of the Merlin (UK–Italy) and Storm Shadow (UK–France), one might be pardoned for a certain scepticism as to the likely timeliness,

---

* Vampire is the NATO brevity code word for the phrase 'hostile anti-ship missile', which would be a bit of a mouthful for use on a radio circuit during an air attack.

economy or even ultimate success of this project.* Still, if you throw enough money at a problem, you can generally solve it after a fashion, in the end.

And my word, we're throwing some money at this one. The Type 45 will be extremely expensive; the cost has now reached *a billion pounds for each ship*. They could call the first one Clampherdown, if we changed the wording of the poem slightly. Actually, she is to be named *Daring*, but it'll still be a billion pounds gone each time we lose one, rather than a million as in Kipling's day. That's the same price as four or five new aircraft carriers, for just six destroyers, and this is where the idiocy of the whole thing starts to become clear.

Destroyers are the most technically difficult, most expensive possible way one can imagine of defending against air attack. The lesson of the Falklands was not that we need better destroyers; it was that destroyers don't work, not cost-effectively anyway. No matter how high up a ship's mast you put an air-defence radar, it won't be very high; you'll always need a computer which is incredibly quick on the trigger to even get a shot off, and then you still have to make a head-on kill against a tiny, speedy target. Every time without fail, remember, or it's a *billion* pounds in steel, lost to the scour of the tide, and a couple of hundred British sailors dead. And the next strikes fly through to carve up our troopships or whatever.

Why on earth would you do it that way, unless you had a mad passion for destroyers? (A-ha! Light begins to dawn.) Why not put the radar up in the sky, where it should be? Where it can detect the enemy missiles – or the plane or ship carrying them – hundreds of miles away, rather than a measly dozen or so? Then you have ample time to destroy the missiles in job lots, before they are even launched. If you can't do this, you can certainly shoot the Vampires down from behind using fighters, a relatively easy feat compared to a split-second head-on kill – any capable

---

* The more so as the British ships at least are to run Microsoft software – another bizarre decision. It's risky enough depending on Windows to preserve important documents; I certainly wouldn't choose to trust it with my life. That said, I find my Windows PC a model of reliability compared to any of the several combat computer systems I encountered in the RN of the 1990s; so the navy will probably prove to be an easy customer to please, as ever.

modern air-to-air missile can manage this already. No need for a miracle radar, Wyatt Earp-style computer and hypersonic wonder-missiles; no need for billion-pound, one-trick ships. Just a regular radar aircraft, communicating with some nice off-the-shelf jets and missiles, flying from a proper carrier. All of which pieces of kit can do many other things for you as well, not just this one job.* What could be more flexible, more 'network-enabled', more 'any sensor, any shooter' than that? (These are fashionable procurement buzz phrases at present. As usual, they are not translating into real action of any sort.)

The Royal Navy, however, run by former frigate and destroyer captains, would rather shoot things down the difficult, expensive way – with destroyers. The die is cast: the Type 45 contracts have been let. (You'll never guess who got this extremely lucrative job. Well, perhaps you will, by now: BAe, of course.) By comparison, the navy is not nearly as solidly behind the future carriers. These far more useful ships have been under constant threat of cancellation, and seem unlikely to get a proper airborne-radar aircraft for the foreseeable future even when (if) they arrive. It is even far from clear whether the F-35 – the plane which the new carriers are intended to operate – can be made to work as a jump-jet at all.

Probably another reason the RN is dragging its feet on the new carriers is that it believes it has lost control of their aircraft. Even if all turns out well none of the jets will have NAVY written on them. Rather, they will be operated in line with the present Joint Force Harrier organisation, in which the navy and air force jump-jet squadrons have been combined and placed under RAF management. The head of the Fleet Air Arm was initially moved to a position high in the RAF's structure as part of this move, which helped to sell the scheme to the navy. A couple of years later, however, a further RAF reshuffle squeezed the admiral out, leaving the navy's Harriers firmly under air force ownership – a masterly

---

* Even the present improvised helicopter-borne flying radar turns out to be marvellously adaptable. Search-radar Sea Kings flying from our present teeny carriers were able to detect Iraqi armour leaving Basra in 2003 and sic other ship-based helicopters onto it. Over fifty tanks and infantry vehicles were knocked out. This is almost a pocket JSTARS capability (see Chapter 6); destroyers will never have this sort of all-round usefulness.

bit of bureaucratic footwork by the air force. With the Jungly helicopters also having been placed in other hands, Naval Air Command is now a pale shadow of what it once was – especially as the Junglies and Harriers were far and away the naval aircraft most likely to see actual combat.

Joint Force Harrier is a new thing and it remains to be seen how things turn out. Navy diehards see it as the first move in the RAF's renewed campaign to swallow up the Fleet Air Arm, with presumably dire results as in the 1930s (see Chapter 4). It is always possible, though, that the reinforced Harrier ethos will acquire more influence over the rest of the RAF and make them rougher and tougher. RAF Harrier squadrons are very much the lean, mean part of the air force, sometimes living under canvas close to the ground fighting rather than in comfortable messes or plush hotels. Service in carriers is similarly seen as arduous by the RAF, incredible though this seems to those of us who spent our time at sea in much smaller ships.

Frankly, provided the carrier squadrons spend enough time at sea to know what they're doing, it really doesn't matter to most taxpayers whether their uniforms are dark blue or light blue, or pink for that matter. But it matters bigtime to the navy. Why spend serious money on ships which will effectively be no more than occasional bases for an RAF organisation? A carrier shorn of navy flight personnel really is, visibly, nothing more than another specialist fleet auxiliary vessel, taking the air force's kit to war as others do for the army and marines. And the same cash could get you another couple of lovely destroyers or several even more useless but equally lovely frigates. Who cares whether carriers are the best way to get the work done, are they the best thing for the *navy*?

So, bad though their reasons are, one can see why the Admiralty has put the carriers and all who sail in them on a back-burner, and is focusing on destroyers. Effective air-defence destroyers may be almost impossible to achieve and useless for any other purpose, but at least they won't be snatched by the RAF. However, as a way of serving the state's purposes, as distinct from the navy's, the destroyer leaves much to be desired. It isn't as though destroyers are the only alternative to fighters, either; doing without the Type 45 would not be to completely rely on the flyboys. It is only the navy's book, remember, which says you must have a middle layer of air defence, and that book was written by destroyer men. In any case, there is a third layer of seagoing anti-air available. Just as well, really, for the next few years, considering the cold-weather-only Sea Harrier and the doesn't-work-at-all Type 42. Attempting to have both outer layers has resulted in us effectively having neither for the last decade or more, lessons of the Falklands be damned. The third, inner layer is point defence, where short-range guns or missiles on each ship attempt to shoot down missiles or planes as they close in.

In the Royal Navy, the point defence weapons are the Phalanx and Goalkeeper automatic gun systems and the short-range Sea Wolf missile. The guns are good, cheap kit, offering useful protection (American and Dutch–American respectively). They are easily bolted onto any ship; most navy warships and a lot of RFAs have them. The ageing, expensive Sea Wolf is less impressive. It had a poor record at best in the Falklands, and nobody but us has bought it. This missile is fitted only in frigates, and they are thought to need the guns as well, which probably says all that one needs to about how good Sea Wolf is. (Another fine BAe product.)

The central thing about point defence weapons like these, however, is that they protect only the ship they are mounted on. The fact that a ship carries point defence is, therefore, not a reason to have it in a task force; you don't send a ship out into danger just to protect itself. What this means, as far as air attack is concerned, is that you don't have any sensible work for frigates. Given the Royal Navy's weakness in fighters and destroyers, however, we sometimes use frigates as 'bullet-catchers' in front of more useful vessels to take the hits. Obviously, this is hardly ideal, as they are rather expensive and have hundreds of sailors on board. Empty oil tankers, which have crews of less than twenty, would work as well, and be immensely cheaper. In any case, most of the ships that require close-in protection have their own point defence nowadays, or could easily be fitted with it.

So, the most significant threat our ships face is air attack. Frigates are basically useless here, and the destroyer faces an almost insurmountable technical challenge. Our current long-obsolete 42s are utterly incapable of their task. Our seagoing fighter screen is cleverly improvised but only works in cold weather and is being got rid of. New destroyers, perhaps a little more effective, will be available in a few years, but they are so expensive that they threaten our ability to buy anything else. As a result, we will be without fleet fighters for some time, and, critically, we will continue to be weak in seagoing airborne radar, which could solve so many of our problems.

There is one final thing to be considered before we write off the escort flotilla as a bad job. All our frigates and destroyers mount single 4.5 inch guns, essentially rapid-firing 114mm artillery pieces. These weapons are of little use for fighting at sea, but they can shell targets on land, normally under the control of friendly troops ashore. This is Naval Gunfire Support (NGS). It is an activity with a high profile in naval circles, though not really anywhere else. NGS, you see, is the only combat action that a frigate is ever really likely to carry out. It is pretty much a frigate captain's sole chance of winning a serious medal; at least one such has recently been awarded for bombarding the scarcely-very-dangerous coast of Sierra Leone.* A naval 4.5 inch gun is said, in naval circles, to provide equal firepower to an entire battery of army artillery. (The spectacle of Royal Navy officers attempting to argue that 4.5 inch guns are serious firepower is rather sad. The lordly gunnery men from the days of the 15 inch battleship must be turning in their graves.)

In any case, the frigate-equals-a-battery-of-artillery statement isn't actually true. The naval weapon is, in fact, roughly equivalent in firepower to half a battery of the *very lightest type* of army gun, the 105mm weapons in the light brigades. The naval

---

* I have to declare a personal interest here. My grandfather was awarded the same gong towards the end of World War II, but he had to go through years of blood and slaughter to get it, including service on the Arctic convoys and at D-Day, with Hitler's Kriegsmarine and Luftwaffe as the opposition. Not quite the same thing as sitting in an African river, shelling raggedy-arsed teenagers armed with rusty AK47s. Even Admiral West, the current head of the navy, must be grinding his teeth a bit – he had to have his ship sunk under him in 1982 to get this same medal. There is clearly an inflationary effect at work on the value of decorations, just as with ranks.

gun can fire 25–30 rounds per minute, about the same as four light 105s. Half a battery of 105s is not a lot of artillery; it's about the smallest amount one would ever find on the land battlefield, actually. What's more, a ship carries only a few hundred shells, enough for about ten minutes' firing. Only targets within nine miles or so of deep water can be reached, and as 4.5 inch is not a normal artillery calibre only a poor selection of shells is available: realistically, these guns will never fire even base-bleed ammo, far less rocket-boosted terminally guided rounds. The ship does not move any faster than heavier army guns, and isn't airportable like the equivalent 105s. And the ship, close inshore, becomes a huge, easy, vulnerable, dream target for the enemy – if they have any serious weaponry, that is, unlike the West Side Boys. All in all, it just isn't that useful. Even in the Falklands, probably the best-imaginable campaign for naval gunfire, Royal Navy escorts using these same guns could add only a small increment to the firepower of our troops ashore, and had to run severe risks to do so.

Naval gunfire, then, is a fairly insignificant capability. In no way does it justify having escort warships; it doesn't even justify the expense of sending them round the world to fire their guns once you've bought them. There would have been many cheaper and better means of providing fire support for our 2003 landings in the Al Faw peninsula than sending frigates thousands of miles to fire a handful of shells each, as we did.

Frigate and destroyer advocates usually fall back on counter-drug and sanctions-enforcement operations at this point. It is true, the frigate which Britain keeps on patrol in or near the Caribbean has intercepted numerous large drug shipments destined for the USA. One would imagine that the Americans are suitably grateful to the British taxpayer for this assistance, although perhaps a little bemused as to why they get it. Similarly, British escorts have found much employment over the last decade in boarding and searching merchantmen in the Gulf and elsewhere, seeking to prevent Iraq from exporting oil and importing arms, for example.

However, even if the drugs trade and the sanctions-busters had both been thoroughly suppressed (not the case) this is hardly suitable employment for such ships. A Type 23 frigate's cost is hard to pin down, but it's a lot. These vessels were originally reported to Parliament as having cost £195 million each. A few years later the figure had dropped to just £95 million, which smacks rather more of creative accounting than it does of anything else. Neither price, one may be sure, includes various expensive extras such as the £30 million-per-ship Sonar 2087, or the £100 million-plus Merlin helicopters they carry, or the £5 million-per-ship anti-torpedo systems now being bought. No matter whether a Type 23 costs £100 million or, more realistically, a quarter-billion or so, it has to be one of the most expensive possible ways to do coastguard and customs work. And a Type 23 is cheap as chips compared to a destroyer.

Using warships fitted with expensive radars, sonars, combat computers, missiles and torpedoes, crewed by hundreds of highly trained military-technical specialists, to chase smugglers is ridiculous. One might characterise it as using a sledgehammer to crack a nut, if the escort warship was a useful tool like a sledgehammer. As it is, escort warships are more like solid-gold sledgehammers: horribly expensive and not very useful even when a big hammer is what you need. The cracking of nuts certainly can't justify the purchase of gold sledgehammers: and when a proper task calling for sledgehammers comes along, you'll only have been able to afford a few, and they won't work.

And that brings my naval career to an end. The only work the service had for me was as an escort-ship specialist – what the Royal Navy calls a principal warfare officer, a PWO. But the escort warship is a useless beast, despite its vast expense and large crew: the tasks it is designed for range from the rather unlikely (air defence) to the fantastically improbable (sub-hunting), and it is no good at them anyway. Even if such jobs come up, something else can always do them better, assuming that the escorts' terrific expense hasn't led to that something else not being there – which seems set to happen more and more.

The British taxpayer is forking out immense sums, then, in order to buy and run escort warships whose only real use is as venues for diplomatic cocktail parties. This is their main employment nowadays, in fact. How very appropriate then, that the other meaning of 'escort' should be a person to whom one pays large sums for some brief entertainment. I don't mind hosting cocktail parties, but

I didn't want it to be my only useful contribution. Much though I enjoyed wearing the blue suit and drawing the pay, much though I would like to be comfortably pensioned at an early age, as I would have been had I stayed, I do have to face myself in the mirror. The only career option for me in the navy was to become an escort – sorry, escort *officer* – a PWO, an expert in the use of golden sledge-hammers – well then, it was clearly time to leave.

The Royal Navy's love of escorts is not something it will grow out of on its own. It has reluctantly decommissioned a few of these ships just lately – as part of its share of the 2004 cuts fiasco and on other occasions. Most, however, were antique Type 42s which will soon be replaced. Even with the imminent disappearance of three Type 23 frigates – hardly a great loss, but it is embarrassing to be throwing away newish kit which has only been working for a few years – the planned future fleet will still have at least twenty-five escorts.* Escorts, then, will be thinned by a matter of 15 per cent or so; in the same period the vastly more useful minehunter flotilla has been slashed to ribbons, with cuts of 30 per cent. And the escorts' future is assured. New destroyers are building, and the replacement frigate is already taking shape. By contrast, commendable mental flexibility is being shown regarding the minehunters – the talk is all of bolt-on systems to be placed on RFAs, or remote-controlled robots, or such like. I should emphasise that this outside-the-box thinking regarding mine warfare is obviously valid. Why build expensive ships to do a job if it can be done better by something else? Unless one is talking about frigates or destroyers, of course.

Why does the navy love escorts so truly, forsaking all others, even unto death and humiliating loss?

---

* The navy will tell you that the first Type 23 frigate was ready to fight in 1990. Actually, however, the main combat computer didn't work. This is every bit as important as it sounds: rather than looking at a display showing ships, subs, missiles, etc., the officer in charge of fighting the ship was forced to look at a piece of paper or acetate on which a number of people would be scribbling information shouted to them by others. The ships were already terribly late, however, and the navy decided to put up with this rather than admit to further problems. The computers weren't sorted out for years. You can see how even Microsoft might be a step forward.

Some of it is simple bureaucratic job preservation, of course – like the RAF, with its wing-commanders in charge of squadrons. The command of a frigate or destroyer is the equivalent job for the navy, like a battalion/regiment CO in the army. No frigates or destroyers would mean no credible command slots at this rank, which would, in turn, decrease the supply of admiral material in future. The navy likes to have a goodly number of frigates so that it can ticket-punch a lot of officers' career portfolios with commands at medium rank, making them potential admirals.

Still, perhaps we could get by with a few less admirals if we really tried. Even at its uttermost stretch, the RN can only put to sea fighting fleets which might require, say, two admirals and three commodores to command. Only three flag officers hold sea commands in normal times. However, we are currently fortunate enough to have forty-six admirals and no less than eighty-eight commodores on the payroll. Even a very severe reduction in the number of candidates for flag rank would seem to be acceptable. Admiral West has lately stated that it costs him £8.8 million a year to run a frigate, and that he very much regrets having to decommission three of them for lack of this money. He could save at least one quite easily, by firing half his admirals and commodores – their pay alone is something in the order of £13 million p.a., quite apart from the other manifold expenses of having them. We may finally have found something the navy likes even more than frigates: desk jobs ashore for high ranks. The seagoing navy would no doubt find it very hard, not having all those flag officers ashore sending them paperwork and heli-coptering in for visits all the time, but they'd probably grin and bear it.

This will never happen. The navy is quite determined to main-tain the admiral factory – the escort fleet – running at full blast, so the oversupply of flag officers will no doubt continue.

There is also, perhaps, a slightly more honourable aspect to the Senior Service's love for escorts. They aren't only a career ticket-punching facility, popular though that is. These ships are also the last surface vessels left which fight for themselves to some degree. A carrier sends its aircraft away to fight; an amphibious ship does the same with its marines. Neither will ever engage the enemy itself unless something goes horribly wrong; indeed, both types of vessel are almost unarmed. Carriers and amphibs are logistics platforms rather than fighting ones – they were in the last chapter for a reason, and as we saw they have already been partly civilianised. Submarines are all very well, and certainly useful for a number of things, but not many British sailors or officers genuinely like them. It is a little-known fact that a lot of Royal Navy submariners are actually pressed men.* Minehunters don't fight at all, in the sense of actually killing people, although the being-killed part of the job is very much on the cards.

By contrast, a frigate or destroyer, for all that it will – in real life – tend to operate mainly through the agency of its helicopter, bristles with weapons. It looks and feels and trains like a proper fighting ship, in contrast to just about anything else in the surface, mainstream navy. And, institutionally, the navy is – thinks itself to be – an organisation for operating fighting ships. It was doing that for hundreds of years before all these nasty modern innovations came along, and by god it plans to keep doing that as its main activity whether it makes sense or not. Fighting sailors like Admiral West want to pass the torch on to others of their own ilk, not to a bunch of pasty-faced submariners or people who drive offshore heliports and car ferries and really ought to be in the auxiliary fleet – if they aren't already.

The trouble is that technology has moved on, and fighting sailors – in the pure sense, as operators of combatant surface ships – have become rather obsolete. Admiral West and his contemporaries should really be looking to the naval aviators and the submariners as their natural successors, not frigate captains.

---

* This might seem to be impossible in a volunteer navy, but it isn't. The RN craftily delays the process, taking new recruits and putting them through all their basic training, in some cases – such as officers, but others too – a process lasting well over two years. Only once this is done does it select people for submarines. In some training batches there are sufficient volunteers, but it is normal for many new submariners to be more or less unwilling. They could theoretically leave, but by now they have made a major investment of time and identity in the navy, and most of them submit to the submarine press gang. They are allowed to transfer out of subs after a few years, but by then they are usually reluctant to forfeit the substantial submarine pay, and they would have to start all over again in another branch. Once the sun-dodgers get their hooks into someone they generally succeed in making a convert of him eventually.

Such officers can reach the upper levels of the navy, but they must first metamorphose into frigate men, largely at the cost of their previous identities. Radical change is extremely unlikely; Admiral West is no Fisher, and nor are any of his colleagues.

In the end, the Royal Navy as a whole provides many useful arrows for the public quiver: sea-based aircraft, submarines, mine clearance, the Royal Marine Commandos. The fighting people of the navy are second to none on the face of the oceans at what they do, even the PWOs. If you need something hit hard, it will get done, although the soft golden hammers and the people swinging them will be badly damaged if it is anything tough, as in the Falklands. All honour, then, to the seagoing combat navy – about 45 per cent of those wearing naval uniform, almost exclusively lower ranks, and quite a lot of civilians. Sadly, though, they are poorly managed. Those who set policy persist in wasting most of the navy's budget, and much of its splendid manpower, on pointless ships that can do little or nothing useful. As a result, we find ourselves unable to afford critically necessary systems.

And the policymakers are pretty much unregulated. The navy is, broadly speaking, allowed to decide for itself on these matters. Unsurprisingly to anyone acquainted with the habits of government bureaucracies, it generally decides to stay as it has always been, unless given a sharp poke by some outside force. Historically, the outside force has often been an enemy, but this is not a good or reliable path to naval reform. A better mechanism is informed public debate, as last seen a hundred years ago, but today's Ministry of Defence is pretty safe from that.

CHAPTER

9

Brass Hats and Rear Echelons

Stick close to your desks and never go to sea,
And you all may be rulers of the Queen's Navy!

> The First [Sea] Lord's Song, HMS Pinafore,
> Gilbert and Sullivan

We have finally looked at all the fighting units in the British armed forces, and we have an idea of what they can do for us. We have also seen that these fighting units, even with all their supporting bits and pieces, don't contain all that many people. The army, at its uttermost extension, can put no more than two divisions into the field. Such a small-corps-sized force would require only four generals and would comprise no more than 65,000 people, many of whom would be marines or called-up reservists. This is to be very kind, very optimistic. The deployment of a single 30,000-strong division in 2003 strained British capability severely, and a recovery period was necessary afterwards. That force included thousands of marines and large numbers of reservists: no more than 25,000 army regulars.

So, at the very best interpretation, the full-time British Army can deploy no more than 55,000 – more likely 30,000 to 40,000 – of its people in operations overseas, including just four generals. Amazingly, however, there are over 100,000 full-time regular soldiers, and more than *sixty* of them are generals of two-star rank or above. Every infantry private in the army currently rotates rapidly through a grinding cycle of training, operational deployment, a period of leave to spend his abysmal pay and then training to deploy once more. By contrast, a deployment for a general is a rare event indeed. What a general does is work at a desk in the UK, and he has a great deal of company in this. (Don't think I'm just down on the army here. The situation is worse in the other services.)

What are all these surplus uniformed people doing with themselves?

Perhaps they are supporting the field forces. It is correctly said that a large number of rear-echelon people are necessary to put each fighting soldier into the field. Hold on, though; support branches are already included in the figures above. Of the 30,000 land-forces troops Britain put on the ground for the invasion of Iraq, no more than 8,000 were members of 'teeth arm' battle groups or attached artillery. Only a few even of these were pure, rifle-section men with guns – 2,500 at most. All the rest were brigade and division headquarters troops, engineers, signals and logistics people, media relations, civil affairs, medics, rear-area security and so on. These are the people who correspond to the various non-core activities in a civilian company or other bureaucracy: the office and facilities people, sales, PR, marketing, IT. Like their civilian counterparts, they include a lot of management.

Fair enough. This is how you can tell a serious army: it has these people, and as a result it can use advanced military technology, move itself about even through wrecked infrastructure and do other necessary things – although one does occasionally suspect that quite a few could actually be civilians in the UK rather than uniforms in theatre. But let's pass over that. Let's assume that everyone in the Iraq deployment genuinely needed to be out there. Even then, supposing we made a supreme, all-out effort and deployed two full divisions, we would still be sending no more than 60 per cent of the full-time regular army. Probably much less: the proportion of reservists would likely rise for such an effort. Scores of thousands of full-time career soldiers would still be left behind in the UK. Similarly, if you deployed every single useable unit in the navy and RAF, you would still find swarms of serving, active-status regulars left over.

The situation is perhaps most extreme in the case of the RAF, which possesses something in the order of 350 deployable combat planes and helicopters. The Iraq operation involved the deployment into theatre of no fewer than fifty-five RAF people per aircraft involved. Every possible supporting specialty or branch was represented: air-traffic, police dogs, fitness instructors and Uncle Tom Cobbleigh, all with plenty of associated – and no doubt highly necessary – management, in the form of non-flying officers. Even with this sort of lavish manning, however, no more than 20,000 of the RAF's 52,000 uniformed people will ever be required to leave British shores. The navy is only a little better overall, although somewhat less prone to feather-bedding the deployed echelons.

This is all the stranger when you reflect that the supporting chain reaching from Britain to a deployed force is mostly civilian-manned. Certainly it is normal for that (large) part of the logistics effort which stays in the UK to be civilian, as we saw with the 30,000 civil servants of the Defence Logistics Organisation. It is hard to fathom what all the soldiers who will never deploy overseas might be for. Likewise their navy and RAF counter-parts.

Some of them, of course, are instructors, employed in training our service people. More yet are under training. This accounts for nearly all the non-useables holding lower ranks, and some at medium levels such as warrant-officers and lieutenant-commanders. Not too many instructional jobs call for ranks higher than this, though. A few courses are taken and taught by very senior officers, but not that many. And really, a lot of instructor jobs hardly seem to call for current, active-duty uniformed personnel. Many of these posts require uniformed *experience*, but this could easily be provided by hiring ex-service personnel with the right background. Such schemes already exist, in fact, but they don't seem to be in very widespread use.

Very sadly, the training system – the true glory of our armed forces – is too often subject to abuse by feather bed makers and empire builders. I have seen many, many examples. The army runs two entirely separate bomb-disposal career tracks, each with its own large school, faculty, examination scheme etc. I had to qualify in each of them, irritatingly: it was necessary at different times for me to operate on both turfs. Naval training, too, is often ridiculously lengthy and repetitive. I was taught how to use tide tables, and then tested formally to see if I had grasped this very basic technique, no fewer than five times by five separate organisations during my basic training*. I could go on all day; and this would only be the examples that one serviceman has encountered. Many in the vast bureaucracies of the MoD would assert that efficiency drives of the last ten years have cut training to the bone. I would say, not even close. We have scarcely kept pace with the bloat. As we all know from bitter personal experience, fat once gone doesn't stay away without constant vigilance. This is even truer of MoD bureaucracy. The navy actually managed to rid itself of its Instructor officer branch in the mid-90s. This was a largish branch of uniformed officers who did almost no service at sea, spending pleasant careers in training schools ashore. They were obvious candidates for civilianisation, and indeed this briefly happened. Instructor officers were no longer recruited, and at last one community of overpaid civilians in uniform seemed set to wither away. Within a few years, however, they were back. Now they are known as the Engineer (Training Management) branch, and we are signing them up again hand over fist, even as infantry battalions close down and ships decommission. (Perhaps I'll just take to drink.)

All that said, much of the training structure is superb. It is overmanned, wasteful and rank-inflated, parts of it are used as dumping grounds for the unimpressive or unimprovable, but much of its output is world-class.

There are many other UK-duty-only junkets apart from training, however. Immense numbers of people, often mid-to-high ranking officers, are employed doing basic administrative tasks which do not require their expensive military skills and do not merit their comfortable pay and conditions. The armed services possess hundreds of bases and facilities in the UK; every one has a base

---

* Back in 1994, as I sat in a classroom being shown how to use the Admiralty tide tables for the fifth time in less than two years, my attention did wander slightly. The instructor noticed, and employed the time-honoured pedagogic gambit of sarcastically enquiring whether I'd care to come up the front and continue the problem he was working through, since I clearly knew it all already. He was distinctly surprised when I did so, and enquired how it was that I was such an expert. I pointed out the large number of times that we had all been taught this technique. 'Goodness,' he said. 'What an unusual sub-lieutenant, to have learned something after only being taught it four times.'

commander, usually holding an exalted military rank. He – nearly always he – does not command anything. The base commander is actually in charge of security guards, cleaning, gardening and so on. The grunt work in all these areas is done by civilian employees, usually working for contracted companies. In civilian life, the base commander would be a low-level administrator. In the services, he is an insanely important person, usually sufficiently senior that he is quite untouchable. It's as though the building manager had taken over the company. And the snug billets for pension-chasers are not limited to these senior posts. I have encountered submarine-qualified, submarine-paid officers running dockyard parking-permit bureaux; or multimillion-pound aviators arranging class timetables – and doing it damned badly, in some cases.

There are many more mid-to-high-ranking officers toiling away in the fields of procurement and logistics. Again, they have few or no uniformed subordinates: the work is actually done – to the extent it *is* done – by civilians. The military officers are said to be necessary as their front-line experience, gained in younger days, is critical to the process of making sure that the right kit gets bought. They also supposedly ensure that our fighting people receive proper support. A lot of officers from the technical and logistic branches are found in these jobs, as would seem sensible on the face of it. The problem with using them as the front line's representatives back in Blighty is that they don't actually have much acquaintance with the front line. Naval engineering and supply officers, for example, typically do just two jobs aboard ship in their entire careers, amounting to perhaps three or four years' service. Their other thirty years in uniform are mostly spent behind desks in the UK, very often involved in the procurement of new ships, despite the fact they know so little about them. Non-flying air force officers have an even sketchier notion of where the sharp end is and what it might be like there. The combat arms couldn't operate without technical and logistic back-up in theatre, but they often fail to see why there should be another ten uniformed admin johnnies and engineers back in the UK for every one who is out there with them.

One shouldn't assume that combat officers are greatly more virtuous. An army officer of the teeth arms is thrown straight in at the deep end, true; his first job will be in charge of a rifle platoon or equivalent, although it might be more accurate to say that this is a probationary period during which he is assessed and trained by his sergeant. He might command another platoon-equivalent shortly afterward, although in all likelihood this one will not actually operate as a unit under his direction. The next time our soldier holds any sort of command will be at the rank of major, two or three promotions and likely a decade later. In the interim he will have spent time in fighting teams, but he will also have done a good deal of less dangerous, less demanding work elsewhere. And after his major's command, he may never see real service again. His best chance of doing so is to be promoted to lieutenant-colonel – far from certain – and then be given a regular army unit to run – very difficult indeed. The passed-over major or half-colonel will continue to hang about on full pay, however, perhaps until the age of fifty-five, with his bulletproof government pension swelling all the time.

Similarly, naval officers of the Warfare or Executive Branch* go to sea or to active air squadrons straight after their inordinately lengthy training. They stay in fighting ships for the remainder of their twenties, although they will not be in charge of much. At some stage in their thirties they come ashore, never to be employed at sea again unless in very scarce, coveted command slots or on the staff of a real seagoing admiral (even rarer). Again, a lot of these beached naval officers will be retained until the age of fifty-five.

Things are, if anything, worse in the RAF. An RAF aviator, already in a minority compared to the blunties, may rise to squadron command, generally in his thirties. Here his actual combat job is to fly his plane; in the air he is unlikely to command more than one or two other aircraft, and even this is by no means a certainty. Fair enough, it's dangerous and testing work, though

---

* This is the branch for mainstream naval officers, as opposed to Engineers or the Supply Branch. It was called Executive until the mid-90s because only these officers can hold command at sea, but then the name was changed to the Warfare Branch, even though this might well describe everyone in the armed forces. Warfare officers handle and navigate the ship, or fly its aircraft: they operate the weapons.

several of his subordinates will also be doing it – indeed, may well be better at it – and it hardly seems to compare with the equivalent army job of directing a 700- or 800-man battle group. After this posting it is vanishingly unlikely that the airman will ever fly a real mission again, whether he makes air marshal or gets passed over. In either case, he is likely to serve out a full career. This is especially wasteful if he is a scarce, expensive pilot. It is difficult to think what he might do at a desk which is quite as useful as flying a jet. It doesn't need to cost six million quid to train a mid-level administrator.

So, we employ a lot of uniformed people over and above what we need. Sometimes this is reasonable. The slight overbearing in infantry privates – soon to be slighter – allows for these men to be trained in the first place, to carry out concurrent tasks, to very occasionally get some time off and progress their careers. But mostly it isn't reasonable at all. The surplus gets more and more out of control as we go up the ranks, particularly up the officer ranks. Junior combat-branch officers do a reasonable amount of genuinely military work early in their careers, but at some point in their thirties, often quite early, it is normal for them to effectively retire from active duty. A very few will participate in useful, deployable teams at high rank, but most won't. Officers of the technical and adminstrative branches do even less than this. As we climb through the junior to the middle officer ranks, the proportion of swivel-chair hussars rises wildly beyond what is justifiable.

Once we arrive at the highest ranks, the situation has become ridiculous. The army's two combat divisions – one of which is at least partly fictional – might call for ten or fifteen brigadiers, two or three major-generals and a single lieutenant-general to run them. Maybe we should also have some extra generals – say, two or three times this number. What we actually have is more than *ten* times as many. There are no fewer than 180 brigadiers, forty-six major-generals and a cool eleven lieutenant-generals in the British army, and a fistful more of each in the marines, despite the fact that there are only enough marines to make a single brigadier's command. On top of this, there are several four-star full generals. The navy is worse, with a *twenty*-fold surplus, and the air force worse still.

The RAF's higher organisation has been mucked about with times beyond number, but nothing can disguise the fact that none of it is designed to do things any more. It is merely a pyramid of managers writing promotion reports on managers: or, more accurately, many pyramids – only one of which has any planes. Long, long ago, RAF squadrons were arranged into wings, and wings into groups. A group-captain might command a group back then, and a group might have a job or mission, such as bombing Germany. Bomber groups formed Bomber Command, fighter groups were in Fighter Command, etc. These days, even a squadron is a fairly notional thing. It doesn't normally deploy together, let alone operate together. However, a wing-commander of the minority wings-on-chest type might deploy overseas in charge of a hastily assembled bunch of aircraft and people roughly equivalent to a squadron. If there were more than one of these, we might send a group-captain in overall charge. This is about the limit of the RAF's actual combat command echelons, although they usually manage to sneak in an air marshal or two above the group-captain, if it is a big operation. Needless to say, there is no shortage of officers at these levels: the RAF has 340 group-captains and forty air marshals, plus ninety-two air commodores. Such actual RAF operational organisations are temporary, however.

All *permanent* RAF organisations above squadron – even, perhaps, the squadron itself – are purely administrative. The army's handful of fighting brigades and divisions and the navy's three seagoing flag commands have no real RAF equivalents at all. Surprisingly, this is even true of the defence of UK airspace. There is no single RAF commander with this as his main task: it is handled – as well as it can be with Tornado F3s – by several different contributors. Despite this, the RAF likes to pretend that being in charge of some of its many UK stations, groups and what not is the same as running a navy task force or army brigade, an actual mission-oriented fighting formation. This allows it to claim that air marshals are as experienced in operational command as admirals and generals are.

In other words, nearly all our mid-to-senior officer ranks are not employed on any work that really justifies having them. The proportion of desk jockeys at any given rank often runs above

90 per cent: it seldom dips below 80. Even junior combat-branch officers, who are fairly likely to have a real job, are employed more as administrators than is good for their performance as military operators. This last is doubly puzzling, given the existence of whole empires of uniformed and civilian admin people who are supposed to take this burden from them. Above the junior levels it gets worse and worse. Anyone of lieutenant-colonel/commander/wing-commander rank or higher is almost certainly a uniformed bureaucrat *now*, no matter his or her past record. Such a person may well have been a swivel-chair specialist for most of his or her previous service as well.

The situation is so smelly that it actually counts *against* an officer that he is best suited by temperament and ability to hold command rather than push paper and give Powerpoint presentations. A comment on an annual report such as 'If promoted, would be best employed in command' is intended to mean 'Don't promote him; he is fit for only a few of the jobs at the next rank.' No matter that those few jobs are the only ones of much importance. No matter that they are supposedly the reason we have all the others.

Well, so what? Why not have plenty of extra uniformed officers doing admin and thinking deep thoughts back in Britain? Surely they've earned some time at home after all their hard service? Surely we need them to see that all the civil servants and contractors don't rob the taxpayer blind and fail to do their jobs? Surely it would be far too cruel to tell keen young officers that realistically they have no chance of ever rising to high rank? By all means, let's create lots of brass-hat jobs even though we've nothing for them to do. (The term for these jobs in the navy is 'Flag Officer Car-parks', a position which remains mythical – for the moment.) After all, civilian organisations have swarms and swarms of middle and upper management – why shouldn't the forces?

These arguments fail to stand up.

Firstly, most armed-services officers haven't actually done much arduous service: certainly not enough to merit twenty years of mellow, aimless semi-retirement on full pay, working a three- or four-day week with splendid holidays, pension and perks. This is the life of a passed-over officer. The high flyer will spend a lot more time hanging around the office, wear out a lot more printer cartridges and end up with a bigger house, but otherwise follows a similar course. One should remember that every uniformed serviceman or woman is paid an 'X-factor' (currently running at 13 per cent of salary) which is supposed to allow for 'such things as, for example . . . liability for duty at all times . . . and the danger, turbulence and separation which are part of Service life' ('An Introduction to Military Pay', MoD).

A lackadaisical office routine in the UK hardly seems to qualify. And, make no mistake, the swarming desk jockeys in uniform are never turned out even for the easiest, safest military operations. This became obvious during the 2003 firemen's strike, when some 19,000 service personnel stepped in to replace the absent firefighters. This is not 'dangerous' or 'turbulent' work in service terms.* Firefighting does, however, call for a certain amount of physical activity. It was not thought wise to put the forces' scores of thousands of lardy old swivel-chair artists to this test; instead, the job was handled almost exclusively by younger front-line combat personnel, despite the fact that the Iraq invasion was looming and these people were in short supply. Warships were tied up so that their crews could drive Green Goddesses; army combat units handed in their tanks and rifles in exchange for hoses and helmets. Meanwhile, most of the remaining active units departed for Iraq. Throughout all this, through the fires and the invasion, thousands upon thousands of majors and colonels and commanders and group-captains stayed right where they were: behind desks in Britain. There couldn't have been a better illustration of how relatively few people in Her Majesty's armed services actually deserve the 'X-factor'.

The shiny-bottomed crowd aren't accomplishing anything else much, either. Although present in vast numbers, the uniformed rear echelons in the UK have utterly failed in their supposed tasks.

---

* Firefighting has the reputation of being a dangerous job, and so it is in civilian terms. However, it is pretty safe compared to being in the forces, if you look at deaths per thousand per decade from hazards of service. Insurance industry tables don't always reflect this, probably because insurers refuse to cover armed-services people against the risks of their trade. As for turbulence, firemen get to go home every twenty-four hours. No sudden six- or eight-month absences for them, either.

They have not controlled or even really influenced the various communities of civilian pirates which live off the defence budget. Despite strong uniformed representation in the procurement apparatus, the front line has been provided with equipment which has been late, defective, galactically expensive, either sparse or over-supplied and frequently misconceived to begin with. There are plenty more uniforms at management levels in the logistics empire, but it remains as complicated, bureaucratic and slow-moving as ever. The only real change is that actual holdings have been slashed, so that even bribery can't necessarily get stores issued any more. (The bribery of today is usually a matter of a packet of chocolate biscuits, or at worst a bottle of whisky, rather than big sums of cash money as in times gone by.)

Far from being helpful to front-line people, the presence of many high-ranking officers within the procurement and logistics fiefdoms is extremely inconvenient. These senior men cannot make their civilian colleagues or contractors do their jobs properly, but they are well able to lean on the sharp-end operator to make do with the results. Thus, if a rifle won't chamber cartridges reliably, soldiers are trained to 'forward-assist', and the weapon is accepted for the army. If a mine-clearance sonar won't track underwater transponders despite being designed and purchased just for this, operators are encouraged to work without it and the equipment is passed as ready for service regardless. If a fighter has dreadful performance, pilots are told to adapt their tactics and the plane goes on to be ordered in such numbers that many will never fly. All these are real examples, and if you've read this far you know that they represent the rule, not the exception.

Boy, I'm certainly glad all those forces officers were there in the procurement agency to make sure we had good, working equipment, aren't you? What a bang-up job they did.

And the story isn't any better with logistics, as anyone with recent experience of the Defence Logistics Organisation will tell you. Perhaps the DLO might be a bit more helpful if its boss gave a hoot what other forces people thought of him. As he is currently a four-star air marshal, and thus has no need to consider the opinion of anyone below ministerial rank, the often slothful and bloody-minded bean-counters of the DLO seem unlikely to mend their ways.

Moving on, the creation of jobs in order to assure promotion prospects is idiotic on many levels. It dilutes expertise and experience, for a start. It tends to rob whole classes of personnel of the main attributes which make them worthwhile. The fact that British colonels and generals are employed almost entirely behind desks and in committees can hardly help their performance on those few occasions when they have to make decisions for themselves under pressure. Spending much of their careers in civilised, officers-only environs will scarcely sharpen their skills in the very specialised, very demanding, often quite stressful business of getting the best from the British ranker. As for the navy, I have seen first hand the effects of putting officers fresh from desk jobs in command at sea. They tend to be nervous ship-handlers at best, cack-handed at worst; many of Her Majesty's ships and submarines have crashed into things under the control of anxious bureaucrats. One can easily produce research to support such anecdotal evidence:

> This brings up yet another hazard of modern war – government by committee . . . four of the worst military disasters in recent American history are directly attributable to the psychological processes which attend group decision-making . . . the sort of person who, as we have seen, makes the best military commander – the outspoken individualist – clearly cannot give of his best in a group situation . . .
>
> *From* On the Psychology of Military Incompetence, *Dr Norman F. Dixon, UCL Psychology faculty and officer in the Royal Engineers 1940 to 1950*

Promoting people only or mainly because they are perceived as being good at staff work is a bad idea.

Another unpleasant consequence of there being god's own plenty of meaningless top-level jobs is that everyone who can manage to get one of the scarce commands at lower levels becomes a shoo-in contender for very high rank. As the navy has well over forty admirals and nearly ninety commodores but less than thirty frigates and destroyers for commanders to command, every frigate or destroyer captain can be reasonably sure of being at least a commodore one day – provided he doesn't make any mistakes.

In a normal, pyramid-shaped command structure, there would be fewer admirals than seagoing captains by a large margin. The decision as to whether a sea captain was going to be an admiral would be made *after* he had held command, not before. The captains would need to make their names stand out if they wanted promotion: they might need to show initiative and dash.

In today's navy the seagoing captains have done all that they need to by getting selected. Sadly, many were probably given their ships based on brilliance at paperwork in the past and perceived suitability for more paperwork at a higher rank in future. The actual command itself becomes merely a ticket-punching exercise, to be got out of the way with as little bother as possible. In particular, no risks are ever taken and nothing is ever done without clearance from higher authority. Given that the ship's output of paperwork will thus become the thing it is best known for, rather than anything it actually does, this is focused on with manic intensity.

Serving under these captains can be very disappointing to anyone who has read about the Royal Navy of former times, back when the best hope of promotion was to be seamanlike, active and not afraid of a risk or two. (Here I'm referring to the Napoleonic wars, and perhaps World War II to some extent. At other times in the last two centuries things have tended to be much the way they are now, as Gilbert and Sullivan so ably remind us.)

From all that I hear, this syndrome is also quite marked in the army. A battalion commander is similarly a made man if he can just avoid trouble and keep the paperwork neat. He will not usually relish the command he has worked for all his career; seldom is he sad at the prospect of leaving his supposedly beloved regiment for staff duty at a higher rank. No, he is merely burnishing his résumé, and the whole battalion are tools to that end. This is no new thing, of course. As Siegfried Sassoon wrote in his *Memoirs of an Infantry Officer*:

Kinjack left us . . . They all come and go; stay in the Batt. long enough to get something out of it, and then disappear and will hardly give a thought to the men and officers who were the means of getting them higher rank. It's a selfish old world, my friend. All

successive C.O.s beg me to stay with the old Battalion they love
so well. I do. So do they, until they get a better job. They neither
know nor care what happens to me (who at their special request
have stuck to 'the dear old Corps') when I leave the Service.

So the current top-heavy rank structure doesn't just mess up
our equipment and supplies. It also tends to put anxious, risk-
averse bureaucratic types in charge of what few operational units
we actually possess. Occasionally, by a fluke, we get officers who
see command as an end in itself – as what they actually joined
up for, an officer's primary purpose – rather than as a stepping
stone to a bigger desk on a higher floor, but this is rare.

The situation isn't helped by the superfluity of ranks. The army
only has five real management levels for officers: platoon,
company, battalion, brigade, division. There are *ten* ranks,
however: second lieutenant, first lieutenant, captain, major,
lieutenant-colonel, colonel, brigadier, major-general, lieutenant-
general, general. Or perhaps eleven, as the chief of defence staff
is effectively still a field marshal or equivalent*. This set-up pretty
much guarantees that you will have far too many officers, even
if there were tight control over the numbers at each rank (which
is not the case).

The army really only needs five officer ranks, then; it certainly
doesn't need ten or eleven. The other services don't require any
more. Fewer, if anything. This was pointed out in the early 1990s
in an independent review into armed-services personnel policy.
The much-loathed Bett Report recommended that the rank structure be flattened out somewhat. People who might feel that the
armed forces' vast top-heaviness can be justified by comparison
with civilian organisations should note that Sir Michael Bett had
been deputy chairman of British Telecom and personnel director
of both the BBC and the General Electric group – and still he
was amazed at the multiplicity of the Forces' management layers.

The Bett Report was nonetheless roundly rejected by every

---

* Although he has at least forfeited the most outrageous perquisite formerly
given to five-star officers: that of remaining on full pay for life. On retirement
he now has to squalor along on a mere £90k or £100k pension, index-linked
and bulletproofed. Probably won't need his senior citizen's bus pass much.

right-thinking officer or armchair strategist, usually on such grounds as:

'in the confusion of battle there is not time to work out who is the most senior of the five officers crouched in a foxhole. A full range of ranks is needed'.

Professor Christopher Bellamy,
co-director of the Security Studies Institute.

The SSI is MoD-funded, and caters very largely to senior British armed-forces officers.

There are several problems here. First off, at least the top five grades of commissioned officer are *extremely* unlikely to be found in any such situation, so the foxhole argument doesn't really stand up as a reason for having four or five different kinds of general. Frankly, if you can find me a foxhole with five British generals crouching in it, I'll find you a situation that has gone wrong beyond all hope of recovery – in all likelihood because the occupants of the foxhole have cocked it up. Knowing which of them is senior just by looking isn't going to mend matters.

Second, in the exceptionally unlikely event of finding five officers in the same foxhole who didn't know each other already, one might hope that they would be wearing field kit. Marks of rank on field kit are deliberately hard to read, snipers being more of a worry than seniority in most real combat situations. A lot of the more sensible sharp-end officers hide their insignia altogether. Thus, our implausible group is not going to instinctively sort itself out in a dark foxhole by virtue of holding a range of different ranks. No quicker than they would by comparing seniorities, anyway.

It isn't as though the ranks were invented sensibly to begin with. Nobody ever sat down and said, 'Right, here's the army, what set up shall we have so as to officer it properly?' Lieutenant-colonels, for instance, only exist due to regimental colonelcies having been lucrative sinecures in the 17th and 18th centuries. A colonel in those days, while normally making a great deal of money from his position, was not expected to accompany his regiment on campaign. He would have a lieutenant-colonel to handle any actual fighting, just as the fortunately beneficed Anglican clergymen of the day might hire curates to do religious duties for them. Regimental administration has been somewhat reformed since then, but we still – bizarrely – have two grades of colonel; and this is not the only obscure bit of historical baggage in the army table of ranks. (Remember, a major-general was originally the boss sergeant-major.) The suggestion that all of this fits naturally with the requirements of modern warfare is absurd.

Regrettably, the army's arcane system eventually spilled over into the navy, which only had four ranks below admiral well into the 19th century. Since then, a further three have appeared in order to match up with all the army ones, a process only completed in 1996. When the air force came along, another dictionary was dreamed up to match, although the RAF's H. G. Wells-style titles aren't popular worldwide: most air forces use army ranks, like the USAF.

Anyway, the Bett Report was largely ignored, and in many respects things might actually be said to have gone backwards since the corrupt old days of the 18th century. The British armed forces had a vast oversupply of officers even then, but at least we didn't give them all jobs. Most spare officers in the old days were simply put on half pay and told to go away until the state had need of them. This is hardly ideal as you find yourself with thousands of loafers hanging about drawing half pay, which costs a lot of money. But it's far better than having to give them all *full* pay until retirement and only then put them on half pay – probably at a higher rank – as we do now. And nowadays we have to find desks and offices and such for them all, which costs even more, and they beaver away producing paperwork which wastes a lot of time – sometimes to the extent that the real officers ask to have extra people out in the field with them just to deal with all the administration. If you relax your guard, the swivel-chair crowd spend their time thinking up reasons to promote themselves and to have even more desks and offices; the Joint Helicopter Command springs to mind. Perhaps it would be better after all to pension them off and lock them out of the building, as our enlightened predecessors did.

Another problem here, as with everything to do with effective military action, is the separate existence of the three services.

Many senior officers exist simply to keep them separate. We find ourselves with three four-star officers as service chiefs. Each of these men has a three-star subordinate to actually control the service's combat units day-to-day, with associated twenty-four-hour operations rooms full of big maps and computers. In these, many officers stand about swilling coffee and looking bravely tired, their hair becomingly ruffled to indicate that they have the weight of the world on their shoulders. There is another three-star for each service, in charge of all the 'base commanders' and training schools and suchlike. And there is an overall authority, the chief of defence staff, theoretically a four-star officer (though paid and treated as if he were a five-star). He has a deputy, the vice chief of defence staff, who is also four-star. One might imagine their role to be that of ensuring that the three services operate together in the national interest. Perhaps it is. However, they have a lot of help. There is the chief of defence procurement, a former three-star officer, and the chief of defence logistics, a four-star: and all the massive bureaux and mighty multi-star brass hats and scampering staff goblins of the MoD and Central Staff, there to provide sensible overall coordination of all three services' efforts. (They aren't doing all that great a job, as we have seen.) This would seem to leave the chief of defence staff with nothing much to do but actually command the forces on operations.

But he doesn't do that either. There is a Chief of Joint Operations, a three-star post. This man is in charge of the Permanent Joint Headquarters, a relatively new organisation. Until the mid-1990s, any operation under British control would be run from whichever single-service command HQ managed to grab it. The Falklands War was directed by the navy's C-in-C Fleet, and the British part of Gulf War I was run by the RAF's Strike Command. It is not coincidence that the chief of defence staff in 1982 was an admiral, and his successor in early 1991 an air marshal. This kind of inter-service bickering and triplication of effort was hardly efficient, and led to much grumbling on each occasion from the two services who didn't get to be in charge.

As ever, the solution to an oversupply of senior officers was seen as being more senior officers. Nowadays, if British forces go anywhere to do real operations, the chances are that they will do so under the control of the Permanent Joint HQ rather than C-

in-C Fleet, Strike Command or HQ Land. There are some exceptions to this rule, which, funnily enough, means that the older
HQs remain – 'jointness' actually turns out, quite often, to mean
the creation of a fourth organisation, rather than the combination and rationalisation of the existing three.

The Permanent Joint HQ, apart from CJO himself, contains a
further trio of two-star officers – two real uniformed ones and a
civil servant who considers himself to be of equivalent status –
and no fewer than nine further one-stars with various lackeys and
retinues, totalling well over 600 people. These latter hangers-on
will commonly be of a rank to command major units themselves,
but in the rarefied atmosphere of the staff they are largely reduced
to preparing briefings. Even such tasks as making tea, doing
photocopying or carrying bags will often be handled by officers
of some seniority. One need hardly say that the PJHQ's home in
the London suburbs also has an entirely separate RAF group-
captain in charge of it, with other high-priced uniformed minions
to oversee the security guards, cleaners, gardeners and so forth.

As top-heavy staff organisations go, PJHQ is more credible
than most; it directs our real combat people about their operational business, if any British organisation does – likelier alternatives are NATO, the UN or various American HQs. This is what
'staff work' proper is supposedly about, although thousands more
officers at many other HQs like to feel that they too are in charge
of British units – or 'assets' as the staff wallahs like to call them.
This can be confusing for the relatively few units which are ready
for use at any given time. Once, as operations officer of such a
ship, I was compelled to brief my CO that he was simultaneously
attached to no fewer than five different chains of command.

Such situations have led to a lot of ridiculous hair-splitting in
which the various chiefs who want to claim a given asset hold
different types of command authority over it. NATO doctrine
alone uses five different definitions, and many national forces
have separate ones of their own. This allows each of the HQs to
have a marker for the given unit on its big map, or an icon on
its big computer plot, and all the chiefs can thus simultaneously
claim that they control mighty forces – even when there are more
chiefs than units, as is common, and in reality they are taking
turns to play with the toys.

Of late years, the staff chaps have come up with a new notion for getting some more pieces onto their game boards: they have decided that special forces is a whole new field of war. Thus we have air, land, sea and now special forces. Formerly, one needed at least a company of troops, or a ship or a couple of planes or something, before anything appeared on the big plot for the three-star officer to ponder over his coffee and the staff chaps to assiduously monitor through the night. These conventional units, though, are expensive and scarce, and it might not be one's turn to play with them.

Special forces are far better. Nowadays a four-man SAS team – or even a single operator – can produce a satisfying symbol on a whole new plot, possibly justifying even more highly priced staff brains pontificating and briefing one another and sitting up late watching CNN. Brilliantly, *these* assets can be sent anywhere and do anything without any great likelihood of reports in the Western media. Thus, one can pick and choose the politicians and journalists one invites to the ops room to view the plot, or whom one briefs 'off the record'. They will be suitably impressed and grateful, and will feel so chuffed at being genuine Whitehall insiders that they will be your friends for life. Splendid. Never have so many senior officers owed their jobs to so few actual troops.

The simple, pyramidal tables of organisation which one finds in sensible hierarchies have to go out the window to accommodate the myriad HQs and staffs; nowadays, balanced on top of the pyramid of the actual field forces, we normally find a vast spheroid of pointless rear-echelon supervision and 'assistance', with lines going all over the place. (See Diagram 1, page 241.) Even the deployed Joint Commander is saddled with a miniature inter-service conflict in the making: he must take with him superfluous land, air and sea sub-commanders whom he must work through whenever he wants to tell his actual combat units to do anything.

The terms 'staff' and 'staff work' are much abused in the British forces. At worst, staff has come to mean any employment for military personnel other than in operational units, and we find all kinds of people claiming to be staff officers: instructors in training schools, for example, are prone to the delusion that they too are staff. Indeed, formally speaking, all British army officers of the combatant arms leave their regiments when they are promoted colonel and become members of the Staff Corps, now to devote themselves to scientific military thought rather than blind tribal loyalty. However, this is not true in any practical sense. They continue to wear their old berets and other insignia, and most spend their remaining careers as rabid partisans of their original regiment and arm, much like their air force and naval colleagues.

Similarly, staff work often comes to mean any paperwork or administration. When giving a junior officer a tiresome job, such as drafting a lengthy document most of which is unlikely to be read by anyone, it is thought to make him feel better if he is told that it is staff work rather than mindless drudgery. To his CO giving him the job, the magic word 'staff' is redolent of promotion, preferment and all good things. It conjures up a glittering world where one is untroubled by recalcitrant non-commissioned people, where worry and danger are in a context of plans and briefings and arrows on maps rather than one of car ferries on collision courses, or over-stressed teenagers with loaded guns, or warning captions, or worse things still. The CO can't understand why the idea of briefly being a staff officer doesn't inspire his junior.

Of course, the chances are that the junior doesn't have any long-term career aspirations as yet. Such a fellow still 'has his head down in the tactical weeds', according to the lofty staff types, whose noses are supposedly sniffing the fresh breeze up at the 'operational level' of war.* The junior man out at sea or in his foxhole (*he* might actually be found in one – he might even have dug it himself) or up in the sky is often unconvinced. He can't rid himself of the suspicion that the staff types have their heads stuck

---

* This is a thing invented by army staffs back in the 20th century to fit between tactics and strategy. There are no jobs for generals and staffs in tactics – even corporals do tactics nowadays. Since the advent of long-range instant communications, however, the strategic role of senior military officers has also tended to evaporate, as heads of state and other politicians often take this over directly. Thus it became necessary to dream up the operational level of war, which is what staff people now like to think of themselves as being for. This has perhaps been rather undercut lately by the notion of the 'strategic corporal', a realistic bit of jargon which acknowledges that quite often nowadays even grandest strategy may be decided according to what happens at rifle section level, rather than the other way round.

firmly somewhere a lot darker than any mere tactical weeds. This opinion is normally based on bitter experience.

> When the units started to collect their vehicles and stores from depots which were spread around the country and manned mostly by civilians who took the week-end off, it was found that mobilisation scales were out-of-date, that numerous items were out-of-stock and that many of the vehicles were, to say the least, decrepit . . . help had to be sought from Pickfords . . . it took four weeks to move and load [aboard ship] ninety-three tanks . . .
>
> *Account of the preparations for*
> *the Suez operation of 1956*

And lest you think that things have changed:

> The container park near the Kuwaiti ports was likened to a Christmas morning where the children had gone downstairs first and removed all the labels from the presents so nobody knew either what was inside or who they were from until they'd been opened . . . Our ammunition arrived much later in the shipping order than I would have liked; it would have been embarrassing to have had guns with no bullets.
>
> *Second in command of 1 UK Division*
> *for the Iraq invasion of 2003 describing the*
> *situation during arrival in theatre.*

A good job, then, that Saddam's boys chose to stay on the defens-ive while we sorted ourselves out. If we'd tried that against the Germans in the old days, the results don't bear thinking about.

We have hundreds – if not thousands – of logistics staffers in the Joint HQ, Land, Strike, Fleet, the DLO and other places. All of them are there so that things such as the Kuwaiti container park will be slickly organised, and the field operators will not have to rootle about at random for their supplies (and possibly get the chance to snaffle things meant for others, leading to even more confusion). It isn't as though a deployment to Kuwait was an unlikely scenario, either: and there are yet more legions of high-priced talent who do nothing but produce plans for such things. We could probably have spared at least a major to sit on top of every stack of containers as it travelled from the UK to Kuwait and remember what was in it.

And yet, despite it being an obvious task which should have been anticipated and thoroughly planned to death years before, despite the involvement of no fewer than five mighty, expensive brain trusts, we get dangerous chaos. The suspicions of the field operators turn out to be correct, even after the establishment of the PJHQ was supposed to have solved everything. Combat people still deride staff types as 'PONTIs',* and it seems that they are often justified in doing so.

All in all, one can't help thinking that if we only had one brain trust in charge of arranging the container park in Kuwait, rather than five separate ones, it might have been a bit better organised. Fewer desk jockeys, rather than more, might be the way ahead. Even if performance in planning and organisation didn't improve, we'd certainly save ourselves a lot of money and spare ourselves a lot of annoying double-talk. But this would be to cruelly savage most long-serving officers' promotion and employment prospects: it doesn't seem likely.

Perhaps we should leave this subject with a final illustration of the curious viewpoint that the rear echelons develop. The home of the PJHQ is in a compound at Northwood, about fifteen miles from the centre of London. There is an ornamental pond and gardens, and a comfortable mess. The actual headquarters is mostly far underground, in an invulnerable bunker hardened against nuclear attack. Northwood is a *very* safe place, then – safer than your house, in all likelihood – and really rather comfortable and pleasant. This is where PJHQ's 600 brilliant minds spend most of their time. Their website gives a clue as to how they see their work: 'With the modern command, control and communications facilities installed here to allow the Chief of Joint Operations to direct national operations world-wide . . . **Northwood is very much in the front line.**'

There seems to be little hope.

---

* Persons Of No Tactical Importance. At least one recent attendee on the Advanced Command and Staff Course has described it as 'PONTI Hogwarts'.

Diagram 1: British Forces' command structure (for Iraq invasion 2003)

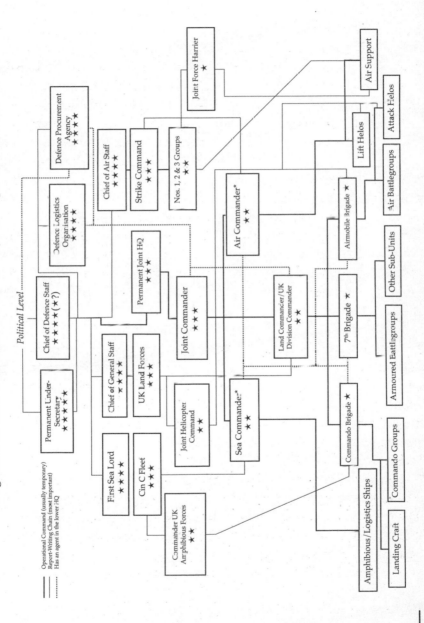

Operational Command (usually temporary)
Report-Writing Chain (most important)
Has an agent in the lower HQ

Political Level

Permanent Under-Secretary ★★★★

Chief of Defence Staff ★★★★ (★?)

Defence Procurement Agency ★★★★

Defence Logistics Organisation ★★★★

Chief of Air Staff ★★★★

Strike Command ★★★

Nos. 1, 2 & 3 Groups ★★

Joint Force Harrier ★

First Sea Lord ★★★★

Cin C Fleet ★★★

Chief of General Staff ★★★★

UK Land Forces ★★★

Permanent Joint HQ ★★★

Joint Commander ★★★

Air Commander* ★★

Air Support ★

Commander UK Amphibious Forces ★★

Joint Helicopter Command ★★

Sea Commander* ★★

Land Commander/UK Division Commander ★★

Airmobile Brigade ★

Lift Helos

Attack Helos

Amphibious/Logistics Ships

Commando Brigade ★

7th Brigade ★

Air Battlegroups

Landing Craft

Commando Groups

Armoured Battlegroups

Other Sub-Units

* Both sea and air commanders had other units at their disposal, but these were largely irrelevant or useless frigates, destroyers, Tornado F3s or deep-strike GR4s, etc.

CHAPTER
10

The British Defence Industry

'The business of government is to keep the government out of business – that is, unless business needs government aid'

Will Rogers, American comic and commentator

So far we have seen all the main combat systems in the British armed forces, from rifles to aircraft carriers, and in many cases we have an idea of what might replace them (nearly always an unimaginative copy of what we already had). Most readers will have picked up on the fact that the name 'British Aerospace' crops up again and again and again – seldom in connection with anything good. It makes sense to take a look at this firm, the more so as in doing this we will cover almost the whole of the remaining British defence, aerospace and shipbuilding industries.

The British Aerospace story begins in the late 1970s. Only a few aviation manufacturers were left operating in Britain at that point, and it was clear that without government intervention most of them would go to the wall sooner or later: the domestic aircraft and missile industry was on the point of collapse. It should be borne in mind that this was to some degree because of shoddy or useless output. The Comet jetliner had a nasty tendency to fall apart in mid-air; the first generation of British guided missiles was comically ineffectual; the Lightning fighter was sexy and beautiful but poorly armed and unable to stay airborne for long. In a Western-world marketplace which realistically needed only a few missiles and aircraft, such products could find few buyers.

So, in 1977, the government stepped in. The British Aircraft Corporation, Hawker Siddeley Aviation, Hawker Siddeley Dynamics and Scottish Aviation, most of which were themselves the result of mergers, were merged and nationalised to produce British Aerospace. The plan was that this company would be given massive injections of government cash, and so kept viable. This would maintain two important things for Britain: the ability to make our own high-technology weaponry rather than having to import it, and the existence of a credible British civil aircraft industry. The cash was certainly injected, in the form of straight-forward subsidies, massive government orders and other sweet-heart deals. Neither of these two aims, however, has been achieved today, as we shall see.

The Labour government, in accordance with socialist thinking back then, would probably have been happy enough to let British Aerospace continue as a state bureau indefinitely. But soon enough it was the 1980s; Labour was swept aside by the Conservatives, and the long government privatisation drive began. BAe, its debts written off, its pockets stuffed with government cash and its books with grossly inflated MoD orders for dubious kit such as Sea Dart and Tornado, was now a prime property. (Literally: it had also inherited large amounts of valuable real estate.) The company was sold off beginning in 1981, although the government retains a special £1 share which is supposed to keep it under UK control, and in theory there are limits on foreign ownership.

BAe now took on several roles. It became asset-stripper to the British government, for example. One instance of this was the sale of the government's many gun and cannon factories to BAe under the name Royal Ordnance in 1987, as we saw in Chapter 1. The Royal Small Arms Factory at Enfield Lock in North London, the last small arms maker left in Britain, was part of the deal. It would have cost money to bring the plant up to date and, even more importantly, it was sitting on prime real estate with excellent commuter connections to central London. The factory closed within a year, before it could even finish making its useless SA80 rifles for the British forces. Enfield Lock is now the site of Enfield Island Village. The lucra-tive second tranche of SA80 rifle production was carried out every bit as badly as the first had been, at another Royal Ordnance/BAe plant in Nottingham.

This asset-stripping role was not confined to the defence sector. BAe's close relationship with the government again stood it in good stead in 1988. The British mass-market car industry, another casualty of the 1970s, was now owned by the government just as BAe had been. Various grand old British automotive names had been merged to form the Rover Group. The government put in a cash injection of no less than £547 million – not far off a billion in today's money – wiping out the group's debts and turning it into a tasty going concern. It was then sold to BAe for a grand total of £150 million. A subsequent report by the national audit office noted that Rover Group made BAe a profit of £65 million within a year and that BAe had been able to sell off Rover Group assets to the tune of £126 million almost immediately. A pretty sweet deal for BAe: they get a major, money-making asset worth something in the region of a billion pounds and it not only doesn't cost them anything, they effectively get £41 million for taking it off the government's hands! They sold their remaining 80per cent stake in Rover six years later for £800m.

Naturally, taking over Royal Ordnance and Rover involved firing large numbers of people, one thing that the government had not felt able to do. There were also several BAe factories which weren't doing anything much, hadn't done anything much for years, and didn't seem likely to do anything much in future: these even bigger workforces had to be sacked too, if BAe was ever to show healthy accounts*. The company's boss at the time, Professor Sir Roland Smith, planned to deal with

---

* I was briefly employed at one of these plants, the civil-aircraft factory at Hatfield, as a management trainee from 1988–1989. I was let go well before the site closed, among other things for pointing out that nobody there was actually doing anything. The Hatfield site had originally been home to the legendary De Havilland company, but the failure of the Comet in the 1960s did for them. The civil side of Hatfield had trundled along amiably for decades since then under Hawker-Siddeley and then BAe without achieving anything that might have justified its many thousands of well-paid staff. BAe finally grasped that nettle in the early '90s: the site is now being turned into a university campus.

the redundancy payouts by selling off some of the company's
enormous amounts of real estate; in the late 1980s the property market seemed a lot easier to make a profit in than the
high-tech engineering one. Pleasingly for those who feel that
engineering is a more laudable field of activity than property
speculation, the scheme backfired badly. Many readers will
remember the real-estate crash of the early 1990s. BAe took
such a severe beating that it very nearly went under, and
Professor Smith was unceremoniously dumped. Astonishingly
to anyone not acquainted with the world of high finance, he
went on to take charge of other large concerns, and was later
made honorary professor of management science at Manchester
University. He died in 2003, revered as a titan of British
business.

BAe survived, although at one point it appeared that it might
be taken over by its great rival of the early 1990s, the General
Electric Company (GEC). This would have been a case of the
greater of two evils. BAe wasn't much good at making hi-tech
kit, but GEC was worse. It had just emerged from the Nimrod-
AEW fiasco, in which it had taken over a billion of public money
over ten years, and succeeded only in producing the world's
ugliest pieces of flying junk. In the event, BAe fought off the
takeover bid, and a few years later bounced back to take over
GEC.

Meanwhile, having finally disposed of great swathes of the
remaining British engineering workforce, British Aerospace
ploughed on. The corporation still seemed unable to make any
decent aircraft or weapons, or to turn much of a profit. People
often wonder how it is that BAe has managed to grow into the
second or third largest arms concern in the world. One answer
to this conundrum is the infamous Al Yamamah weapons
contract, described by the *Financial Times* as 'the biggest UK
sale ever of anything to anyone'.

Al Yamamah was awarded to BAe in 1985 by Saudi Arabia:
the deal was brokered by the British government, as is common
in these cases. The contract centred around the supply of dubious
Tornado jets, both bombers and fighters, but other items were
also included: most notably trainer aircraft and three Sandown-
class minehunting ships. Critically, Al-Yamamah also included

munitions, maintenance, through-life upgrades, and massive provision of training and other support facilities. Even as late as 2004, BAe was getting annual revenue of over £1 billion from Al-Yamamah, and total receipts have been estimated at anywhere from £22 billion on up through £50bn since the deal was set up. Lately the Saudis have been making some belated attempts at getting value for money, but BAe continue to be a massive drain on their public finances.

As for how BAe managed to get themselves such a peach of a deal from the Saudis, especially in light of the poor perform-ance of the Tornado – particularly the F3 fighter – that is a tale in itself. Even after the British government had given the lament-able F3 some undeserved credibility by ordering a large number of jets for the RAF, most foreign governments could see no reason to buy it. The Saudis did, though, despite the fact that the RAF's F3s were then flying about with their nose cones full of concrete, and everyone knew that the radars which should have been there would not be serviceable for years. They also bought even larger numbers of Tornado bombers, with 'runway-denial' low-level suicide weapons all complete.

Most people knowledgeable about defence systems can see no legitimate explanation for the Saudi government's purchases. It is generally felt that the Saudis must have had some powerful hidden reason to buy jets with a terrible reputation, in a parts and service lifetime package which is still bleeding their treasury viciously two decades later. A few suggest that the Saudis went with the Tornado because the US Congress had refused to allow them American planes. Such a prohibition did occur but it was only temporary: as evidenced by the fact that the Saudis now operate large numbers of cheap, excellent US-made F-15s in addition to their dreadful, expensive British Tornados. Anyway, nothing was stopping the Saudis from buying French or Swedish or Russian.

So what was the motivation to buy British? It has been widely reported that the Saudi royal in charge of Al Yamamah was provided with 'a lifestyle beyond that of most film stars'* at

---

* This according to Peter Gardiner, boss of the private travel company Travellers World, who laid on 5-star hotels, chartered aircraft, limousines and so forth on BAe's tab.

BAe's expense, and other Saudis are said to have received large kickbacks. The scandal is ongoing, and both the Serious Fraud Office and the Ministry of Defence police are investigating the matter as I write. BAe, of course, denies all wrongdoing. Sir Richard Evans, BAe's chairman, has stated to the Parliamentary Defence Select Committee that 'we are not in the business of making payments to the members of any government'. This is a manifestly true statement. It would be just as true to say, for example, that BAe is not in the business of buying office computers or printer paper. It still buys a lot of them, though. But BAe insists it is falsely accused and told the *Guardian*: 'We operate in line with the laws of the United Kingdom and all other countries we operate in.'

However the MoD-plod and SFO investigations turn out (neither organisation has a particularly impressive track record, and both have good reasons to report that all is well – the Al Yamamah deal was set up by the British government, remember) there are only two possibilities. Firstly, that BAe used bribery. Secondly, that the Saudis decided to buy the worst kit on the market, at an absurdly inflated price, *for no reason at all*. I know which one I'd bet on.

Still, one has to keep a sense of perspective regarding Al Yamamah. BAe, or BAE Systems as it nowadays prefers to call itself, has surely taken tens or even scores of billions from the Saudis, and provided very little in the way of useful kit. Few will weep for the House of Saud, however, or find the fact that they are poorly armed a cause for concern. Rather more to the point, Al Yamamah is small beer compared to what BAE has done to the British government. The Saudis only bought a few jets, ships and accessories from BAE; the UK's MoD has bought just about everything that BAE has ever offered for sale, often in larger numbers than our armed forces actually wanted. The *Financial Times*' description of Al Yamamah as 'biggest ever' is only correct in terms of a single export deal; the many, many deals BAE has done with the British government have been far more lucrative in total. The Eurofighter gravy train, to name just one, first pulled out of the station at the same time as Al Yamamah – and will keep running for a good many years yet.

And it gets worse. The huge piles of government cash gifted to BAE over the years have been used in an aggressive programme of acquisitions. BAE has bought up just about the whole of the remaining UK defence sector: the very few UK arms factories not part of BAE are now owned by foreign companies. If you want to buy weapons made by a British firm, or at any rate a nominally British one, you must go to BAE. 'British Aerospace' is nowadays something of a misnomer. BAE is not merely an aerospace company; it makes weapons systems used on land and sea as well. Armour, artillery, warships, submarines, torpedoes, mines . . . all of these are nowadays made by just one British provider: BAE.

As a side effect, BAE controls almost all remaining British shipyards. Commercial shipbuilding, like many another industry, has very largely moved to the Far East. British concerns, forced to pay their workers comparatively well, can normally only win British government business and thus are mostly builders and maintainers of warships and fleet auxiliaries. The only British building yards with big navy and RFA orders – the only ones likely to survive for long – are now owned by BAE.

This situation is not good from the viewpoint of a British fighting operator – and from other viewpoints too, no doubt. However, the disappearance of British manufacturing industry seems to have the inevitability of the tide going out, and trying to hold back the tide is well known to be impossible, even given governmental powers. It has been the case for many decades that if you wanted to buy a weapon in Britain, there was normally only one factory that could make it: Enfield for rifles, Waterlooville for torpedoes, and so on. This one plant could be reasonably sure of getting the job because British MPs don't like seeing money spent abroad when it could be buying them votes. As a result, the quality of British forces equipment has long been erratic (see the tables on page 254–5). But things are much worse now: all these individual companies have been united into a single unholy monster with an almost unbreakable hammer-lock on the MoD's purchasing bureau. BAE decide what will be bought and for how much, regardless of what the armed forces or even the government may want. Here is Admiral Sir Raymond Lygo, former BAE chief executive, on the subject:

Whatever you want to get through government, you have to first of all establish what is the Treasury likely to approve in terms of money . . .

So you say, 'Right, we can do this and we'll do it for the price,' and then the programme goes ahead. But you know automatically that it's going to cost more than that . . .

And so after a year you say, 'I'm terribly sorry but the costs have now risen for this reason and the other reason.'

There are always a thousand reasons because [the MoD] will never stop mucking about with the contract so you've always the comeback of saying, 'that is not the contract we agreed.'

And so then the price goes up and they have a decision whether they are going to continue or cancel. And the cancellation costs will be greater than continuing with it . . . That's life in Whitehall, I'm afraid.'

Interview on BBC Radio Five Live

BAE sets the agenda from start to finish. The pathetic negotiators of the Defence Procurement Agency are led by the nose until every possible penny has been squeezed from the taxpayers, regardless of what may be required by the national interest. BAE management are often veterans with experience on the government side of the table, such as Admiral Sir Raymond himself back in the 1980s. BAE nowadays employs other former senior officers, such as former air marshal Sir John Day. Sadly, the reverse is never true. BAE people are never contemplating a career with the Defence Procurement Agency.

Whenever this point is made, we are assured that everything has been fixed. We are told that 'smart procurement' has been in place since 1998, and all is now well. BAE no longer drives the programme.

This is quite simply not true. Even the air marshals of the RAF don't want 232 Eurofighters, for example (nobody else wants even one). They would like seven squadrons of a dozen, a further slightly bigger squadron for training, and some spares for when they have a prang. Say 115, 120 jets at most. The RAF does not have the pilots for any more and doesn't plan to train them: it hasn't the people or the budget to operate 200 plus of these planes. The air force would have to become an entirely Eurofighter force to do so – and thus almost entirely irrelevant. Yet in 2004 – six years after 'smart procurement' had allegedly been introduced – we increased our order from 55 to 144 Eurofighters and, barring a miracle, we will increase it again soon to 232. At least a score of these wildly expensive jets, which only a minority even of the RAF considers necessary, will never fly; quite likely, over a hundred of them. What's 'smart' about that? Who on earth, apart from BAE, benefits? (The book answer is that 'smart procurement' doesn't apply to Eurofighter because this project began in the 1980s. Under rules such as these we have at least another decade or so before the new system actually produces any real results – assuming anyone remembers it by then.)

The project that advocates of 'smart procurement' would rather discuss is Sonar 2087, which we saw in Chapter 8. This programme is intended to provide new pinging sonars for the navy's Type 23 frigates to find submarines with, because the ones originally supplied are rubbish. Sonar 2087 is lauded as a work of genius because it was 'de-risked'. This means that a prototype was actually built and tested before the decision was taken to start making sonars in any numbers and fitting them to ships. Brilliant stuff this, according to the friends of the Defence Procurement Agency – groundbreaking, really. The reaction from most normal people tends to be more along the lines of, 'You mean it *isn't normal practice* to test prototypes and find out whether the thing works before going to production?'

De-risking, then, the centrepiece of 'smart procurement', is quite simple: don't order dozens or hundreds of anything until you know it can work. It is hard to congratulate the DPA for such basic stuff. (It wasn't even their idea, anyway: they had to hire consultants.) And de-risking hasn't dealt with the main problem of Sonar 2087, which is simply that it isn't required. The frigates have no submarines to hunt in the first place, and if any should appear their hash will be settled by aircraft or our own subs, not by frigates. So Sonar 2087 is hardly a triumph for common sense.

The Procurement chaps also like to talk up Sonar 2087 because it is being made by Thales, the French defence group, which appears to show that we are no longer in thrall to the jobs-for-the-boys principle. However, this doesn't stand up under examination. Thales have the contract because they bought the one factory in Britain which makes sonars before BAE could buy it; this is where the work is being done. The job was not actually open to competition in any real way.

Today's situation doesn't bode well for quality, either. Occasionally in the past British makers would produce some decent equipment, despite not really having any competition. BAE, which now owns nearly all of them, has never made anything itself which really worked well, as the tables below show, and it has ruined a number of perfectly good products and companies after taking them over. Early versions of the Hawker Siddeley Harrier jump-jet, for example, were absolutely amazing for their day. This plane was later competently upgraded by McDonnell Douglas, at the behest of the US Marines, and in this form it is still a good aircraft. The BAE modification – the Sea Harrier FA2 missile upgrade for the Royal Navy – could only lift its excellent American missiles in cold weather, and it was delivered years too late for this to be of any use. BAE management threatens to reduce the current goodish British torpedoes and a few other minor successes to the lowest common denominator as well.

So, the main purpose of British Aerospace, the reason for the government's massive and unceasing support for it, has not been achieved: Britain cannot any longer make proper up to date weapons – certainly not without foreign assistance. British weaponry, twenty-five years after the appearance of BAe, is mostly expensive rubbish, and all the signs are that it will get worse. The extent to which British forces are properly armed is largely the extent to which they have been allowed to buy abroad, which normally means buy American. Several manufacturing capabilities have already disappeared from Britain altogether, or passed into foreign hands: helicopters, small arms, naval sonars and light army-type missiles are the most obvious examples.

The secondary purpose of setting up this monstrous cartel – the maintenance of a viable British civil aircraft industry – has pretty well failed as well. For practical purposes there are now two major civil-aircraft makers in the world. BAE owns 20 per cent of one of them (Airbus), and makes wings for it; that's pretty much all Britain has retained in this line. There is also a genuine, viable British jet-engine maker, Rolls-Royce, which is grounds for real industrial pride, but BAE can claim no credit for this.* British civil shipbuilding has gone almost completely by the board, with those non-naval yards which haven't closed surviving on crumbs of maintenance and refit work, or making yachts and the like. Real, working commercial shipping is no longer built in the UK.

Really, then, we have received no benefits at all for the vast sums we have poured into BAE over the decades. Our civil aircraft and shipbuilding industries have disappeared anyway, and we have lost our national ability to arm ourselves despite having paid well over the odds to retain it. We have become totally dependent on foreign partnerships if we wish to make weapons of any complexity; sometimes, even, to make very simple ones such as rifles. Indeed, to a large extent, we have failed to arm ourselves properly at all. On land and sea and in the air, our excellent front-line servicemen and women struggle with badly designed, defective equipment. Massive hangars are crammed with British jets which will never fly at the same time as one of our three carriers is mothballed for lack of jets, and inadequate numbers of useful, mostly foreign-designed planes and helicopters struggle to do the work. Our legendary infantrymen, hard pressed as they are, turn in their colours so that we can afford even more BAE jets, to sit in even more hangars.

And still BAE is heavily involved in all the big projects currently under way. Why?

Some people still rabbit on about 'building your own' despite the fact that this part of the debate is largely over from the viewpoint of those who actually use weapons, rather than make them. As far as combat operators are concerned, with a very

---

* The real, serious Rolls-Royce, one of only a few firms in the world which can really build gas turbines and jet engines. Not to be confused with the luxury car brand, of no great importance, which was sold to Germany a few years back.

BAE products in British service

System	Any good?
SA80 Rifle	Dross, finally rectified in Germany
Tornado bomber	Misconceived from the start, still poor after much upgrading
Tornado fighter	Awful, many bought only to be mothballed
Eurofighter	Not required, very late, very expensive, too many on order already
Storm Shadow air-dropped cruise	Not required, very expensive, unreliable
Sea Wolf missile	Expensive rubbish
Rapier missile	OK-ish
ALARM missile	Needlessly complex and pricey
Warships and auxiliaries	Six built under BAE management so far, at least two badly botched
Nimrod patrol aircraft	Existing version OK-ish, but many bought only for mothballs

Other in-service British products

System	Any good?	Maker	Fate of Maker
Warrior AIFV	Good	Alvis Vickers	Taken over by BAe
Challenger II tank	OK, irrelevant	Alvis Vickers	Taken over by BAe
Harrier jet	Excellent	Hawker Siddeley	Taken over by BAe
Naval torpedoes	OK	Marconi	Taken over by BAe
Merlin helicopter	Not yet	Westland	Sold abroad
Lynx helicopter	Good		
Apache helicopter	OK, stupidly pricey		
Sea King/Puma	OK, now worn out		
TIALD targeting pod	Poor	GEC	Taken over by BAe
AS90 howitzer	OK, irrelevant	Vickers	Taken over by BAe
Sea Dart missile	Basically rubbish	Hawker Siddeley	Taken over by BAe
Starstreak missile	Seems OK	Shorts	Sold abroad
Warships and auxiliaries	Mixed bag	Yarrows (15)	Taken over by BAe
		Swan Hunter (18)	On the ropes
		Vickers (20)	Taken over by BAe
		Cammell Laird (6)	Closed
		Vosper (25)	Leaving the market*
LAW94 rocket	OK	Hunting/Insys	BAe subcontractor**

* Warships built by Vosper have mostly been small ones. The company is moving out of shipbuilding and now estimate that 75 per cent of their business is in other areas.

In-service systems without British involvement

System	Any good?	Maker	Country of origin
Minimi light machine gun	Good	Fabrique Nationale	Belgium
Underslung grenade launcher	Seems fine	Heckler and Koch	Germany
Hercules transport plane	Excellent	Lockheed	USA
C-17 Globemaster transport plane	Excellent	Boeing	USA
Chinook helicopter	Excellent	Boeing	USA
Current air-to-air missiles	Good	Various	All from USA
Current air-to-ground weapons	Good	Various	All from USA
Harpoon naval missile	Good	Hughes/Raytheon	USA
Tomahawk cruise missile	Excellent	Hughes/Raytheon	USA
Phalanx naval air defence gun	Good	Hughes	USA
Goalkeeper naval air defence gun	Good	Signaal/GD	Netherlands/USA
MLRS artillery rockets	OK, messy	Lockheed	USA
MILAN infantry missile	OK	Euromissile***	France/Germany

Future kit

System	Necessary?	Prognosis/summary	BAE involved
F-35 jump-jet	Yes	Avoidable problems	Yes
Type 45 destroyer and missiles	No	Expensive, stupid	Yes, both
Future carrier	Yes	Half-arsed, struggling	Yes
Astute-class subs	Maybe	Late, well over budget	Yes
ASTOR radar planes	Yes	Half-arsed, very expensive	Yes
FLA-A400M transport plane	No	Awful value for money, late	Yes
Future air-to-air missiles	Not really	Bad, Euro-consortia	Yes
Nimrod replacements	No	Awful mess	Oh yes
Future army missiles and rockets	Some	Pretty good	No
Sonar 2087	No	Should work to spec	No

** Insys is notionally the lead contractor on the new LIMAWS artillery rocket system, but in fact both rockets and vehicles are to be made by other firms. Insys' 'lead' role in LIMAWS is presumably intended to mask from most casual observers, like MPs, the fact that the MoD is buying American. Other than this, Insys is purely a sub-assembly maker.

*** The French bit of Euromissile is now attached to the BAE empire, but this happened after the MILAN was produced.

few exceptions, to be British armed is becoming similar to being unarmed. However, away from the front line it is often still taken as a given that Britain – maybe with European assistance – really can make its own useful weapons, and that this is a genuine (if expensive) option. If Britain doesn't make its own weapons, goes the reasoning, it may be unable to fight. Modern weaponry is said to need a constant flow of spare parts and other manufacturer support to remain functional. If Britain is to be a truly sovereign nation state, able to make its own policy, it must build its own arms. This means that BAE, now the only British weapons maker, must continue to receive most if not all of the MoD's business.

The trouble with this is that Britain simply cannot support the full spectrum of modern weapons manufacture; it hasn't been able to for decades. BAE already cannot build a new missile or a new plane; it must ally with other, foreign, defence firms to do so. It can sometimes make simpler items such as radars, ship hulls and so forth, but these alone can seldom be assembled into a modern fighting platform. In terms of weapons manufacture, Britain has already lost its sovereignty. Indeed, almost everybody has, except America and maybe, for a little while more, France. So much for that argument.

The next line of defence for the buy-British advocates is usually Europe – which is odd, as until this point in the argument their stance has been British-Isolationist. Very well, they say, Britain alone can't support a serious modern arms industry – one that can compete with the Americans, that is. But *Europe* could, if we all just pulled together. That would be better than being forced to rely on the US, wouldn't it? The building of a European military superpower to rival or even confront America isn't a goal which is commonly stated plainly, but in essence this is sometimes thought to justify our continuing to spend vast sums on British arms plants. Disagreement between Europe and America is the only possible reason for the industrial democracies of the world to maintain two vast, independent weapons industries rather than just one. Better BAE and its sometime continental associates than Lockheed, Boeing et al. – that's the idea.

There are many holes in this argument, even if you think that superpower rivalry is a good thing (please god, hopefully you don't).

Firstly, Europe can't, in fact, match US defence spending. The US spends far more on defence than the whole rest of the world combined. On trends through 2003, the US will have got within spitting distance of spending *twice as much as the whole rest of the world* in 2004.* (This leaves the British two-power standard of the 1890s looking puny and unambitious. The US armed forces really should be able to do more than just beat the next two biggest; they ought to be able to conquer this whole planet and another one like it – provided, of course, that the other planet lacked a USA of its own, and that money was the only factor in military power.**) The governments of post-World War II Europe have never spent as much proportionally on their militaries as the US, nor have they had anything like as much revenue to begin with. Europe, even if it could get its act together, will never be able to afford a defence-industrial sector which can match America's for either quality or quantity. As far as conventional military activities are concerned, the Pax Americana is a fact and we are all living under it. (Of course, there are exceptions. Nuclear-tipped ICBMs, for the moment, confer immunity from direct American confrontation up to a point; this is why everyone is so keen to get some.*** And the Yanks still find the men-with-guns level of operations as troublesome as ever.)

Secondly, there is no technological independence any more. You can make a rifle without using US parts, sure. (Well, British engineers can't, actually – even the abject SA80 was based around an excellent American design, which the men from Enfield

---

* CIA World Factbook and Stockholm International Peace Research Institute data both support this assessment.

** It isn't, of course. As the old saw has it, good soldiers can usually get you some gold, but gold won't always get you good soldiers. The Americans do have some good soldiers, in fact, but not in numbers anywhere near proportionate to the gold they spend.

*** Everyone really is keen to get them; *this* isn't scaremongering or lies. So much flimflam has lately surrounded the whole area of weapons of mass destruction that people sometimes assume it to be a non-issue. Chemical artillery shells are a bogeyman to frighten children with – the Kaiser had them in World War I, for goodness' sake – even where they actually exist; bio-weapons likewise. But long-ranging missiles and nukes are the real deal. If I was running a government, I'd want some.

somehow managed to ruin – but most countries can.) You'll struggle to build a decent night sight for your rifle, though, or a reliable encrypted radio for your rifle-section leader. Even if you get that done, you aren't realistically going to make a useful jet fighter or weapons for it without parts and probably expertise from the States. For that matter, everybody – even the Americans themselves – will find it wildly inconvenient to attempt any of these things without using components manufactured in China or Japan, or software written in India, or all sorts of other things from all sorts of other places. The global economy isn't just on the way; it's here, as far as high-tech manufacturing is concerned. Nobody is really independent, not even the Yanks.

Furthermore, the idea that weapon systems can't be used contrary to the wishes of their country of manufacture isn't *necessarily* true: it's only true if you manage your support echelons idiotically, as we do. Certainly, complex kit needs spare parts, but there isn't much to stop you from ordering a big supply of these when you buy the planes or whatever, or from cannibalising bits within your fleet. This can be seen from the way the Iranian air force was able to keep flying its cutting-edge American F-14 fighters against the Iraqis all through the 1980s, scoring kills with all types of weapon. It didn't matter that the USA had withdrawn support for these planes on the fall of the Shah, and indeed had placed Iran under a 'total' arms embargo.* A lot of military equipment doesn't require even this much effort, and is easily used against those who made it. Many, many Russian soldiers have been killed with AK47 rifles and RPGs, while American Stinger missiles have been used against US aircraft on several occasions.

You'll need quite efficient technical people of your own to service your foreign-bought high-tech gear to the level where you don't need manufacturer back-up, but in a First World country this shouldn't be a problem. Many modern forces don't bother, of course: we British, despite having enormous numbers of expensively trained uniformed technicians and civil-service or partly

---

* It isn't clear how much the Iran–Contra affair contributed to the Iranians' early success in maintaining their F-14s. It is clear that up to thirty of the seventy-nine F-14s supplied are still flying to this day, decades after even secret US support must have been cut off.

civil-service boffins, are often reliant on manufacturer tech back-up actually on the battlefield. It takes many years, usually, for the British forces to develop any serious expertise in a new system, whether foreign *or* British. Good techs learn fast, and are jewels beyond price, but these people are fairly rare – as rare as the really bad ones, who are so far behind the game that they aren't worth taking with you. I have served with both, and with the more normal forces tech who knows some of his kit well and some of it less well.

Even if the British forces managed to get a more serious grip on their modern equipment, however, they would be – are – hamstrung by the 'just enough, just in time' stores policy now universal in the Defence Logistics Organisation. Even if you manage to find a tech who knows what bit to replace in order to mend something, and he isn't forbidden to do so by some asinine MoD written hand-book (yes, this too is common) it isn't any use if he can't get the part. And he won't be able to get it, because the so-brilliantly organ-ised logistics chain reaching all the way from the front line back to Britain does not end at a big store full of parts. It ends at a man behind a desk who knows the manufacturer's phone number. *That's* what 'just enough, just in time' means.

But this isn't necessary, it's just the way we do it. The DLO finds it infinitely easier to control costs by slashing inventory than by firing any of its byzantine bureaucracy, so that is what it has done. The Defence Procurement Agency finds it much easier to negotiate sweetheart, life-of-system contracts than to buy a proper set of parts and manuals to begin with – so that is what it has done. Much of the time, despite buying British until our noses bleed, we wind up in the same situation we would have been in had we bought American and then found ourselves in complete disagreement with Washington, to the point where they cut off our spare parts. So, really, we might as well buy American and have done with it. At least that way we'd be able to fight when-ever the US was onside (most of the time) rather than only when BAE/Euro arms partner du jour has a few spare bits on the shelf – seldom, because often nobody else buys their stuff.

People in the pocket of the British defence industry will tell you at this point that none of this is true and that the horrid US government refuses to release full technical data to foreign buyers of American weaponry. They will cite the current mild brouhaha regarding the source software code of the F-35 jet, for instance, which some say will not ever be released to the British. And true, it is a fact that the US has made an effort to design the plane so that overseas customers will not be able to modify it or use its technology in other designs.

But source software code isn't all that important – you aren't going to need it to fix short-term, battle-timescale problems. Monkeying with flight or weapon software is not something you do in a hurry. A swift reinstall would be about all we'd really need. I would be a lot more worried about hardware – about spare engines and tyres and circuit boards and flexible hoses and munitions – that is, I would if I thought for one moment that our DLO intended to hold any useful stock of such things. I would also, once again, point out that if the Iranians can use F-14 Tomcats against Washington's wishes, we should bloody well be able to use F-35s. American attempts to restrict military technology have seldom been very successful – the GPS navigation satellites are another case in point.* And I would round off by pointing out that BAE usually refuses to release useful technical information to the British forces as well, so one gains nothing in this respect by buying from them. As an example, British bomb-disposal operators in the Balkans during the 1990s were unable to obtain any information on the late-model BAE bomb fuses they were encountering: BAE refused to divulge it on grounds of 'commercial confidentiality'. Our bomb-disposal men had to use improvised, needlessly risky and destructive render-safe procedures as a result. Thanks a million, BAE.

---

* GPS was originally intended to offer no better than 100–150 metre accuracy to anyone who didn't have special codes – that is, anyone not in the US military. This restriction was laughably easy to get around, however. In some circumstances, non-US-military users were able to obtain greater accuracy than American forces themselves. America gave up in the end, and unlocked the system for anyone to use, although they retain the option of turning it off altogether over certain regions. (This would prohibit just about all US military activity in such a region – it isn't really a threat.) GPS will soon be tied in with the European Galileo satellites, offering an even better service and reducing US control still further.

Finally, even in this dream world where you have managed to purchase your mythical high-tech weapon which is not dependent on anything made in America, and it works, you still can't use it if the Yanks really don't want you to. They aren't particularly good at controlling the use of low-tech stuff like rifles and RPGs and bombs, but they are absolutely marvellous at high-tech prevention. Both the no-fly zone and the no-tank zone are American coinages, and they could easily implement no-ship zones as well.

So let's say you've decided to go to war with your Eurofighter, or your Type 45 Brit–Euro destroyer,* and the Americans really seriously disagree. They'll stop you. Eurofighters aren't going to beat F-22 Raptors, or even the current US jets in long-range missile exchanges, and anyway Eurofighters are dependent on US-made AWACS planes to operate. Any feasible number of Type 45s could be blasted to scrap by a US strike package in a matter of minutes, even if the ships actually work according to spec. Of course, you could then threaten a nuclear launch against America, if you were really committed to this war of yours, but if you're that crazy you could have done so when the US withdrew tech support for your American-supplied ships and planes. There wasn't any need to piss away hundreds of billions buying 'independent' conventional weapons. All that money really got you was the ability to carry out a very narrow class of operations: ones requiring high-tech weaponry, disapproved of by the US to the degree that they will cut off technical support but not enough that they will use force to stop you. In other words, you have bought the capability to mount another Suez fiasco. How very useful.

None of this stacks up. If such foolishness were really the only reason to buy British–European, we would be largely armed by America, to our very great benefit in terms of military punch and credibility, and to the very great relief of our public purse. All of the argument about building your own and independent capability is smoke and misdirection: a not-very-serious fig leaf for the real reason why we buy British, or buy Euro in such a way as to get all our money spent in Blighty.

---

* Runs on Windows, remember. Bill Gates will probably be able to shut the ships down remotely, assuming they haven't already crashed on their own.

The real reason, of course, is jobs for the boys and girls, no more and no less. Well-paid jobs in nice big clusters at arms factories: this is what MPs hope to buy when they give money to British defence contractors. Actual weapons, politically speaking, are just the cherry on top. What MPs seem not to realise is that they aren't gaining influence for themselves and their parties by doing this; they are surrendering political power to the arms makers and becoming their pawns. The jobs, once they exist, control the surrounding MPs absolutely, and all the rest of Parliament to a very serious degree. The political supervisors of the MoD spend most of their time making sure that it buys British: they care very little about anything else it might do or not do.

No bones are made about this. Consider Rachel Squire, Labour MP for Dunfermline West, right next to the Rosyth dockyard. The Rosyth bullet might be thought to have been bitten some years ago: it closed as a naval base and as a heavyweight shipyard during the early 1990s, under the Conservative government – nobody votes Tory around there, you see. Many jobs were lost, despite the fact that Labour reversed as much of the policy as they could on coming to power (Gordon Brown, chancellor of the exchequer and *eminence grise* of New Labour, also has his constituency seat within sight of the yard). Rosyth survives on generous helpings of naval refit work, most inconveniently for the navy now that it no longer bases ships there: and Rachel Squire would like to see it expand all over again. Here she is, addressing the head of the navy on the subject in open committee:

> You will not be surprised, Admiral, if I want to pick up a bit more on the future of aircraft carriers . . . because of . . . my interest as a local MP for the Rosyth dockyard and my hopes, along with other MPs [*that is, Gordon Brown, Admiral, and don't you forget it*] for getting a major share of the work . . . I was looking at a Warships Magazine interview . . . you were asked then about the new carriers contract that was placed at the end of January 2003 and the merits of competing companies . . . you were quoted as saying. 'What matters to me is that the Royal Navy gets the first carrier by 2012. Who builds the ships is neither here nor there

. . .' I would like you first of all to perhaps reinforce that you do see the work being done in the UK . . .

Examination of Witnesses by the Defence
Committee of the House of Commons,
Wednesday 24 November 2004.

And this person was allowed to be a member of the Defence Select Committee, heaven help us. Conflict of interest hardly seems to cover it. What does it matter what the new carriers cost or whether they are any good? Rachel Squire's top priority is whether or not Rosyth gets any work, and, by extension, whether she keeps her own job. She appears somewhat less concerned about the problems of the sailors and aviators who will one day depend on these ships for their lives. This is not right. She and her fellow committee members were not given powers to grill the First Sea Lord so that they could benefit their constituencies: they were supposed to be finding out whether Admiral West and his colleagues were running the defence of Britain properly.

This is only one minor example, and Rachel Squire is, after all, only doing what the voters of Dunfermline sent her to Westminster to do. If she ever went back to her constituency and said 'chaps, it seems that a Dutch or American yard could make us a much better carrier for the same money, so I'm afraid I recommended that's what we do' she would probably never return to Westminster. Nonetheless, this sort of thing is a hell of a way to decide who builds our new carriers (assuming they ever get built) and it illustrates the terrible weakness of democratic government in overseeing these matters.

Since democratic government, imperfect as it may be, is the only decent game in town, we must try to make it work better. The traditional remedy for unsatisfactory political performance, of course, is to vote for the other party next time. Unfortunately, when it comes to defence, this is unlikely to really change matters. Let's leave Labour for the moment, and give the Conservatives a turn under the lights.

The Right Honourable Michael Portillo MP was Conservative secretary of state for defence from 1995 to 1997. One of the many things the MoD did during this time was decide to upgrade the RAF's Nimrod maritime patrol aircraft; contracts were signed in 1996. This decision was curious in itself. Admittedly the Nimrod was very definitely showing its age, but one must remember that a maritime-patrol aircraft is principally intended for fighting enemy submarines – in other countries which operate them, they are owned by the navy rather than the air force. This was a cold war mission against the Red Banner Northern Fleet. By 1996 the commie submarines were already out of the picture, and so the decision to spend a lot of money on new anti-submarine planes seems odd.

It appears less odd, though, when you reflect that BAE would have been pushing the Nimrod upgrade deal through for some time by then. The original MoD plan had been for the Nimrods to be replaced by whatever the US Navy chose to succeed its similarly aged P-3 Orions, but the USN cancelled its P-7 programme in 1990 and nothing concrete has yet emerged in its place. This is understandable, given the disappearance of the communist threat and the suggestion by many that unmanned drones – or even nothing at all – would be a better idea for this role than vast, expensive manned aeroplanes. Britain, however, was undeterred by such real-world thinking. In 1990, with the folding of the P-7, BAE saw a chance to get a large amount of public money, and they successfully pushed the programme on, just as Admiral Lygo described on the BBC.

So, in 1996, Michael Portillo signed off on a £2.2 billion 'fixed-price' contract under which BAE was supposed to rebuild, rearm and update the RAF's twenty-one Nimrods – over a hundred million pounds per aircraft. The planes would enter service in 2003, and the programme was to include 80 per cent replacement of the airframes in addition to completely new mission systems electronics. The refurbished Nimrods would effectively be new planes, which was only reasonable considering the MoD was to pay new-plane prices and then some. A fair 1990s price for maritime-patrol planes is hard to set, as nobody else was barmy enough to buy any, but £100 million each is definitely on the high side.

The rest of the process followed as night follows day. Costs rose massively, delay piled upon delay. The 'fixed price' has climbed steadily since 1996, and the MoD now estimates the programme's overall tag as having increased by a whopping 60 per cent, to £3.5 billion: this despite the fact that the project became one of the first to be run under the 'smart procurement' principles in 1998. In fact, the true figure is worse, as it has also been agreed that the RAF is now to receive only twelve aircraft. Thus the cost per plane has almost tripled, to an amazing *two hundred and ninety million pounds*. This will make the 'new' Nimrods far and away the most expensive and pointless aircraft in the British armed forces, surpassing the Merlin helicopter and even the Eurofighter.

Just to set the seal on the awfulness of the Nimrod upgrade project, the delivery date has slipped to 2009 at the most recent forecast, and the planes won't be operational for some years after that: by which point one may be reasonably sure that they will be obsolete on top of not having really been necessary to begin with.

Marvellous. 'Smart procurement' at work, then, appears to add up the usual prolonged gorge at the public trough for BAE, the more so as they also have agreements to provide servicing and training support once the Nimrods are finally working. BAE can expect to carry on taking government money on the back of the Nimrod programme for decades, on top of their billions up front.

Really, then, it should be unthinkable for the minister who oversaw the award of the Nimrod MRA4 contract to subsequently become a non-executive director of BAE, as Michael Portillo has done. He gets a nice cheque from BAE every year: not an obscene sum perhaps, but the kind of money that most people have to keep families on – and, unlike them, he is not required to do much work for it. No crime has been committed here: no regulation has been broken. Perhaps it's only me who thinks it bad form on Mr Portillo's part, given the way Nimrod is working out for taxpayers and the RAF.

What's really upsetting about Nimrod is that BAE can't even manage to turn a profit on it. Even having tripled the price of the planes, BAE has already had to take serious write-downs on its accounts from Nimrod, and more bad news is expected in the City. The programme is seen as a terrible millstone by the company, as is its ongoing effort to build the new *Astute*-class attack submarines. So far from being a high-tech powerhouse, BAE seems to struggle desperately whenever it is asked to actually make anything complicated.

BAE, in fact, finds working for the UK Ministry of Defence terribly onerous. The MoD simply isn't rich enough to support a company like BAE in the style to which it would like to become accustomed, no matter how cruelly British taxpayers are bled, and the MoD tends to be so picky about what it wants that the results can't then be sold to anyone else – the more so as it has a habit of ordering things which no one in their right minds would even think necessary, like anti-submarine systems all though the 1990s. With the flow of black gold from Arabia starting to dry up at last, and at least a few people in the MoD getting mildly sick of being mulcted for every penny whenever they buy something, BAE needs to think again about what it does for a living. (The black gold wasn't just a metaphor, by the way: under Al Yamamah, the Saudis pay BAE in oil rather than currency.)

Essentially, the world weapons market is starting to shake out into two main camps: a few big combines who work for the Pentagon, and another few who make collaborative systems for sale to European defence ministries. Both kinds of weaponry may be sold elsewhere later on, but in order to cover development costs you must deal initially in one of the big markets.

The trouble with the Pentagon, from BAE's viewpoint, is that there are a number of massive defence cartels there already, with all the political pull that comes from employing legions of well-paid Americans and from having played more or less naughty games in Washington for decades. Perhaps more to the point, there has until very lately often been actual competition in the US domestic arms market, and as a result American weapons really are – normally – much better. Breaking into a set-up like that is very difficult.

Europe is even worse. The Pentagon brass are an annoying bunch to work for, but at least they are a semi-cohesive group with huge sums of money and a certain amount in common. Nothing like this exists in Europe. Instead, when you want to sell death-tech to the Old World, you must deal with a dozen different governments and probably several multinational bodies, all with different requirements, none of which have much money individually. You must arrange that well-paid jobs are created in all their territories or they won't give you the time of day. You must somehow lock all their associated military people, many of whom loathe each other like poison, into a room and refuse to let them out until they agree on what it is they want. Then you must stay on top of the situation for years, as both military folk and politicians will change frequently and often have bright ideas or changes of heart. Really, herding cats for a living would be much easier. And, at the end of it all, you won't have made nearly as much money as you would working for the Pentagon. That is, if you get there, as it's all too probable that the project will either collapse at some point or get so badly cut back that it becomes unprofitable.

Unsurprisingly, BAE seems to have decided against Europe, pulling back from a merger with the mighty pan-European EADS in favour of buying up American companies with Pentagon contracts. EADS, European Aeronautics, Defence and Space, is one of the two remaining continental heavyweights, following many mergers. Its core operations are German, but much of it is distributed across the whole of industrial Europe. EADS owns the 80 per cent of Airbus that BAE doesn't, and it is the rest of Eurofighter as well. The other company still on the playing field is the France-based Thales, which has grown courtesy of the French government. France would like EADS and Thales to merge. EADS is partly French already and EADS–Thales would be a global monster to rank with Boeing. It would also be more or less an arm of French policy, despite much of its muscle being German. The Germans are understandably less thrilled with the notion.

It will be interesting to see how the mating dance of the leviathans turns out, but we are digressing slightly. The important thing here is that Britain cannot somehow maintain a viable national arms capability on its own, and it is very questionable whether Europe can do this even if becomes more centrally organised – that is, more French, as far as defence goes. Furthermore, probably more importantly as far as Westminister politicians are concerned, buying whatever comes from British arms factories has *utterly failed to sustain British manufacturing jobs*. Already the civil aircraft and shipbuilding industries have gone, and much of the domestic defence sector as well. We shouldn't forget the

Rover Group, stripped and sold off by BAE after being handed over as a gift from the British government. Rover, the last British volume car manufacturer, is in its final death throes as I write, and according to the Cambridge-MIT Institute, 'British Aerospace clearly played a major part in Rover's demise.' BAE itself has haemorrhaged UK staff and closed UK factories for almost all of its history, and the trend is continuing. The company now employs only 40,000 people in the UK as opposed to nearly 60,000 over-seas. It's not just the 'Aerospace' part of the name that's a dead letter now.

BAE isn't really a provider of classic manufacturing jobs any more, either. As an indication of the kind of company it is turning into, over 10,000 of its people are now software engineers. BAE has, in fact, been moving offshore and out of manufacturing for some years now. The resulting multinational service corporation scarcely deserves the blind loyalty that the British government continues to give it – the more so as this loyalty has severely handicapped our fighting forces, who actually *are* quite good value for money.

Forty thousand volatile jobs, most of them white-collar, are simply not a significant factor in the British economy; this is a trifle over 0.1 per cent of all the jobs currently existing in the UK.* Keeping this miniscule fraction of the nation's workers employed cannot possibly justify the wasting of billions every year, far less the associated weakening of our nation's defences.

Some people, of course, will tell you that the UK arms busi-ness indirectly employs hundreds of thousands of people – this figure surely including themselves. These BAE mouthpieces also contend that British arms exports run to tens of billions every year. The earnings are more likely to be in the £5 billion region according to the government's arms-sales-encouragement bureau,** which could scarcely justify the misuse of our £30 billion defence

---

* Office for National Statistics. Workforce jobs in the UK as of Sep 2004 stood at 30,399,000.
** DESO, the Defence Export Sales Organisation, a state agency whose mission is to help British manufacturers sell arms abroad. We don't seem to have anything like as many government resources assigned to selling anything else: but then, as we have seen, British weapons are remarkably bad and need a lot of selling.

budget. But no matter: if these invisible hundreds of thousands of UK arms workers are, as their lobbyists tell us, earning vast sums abroad, they surely don't need the custom and assistance of the British government to stay in business. I have no quarrel with British arms manufacturers selling their products overseas, especially given that most of their products don't work: I would far prefer that warlords and dictators were equipped with crappy SA80s and Tornado F3s than with deadly, effective AK47s and MiG-29s. (Nobody would ever make such a foolish choice, of course, apart from the Saudis: this is why the myth of massive UK defence exports is so farcical.) It is the arms makers' insistence on being perpetually underwritten by the British state that I object to. Let BAE leech off the Pentagon if it can, but the British free-lunch counter has to close. The armed forces should be encouraged to buy from whoever can make the best and cheapest kit, which at the moment will mostly be America. (Not always, and probably not for ever now that competition in the US domestic arms market has been largely eliminated, but definitely for a while.) Rachel Squire, Gordon Brown and their colleagues in Parliament should remember what BAE did to British engineering in the 1980s and '90s – closed much of it down and asset-stripped it – before they sell their souls to the devil even one more time. Although they may actually like to thank BAE for the closures: at least they aren't having to find subsidies and make-work for all those people any more. If the Rosyth dockyard should start hiring again, as it seems likely it will, this will merely lead to more suffering down the road. I wouldn't take a job at that yard if I lived there – it wouldn't last. It is only cruelty, really, to give the young working men of Dunfermline hopes of a career for life cutting steel on good wages. Better they should learn other trades, in a world full of hungry folk eager to cut steel for a pittance.

Wider British economic policy is beyond the scope of this book. I have no idea whether Britain can survive without manufacturing industry, although it looks as though we might find out fairly soon. But manufacturing industry which can only survive by selling expensive rubbish to the British government is no more than a big dole office; it cannot possibly be the answer. By all means subsidise UK industry and take some of the defence budget to do it, if you like. I suspect you'll get nowhere – you'd need to find some way of getting kids to learn maths, for a start. But let the remaining defence budget be spent on proper weaponry, mostly from overseas. You could still buy more and better kit than we have now, spending half the money. Let the Department of Trade and Industry do what it says on the tin, and run the Ministry of Defence as a *defence* organisation. Surely it can't only be me who would vote for that.

Speaking of voting . . .

CHAPTER

11

Politics

A prince ought to have no other aim or thought, nor select anything else for his study, than war and its rules and discipline; for this is the sole art that belongs to him who rules . . . it is seen that when princes have thought more of ease than of arms they have lost their states. And the first cause of your losing it is to neglect this art . . . a prince who does not understand the art of war, over and above the other misfortunes already mentioned, cannot be respected by his soldiers . . . He ought never, therefore, to have out of his thoughts this subject of war, and in peace he should addict himself more to its exercise than in war; this he can do in two ways, the one by action, the other by study.

The Prince, Niccolo Machiavelli

The armed forces are parts of the government. The Ministry of Defence civil service is part of the government. British Aerospace – BAE Systems, the entire British defence-industrial sector – is a creature of the government's creation and has grown to its present bloated eminence on government money and government-brokered deals with other governments.* It is the government, then, that we have to thank for the present state of our defences: the government, as represented by Her Majesty's ministers, legislators, civil service and senior forces officers. It is these people, each year, who take thirty billion pounds of our money and tens

---

* Often these too involve British government money, as when the UK gives grant aid to a Third World country but makes sure it is spent on British defence equipment. Local politicians are often allowed to take a cut for their personal enrichment.

of thousands of our young men and women – whom they then often work like slaves, at least for a few years – and manage to produce the present embarrassing mess.

At the political level we have four defence ministers. There is the secretary of state for defence himself, now Dr John Reid – the 'Dr' is a PhD in West African history. Below him we find the minister for defence procurement (referred to as Min DP in staff jargon, which usually comes out as 'Mindy P') and the armed forces minister (Min AF). This neatly sums up the reality that the defence procurement pork barrel is at least as important politically as the armed forces themselves, one of the benefits of living in an advanced country which has managed to subordinate the military to the civil power.

There is another junior minister too, Min Veterans, with a remit to oversee ex-servicemens' issues and the like. In fact, this portfolio might better be described as 'minister for distracting the press' or 'minister for rotten eggs'. Min Veterans may expect to spend much time standing in the pillory during lawsuits and media probes attendant on such issues as Gulf War Syndrome, the mythical dangers of depleted-uranium munitions, supposedly inadequate counselling for post-traumatic stress after various past conflicts, failure to pay widow's benefit to unmarried soldiers' girlfriends, former servicemen used as guinea pigs in weapons tests of the 1950s and so on. Long-ago villainies and dubious medical debates are much easier to write up and sue over than real, current issues, so correspondingly large amounts of media and legal attention are given to them. Hence the existence of Min Veterans.

Apart from the actual ministers there are various other politicians attached to the MoD: parliamentary secretaries and special advisers and such.

All these politicians are largely free of direct influence from the armed forces, provided they don't try to change the forces' internal organisation. This is, of course, absolutely right and proper, the crowning glory of the modern British state. Sadly, the political classes are very much in thrall to their predecessors' awful creation BAE Systems, as we have seen. Forty thousand British citizens employed by BAE and a few tens of thousands more working for Thales UK, the Rosyth dockyard and so on possess infinitely more political clout than the 200,000 servicemen and women of the armed forces. It seems to be an axiom of political life in this country that British voters would always rather risk dead servicemen and national defeat in a few years' time than jobless arms workers right now. Actually it may be more correct to say that Min DPs are well aware that they personally will have moved on by the time their decisions kill any servicemen. They are also comforted by the long tradition of British forces miraculously achieving victory – or at least avoiding defeat – despite atrocious support and dreadful equipment.

Just below the political level we have the permanent bureaucracy: the 500 admirals, generals and air marshals and the 300 plus MoD civil servants who rate themselves as holding equivalent ranks. The mandarins are equal in number to the senior officers of any two services, despite the fact that their civil service subordinates number less than half the forces' total strength. The MoD civil service is therefore – amazingly – even more top-heavy than the forces themselves are. Furthermore, the head mandarin, the permanent under-secretary, considers himself to be at least equal in rank to the head of the armed forces; in his heart of hearts, he probably thinks he is a five-star field marshal. Certainly, the MoD's table of rank equivalences strongly suggests that if the PUS isn't a five-star, he is an extremely senior four-star. None of this means that the civil servants are in charge of the armed services, but it does mean that if the uniformed men wish to make any serious change, all three services must cooperate with each other – not a likely occurrence.

The permanent bureaucracy is every bit as malign as the short-sighted politicians it nominally serves. Empire-building, internecine conflict, cover-ups, lying, foot-dragging, ridiculous amounts of red tape and plain old incompetence are rife in all quarters. It is the bureaucracy which has arranged the permanent unofficial budget carve-up which is one of the most serious factors paralysing the Ministry of Defence. The rule is that the three armed services split the defence budget equally. It doesn't matter what the technological or geopolitical circumstances may be; it is one third each. Under such a regime we would probably carry on buying anti-submarine equipment, for example, even if we were invaded from space. This is not stated plainly – as one would expect, the MoD's accounts are presented in bafflingly abstruse forms – but it is the reality. Any sensible post-cold-war defence policy would have de-emphasised the navy and RAF somewhat and given the army greater resources. This has not occurred. Don't just take my word for it.

> Another consequence of [the RAF's] political success in the Ministry of Defence is that it has achieved, almost stunningly accurately, 33 per cent of defence expenditure, along with 33 per cent for the Royal Navy and 33 per cent for the Army. When I arrived as a special adviser at the Ministry of Defence and looked carefully at the statistics, I was amazed at how consistent that picture had been for a long time. The services had cleverly seemed to carve up the cake almost equally between them, as if, regardless of the strategic or technological circumstances, a deal had to be done between the chiefs of staff.
> Crispin Blunt MP (Tory, late of Wellington College, the 13th/18th Hussars,* the Ministry of Defence and the Commons Defence Select Committee)

'As if'. *Of course* a deal has to be done, and given that there is no active defence authority above the three chiefs of staff, one third each is the only possible answer. Each of the three has right of access directly to the prime minister, a rare Whitehall privilege. It is questionable how much authority the Defence Minister himself has over them, let alone such ciphers as the chief of defence staff, their nominal boss. The chance of the forces ever producing admirals, generals or air marshals who consider the national interest above that of their own service is slim; such men would not be promoted in the first place. This is the terrible, crippling downside of the much-vaunted 'single-service ethos', the regimental spirit which makes British officers such competent field operators (quite often, anyway) and so generally useless for planning and policy.

It is also the permanent bureaucracy which saddles us with military doctrines designed not to serve sensible purposes but to justify equipment and people which will belong undisputably to their own sub-tribe. Thus we see the army with its incredibly manpower-

---

* One of the ancestor units of today's Light Dragoons, one of the light-tank formation recce/surveillance and target acquisition cavalry regiments.

intensive and unwieldy tanks and big guns, such that we can put 30,000 soldiers on the ground and only a few thousand of them will be riflemen by primary trade. Thus we see the navy, which has focused on escort warships almost to the exclusion of having anything for them to protect, even if they were capable of doing so – which they aren't. Thus we see the RAF, which has provided almost none of the things it is supposed to lately: no credible air superiority, hardly any effective battlefield support, pitifully weak air transport – and all these neglected in favour of a sometimes criminally destructive, occasionally suicidal, always fairly useless deep-strike capability. Indeed, it sometimes appears that the forces haven't even progressed as far as the cold war; their favoured posture has a strong whiff of World War II about it.

There has been creeping reform. Unbelievably, the current MoD is lean and efficient compared to the set-up in the 1950s, when absolutely nothing was in common and there were three entirely separate ministries all complete, one for each service. As the long decades have slipped by, parts of this have been chipped away. But the three-way cake-slice is still there, perhaps more firmly than ever; the services still prioritise the battle against each other over any real or prospective battle against the nation's enemies.

Almost worse than this, the incredible inertia of the procurement and planning process persists and may in fact have worsened. As I write in 2005, nearly fifteen years after the Red Banner Northern Fleet ceased to be a serious threat, massive amounts of new, astonishingly expensive anti-submarine equipment are still coming on line. This has been continuous ever since the commie submariners started to close down and much more anti-submarine gear is in the pipeline; the rebuilt Nimrod MRA4s probably won't be operational in the first half of the next decade, at the rate BAE is going on them. Twenty-five years to react to the closure of the Soviet submarine fleet is unacceptably, ludicrously slow. Using the Defence Procurement Agency against real-world threats is like trying to run over weasels with a glacier.

So don't *tell* me everything's all sorted out now, and the bad old days are over, and British arms manufacturing is a success story, as people do nearly every day.

'The UK defence industry is that rarest of things, a British manufacturing success story'

> BBC Business News, *25 March 2005*.

Success story in terms of profits, maybe. In terms of producing
cost-effective weaponry, never. This sort of thing makes me really
mad, after more than ten years in uniform struggling with awful
British equipment. It makes me madder still, now that I have to
pay taxes myself rather than just live off them. (Another irritating
thing that forces desk jockeys and civil servants and arms-industry
types often say is, 'I pay taxes too.')

And there is worse than infighting and inertia and public
misperception to contend with. There are also the incompetence
and the cover-ups. We are now arriving back where we started:
at the true, underlying reasons for the infantry cuts announced
in 2004 and still working through the system.

The story begins years before, in a number of places and times.
The Nimrod and *Astute* and Eurofighter programmes began in the
1980s and '90s, along with many others. Because BAE Systems is
incapable of bringing in a project on time and at cost, because
other European governments did not honour their commitments,
because the MoD negotiating posture is that of a drunken sailor
with his pockets full of cash, all these things were late and over
budget. In particular, expenditure on the horrifically expensive
Eurofighter, which should long ago have died down to a maintenance level, did not peak until financial year 2004–05. Spending
on Nimrod MRA4, which should also have been largely past and
gone, also rose to a nasty, belated high that year, and the *Astute*
bills had only just started to drop from a 2003–04 peak. This is
because defence projects are not paid for all at once – the invoices
are settled over a period of years or even decades, according to
what stage things get to. Other late, over-budget projects added
their mite. Eurofighter was, and is, the biggy, however.

The brilliant minds of the MoD chose to deal with this situation by ordering even more big, expensive things right through
the turn of the century – the Type 45 destroyer, various anti-
submarine gadgets and upgrades, the F-35 strike jet – to name
but a few of the biggest. By sheer bad luck, completely out of

the blue, 'smart procurement' made partial progress with these things. Money wasn't actually saved, or anything like that, but these later schemes did manage to move forward comparatively briskly to the stage at which big invoices were going to be presented for payment quite soon, even as the old projects were still dragging on and costing far more than planned.

It began to become clearer and clearer from around 2001 or 2002 that there was going to be a terrible financial pile-up in the MoD from the 2004 financial year onwards – it was in 2001 that the rumours first filtered down to my level, anyway. A whole bunch of really big bills were going to be presented all within a few years. There was no way that the defence budget, even with a biggish increase, could cover them, not on top of regular running costs anyway.

There wasn't an awful lot that could be done about this enormous, glaring cock-up without people finding out – or so it seemed. Many of the MoD's expenses aren't really under its control and must be settled every year no matter what. Everyone must be paid, for example, including the pensioners: and the pension bill is already beginning to swell alarmingly.* Expensive maintenance can be shaved somewhat, but not too much, as nobody wants a reactor accident or a sudden rise in aircraft crashes. Besides, maintenance contracts are often valuable regional pork; MPs will howl if you touch them. A lot of expensive multinational exercises happen as regular as clockwork, and while *third*-rate nations may pull out of them, this is impossible for Britain – certainly without people noticing and wanting to know why. So there wasn't much scope for making savings on the quiet.

The brass hats and mandarins could have tried coming clean about the whole thing, of course, and blaming BAE, which had certainly been responsible for much of the problem, but, as Admiral Lygo showed us in the last chapter, BAE always has its back covered. MoD-written contracts are always so vaguely drafted, and amended so many times, that contractors are seldom if ever in the wrong. It doesn't matter how useless the products are or

---

* As one might expect, given how sweet an armed-forces pension can get to be if you stay in uniform long enough.

how late and costly they may be, the MoD has always requested in writing that they should be as they are. (Remember Boeing and the Chinook HC3s?)

So it was clear that the defence budget would be a billion or more short in 2004, probably worse shortly after, and it would be no good trying to blame BAE. Some small cuts were made here and there – minehunters and suchlike – but not enough to cover the shortfall. Major surgery was going to be needed: and people were going to want to know why. 'Because we here at the MoD can't add up or bring projects in on time,' clearly wouldn't do as an answer.

When the Iraq invasion was green-lighted in 2002, a way out of the impasse seemed to have presented itself. The chancellor of the exchequer, Gordon Brown, stated from the outset that the costs of the operation would not have to be met from within the MoD budget. Extra funds would be available from Treasury reserves. Funnily enough, it was at around this point that the MoD made up its mind that if it were to participate in the invasion it wanted to make a serious contribution. This seemed odd at the time, given the reservations of many senior British officers regarding the wisdom of invading Iraq – at any rate, invading it without any plan for afterwards. There had been much talk of Britain sending only a token force, just to show solidarity with the US, as the Australians did. A major British deployment, however, would naturally mean major extra funds from the Treasury, and this would offer scope for the MoD sneakily to add some of the troublesome procurement bills to their Iraq expenses.

The Iraq invasion duly took place, with a full British division on the ground plus ships and aircraft in proportion. A suitably eye-watering expenses chit landed on the chancellor of the exchequer's desk. It seemed that those cheeky scamps down at the Ministry of Defence were going to get away scot-free.

However, Gordon Brown, the Iron Chancellor, was not so easily rooked. He turned down a large part of the padded expenses. Though he was also planning a substantial increase in the defence budget, it wouldn't be enough to make up the difference. The charlatans of the MoD were thus left in dire straits: they had no idea what to do. In the end, the chancellor, firmly but kindly, was forced to step in – for their own good, they were in a complete dither – and show them how to save the money. This, at least, is how the Treasury describe the chain of events early in 2004.

The MoD's version is that the cruel chancellor welshed on his promise to cover the Iraq bill, rejecting several perfectly legitimate items. Having done such a nasty and uncalled-for thing, he might at least have had the decency to cough up a bigger budget increase, a measly billion would have done it. It's only fair, guv. We've all been toiling away in the hot Iraqi sun, or anyway watching it on TV in our offices . . . Go on. Please. (Obviously I'm paraphrasing here.) But he wouldn't. Instead he held a spending review – a process whereby the Treasury can effectively take over another government department, at least for a while – and dictated a programme of defence cuts, all to a background of total silence from Number 10 Downing Street.

What is certainly true is that the 2004 slashfest was indeed planned at the Treasury rather than in the Ministry of Defence: by Chancellor Brown, then, rather than by Secretary of State for Defence Geoffrey Hoon (Dr Reid's predecessor). This became embarrassingly obvious when the cuts were leaked to the press before being announced in Parliament. When the MoD was asked to comment on the leak, it was able to say with complete truthfulness that it had no idea whether or not the rumours were true. How could it, when it wasn't in charge of the process any longer? The MoD, at this stage, was in the position of a commercial company in the hands of the receivers. Geoffrey Hoon was effectively on gardening leave.

At the time, I personally wasn't all that upset. Gordon Brown had the reputation of being a strictly no-nonsense, take-charge sort of politician. And while nobody would try to claim that the Treasury is a force for good in the world – certainly not to the degree that the armed forces are, for example – most people agree that the Treasury is at least able to add – better than the MoD anyway. It seemed as though Brown and his flinty-eyed Treasury hatchetmen might clear away the MoD bumblers' financial car-crash with some efficiency. We might see some considerations of cost-effectiveness and value for money at last.

As ever, I was disappointed. I had forgotten, for a start, about the three-way cake-split and the service chiefs' direct access to the prime minister. Tony Blair was only too happy not to be involved in this particular fracas, and Gordon Brown only too happy for him not to be. Apparently Blair did ask 'his' chancellor for a meeting to discuss the matter, but Brown was too busy. Nothing further was heard from Number 10. The bad news would have to be split equally between the services, then, or there was a risk that the disadvantaged chief or chiefs of staff would beard Tony Blair, forcing him to take charge of the unseemly row going on in his cabinet.

Thus, it was clear that the army would have to take some cuts as well as the RAF and navy, much though this was evidently stupid given the situation in Iraq and other places. (Evident to everyone except the RAF and the navy, that is.) Worse, far from being a hard-headed tough guy with the public interest and value for money at heart, Brown turned out to be an old-fashioned pork-barrel machine politician – certainly as far as these cuts went.

One should recall that the gap in the accounts was not, in government terms, so very huge: around a billion pounds, not more than 4 per cent or so of the defence budget overall. There were literally dozens of ways that fat could be trimmed from the MoD to save this money. One excellent idea would have been to close some of the forces' many surplus bases and facilities in the UK. Some rationalisation of these has taken place over the past few years, but there is still plenty of scope: a billion's worth of savings spread across all three services wouldn't be difficult to achieve at all.

But bases and facilities equal jobs and money in the UK: votes. Swarms of cleaners and security guards and gardeners and clerical staff would lose their jobs, not to mention the various local industries dependent on a base – strip clubs, rip-off late-night bars and clubs, tattooists, second-hand car dealers, people who sell white goods on the never-never, all pillars of the community. The year before an election, Gordon Brown had little stomach for closing bases. One RAF station was initially marked for closure, just for the look of the thing – RAF Coltishall, funnily enough in a constituency where Labour had not the slightest chance. Just closing one airbase wasn't going to make the necessary savings, though: more would have to be cut.

But this still needn't have been a problem. Bases are not the only thing one can get rid of. Indeed, they look valuable compared to some other items on the defence budget. As we have seen throughout this book, there are always a huge number of bloated, pointless, shockingly expensive equipment projects grinding slowly through the system. Given that Gordon Brown and his Treasury henchmen didn't have the guts to close bases, they could have axed a project or two. The Nimrod MRA4 update would seem especially ripe for the chopper. It is a Britain-only project, unlike the Eurofighter, so there wouldn't be any diplomatic fallout and a lot of money is due to be spent on Nimrod in 2006. Getting rid of it would achieve a big saving just when one was required.

But oh, the wailing and gnashing of teeth if Nimrod were cancelled! BAE would at once threaten to fire a few thousand UK employees, just to make it clear who had the whip hand. There would be dire statements of doom from the unions *and* the CBI* about the death of British manufacturing industry – a death which has been going on noisily for so long that it is becoming reminiscent of opera. One might also expect much chuntering in the press about valuable high-tech skills to be lost abroad and so on.

The idea here seems to be that all high-tech skills are interchangeable: all boffins can turn their hands to anything from space shuttles to personal stereos, like Professor Frink in *The Simpsons*, so it doesn't matter what kind of boffin you have as long as you have some. Thus it is a good idea for its own sake to spend billions establishing a big group of people who can lovingly restore a dozen 1950s-vintage airliners and fit them out with some of the most specialist hardware known to man.** These people, being boffins, will then naturally be able to mass-produce up-to-date digital video recorders or fridges or whatever – after all, it's all *technology*, isn't it – at lower prices than factories in China can do it, and the British economy will bloom like a rose. The very fact that this kind of thinking can affect national politics suggests that one may as well give up on salvaging Britain's technical know-how.

Almost nobody, during such a brouhaha, would mention that Al Qaeda doesn't have much of a submarine branch, and even if it did we already have loads of ridiculously expensive Merlin heli-

---

* Confederation of British Industry – the fat cats' club. Not usually friends of the unions, but the two factions occasionally get together for the purpose of gouging the taxpayers.
** The 'new' Nimrod MRA4s will still be De Havilland Comets full of electronics, like their predecessors.

copters and attack submarines to tackle it with. The utter absence of need for a new anti-submarine patrol plane would not figure in the debate at all. Cutting the Nimrod would have been election poison, ridiculous though that is. It ought to have been a guaranteed landslide-winner. And all the other stupid, pointless, wildly expensive programmes would be just as invulnerable. Eurofighter and the A400M Euro-transport plane seemingly cannot be touched as this would anger foreign governments (strange, given the fact that Britain usually signs up for these deals on the grounds that they will *prevent* our policy being dictated from foreign capitals).

In the end, if you haven't the political will and integrity to close surplus bases, you're unlikely to have enough to axe worthless projects. This certainly was the case with Gordon Brown. The Iron Chancellor, disappointingly, didn't have much iron in him after all.

So it was clear that no fat would be cut from the MoD under Treasury management, which meant that muscles and teeth would have to go instead. Fighting units would be shut down. In order to minimise aggravation from the service chiefs, with its attendant risk of involvement by Number 10 Downing Street, the losses would fall equally across the three services. Thus, the navy lost a few more antique destroyers and pointless frigates. The RAF got rid of half its Jaguar strike jets (useful but old) and a dozen Tornado fighters (nearly as old but not nearly as useful). And the army, forced to cut something, decided that it must be infantry, of all things. Even the one, lonely base closure – RAF Coltishall, the only actual efficiency saving in the whole package – was eventually repealed, at least until after the election.

This adds up to the loss of approximately 15 per cent of the nation's fighters and strike planes, 10 per cent of its escort flotilla and 10 per cent of the army infantry: all gone in order to save 3 or 4 per cent of the defence budget. To be sure, some of these things are so obsolete as to be almost useless, such as the Type 42 destroyer. The Jaguar jet, though, recently upgraded at some expense, isn't that bad, and British infantrymen aren't obsolete at all – quite the opposite. And *all* these things are more useful, come a war, than 80,000 MoD civil servants; they are all more useful than scores upon scores of underused UK bases; and these latter are in their turn more useful than much of the junk on the MoD's current shopping list.

But Gordon Brown didn't care. He had a billion to save, and

fighting units are easily got rid of by comparison with bases or procurements. The only people who really care that they're gone are certain elements in the armed forces, who are few in number and do not form a cohesive bloc.* Better yet, unlike unions and fat cats and local communities and all the other vested interests, armed services people are not permitted to publicly criticise government or departmental policy. Any serving member of the Forces who dares to do so will be sacked. (It was only the fact that I had already tendered my resignation which stopped this happening to me when I first broke into print.)

All this makes it easy to see why the not-so-iron chancellor chose to pull out fangs and cut off limbs rather than do any liposuction on the MoD's great fat tail, although it doesn't make it creditable. Once all is said and done, one cannot expect the chancellor and the Treasury to give much of a hoot about the state of the nation's defences – it isn't their job. Balancing the books is all they really care about. Gordon Brown merely wished to sort out the MoD's budget crisis at the least political cost, and within that brief he did very well. The episode makes him appear a tolerable chancellor, if not much of a prospective prime minister.

Which brings us back to the denizens of the Defence Ministry, who *should* care about defence, and who had created the mess in the first place. They absolutely deny this, of course. Off the record, MoD insiders will whine and grizzle interminably, often blaming the whole imbroglio on 'resource account budgeting', which is an astonishingly boring and obscure financial system brought in lately at Treasury behest. The fact remains that Hoon and his MoD minions were over budget because they and their predecessors had ordered far too much ridiculous stuff along cakesplit lines and let costs balloon out of control.

One can be reasonably sure of the defence functionaries' guilt because they have been quite willing to go along with the fiction that the cuts were their idea. If they really thought they were in the clear on this one, it seems unlikely that the chaps at MoD

---

* Not a majority by any means. Most forces people would rather sit about in a cushy rear-echelon billet in the UK than work like slaves under unpleasant and dangerous conditions in a combat unit. They get paid the same either way. Not theirs to reason why, if no one asks them to do or die.

Main Building would be willing to take the blame. But in fact, once Gordon Brown had picked out who and what was to go, the list was sent back to Main Building for Geoffrey Hoon to present to Parliament. After a brief, frantic period of late-night head-scratching, the cuts were dressed up in an MoD white paper called 'Delivering Security in a Changing World', which the Secretary of State duly presented to Parliament in June 2004, just after the chancellor's budget speech.

'Delivering Security in a Changing World' is a remarkable document. Twenty-eight pages long, it suggests that Geoffrey Hoon sat down with the service chiefs at some point in early 2004 and said something along the lines of 'Right chaps, I've decided that network enabled capability is the way to go. What must we cut in order to afford that?' And the chiefs, impressed with such a dynamic, incisive vision, got rid of a few things they didn't really need.

You may be saying to yourself at this point, 'What on earth is network enabled capability?'

The short answer is, it's a fashionable staff-jargon buzz phrase, like 'effects-based operations'* or 'littoral warfare' or 'transforma-

---

* 'Effects-based operations are operations conceived and planned in a systems framework that considers the full range of direct, indirect, and cascading effects, which may – with different degrees of probability – be achieved by the application of military, diplomatic, psychological, and economic instruments.' (Rand Corporation). More succinctly, you might say that effects-based operations are ones where you try to achieve a given end, focusing all your efforts toward that end rather than just on some part of it at the expense of the rest. For example: we would like to achieve a democratic and peaceful Iraqi state with a thriving economy, friendly to all the world and especially us. Toppling the previous dictator is only part of the job, defeating his forces is only part of that sub-job, and if you act as though either of these were the whole thing – eg, by blowing apart a whole building merely because you have taken fire from that direction – you are unlikely to achieve your desired end state.

This philosophy formerly went under the name 'selection and maintenance of the aim', and then as now it was honoured more in the breach than the observance. The staff brains like to change the names of basic ideas quite often, however. It's a lot easier than actually implementing them. Also, thinking up the new jargon and writing massive theses about it provides a lot of pleasant jobs, and regular changes make it clear who has been actually reading all the bumf. Presumably he should be promoted rather than one who has merely been doing things.

tion'. It is meant to be the thing that lets you do 'any sensor, any shooter' warfare. Boiled down, it means everyone communicating with each other. In the modern era, this needs to be happening more and more with high-speed data links rather than simply people speaking on voice channels. For instance, the navy's airborne radar helos had until lately to pass all information by voice. When you have, let us say, a dozen different blips on your screen, all moving at 600 mph, you need to be an almost super-human motormouth to keep everyone else even partially in the picture by such means. Nowadays a computer data link transmits the helicopter's radar picture instantly to displays in the carrier, all the other ships, possibly fighter planes, etc. Much better.

Another example is the new Bowman digital comms infrastructure for the land forces, just now arriving, disgustingly late and over budget. (Main contractor through the 1990s: Plessey. Owned by: BAE Systems.) Here the idea is that all radios at rifle-section level and higher will be encrypted and able to do such things as transmit their GPS location to other friendly units automatically.* Commanders will know where all their people are without having to hassle them over the radio all the time and scribble on maps in wax pencil; they'll simply look at the nifty map display in their command vehicle or post. Everyone will be able to accurately finger an enemy unit for shelling or air strikes or whatever, in much the same way that artillery observation-party vehicles already do.

Great stuff, then, but hardly cutting edge. Network enabled capability is actually nothing more than sending information over communication links. This is already commonplace in the civilian world. The British rifle-section leader is just now getting a very expensive Bowman radio which will enable him and his bosses

---

* Amazingly, nearly all land-forces communications below brigade level have been in clear until now, easier to listen in on than a modern mobile phone. This has been less of a worry than one might imagine, however, as most of the army's radios work only intermittently and anyway hardly anything of importance is ever transmitted. British land forces still have a strong tradition of cascading information up and down the command chain in face-to-face briefings, and then at least trying to let junior commanders go out and get the job done without constant badgering from on high.

to have secure voice and data links, provided that the rest of the infrastructure is in place. The same young man has owned a mobile phone capable of doing the same things for years, although he probably doesn't use most of its capabilities. If he happens to be a gadget geek, he may well have been doing all that Bowman does for a long time.

Funnily enough, given that it's nothing particularly special, network enabled capability isn't all that expensive, even when the DPA is buying it. Furthermore, much of it has already been bought. Warships have been digitally networked for decades, albeit unreliably and often with cretinously cumbersome displays and links within the ship itself.* Most aircraft also have some kind of data linkage these days. The only two ongoing network-enabling-type projects expensive enough to really be visible in the MoD's accounts are Bowman and the Skynet communications satellites, and they are both cheap as chips compared to heavyweights like Eurofighter, the Type 45 destroyer, *Astute* and Nimrod. Not one of the top ten major projects lined up for the future, according the the MoD's own forecast, is network enabling as such.

In other words, Skynet + Bowman = network enabled capability = less than 15 per cent of the cost of the four real big-money projects just now (Eurofighter + Type 45 + Nimrod + *Astute*). Network enabled capability, while it will be significant in combat – at least, combat of the seldom-seen high-intensity sort – is not at all significant in budget terms. To pretend that the 2004 cuts of infantry and jets and ships were made in order to pay for NEC is a palpable untruth. To pretend that these cuts were part of a considered defence policy rather than an exercise in path-of-least-

---

* A common spectacle in all Royal Navy warships of the 1990s was harassed officers and ratings reading endless streams of numbers off a screen or printout from one device and typing them into another, or speaking them into a microphone so that someone elsewhere in the ship could do so. This sort of idiocy is slowly, slowly being tackled, but every time you automate one feed you will normally find that some admiral or other is now demanding a further regular slug of data, and his people have decided that you should supply this by manually typing it into a Microsoft Word document or Excel spreadsheet which they have 'designed'. Quite often you are to do this while you are actually fighting the ship. The admiral usually considers this to be evidence of advanced IT skills among his staff, and gives them a promotion.

resistance crisis management by the Treasury is not merely spin, but outright falsehood. 'Delivering Security in a Changing World' then, is a classic piece of Whitehall flim-flam. Like all such documents, it is long on waffle and short on checkable statements of fact. Bureaucrats who draft such rubbish and politicians who endorse it can scarcely complain about the plummeting level of public trust in the governmental process.

The truth is that the cuts were made in the most short-sighted, most politically expedient possible way by Gordon Brown's Treasury. This was necessary due to galactic incompetence in Geoffrey Hoon's Defence Ministry. The situation was severely aggravated by the fact that the prime minister, who is supposed to be in overall charge of both, took no active role whatsoever.

And lest anyone is seeing this unsavoury episode as an argument in favour of the Conservative Party, one should bear in mind that it was the Tories who ordered the Eurofighter and carried it to the point where it was pretty well impossible to get rid of – and it is the Eurofighter more than any other single thing which lies at the root of today's problems. The Tories really haven't a leg to stand on when criticising Labour's utter mismanagement of the present defence-financial crisis as it is in large part their own fault. They also, remember, gave us the Nimrod MRA4, another cretinous stroke of policy.

This cross-party culpability for the current mess may give a clue as to why neither of the main parties offered much in the way of detailed defence ideas to the public in the run-up to the 2005 election. Labour merely pledged a further whacking £3.5 billion budget increase, which should just about cover the spiralling dino-project costs and put paid, literally, to the ongoing Treasury–MoD row. The Tories proposed only £2.5 billion, much of which they thought might be found from efficiency savings within the MoD, by firing surplus bureaucrats. Presumably they have a less clear idea of how badly the MoD is in the hole, and during their long spell in opposition they have forgotten how hard it is to chip the barnacles of government off their comfortable slimy rocks, although the principle is splendid.

The Conservatives also considered that they could save the infantry's lost regiments, even expand the infantry – but still put an end to the arms plot (see Chapter 1). This does seem to mean that they would assign permanent roles to most infantrymen for their entire careers, effectively creating third-class infantry units; there are already first and second class, as we have seen – Paras and commandos plus all the rest.

This doesn't seem very sensible. Who would join a regiment permanently assigned to a plain-vanilla, non-brigaded light role? The paras and commandos and armoured/medium/mechanised types would have all the fun of invading places and the training to do so, and the rest would have to patrol the streets afterwards, guard prisoners, or do all the frustrating hands-tied UN peace-keeping – or similar no-fun, low-status work. Spend an entire military career cleaning up after the well-funded elites, as a sort of heavily-armed security guard? I wouldn't fancy that much. More witlessly yet, the Tories also planned to save the three useless frigates currently marked for the axe.

The Liberal Democrats offered one solid promise which got them my tactical vote, much effect though that had. If they had somehow won the election, they promised to scrap the third tranche of Eurofighter, which they reckoned would save a couple of billion. The RAF would thus only have had to mothball a score or so of these jets over and above its attrition spares, and the cost per plane would have come in at £125 million or so, which, ridiculously, would have been the best result achievable. The Lib Dems also planned to save the infantry regimental system – and do away with the arms plot somehow at the same time, just like the Tories. To be fair, Labour will still have the problem of third-class light infantry, given that there are still going to be lots of one- and two-battalion permanently light-roled regiments under their plans.

It would be nice to think that the Lib Dems would do better than the others. However, it is hard to rid oneself of the suspicion that they only made their Eurofighter promise because they didn't think they would have to honour it. Essentially they are only free of BAE influence because BAE, along with most other political entities, does not believe that they have much chance of winning power. Even if they ever manage a place in a coalition government, it is hard to see one of the other parties letting the Lib Dems run defence without interference. In the end, the only reason they are relatively untarnished is that they haven't been at the trough lately.

The Lib Dems, too, have a touching faith in integrated Euro-forces, which is hard for anyone who has worked in the floppier, more European bits of NATO to really get on board with. And the notion loses credence, unhappily, each time another country joins NATO and the EU. It would seem more reasonable to try and get the British forces working together in harmony and efficiency before attempting the even more difficult task of international rationalisation. It *might* be possible to get the Royal Navy, British Army and RAF to work together some day, although I won't hold my breath. But the Lib Dems pass over this as a mere stepping stone. The desired end of many advocates of Euro-force integration, including Paul Keetch, the Lib Dem defence spokesman, is for European nations to specialise in different military areas rather than each struggling to maintain a full spectrum of kit and capability. The resulting pie fight can barely be imagined. Who's going to have the guts to go up to, for instance, Turkey and say, 'We've decided that your national specialism is pioneer corps. You won't need any fighter pilots, or special forces, or anything else fun. The Turkish army digs latrines from now on. If you want to do anything cool, you have to join the French forces.' And if you survived that, you'd have to somehow make the French take Turkish fighter pilots over French ones. Well . . . Mr Keetch is made of sterner stuff than me. And a minister who had cancelled a hundred Eurofighters would be *persona non grata* at a lot of continental capitals for many years if not for ever, so Lib Dem defence policy isn't exactly cohesive.

Neither Lib Dems nor Tories, as is common with opposition politicians, make clear how they would fund their reversals of Labour policy, and nobody is offering more than policy reversals, really. Proper, serious reform is not on the menu.

Very well. Politicians tend to do badly when it comes to overseeing the defence bureaucracy, and the bureaucracy itself is, if anything, worse than the politicians. It isn't just that they're all useless boneheads, either. One of the most annoying things about the whole bloody business is that, in fact, both these groups contain a fair proportion of able people, keen to do their jobs right. Even BAE has quite a lot of employees whose aim in life is to earn a living making good weapons at a fair price, and who wouldn't wish to see them in the hands of anyone but the accountable militaries of proper, stable democracies. But somehow the end result is always wrong.

One reason for the constant, stumbling, cross-party mess which we nationally make of defence policy in this country may be that it is largely invisible to the wider public. There is very little effective scrutiny of the subject, particularly of the nuts and bolts of it. Surely this can't be true, you may be thinking. There are the MPs of the House of Commons Defence Select Committee, for example. Their role, during that part of their time which they devote to committee duties, is to keep an eye on the MoD and make sure it is properly run. They have the power to grill major bureaucrats and demand answers from ministers. Why, their documents are extensively quoted in this very book.

True, and well done you for noticing that they exist. Not many British voters are aware of them, or have read the many critical reports that the committee has issued in late years, condemning MoD and ministerial mismanagement in quite stern terms as these things go in Whitehall. This is all the more notable given that most current members are Labour MPs, and they are thus implicitly criticising their own party's front bench. Unfortunately, several of these MPs are pretty well crippled as impartial critics of the defence establishment, due to having bases or factories in or near their constituencies. This presents them with a massive conflict of interest, of the sort that would cause a lawyer or a judge to decline a case. Sadly, political standards are not as strict as legal ones, and such MPs feel no embarrassment. Some, like Rachel Squire, have quite blatantly used their positions on the committee to push for the diversion of defence funding to where it will benefit their constituents' job security – and of course their own. As well as direct conflicts of interest like these, there are more general factors which might make the committee less able to really do its job. Several of its members have past careers with the unions, for instance, as one might expect of Labour MPs. This does tend to mean that they will never recommend buying anything foreign made, no matter how useful or even critically necessary the armed forces might find it. The committee's new chairman since the 2005 election, dispiritingly, is James Arbuthnot – the man who decided to buy our Apaches at triple price when he was Minister for Defence Procurement (see Chapter 4).

One of the biggest problems here is that few MPs really know much about the modern-day landscape of military force. This includes ministers and shadow spokesmen often enough, as well as the select committee. We are unusually fortunate in that one of the new committee members since the election is a Territorial Army officer who actually went to Iraq in 2003. His input will be valuable indeed. However, Major Swayne – a banker in day-to-day life before he was elected – is an unusual case. None of the other thirteen committee members have any significantly useful knowledge or experience. Most MPs with any interest in defence have only ever 'served', as they like to put it, in the Armed Forces Parliamentary Scheme. This involves being shown around one of the three services under close supervision and pumped full of self-serving propaganda by the upper echelons of that service. And that's usually it. That's the limit of their qualifications to supervise the nation's efforts in one of the most technically involved, most demanding fields of human activity: one in which even lifelong professionals commonly make immense blunders. It is no exaggeration to say that having read this book you know more about defence than 99 per cent of MPs. Perhaps just one tiny example may serve to bear this out:

'This may be the appropriate moment to pay tribute to the flying skills and dedication of those based at RAF Lyneham, whose Hercules, of course, were the main aircraft used in the Berlin airlift.'
Mr James Gray MP (Tory, North Wiltshire – RAF Lyneham's local MP) House of Commons Hansard Debates, 23 April 1998

Holy cow. The Berlin airlift took place in 1948–49, as most people are at least dimly aware – especially those like Mr Gray who list British history among their interests. The Hercules is an old warhorse, sure enough, but it isn't *that* old. The first *prototype* of the Hercules didn't take to the air until the following decade, and the RAF didn't receive it until the the decade after that. Turboprop transport aircraft like the Hercules simply don't belong to the same historical period as the Berlin airlift. It's as though one had congratulated RAF Spitfire pilots for winning World War I.

But Mr Gray is a veritable military guru, as MPs go. He later became opposition spokesman for defence, and at the point when he made this notably ignorant utterance had already completed a tour with the Armed Forces Parliamentary Scheme. This is not even to mention his period of 'active service' (as his bio sheet puts it) as a Territorial weekend warrior from 1977 to 1984.

This is an MP well informed on matters military, then, from the party which has by far the closest connections with the armed forces. He thinks the RAF had its current Hercules transport in the 1940s in such numbers that it was the main aircraft used for the Berlin airlift. Presumably, therefore, he also thinks the Paras at Arnhem (the famous 'bridge too far'), just four years earlier in 1944, also jumped from the RAF's present-day transport. Defence procurement is pretty lethargic in this country, I grant you, but it isn't *that* bad.

Unfair. We've all made mistakes, after all – though not usually in the House of Commons, on public record. However, you can rest assured: if you've read this far, you really do – almost certainly – know more about defence than your MP does. You should probably make him or her aware of that.

So, we can see that our rulers, our 'princes' as Machiavelli would say, have not heeded his advice. All of them, of every party, have neglected the primary art of rulership, thinking more of ease than of arms. Having little understanding of defence matters, they are not, as Machiavelli warns, respected by their soldiers: the lower ranks tend to despise politicians, and the higher ranks to ignore, manipulate or frustrate them at will. There really is very little proper supervision of our military establishment in this country.

But this is not 16th-century Italy. There is no danger that the forces' commanders will seize control of the state. They see politics as a step down, an attitude strengthened by the fact that they are paid more than their ministerial bosses and enjoy infinitely better job security.* Even better, our modern princes are actually quite attentive to some of Machiavelli's other dicta – in particular, the ones regarding keeping the people happy. If they think that voters care about efficiently run defences, they are likely to buck their ideas up. So keep working on that letter to your MP.

---

* A four-star officer is paid better than £140,000 p.a. as of 2004: more like £180,000 in the case of the chief of defence staff, still five-star in all but name. An MP appointed secretary of state for defence gets £135,000, and junior ministers less.

CHAPTER
12

Over to you

So we come down, uneasy, to look; uneasily pacing the beach.
These are the dykes our fathers made: we have never known a breach.
Time and again has the gale blown by and we were not afraid;
Now we come only to look at the dykes – at the dykes our fathers
  made.

Now we can only wait till the day, wait and apportion our shame.
These are the dykes our fathers left, but we would not look to the same.
Time and again were we warned of the dykes, time and again we delayed.
Now, it may fall, we have slain our sons, as our fathers we have betrayed.

Walking along the wreck of the dykes, watching the works of the sea!
These were the dykes our fathers made to our great profit and ease.
But the peace is gone and the profit is gone, with the old sure days
  withdrawn . . .
That our own houses show as strange when we come back in the dawn!

'The Dykes', Rudyard Kipling, 1902.

Now you know it all – most of the hard facts, and most of the
things that aren't said because they aren't politically acceptable,
or because nobody especially wants you to know them.

We need Kipling's dykes as much as ever we did – it's a
dangerous world still – but, just as in 1902, we cannot nationally be bothered to pay attention to them. Kipling had the terrible
misfortune to predict his own fate: he actually did lose his son
in the military idiocy of World War I. We would do well to
make sure that our forces are better prepared than the British

Army of 1914, or we may lose a lot more sons and daughters in future.

You should care about the other things the British government does or doesn't do, of course. Consider the health service; know about education; give some thought to your freedom and your domestic security and who might take them away. Watch all of your government like a hawk. But care about your defences at least as much: look to the dykes before it is too late.

So, what's to be done to make things more efficient? What should our no-ideas politicians and MoD dinos be offering?

By now, you should have your own thoughts. You know a bit, having read this far, about all the various different tools of the killing trade: what they cost, what they do, how easy it is to get them into place. But it may help to summarise.

The most technically difficult military task we might set our armed forces in future would be to go a long way off and overcome military opposition from a medium-weight state. This sort of thing, remember, is what you actually have armed forces for. They often do other jobs, being unaccustomed to giving the answer 'No can do.' They will have a stab at pretty much any civil function you care to name: policing, building, diplomacy, even governing. But in general policemen are better at policing, builders better at building, diplomats at negotiating; and military government is never a good idea. To be sure, there is a grey area around what one might call gendarmerie functions, or peacekeeping as it is often known. In general, though, one mainly has armed forces to overcome other armed forces. If they aren't capable of doing so, after all, keeping the peace will probably be someone else's problem. The British Army and Royal Marines are actually quite good at peacekeeping – as good as anyone else is, anyway. That is not our national weakness.

I would suggest that if we can put enough British riflemen on the ground to actually control a situation, as we eventually did in Northern Ireland, that situation will soon be as good as it can be made using military force. This may not be all that good in relative terms, of course: Northern Ireland in the 1970s and '80s was often not so very great a place to live, even with a significant fraction of the British Army keeping a lid on it. It still tends to flare up even today. However, that is about as nice as you can reasonably expect the armed forces to make things. Progress beyond the level of 1980s Belfast must be made by other people: by diplomats, police, lawyers, politicians, paramilitaries – ultimately, by the local community itself. If a situation is already better than 1980s Belfast, one should always give some thought to leaving it alone.

Our army and marines did get themselves effectively organised in Northern Ireland, after some initial errors. (Not many other rich militaries have managed the trick at all.) It took some of our people a little while, but most realised quite fast that they could not do more than contain the problem while others resolved it. Excessive force was never authorised, which helped a lot. Serious armoured vehicles were almost never used – an early example of effective media ops – and while many artillerymen did tours there, it was in the infantry role. Even the SAS, sterling fellows, eventually twigged that it was more useful to capture PIRA volunteers than kill them, even if the courts did occasionally let them go again afterwards.

All this hard-won expertise has now permeated throughout the British forces, top to bottom and side to side. Today's generals cut their teeth as platoon and company commanders in Belfast and South Armagh: today's sergeant-majors were their riflemen. Even I, a sailor, was trained to deal with IEDs alongside operators from all three services at the Felix Centre, one of the many schools which have sprung from the Northern Irish troubles.* The bloody lessons of Ulster have been applied in Bosnia, Kosovo, Sierra Leone and southern Iraq, usually with acceptable results: and in this field, remember, acceptable equals excellent. The British land forces are almost uniquely experienced and effective at

---

* The Felix centre is named for the legendary operators of 321 Explosive Ordnance Disposal Company, RAOC – now part of the Royal Logistics Corps, and officially a 'squadron' – who have been the sole bomb squad for Northern Ireland since the troubles began. Their radio callsign was 'Felix', both for the direct latin meaning and as an allusion to Felix the Cat: a bomb-disposal operator in Northern Ireland generally needing at least nine lives. Traditionally, only operators with a successful Northern Ireland tour under their belts can award a British licence to deal with IEDs. (There is talk nowadays of shifting the gold standard to other theatres, as you might imagine.) The American FBI has sent its people to do the Felix centre course, among many others.

low-intensity containment. Provided, as I say, that enough appropriate people can be found – mostly infantry, but also various
other bits and pieces: helicopters, Felix-trained operators, etc –
things can usually be made peaceful enough that people of good
will may have a chance. And that is all that you must expect
armed forces to do. They cannot make the local lions lie down
with the lambs: all they can do is prevent the bites and scratches
being too painful. At that, however, they are very good.

What the British forces may struggle with is doing their real,
ultimate work – fighting other more-or-less-organised armed
forces, ideally at a long distance from the UK. It isn't much use
being able to keep the ring between warring local factions if one
of them can stand you off altogether using commonly available
military kit. We need more infantrymen, better resourced: but we
do need other things, too.

The merits or otherwise of sitting at home in our peaceful
islands and leaving the big bad world for others to deal with I
will leave to your own consideration. I merely note for now that
the British armed forces are funded for expeditionary warfare,
and it is currently government policy that they should be able to
carry it out. The point has been made, I think, that our forces
are extremely limited in their ability to do so at present. That is
mainly what I wanted to say in writing this book. For what it's
worth, because it's bound to be asked, I will also offer very briefly
my own plan of action.

To begin with, I do not believe that one must focus only on
peacekeeping or only on war-fighting, even at unit level. I do not
find this distinction to be useful. It is my contention that some
things are required across the spectrum of military activity:
infantry of all flavours, utility helicopters, recce drones and so
forth. Other things – Main Battle Tanks, self-propelled artillery,
frigates, destroyers, pure air-superiority fighters, air-launched
cruise missiles – have become almost entirely valueless, no matter
what kind of war one may be fighting.

My ideal plan for the future is designed to give the UK a credible ability to reach round the world and overcome a medium-
weight governmental military without much assistance: and then
to mount a Northern-Ireland level of containment afterwards.
Such operations, if they are to be useful, must often be mounted

fast and decisively. The need to implement them may not be apparent to everyone. Also, we may not wish to wait while various nations attempt to turn the issue into a bargaining chip in other debates, or otherwise practice diplomatic football. Hence the emphasis on being able to act without allied assistance. However, I make no attempt to ensure that Britain can also *equip* itself unilaterally: first because it's impossible, and second because I think that if nobody in the whole world – not even America – is willing to so much as let us have spare parts for an operation, then perhaps we are in the wrong and it shouldn't be carried out.

Given that we must be dependent on foreign consent to some degree, it should be American consent rather than the far harder-to-obtain consensus of the expanding European Union. Also, American kit is much better and cheaper at present, and if we *are* operating as part of an alliance, as one might hope, the most significant member of it will almost certainly be the USA. Interoperability with the US forces is far more useful than inter-operability with anyone else. Finally, as previously noted, if the Americans seriously wish to prevent an operation of ours they can do so, wherever we buy our equipment: this is far less true of Europe. For all these reasons, going the American equipment route offers the greatest British freedom of action, which I take to be a good thing. For all that I have just spent a lot of time criticising the British state, for me the Mother of Parliaments remains one of the very few bodies on earth which should have such power.

Having set out what is wanted, here is how I would get it.

First off, very little can be done under hostile skies. The best way to control the sky is a combined system of fighters and radar planes. The fighters don't need to be superfighters: they just need supersonic speed and a good missile. All the planes, fighters and radar, should be easy to use anywhere: at sea, round the world, here in Britain. In other words, they should all be carrier aircraft. If we were huge and rich like the Americans, we could afford to have non-carrier ones too, but we aren't huge and rich. Britain should never buy another strike, fighter or radar aircraft which cannot be operated from a ship. If we choose our fighter sensibly, it can also be a good attack plane able to deliver smart bombs and cheap, worthwhile anti-armour or defence-suppression missiles. If we choose our carrier sensibly, we will not have to further compromise the design of our fighter/attack plane by also making it a jump-jet.

As things stand, we have done none of this. Our future carriers are to be jump-jet ships, in order to reduce their cost. This is causing the price of their planes (the future F-35 jump-jets) to skyrocket, so much so that we will probably lose money in the end – and we get less capable planes, and badly restrict our options on carrier airborne radar to boot. This is idiocy. We are buying a lot of land-bases-only planes as well, which aren't even multi-role (the Eurofighter). More idiocy.

We should upgrade the future carrier project to a proper, large, conventional take off and landing ship with catapults and arrester wires. Such a vessel probably can't be built in British yards: so much the better. We needn't build up a hopelessly uncompetitive shipbuilding industry on the ruins of our old one and then cut it off at the knees again in ten years' time. We can simply get our carriers from overseas yards, saving ourselves a mint. We should change our F-35 fighter-bomber order to the type that the US Navy are getting, thus torpedoing the jump-jet version and saving time and money for everyone. Simultaneously, we should buy the current American carrier radar plane (E-2 Hawkeye) or whatever they build to replace it, rather than faffing about with carrier radar helicopters that can't get very high and can't stay up very long. We should cancel as many Eurofighters as we possibly can. The combined effect of these decisions would be to save us money and give us a lot more capability.

That's fighters, bombers, carriers and flying radar sorted out. The skies can easily be cleared of enemy aircraft. A good start. But there might be a troublesome SAM network, preventing us from flying freely over the contested territory. Our F-35s can tackle this, but we should also have Tomahawk cruise missiles for the deeper, harder-to-reach bits. Buy a few thousand of them – it'll only cost a billion or so – and we can cancel the Future Offensive Air System, get rid of the Storm Shadow and close down the Tornado bomber force to make up for it. Mount most of the Tomahawks on nice cheap commercially-built ships which also have big flat tops on them and plenty of room, along the lines of the current HMS *Ocean* or RFA *Argus*. The enemy air-

defence network is toast, and we also have lots of space for helicopters and other useful things.

Now we rule the skies at medium heights and above. This
allows us to rain explosives accurately and cheaply wherever we
like, without needing local pals to lend us bases. Our carrier
planes and Tomahawks also mean that no hostile surface flotilla
can keep our fleet away, or even dare put to sea. Just to cover
all bases, keep the current Merlin sub-hunting helicopters and
attack submarines, in case enemy subs should actually show up.
We would seem to have little need now for the destroyer and
frigate fleet: decommission the lot, cancel the Type 45 destroyer,
and buy more Tomahawk-firing helicopter ships and amphibious-
assault floating docks with the money.

This is going well. We are now off the coast anywhere in the
world, invulnerable to all likely threats and with lots of room for
marines, soldiers and all their toys, plus the ability to blast
anything we like on shore. Now we would like to clear away
such old-fashioned iron as the local army may care to bring
forward: tanks, artillery and the like. All we need is to find them
– we have the weapons to hit them already. So let's make sure
our carrier flying radar can also sniff out ground targets, as the
American JSTARS or Global Hawk drone can already. If this
seems tricky, buy some Global Hawks. Use the ASTOR money
for this, rather than continuing with ASTOR itself. Get plenty of
TV/thermal-imaging drones too, to confirm that our targets are
legit. We wouldn't want to be blowing up radar blips just because
a computer thinks they look a bit dodgy. Elite sneaky recon teams,
deployable by air, will also help here, and they tend to be useful
for other things too. Being good fun and cheap, such teams are
mushrooming at a fair old rate already, all across the army and
marines.*

Now we can happily start landing our troops. Given that enemy
armour will swiftly be detected and smashed from above and we
can put smart bombs or Tomahawks on artillery targets, they
won't need tanks or self-propelled guns. We can send all our

---

* Royal Artillery Special OPs, 16 Air Assault Brigade Pathfinder Platoon, 3
Commando Brigade Patrol Troop etc – quite apart from the actual Special
Forces themselves.

Challengers and AS90/Bravehearts to the scrapyard, and the army and marines can have lots more Warriors or Vikings or helicopters as may suit. At a stroke, the land forces have become radically lighter, less hungry for fuel and ammo, and a lot more of them can be riflemen. We can afford helicopters now, no trouble at all: especially if we simply buy them from America (specifying that they must pass UK airworthiness checks this time, please). This will give us approximately ten times as much lift for our money as utility Merlins or other expensive Euro-dross. Let the Italians worry about the one remaining British helicopter factory: they own it.

Some new lightweight, portable 155mm towed artillery pieces are already on order, to replace the current light 105s. By all means keep these to console the artillerymen. Every brigade can still have an artillery regiment, just not a self-propelled dinosaur one. They may not get huge amounts of work in future, but gunners make excellent infantrymen in a pinch, and the forward-observer officers can qualify as airstrike controllers – a few already have. (Don't let them have their new lightweight cluster-bomb rockets, though; we're trying to make the place *nicer* to live in, not turn it into a big minefield.) Similarly, if we absolutely must have a whole regiment of amiable toffs in light tanks for every brigade, fair enough; though a squadron per brigade seems more reasonable.

What if we want to go by air rather than by sea? Well, we'd need more air transport. We can probably afford some now: all the measures to this point will have brought us out ahead of existing plans by a few billion. Let's make our money work harder for us by purchasing C-17s from Boeing rather than A400Ms from BAE: we get nearly twice the lift that way. The C-17 moves much faster and further as well, which effectively doubles the lift again and opens up options. Even if we aren't going to do a whole operation by air, transport planes are always handy and we never have enough. We should certainly get more, and more air-to-air tankers as well, although a few billion won't get us enough for serious air deployments.

Do we then need lightweight, air-freightable armoured vehicles if we're going by air? In other words, do we need FRES (the Future Rapid Effects System)? That's highly questionable. The

Americans already have a FRES equivalent, the Stryker, and it isn't much cop. In order to have any chance of resisting RPGs – the main threat – Stryker needs to have protective gratings bolted all over it, reducing its usability and robbing it of its air portability. It isn't very tough even then: you'd much rather have a Warrior or equivalent. And your Warrior will be there in a few weeks by sea, so FRES is only required for the first few weeks of a major airborne deployment into a high threat area. It's not really worth its projected cost of £14bn, then, let alone whatever the real cost may turn out to be.

Traditional light airborne forces look like a better idea. There are plenty of tricks they can use in a higher-threat environment: helicopters are pretty safe if used in the right way, as we know from South Armagh and Iraq. Another good method of keeping our lads alive even without heavy vehicles is to put the armour on the *man* rather than on his transport. (There has been at least one case in Iraq of a soldier surviving a direct RPG hit on his chest armour.) It's worth remembering that one doesn't have infantrymen so that they can ride about in vehicles: this is merely the way in which they get to work. Once they are doing what we actually pay them for, operating dismounted, the toughest vehicle in the world cannot protect them. Money spent on a range of new body-armour options would probably yield major benefits. And if we don't buy FRES, we can actually afford a decent number of transport planes.

This is great. We can now reach round the world, heavy by sea or light by air, and no likely adversary can stop us. (Sure, the French, Germans, Americans or Chinese could, but we've already invaded all those places more than once – probably time to quit while we're ahead.) When we get there, we will have a much higher proportion of useable troops among our people on the ground, and they will have at least as much heavy hitting power at their disposal as before. We have the military that Britain ought to have.

There is still some tidying up to do. Let's not bother with SAMs, except shoulder-launched ones for emergencies, and those should be used by anyone rather than just by artillerymen. That's another three regiments of troops freed up, and a good deal of cash – at least enough to get everyone a new set of indisputably good small-arms. Institute a separate career track for ceremonial duties in the infantry and cavalry, the way the artillery and marines and certain Territorial units have already done (assuming we must really continue to pay for state pageantry from the defence budget). Get rid of a few officer ranks, and trim the UK bureaucracy severely. There are other minor adjustments: but we're pretty much done with the forces themselves.

Now let's see if we can find some money for other departments, so that they can sort out the utter mess that British industry has been left in after decades of wrongheaded military subsidies. Let's cancel Nimrod MRA4, Sonar 2087, the Future Surface Combatant, the Guided Multiple Launch Rocket System and all the next-generation European air-launched missiles. If we reinvest all that money in – let's say – a British space programme, we might actually achieve some competitive high-tech industry. (If you don't care for that idea, do what you like with the cash; the MoD certainly doesn't need it.) We could shut a whole lot of unnecessary bases, too; the idea of keeping military bases open just because their local communities like the revenue is preposterous. If these communities for some reason are thought to deserve a constant stream of government cash, just give it to them. It'll cost less than running bases that have no purpose, and achieve more social benefit. I never found a local community in ten years which really seemed better for having a base nearby, or whose citizenry seemed glad to have me and my mates around. 'Tommy this, and Tommy that,' and 'chuck 'im out, the brute'* was more their style.

Blimey: that was easy. Why aren't we doing it? Because nobody with any power to influence events wants to, generally for bad reasons.

The army would hate these plans. What? No big tanks? No SP guns? No cluster-rockets? No cloud-punchers? Actually be compelled to cooperate with the air arms or the navy to get anything done? Life wouldn't be worth living, certainly not as a cavalry or artillery officer.

The navy couldn't bear it. To traditional naval eyes, the only actual warships left would be submarines: everything else afloat

---

* Kipling again: from *Barrack Room Ballads*.

would have a strong resemblance to a fleet auxiliary of some sort. If you wanted to seriously claim to be a combatant, you'd have to be an aviator, a submariner or a marine. An ancient way of life, that of the fighting surface sailor, would be pretty well gone.

And it would be even more difficult than it is now to justify a separate air force, reason enough to guarantee total opposition from that quarter. Even if you kept the RAF, it would no longer be a restful organisation employed overwhelmingly in the UK. It would find itself aboard ship or deployed abroad a lot of the time – perhaps as much as the tiny minority of combat pilots already are. And an awful lot of the future RAF would be operating boring transports and helicopters or, even worse, carrier planes. All the bombers would be directed by ground-force commanders. There wouldn't be any lovely deep strikes. No, that would never do.

Even more adamantly opposed would be the various mouthpieces and allies of BAE: politicians, union people, 'defence analysts' and so on. Much of the British arms sector would go to the wall. This would be portrayed as some sort of national economic catastrophe, much though we aren't actually talking about huge numbers of people out of work, nor any genuinely valuable export earnings lost. Indeed, without BAE gobbling up so much of our shrinking supply of engineering and science graduates, we might manage to make some strides in other fields of technology.

So serious reform of the defence sector in Britain would meet with stiff opposition – which brings us back to your letter to your MP. If British voters ever decide that the usefulness and the lives of their servicemen and women are more important than the jobs of a small number of arms workers, we might see some political response. Public consciousness of defence would have to rise very significantly indeed, in a way that hasn't happened for generations, but that isn't impossible. You've read this book, after all.

The difficult bit would be overcoming the bureaucracy. I take the view that there is no way serious progress will ever occur under the present set-up. Far too much power lies in the hands of the three Service chiefs, backed by the terrifically strong tribal loyalty of their juniors. It is difficult to see why the nation should tolerate this sort of thing any longer. The bickering admirals, generals and air marshals, their jealously-guarded prerogatives, their three-way cake split, have caused us too much trouble. All three groups are equally guilty. The navy clings obstinately to pointless surface warships. The RAF insists on unnecessary and foolishly wasteful deep strikes. The army refuses to seriously consider any methods which don't involve ground vehicles and plenty of them. All because their primary loyalty is to their tribe rather than to the state.

The Chiefs of Staff must go. So must most other uniformed bureaucrats who exist only or primarily as tribal chiefs or sub-chiefs. The problem is not, I should point out, with the people who fill these offices, but with the offices themselves. All three of the current service heads have admirable records. They were all lions among lions in their time. General Jackson passed through the furnace of pre-ceasefire Northern Ireland several times and then crowned his operational career with a most successful handling of the Kosovo intervention. Admiral West blithely took the almost defenceless HMS *Ardent* into 'Bomb Alley' in 1982, where she was hit no fewer than nine times before he gave the order to abandon ship. Air Chief Marshal Stirrup flew combat in the little-known Dhofar fighting of the 1970s as a young pilot, and won an impressive Air Force Cross later on. Even so, the steely General Jackson has been unable to reorganise the Guards sensibly, let alone the artillery or cavalry. No one should know better than Admiral West how vulnerable surface ships are without air cover, but on his watch we have burked fleet air and decided that the gap can be plugged with surface ships. Air Chief Marshal Stirrup is clearly a brave man, but not brave enough to reassign his deep-strike force to close support. Most crucially, all three men adamantly refuse to cede any ground. Stirrup and West, along with every other Whitehall warrior in light or dark blue uniform, insisted on army cuts to match theirs in 2004. It would be nice to think that Jackson and the soldiery would have been more magnanimous had the need been at sea or in the sky, but one begs leave to doubt that.

If I were allowed to carry out just one of all the recommenda-tions I've made in this book, this would be it: break the power of the single services and subordinate them to a non-partisan joint authority, one not required to treat all three forces evenhandedly.

This would inevitably lead to better use of resources and personnel. Disagree with me as much as you like about every-thing else, but believe me on that.

And believe me when I say that this is important stuff which we need to get right. The world is not getting safer, it is getting more dangerous. At the moment, when someone wants to attack British citizens on the UK mainland, he must do so by using smug-gled or home-made explosives, or chemical weapons which are even less effective.* But this is not a static situation. There are many more serious, more capable adversaries out there than the various underground extremist groups. Country after country has acquired the ability to cause a nuclear explosion, and more are working on it. Many such nations – North Korea, Iran and Syria among others – already have theatre-range ballistic missiles. Most will find it impossible to prevent their new technical knowledge from leaking out across the world, just as the Western powers and then the Soviets did. The atomic cat is out of the bag: we are now in a race against time.

The day *will* come when a lot of very worrying new players will be close to having some ability to drop nukes into London or New York. Players even more worrying, that is, than the governments of Israel and Pakistan – fortunately, neither of those two can hit London or New York quite yet. Perhaps a nuclear stand-off will suffice in these future cases as it did with the Soviets and does with China. But perhaps it won't, even in the case of governments, which are easy to find and target. The more roguish a state is, the less likely it is to care whether the citizens of its capital city die in a retaliatory strike. And the more unstable or fragmented or domestically threatened a government is, the greater the chance of real, genuine Weapons of Mass Destruction – that is, nukes – passing into the control of out-and-out nutters who don't care if they themselves die so long as they can take a couple of million Westerners with them. To give just one example, Iran's

---

* Contrary to popular perception, even advanced chemical weapons such as nerve agents are normally no more deadly per kilogram than regular high explo-sives. The current exaggerated fear of chemical weapons has little foundation in fact. I say this as one who has personally encountered and disposed of such munitions, much though it unfortunately tends to diminish my own reputation for derring-do.

hardline Revolutionary Guards – much the most serious of that nation's military and paramilitary forces – cannot really be said to operate under the control of their central government.

If nothing is done, unstable or inimical countries will eventually possess suitcase-sized nukes. Some, in all likelihood, aren't far from having ones that can be fitted into a standard shipping container. Such governments, or elements within such governments, have already offered various terrorists support and weaponry of lesser power. There is plenty of scope in future for nukes to be smuggled into the West, with varying degrees of state involvement and deniability. In this case, it may be impossible to accurately or legitimately respond after the fact, so nuclear deterrence is not useful. Nor is a national missile-defence system such as the Americans aspire to. Almost the only reasonable military option – much though it is now anathema in many circles even to suggest such things – would be a pre-emptive invasion.

This is not to say that the Western nations should or even could dash about the world invading anyone who seemed a bit worrying. Quite apart from anything else, the rich democracies as presently set up are incapable of mustering sufficient forces to do so. The West, in protecting itself from attack in future, will be compelled do so mostly by non-violent means: it has no choice in the matter. Perhaps the attractions of mad zealotry, ethnic separatism and dictatorship as ways of running things can be diminished. Maybe the community of nations can develop a more reasonable book of international laws, and get more serious about applying it. Possibly the spread of weapons knowledge can be slowed down – it certainly can't be stopped forever. In nearly every case, difficulties must be resolved without the use of force. Diplomats and politicians surely have their work cut out for the next few decades, as do intelligence and security services, finance and aid departments, the central and international banks and many others.

But when they fail – and it would be nothing short of miraculous if there weren't some failures ahead – we may reluctantly need to turn to other means: to military means. Probably, at least once or twice in the next fifty years, British servicemen and women will be fighting for their lives yet again, facing serious government opposition at the far end of a long supply line. And this may well be because they are actually fighting for *our* lives, to save us from the violence of the enemy and the desolation of war. They may no longer be acting merely to bring down an unpleasant tyrant, or to save other people from the reign of Chaos and Old Night, as they have lately been doing all over the world.

Perhaps, just for once, we could try getting ready in advance, rather than bribing ourselves – and only a few of us, at that – with our own taxes, while donkeys arm to fight the vanished enemies of their youth. Perhaps if the public cared about defence specifics, as they did during the Dreadnought debate a century ago, we might get things right, or right enough – as we did in that case. At the very least, to use a pithy old military phrase, we might get the MoD to pull its head out of its arse for a look round now and again. Nobody nowadays thinks it reasonable to simply take it on trust that the local school is OK; few any longer think that the medical profession, or the police, or any other important government department should be left unscrutinised to regulate itself. But there is a curious national blind spot around defence, perhaps the most basic government capability of all. If this book has changed that even a little, then it has done its job.

Ranks and Commands in the British Armed Services

Royal Navy		British Army/Royal Marines		Royal Air Force		Notes
				Commissioned Officers		Non-commissioned Ranks & Ratings
Admiral of the Fleet*		Field Marshal*		Marshal of the RAF*		'Five-star'
Admiral		General	*Field Army***	Air Chief Marshal		'Four-star'
Vice Admiral		Lieutenant-General	*Army Corps***	Air Marshal		'Three-star'
Rear Admiral	*Major task force*	Major-General	*Division*	Air Vice Marshal		'Two-star'
Commodore	*Minor task group*	Brigadier	*Brigade*	Air Commodore		'One-star'
Captain	*Carrier/Amphib*	Colonel		Group-Captain		
Commander	*Frigate/destroyer*	Lieutenant-Colonel	*Battalion/Regiment*	Wing-Commander	*Squadron*	
Lieutenant-Commander	*Minor warship*	Major	*Company/Squadron*	Squadron-Leader	*Flight*	
Lieutenant		Captain		Flight-Lieutenant	*One aircraft*	
Sub-Lieutenant		1st Lieutenant	*Platoon/Troop*	Flying-Officer		
Midshipman		2nd Lieutenant	*Platoon/Troop*	Pilot-Officer		
Warrant-Officer 1st Class		Warrant-Officer 1st Class		Warrant-Officer/Master Aircrew		
Warrant-Officer 2nd Class		Warrant-Officer 2nd Class				
Chief Petty Officer		Staff/Colour Sergeant		Flight-Sergeant		
Petty Officer		Sergeant		Sergeant		
Leading Hand		Corporal	*Section*	Corporal		
Able Rating		Lance-Corporal	*Fire Team*	Senior Aircraftsman		
		Private/Various titles				

The type of operational unit an officer or noncommissioned officer might be in charge of is shown in italics where applicable.

* This rank is ostensibly disused, although in fact the Chief of Defence Staff – the senior officer of the UK armed forces – remains a five-star position in all but name.

** No Field Army or Corps HQs exist in the British Army, and it would have great difficulty assembling even a Corps from its own resources.

GLOSSARY

AIFV (Armoured Infantry Fighting Vehicle): British portmanteau term for the latest generation of armoured infantry battle transport vehicles, usually known in America as a Mechanised Infantry Combat Vehicle. Modern types have armament equivalent to a light tank, in addition to carrying a section of infantrymen. They were designed for the great battle on the German plains with the Red Army, like the Main Battle Tank and the Self-Propelled Gun. Unlike the tanks and guns, however, the AIFV is usually found extremely useful in modern urban-insurgency fighting, as it allows infantry to move about in hostile areas with little fear of ambush – even ambushes involving mines, large IEDs or mass RPG attacks. The current British AIFV is the Warrior.

Air Assault (also **Airmobile**): A type of army unit intended to manoeuvre on the battlefield mainly by helicopter, generally light-infantry in nature and capability. In the British Army, the Air Assault formation is 16 Air Assault Brigade. This unit was formed by a very minimal reorganisation of the old 5 Airborne Brigade, and it is still very airborne in character: the more so in that it possesses almost no utility helicopters.

Airborne: Strictly speaking, any military force or operation using transport aeroplanes. In a British and American sense, strongly associated with parachute troops. Airborne qualification, in the British services, requires the completion of not only parachutist training but also the infinitely tougher 'P-company' selection course. The three infantry battalions of the Parachute Regiment must complete Airborne qualification as part of their basic recruit training, earning the right to wear the red beret (actually maroon in the British airborne). Two of these battalions are assigned to 16 Air Assault Brigade, and the third has just been moved into the Directorate of Special Forces.

Aircraft Carrier: Broadly, any warship whose primary purpose is to act as a base for aircraft at sea. Usually used specifically to mean ships which can operate jet aeroplanes as well as helicopters, even if only jump-jets like the Harrier. Such ships are normally equipped to act as command vessel for a large fleet.

AK47: Acronym for Avtomat Kalashnikova 1947, Mikhail Kalashnikov's phenomenally successful Soviet assault rifle. The AK47 and its numerous derivatives have equipped a majority of the world's armies, paramilitaries, insurgents and others during the last fifty years. It is an excellent weapon, thoroughly robust, reliable and as accurate as an assault rifle needs to be. Much of its design was copied from the German MP44, the first assault rifle ever.

Allied: Operations and formations involving forces from more than one nation. In a British sense, usually associated with NATO.

Amphibious Assault Ship: A warship (or, in Britain, more commonly a Royal Fleet Auxiliary vessel) built to deliver land forces onto enemy shores. Generally the only vessels able to land personnel and equipment easily without a modern harbour. They are of two types: those mainly intended as helicopter carriers, and those with a small floating dock allowing the use of beach landing craft even in choppy seas. Britain operates both types as naval vessels and as civilian-manned auxiliaries.

Apache: An American-designed attack helicopter, large numbers of which are operated by the US Army. Now coming into service in the British Army also, at unnecessarily vast expense.

Armoured: Armoured forces are those organised around the Main Battle Tank. Everything and everybody in an armoured formation should be able to keep up with swiftly-moving tanks racing across country, and should possess armour protection as well if at all possible. Accompanying infantrymen must therefore ride in Armoured Infantry Fighting Vehicles; associated artillery must be equipped with Self-Propelled Guns. While armoured forces are swift on those battlefields which they are suited to – given enough logistic support – they are unbelievably cumbersome to deploy around the world, and terrifically expensive. They have a very low proportion of rifle infantry.

Assault Rifle: The usual term for a modern military rifle. Assault rifles fire 'intermediate' ammunition such as NATO 5.56mm or Soviet 7.62mm. Intermediate cartridges are less powerful than those used in older combat rifles, but more powerful than the light rounds used in pistols or submachineguns. This means that the assault rifle can practicably deliver short bursts of automatic fire without becoming uncontrollable or burning out its barrel, and has an accurate range of several hundred metres – all that most users need. Such weapons are intended for general-purpose use, not just for assaults. The name arises from Hitler's fondness for the mystique of the storm trooper. The first ever intermediate-power weapon, the German MP44, was described as a '*Sturm gewehr*', a rifle for storm troopers, in order to get his approval. This was translated into English as 'assault rifle', and so the new class of weapons was misnamed.

Astute-**Class:** The new Royal Navy submarines, now being built by BAE. They will be nuclear-powered, and armed with conventional weapons including torpedoes, Harpoon and Tomahawk. The programme has suffered serious cost and time overruns, and is now seen as a serious liability by BAE.

ASW: Anti-Submarine Warfare.

AS90: This stands for Artillery System of the 1990s, the current British Self-Propelled Gun, now being upgraded as the Braveheart.

ASTOR (Airborne Stand Off Radar): A British procurement programme under which the UK is seeking to acquire a ground-scanning radar aircraft like the American JSTARS (Joint Surveillance and Target Acquisition Radar System). The JSTARS plane can fly along at high altitude, and pick out all moving vehicles over hundreds of miles of country: it can often tell which ones are military, too. Such technology allows the practical implementation of 'no-tank zones', or the swift annihilation of any armoured force foolish enough to manoeuvre within JSTARS range. The ASTOR promises to cost more and achieve rather less.

Attack Helicopter: A helicopter designed to strike enemy ground forces rather than to lift loads: for example the Apache. Attack helicopters are operated by the army rather than the air force, in both Britain and the US. They have light armour protection, and will usually be equipped to detect and destroy armoured vehicles from far off, using radar and homing missiles. Attack helicopters also mount cannon or rockets intended for use at short range. Especially in urban terrain or against enemies without many armoured vehicles, there will be a temptation to close in and use these latter weapons. This will tend to make the attack helicopter an easy target for enemy machine guns or RPGs, unless it maintains a high speed. Such aircraft are somewhat burdensome logistically, if not as much so as artillery or tanks. Conventional strike jets would be safer and better value for money, but for reasons of inter-service rivalry the attack helicopter will probably continue to exist.

AWACS (Airborne Warning and Command System): Also known as the Boeing E-3 Sentry. A 707 airliner full of computers and electronics with a big rotating radar on top, made in the USA. This radar can detect even low-flying aircraft or missiles hundreds of miles away and onboard controllers can then direct fighters to intercept. Without such an airborne radar, even the most modern fighter is effectively hamstrung. However, building radar aircraft is not a simple matter, as Britain found out during the ill-fated Nimrod AEW project. The AWACS is the main proven example of its type: it is used by all NATO countries including the UK, and by others as well.

A400M: The current name for the collaborative European military transport aircraft now in development, formerly known as Future Large Aircraft (FLA). A400M is intended for service with British, French, German, Turkish, Belgian and possibly other forces. It will be a fairly basic turboprop design, and will offer only a marginal improvement over modernised Hercules. It is forecast to be very expensive and is not due in service until 2011. Despite all this it is to receive almost all the British funding allocated to military airlift, for the usual reasons of pork-barrel politics.

BAE Systems (British Aerospace): Originally called British Aerospace plc, or BAe, this corporation was formed by the UK government's sell-off of the nationalised aerospace industry in the 1980s. Since then, with massive help from the British government, the company has taken over almost the entire British military-industrial sector, including the vestigial remnants of British civil aerospace and shipbuilding activity. The company nowadays has extensive US interests, and is acquiring more, with an eye to winning lucrative Pentagon business. For practical purposes, BAE Systems may now be thought of as an offshore holding company, primarily focused on the US defence market, which happens to own the vast majority of British defence manufacturing as part of its portfolio. It has an unhealthy amount of power over the UK government.

Ballistic Missile: A large rocket-powered missile that flies on a very high, very fast trajectory. Ballistic missiles possessed by minor powers are usually of 'theatre' range, such as the original German V-2, the well-known Scud or other aged ex-Chinese or Soviet weapons. These can normally reach no further than one or two countries away from their launch site. They carry a warhead not very much heavier than a typical aircraft bomb, which if loaded with conventional explosives will not do significantly more damage. The true power of a ballistic missile is that it is almost impossible to defend against: it descends to strike its target hypersonically, many times faster than sound, and only the very latest anti-air missile systems have any chance at all of intercepting it. Even these state-of-the-art defences, such as the American Patriot, may well prove ineffective (as was the case in Gulf War I, much though media reports at the time did not reflect this). Defence against ballistic missiles has yet to really be achieved, even by the US: hence these missiles' very great popularity as strategic terror weapons among governments of all kinds. It is important to remember, however, that without nuclear warheads one will require thousands of ballistic missiles to do much damage, and only modern types have any accuracy at all.

Bergen: The usual term for a British soldier's rucksack, in which he carries his sleeping bag and other personal kit. Usually a loaded bergen is heavy, even if the soldier isn't a devotee of the 'comfort zone' philosophy and hasn't packed any luxuries. Troops will always try to fight without their bergens if possible.

Blunty: A non-flying member of the Royal Air Force, so called because he or she is seen as being a stranger to the sharp end.

Body Armour: See Enhanced Combat Body Armour.

Bomber: An older and perhaps more honest name for an aeroplane primarily intended to drop bombs. No longer much used. Strike or the even more emollient Interdiction are nowadays preferred as terms for this activity.

Braveheart: The new name for modernised AS90 British Self-Propelled Guns. These updated vehicles still mount 155mm NATO-standard artillery pieces, but the barrels have been lengthened for greater range.

Cavalry: Formerly the term for troops who fought on horseback, it now means different things in different armies. In British service it means upper-class tank regiments who formerly had (or still have) horses, as opposed to the middle-class units of the Royal Tank Regiment. In the US Army it refers to mostly armoured units of non-standard organisation, also descended historically from horsed troops. At the time of Vietnam the US Cavalry was largely Airmobile, but this role has now been handed to a formerly Airborne division, the famous 101st.

Challenger II: The current British Main Battle Tank, a reasonably good example of its type when properly prepared although not thought to compare particularly well with the German Leopard for reliability or the US Abrams for capability.

Chinook: A large twin-main-rotor utility helicopter made by Boeing of the USA. It is at present the only proven, effective, reasonably serviceable lift helicopter in British service and it has been the workhorse of all recent British deployments. It is favoured by the Special Forces. The Chinook is particularly popular in Afghanistan as it is the only military helicopter in widespread service with enough power margin to operate usefully at higher altitudes.

Cluster-bomb: The most common term for a weapon designed to split apart before impact and shower its target area with many submunitions. Each submunition usually delivers both an armour-piercing plasma spike and a cloud of anti-personnel fragments, thus killing or wounding all exposed personnel nearby and usually wrecking even armoured vehicles in the vicinity. Unfortunately, from 5 to 25 per cent of the submunitions will fail to detonate and remain scattered in the target area, effectively constituting a particularly nasty and troublesome field of land mines. Cluster-bomb warheads range from artillery shells with 90 or so bomblets inside to heavy artillery rockets and air-dropped bombs containing hundreds.

Cloud-punchers: The air-defence units of the Royal Artillery.

Commando: In British terms, this word refers to 3 Commando Brigade and those who have achieved the qualification necessary to serve in this formation. The word also refers to a commando infantry battalion, eg 45 Commando. Commando training is an especially arduous infantry preparation, of similar difficulty and conferring similar status to Airborne P-company selection. A British commando wears a green beret. UK Commando forces are particularly focused on amphibious warfare: the core of 3 Commando Brigade is provided by the Royal Marines.

Commons Defence Select Committee: A committee of backbench Members of Parliament who are supposed to scrutinise and supervise the Ministry of Defence. The members typically suffer from low levels of military knowledge, and many are pawns of vested interests inimical to the efficiency of the armed forces. Despite these handicaps the committee is collectively quite perceptive. Unfortunately its reports are not widely read and command relatively little public attention. The Ministry of Defence usually ignores them or even – with enormous cheekiness – publicly disparages them, making a mockery of democratic government.

Cruise Missile: A small robot jet plane carrying a warhead of similar size to an aircraft bomb, which flies to its target at low level and then crashes on it, blowing it up. By far the best and most effective type is the US Tomahawk. Various other countries have produced less capable versions, such as the Franco-British Storm Shadow. Cruise missiles were originally developed to deliver nuclear weapons more economically than ballistic missiles could, but they are nowadays seen more as a way of putting conventional warheads onto targets which are protected by hostile air defences, without risking the lives of airmen. The unit costs of the Tomahawk are dropping to the level where it is now seen as a weapon for routine tactical use, at least by American users.

C-5 Galaxy: The older of the USA's two long-range heavy transport aeroplanes. An absolutely gigantic brute, theoretically able to lift loads of well over 100 tons in an emergency. Though it tends to suffer from lower serviceability rates than the newer Globemaster, and is unable to land on short or rough runways, the Galaxy provides an important part of the USA's strategic mobility. The only other such plane flying in any numbers is the equally monstrous ex-Soviet An-24, which is nowadays available for charter work on the international market. (The British forces are frequent customers.)

C-17 Globemaster: The latest American heavy transport plane. It is a unique aircraft, which employs new technology to allow landing on short or rough airstrips after a flight of thousands of miles. This is normally impossible for intercontinental jet aircraft like the C-17: until the Globemaster was developed the only transport aeroplanes which could land on such strips were slow, short-range turboprops like the Hercules or the A400M. The RAF has five Globemasters, the only heavy long-range military transport planes in Europe. They were officially leased as a temporary measure pending the arrival of the A400M, but this was merely a ploy to placate the powerful political allies of British Aerospace. The leases on the RAF's Globemasters have now been quietly bought out, and this handful of aircraft will be a much more valuable capability for the UK than its entire future fleet of A400Ms.

C-130 Hercules: a medium-sized turboprop transport aircraft made in the USA, which has been in RAF service since the 1960s. It is rugged and capable of operating to and from short or rough airstrips. As a turboprop, it is best suited to shorter-range trips within a theatre of war, which is its main employment in the US forces. The British air force possesses only a handful of proper long-range transports, and so it is compelled to press its Hercules into longhaul service: RAF Hercules frequently travel worldwide, generally taking days or even weeks to do so and requiring numerous stopovers. During the 1990s, Lockheed (the makers) developed various updates, to the point that a fully modernised Hercules is almost a new type of aircraft. Such an upgrade is much cheaper than buying an A400M, and yields only slightly less capability.

Defence: modern euphemism for activities formerly carried out by Ministries or Offices of War. Frequently includes attack and offence, certainly if the relevant government possesses any effectiveness or credibility at all in this area.

Destroyer: An escort warship similar to a frigate, but different in that it mounts an extremely expensive anti-air-defence missile system intended to protect not just the destroyer but also the fleet or convoy it is accompanying. This missile system may work to some degree (as in the case of the American Aegis/Standard, and perhaps the new French–British–Italian PAAMS) or not (as with the British Sea Dart mounted in current Type 42 destroyers). In either case it will make the destroyer from three to five times as expensive as a frigate, approaching the cost of a small aircraft carrier. Destroyers have changed mission and design at least four times since they first appeared in the Royal Navy.

DLO (Defence Logistics Organisation): Vast, inefficient bureaucracy created by nominally amalgamating the three UK armed services' logistics empires during the 1990s. Almost the only noticeable effect has been the appearance of another level of extremely senior uniformed management above the three single-service chieftains, and the slashing of stores holdings in line with commercial 'just enough, just in time' efficiency principles. This has permitted the firing of numbers of inexpensive warehousemen and the sale of large amounts of defence real estate, but has not addressed the gigantic, slothful middle-ranking bureaucracy which was the real problem. Much of the DLO's management consists of serving or former uniformed officers, but its 30,000 rank and file are mostly civil servants.

Droggie/Droggy: A member of the hydrographic surveying arm of the Royal Navy. In former times, surveying and charting was an occasional mission for regular warship crews. Nowadays the bulk of it is done by specialised ships and people. Curiously, these remain in the Royal Navy, despite the fact that other support and even combatant functions are now handled by civilians.

ECBA (Enhanced Combat Body Armour): A new type of flak jacket which can be fitted with rigid plates for extra protection. With the plates, it protects parts of the wearer from even quite high-powered small-arms ammunition. This equipment first saw widespread use in the Iraq invasion of 2003. It received a lot of media attention following the case of Sergeant Steve Roberts of the Royal Tank Regiment. Sergeant Roberts had originally been issued with ECBA, but it was later taken from him to be given to an infantry unit, reasonably seen as a higher priority. Sergeant Roberts was later killed by small-arms fire: ECBA would have saved him. MoD shiftiness and obfuscation regarding the circumstances of his death convinced many that the sergeant's lack of ECBA was due to some major supply error. In fact, the Ministry was simply trying to avoid revealing that Sergeant Roberts had been killed by friendly fire.

Escort: the term for both frigates and destroyers, medium-sized warships which are formally intended to accompany major warships or convoys of merchantmen and protect them from attack by enemy aircraft, missiles, ships or submarines. Escorts generally have a crew of two to three hundred, mount expensive radars and sonars, and carry various specialised missiles. British escorts normally have a light, rapid firing cannon which is sometimes used to offer largely notional assistance to forces ashore. In addition, UK escorts carry a single helicopter, which in most combat situations is the ship's only useful contribution. Escort warships are much beloved of mainstream naval officers, as they are critical to the naval personnel and promotion mechanism: the chance of any given officer achieving high rank is completely dependent on the number of escorts in service during the middle-to-late part of his career.

Eurofighter: Jet fighter developed collaboratively by Britain, Germany, Spain and Italy; now finally coming into British service designated Typhoon. It is a pure air-superiority fighter, designed long ago to operate at short range from Central European airbases against the deadly, numerous MiGs and Sukhois of Voyska PVO. It is ridiculously expensive even by the standards of military aircraft, and late even by the standards of European cooperative projects: it lies at the root of the present British defence-financial crisis. Eurofighters will be difficult to deploy worldwide and largely irrelevant against modern enemies who will possess little in the way of fighter capability. It seems likely that the RAF will be compelled to take delivery of at least 200 of these aircraft, far more than it can conceivably use. Perhaps the worst ever British defence project.

Exocet: An older sea-skimming ship-killer missile of French manufacture. Used to great effect against the British fleet by Argentine forces during the Falklands War.

Fighter: Formerly the word for aeroplanes designed for air-to-air combat against other aircraft. Nowadays used more promiscuously, especially in American service, tending to refer to any one or two seat fast combat jet; no matter if its primary role is actually as a bomber.

FOAS (Future Offensive Air System): The project working to replace the Tornado bomber, probably with something very similar.

Frigate: An escort warship not possessing even the dubious capability of fleet air defence. Theoretically its main role is anti-submarine warfare, although it would hardly be the first choice for this in any real situation. Frigates are actually employed more on coastguard/police type work, chasing blockade runners and drug smugglers (to little effect), or as platforms for diplomatic entertainments and cocktail parties. These ships do, however, provide scarce command slots at sea, and so are much cried up by all ambitious naval officers. There have been frigates in the Royal Navy for hundreds of years (with a hiatus from the mid-nineteenth to the mid-twentieth century). They have tended to be characterised as 'general purpose' ships in recent decades, perhaps because there is no single, obvious, worthwhile task for which they are much use.

Future Carrier: The British effort to acquire two new small aircraft carriers to replace our present three very small ones. This project has already been badly burked: the new ships will not be able to operate normal jet aircraft. This was supposedly in order to save money, but it will wind up costing vast sums as the F-35 must now be made to function as a jump-jet (see Harrier), which would otherwise be unnecessary. Furthermore, the decision to make the ships jump-jet only is likely to rob the future British fleet of serious airborne-radar capability. Despite these painful economies, the carrier project shows every sign of developing massive cost overruns and delays. Much of the difficulty is due, as ever, to inter-service rivalry.

FRES (Future Rapid Effects System): The British Army's ongoing effort to obtain armoured vehicles which are light enough to be shipped around the world by air. The current Warrior infantry vehicle is splendidly tough, often preserving its passengers from massive volleys of RPGs and large IED explosions, but it is very heavy. Thus it must be sent to foreign war zones by sea, which takes a few weeks: hence the FRES. Many commentators note that the 'Stryker', the US Army's equivalent, is not working well: it must be fitted with extra protection to make it even moderately survivable. Even if FRES works better than Stryker, the UK will still not possess any significant amount of military air transport, and has no real plans to get any, which renders the FRES effort somewhat pointless.

Future Surface Combatant: The programme which will replace today's British frigates, probably with something very similar.

F-15 Eagle: The USA's current premier air-to-air fighter, although it has actually seen more combat employment delivering air-to-ground strikes. The best fighter in the world at the moment, although the cream of ex-Soviet MiGs and Sukhois could give Eagle pilots some trouble in the vanishingly unlikely event of their ever getting to close range. (They would almost certainly be destroyed from afar by the F-15's advanced missiles and AWACS backup.) The F-15 is soon to be supplanted by the even more puissant, wildly expensive F-22 Raptor, despite the lack of any obvious reason for this.

F-22 Raptor: The USA's very latest ultra-super-fighter, now with added Stealth, which has somehow survived the end of the cold war and thus the disappearance of any real role for it. The first deliveries of F-22s are just reaching the US Air Force (as of 2005). It may conceivably bump the Eurofighter from the position of most expensive combat jet ever, although the Eurofighter will probably win on the basis of cost to the taxpayer per jet actually used in front-line service.

F-35: Also known as Joint Strike Fighter, Joint Combat Aircraft, etc. This programme is intended to produce three quite different jets for different branches of the US and British armed forces, although they will look similar and there will be a few parts in common. All three types will be supersonic and primarily intended to deliver ground strikes, though they will also be useful air-to-air fighters. The first type is designed to fly from normal runways and is intended for the US Air Force. The second is meant to fly from proper full size aircraft carriers, and is meant for the US Navy. The third type is to be a jump-jet, able to take off from a 'ski-jump' ramp and land vertically like the Harrier: it will thus be able to operate from small, cheap carriers such as the current and planned British ones. As a supersonic jump-jet has never been built before, this third variant is adding very significantly to the cost and difficulty of the whole programme. Nonetheless, the F-35 will probably come out well below even the artificially-low headline price of the Eurofighter, and will be vastly more useful.

Gazelle: A small, light helicopter used by the British Army and Royal Marines as a senior officer's taxi and for training. Formerly it would also carry out casualty evacuation, reconnaissance and even ground attack duties, but this would be unlikely nowadays: the Gazelle cannot carry any very significant payload and is getting rather old.

Goalkeeper: One of two automatic air-defence gun systems employed for close-in protection by ships of the Royal Navy and Royal Fleet Auxiliary. Such systems use their own built-in radar to detect any fast-moving object approaching the ship: they then automatically spray it with high-velocity, high-impact projectiles at a very high rate of fire. The only action required from the ship's crew is to switch the system on when air attacks are expected, and to switch it off when friendly aircraft are about. Such an auto-gun is cheap and quite easily bolted onto any ship: most warships and many civilian-manned auxiliaries have such protection. Goalkeeper is made by a Dutch American consortium.

GPS (Global Positioning System): A constellation of satellites orbiting the earth, paid for and operated by the US Department of Defense. These satellites emit very precise time signals which enable a small, cheap portable receiver anywhere on or above the earth to calculate its own position, typically to an accuracy of around 30m. GPS is used by missile guidance systems, smart bombs, ships, aircraft, vehicles, individual infantry teams and in many other military applications. It has also become indispensable in many areas of civilian life. Military conservatives (especially from branches of service whose existence has been rendered largely pointless by GPS, such as the Royal Navy's navigation specialists) frequently assert that the US might choose to switch off GPS unilaterally in certain regions of the world. This makes little sense, as such a denial of service would prohibit almost all US military operations in that region, and probably trigger a number of airliner crashes, shipwrecks or similar civilian disasters. GPS will shortly be integrated with the European Space Agency's Galileo system.

Guards: A designation used for military units, meaning different things in different countries. In the Soviet Union it was an honour given to Red Army formations that had performed well in combat, often during World War II. In the US it is a shorthand for the National Guard, the closest American equivalent of the Territorials. In the British service it refers to army units with a historical role as personal security troops of the sovereign, such as the several regiments of the Foot Guards and the various Horse Guards outfits. Nowadays the British army possesses five Guards infantry battalions and two Household Cavalry regiments, all of which spend a great deal of time and effort mounting ceremonial guards and parades in London. The actual protection of the royal family is nowadays carried out by special police units. The heavy ceremonial commitments of the Guards and Household Cavalry are widely believed to reduce their effectiveness for real soldiering. These regiments possess immense behind-the-scenes clout, and they were accorded preferential treatment in the cuts of 2004.

Gunship: an older term for attack helicopter. Nowadays refers mostly to side-firing gunships, converted transport planes fitted with an array of guns firing out of the side of the cargo hold. This permits the plane to circle high up and far off while its gunners pick off enemy troops below, often individually. Side-firing gunships are extremely popular with the ground forces they support and are generally judged to be very effective: especially against lightly-equipped enemy soldiers or paramilitaries, targets which conventional air power often has difficulty engaging. Nonetheless, such aircraft are unpopular in air forces, and even the mighty USAF has only 21, mostly assigned to the Special-Ops command. Britain has none.

Harpoon: A sea-skimming ship-killing missile of the same general type as the French Exocet. Harpoon is of American design and is a more sophisticated weapon by far, more like a short-range cruise missile. Later versions can be used to attack shore targets as well as ships. It is the main armament of British frigates for use against other surface vessels, although it would normally be safer and more convenient to deliver the weapons from an aircraft or a submarine.

Harrier: the famous British 'jump-jet', at present the only proven example of its type in service. A Harrier is able to swivel the exhaust nozzles of its engine downwards by more than 90 degrees, providing a vertical upward thrust. However, the engine does not have enough power to support the plane in a hover unless it is without most of its fuel and payload. An armed and fuelled Harrier thus cannot lift off vertically, but it can get airborne from a short improvised strip ashore or a small, cheap aircraft carrier at sea. It can then fly a mission during which it will expend its weapons and burn most of its fuel, and return to make a safe vertical landing. A Harrier is not, therefore, a true Vertical Take Off and Landing (VTOL) aircraft: it is STOVL, Short Take Off and Vertical Landing. Ground-attack Harriers, updated by American designers, are operated to good effect by the Royal Air Force and the US Marine Corps, in both cases assigned to close support of ground forces. Harriers have also been employed successfully as fighters by the Royal Navy, most famously above the Falkland Islands in 1982, when British forces were limited almost entirely to ship-based air support. The Royal Navy's Sea Harrier fighters were later upgraded with new, heavier American missiles by British Aerospace. These missiles made the Sea Harrier by far the deadliest British fighter in air-to-air combat. However, they were too weighty for the Harrier to safely descend vertically with them still aboard in hot weather: jet engines lose power in such conditions. This meant that Sea Harriers could not carry out fully-armed routine patrols (the main mission of a fighter) without jettisoning their expensive weapons into the sea before each landing. The missile upgrade had rendered the Sea Harrier impossibly wasteful in hot climates, and thus effectively useless. The Sea Harrier is now being scrapped, after much debate as to whether it could be fitted with a more powerful engine, leaving the British fleet reliant on shore-based or Allied planes for fighter cover. From

2005 the only aircraft operated by Joint Force Harrier will be bomber versions, at least until the F-35 enters service.

Helo: an alternative military-jargon word for helicopter. Pronounced 'he-lo', like 'J-Lo'.

Hercules: See C-130 Hercules.

ICBM (Inter-Continental Ballistic Missile): A very powerful, sophisticated and expensive ballistic missile using multiple rocket stages to achieve sub-orbital flight and thus world-wide range. ICBM warheads will complete most of their journey outside the atmosphere, covering thousands of miles in only tens of minutes, and then re-enter to strike their targets hypersonically. They are, at present, effectively impossible to shoot down or intercept; particularly where multiple warheads and decoys are used. While the ability to produce a nuclear explosion is nowadays comparatively widespread, true ICBMs are possessed only by the US, UK, France, China and Russia. ICBMs are sometimes designed to be launched from nuclear-powered submarines: this is so that they cannot be easily located and so perhaps knocked out by a pre-emptive strike. (This is the only type of ICBM employed by the UK.)

IED (Improvised Explosive Device): the correct term for a bomb built by terrorists, criminals or paramilitaries, as opposed to conventional munitions made in established weapons plants. IEDs may be triggered in myriad different ways against a vast range of potential targets, and vary in sophistication from simple pipe bombs with igniferous fuses up to quite complex anti-armour projectiles, barrack-busting mortars or massive truck bombs detonated by radio, mobile phones, laser beams etc. IED builders frequently make use of stolen, failed or discarded regular munitions; where these are lacking they may use home-made explosive mixtures.

Interdiction: A word sometimes used in military staff jargon to describe aerial bombing which has not been requested by ground forces. It is a popular concept with air forces as it can be used to argue in favour of a separate command structure.

Jaguar: An older combat jet now approaching the end of its service with the RAF. It is mainly used for bombing, although it can defend itself against enemy fighters if required. A rare example of a successful, effective and reasonably economical European-collaborative defence project, albeit from long ago.

Jarhead: A member of the US Marine Corps. The name comes from the 'high and tight' haircuts popular in the USMC, which have now been carried well beyond the traditional crew cuts of yesteryear. A modern high-and-tight involves the sides of the head being shaven almost to the bare flesh, with a sharply-defined oval region of extremely short stubble left on the top. In many cases this leaves the high-and-tight wearer looking like a bald man wearing a curious flat skullcap – or, of course, a jar with a lid on it. The jarheads like the look, though, and some of them are almost as tough as they think they are, so jocular comment is rare. High-and-tights are also popular with other American elites, such as US Army Rangers.

Joint: Any force or operation employing units or people from more than one of the three armed services. It is also meant to be a way of doing business, all three services working together in the British interest without infighting or rivalry or triplica-tion of effort. In practice, 'Jointness' often means the creation of a new bureaucracy in addition to the existing ones. Joint organisations, exercises or operations are often referred to as 'Purple', a colour not associated with any particular single service.

Joint Force Harrier: A new command under which the Royal Navy's Sea Harrier fighter squadrons were brought together with the Royal Air Force ground-attack Harriers. Joint Force Harrier is part of the RAF. Originally this was sold to the Navy by placing an admiral high up in the RAF's command structure, but in a further reshuffle the admiral was forced out and Joint Force Harrier is now unequivocally under RAF ownership. Meanwhile, the Sea Harrier is in the process of being retired. Joint Force Harrier still contains naval personnel, however, and parts of it still go to sea aboard carriers on occasion. In future, Joint Force Harrier will re-equip with the jump-jet version of the F-35. (See Harrier.)

Joint Helicopter Command: A new command formed to take control of all utility and attack helicopters operated by the three services. It also took over 16 Air Assault brigade. The creation of the JHC headquarters, with all its glistening senior officers and staff, has not addressed the fact that Britain has an insufficient number of helicopters, particularly utility ones, and those we do have are mostly very old and worn out.

Jump-jet: See Harrier.

Jungly: A person or helicopter belonging to the Royal Navy's utility-helicopter squadrons, formerly operated principally in support of commando forces, so called from their earliest combat operations in the Borneo rainforest. Nowadays the Junglies are under the control of the Joint Helicopter Command. They are equipped with aged Sea King aircraft, now so worn out that they are only marginally useful.

LAW (Light Anti-tank Weapon): A one-shot shoulder-fired rocket in a disposable launching tube, which can damage or destroy armoured vehicles if the user is brave, expert and manages to get close to his target without being seen. (This would usually be done by lurking in ambush.) LAWs have actually seen very little use against their intended target: they have mainly been employed against foot soldiers or gunmen protected by bunkers, trenches or urban terrain features. LAWs are often carried for such purposes even when armoured opposition is not expected. While light as rocket systems go, the LAW adds very significantly to an infantryman's personal load. LAW-type rockets are generally employed by Western armies; their adversaries normally favour the RPG.

Lynx: A smallish, high-performance helicopter long used by both the British Army and Royal Navy. In the British Army it was formerly an attack helicopter with a subsidiary light utility role: nowadays the attack work is being taken over by the Apache and the remaining Lynxes will see out their last few years of army service moving small loads about the battlefield. Royal Navy Lynxes will probably continue flying for some time, as the new naval Merlin lacks the ability to carry out the seagoing Lynx's most useful mission, that of making missile attacks against small surface ships.

Main Battle Tank: A modern heavy tank. Such vehicles move very fast cross-country (provided the terrain is suitable) and mount extremely tough armour. Their main armament is a highly specialised armour-piercing cannon designed to destroy enemy tanks: they are not really very useful for any other task.

Unfortunately for the Main Battle Tank and the many people who depend on it for their livelihood and sense of identity, there are better and safer ways to deal with enemy tanks nowadays – most obviously using strike aircraft. It doesn't help that tanks are very difficult to move about off the battlefield. Each one weighs sixty tons or more, meaning that it cannot be air freighted. Main Battle Tanks go by ship as far as possible, and then on rail cars or road transporters until nearly at the front line. (They must not be driven too much under their own power, as they will damage roads and break down often.) Then, once you have your tank on the battlefield, it needs to be constantly resupplied with vast amounts of fuel and ammunition, and it will require a massive maintenance effort to keep it running. These things are also generally true of the AIFV, but the AIFV is often worth all the trouble: the Main Battle Tank, rather less so.

Mechanised: A military word once used to refer to troops that moved by motor vehicle rather than by horse or foot. Nowadays in some countries it refers to the infantry component of armoured forces: US Army 'mechanised infantry' and 'Mechanised Infantry Combat Vehicles' are the same as British armoured infantry and AIFVs. In Britain the word 'mechanised' has a different meaning, referring to second-rate or economy-class armoured infantry. Rather than tough, speedy Warriors, a British mechanised infantry battalion has vulnerable, slow (but cheap) Saxons. In the cold war, Britain employed mechanised/ Saxon units simply as a low-cost means of bulking out its armoured forces. In future, the plan is for the mechanised brigades to transform into the new 'medium weight' forces, which will be equipped with FRES and so easier to deploy round the world than armoured formations, yet harder to kill than light infantry. The concept has some serious weaknesses, however.

Merlin: A helicopter cooperatively built by British and Italian concerns, originally as a naval submarine-hunting aircraft. The programme was dogged by delays and became ridiculously expensive. Merlins finally began to be delivered to the Royal Navy more than twenty years after project commencement, with a price tag of over £100m per helicopter; they are only just beginning to reach operational useability as of 2004. One should note that an armed and fuelled sub-hunting Merlin does not have enough power to achieve a hover in still airs – rather upsetting in a brand-new helicopter. Even more sadly, the Soviet submarine fleet has closed up shop, and the anti-submarine Merlin is now largely without an enemy. There is also a utility version. It can lift a comparable number of soldiers to the American Black Hawk and costs approximately ten times as much to buy. The utility Merlin, like the sub-hunter variant, has suffered delays in reaching real-world effectiveness: despite having been delivered to the RAF in 2001 it was only cleared for use in Iraq during 2005.

Milan: An anti-tank guided missile system which can be mounted in light vehicles or carried by a small team. British Army infantry battalions and Royal Marine Commando units normally have a group of Milan teams attached. Milan has greater effective range against armoured vehicles than a LAW, but it still requires guts and concealment to be used effectively. The Milan will be replaced in the nearish future.

Minimi: A Belgian-designed light machine gun in NATO 5.56mm calibre, used for many years by the US and other armies, as well as by the British Special Forces. Normal British troops were generally compelled to use the light-machine-gun version of the SA80 until 2003, despite its inadequacy. Nowadays, at last, the Minimi is widely issued in the British forces. (The SA80 machine guns were still expensively upgraded, however.)

MLRS (Multiple Launch Rocket Systems): An alternative to conventional cannon for use as artillery. The usual configuration, as in the US and British armies at present, is a medium-weight tracked vehicle carrying a rack of twelve large, long-range rockets, which can all be launched in less than a minute. Formerly, MLRS-type weapons offered a distinct range advantage over ordinary guns, at the cost of some accuracy. The inaccuracy of rockets was dealt with by the use of cluster-bomb warheads, covering such a wide target area that precision ceased to be an issue. Nowadays long-barrelled cannon firing various exotic types of shell can achieve better range than the rockets, but plans are afoot in America and the UK to upgrade artillery rockets to the point where they are almost ballistic missiles, and so the pendulum seems set to swing back again.

National Audit Office: An agency of the British government that investigates and reports upon the activities of other departments of state, especially regarding their efficiency and value for money. It occasionally looks into the Ministry of Defence. NAO reports often reveal serious deficiencies, but generally hedge their conclusions sufficiently for the MoD to escape serious censure.

NATO (North Atlantic Treaty Organisation): A military alliance of the US, the Western European countries, and nowadays many Eastern European ones also. Member states agree to respond to an attack on any one of them as though it were an attack upon them all, handing over control of designated forces to the NATO supreme commander (always an American) for this purpose without further ado. Any other action by the Alliance requires lengthy, perhaps interminable debate, and in such cases member states contribute forces only voluntarily, often with many caveats. Originally NATO was intended to resist a possible assault by the Soviets and their Warsaw Pact allies. Its long standing, the relative wealth and military competence of its founding members, and the fact that it had a clearly-defined purpose for a long time have all meant that NATO is far and away the most credible international military organisation currently extant. For this reason, NATO is sometimes sanctioned by the UN to carry out international military missions in which the UN itself would have little or no chance of success. Most plans for an integrated European military force expect to use the structure of NATO as a basis. Despite all this, one should note that various significant components and sections of NATO are regarded by serious military professionals as being essentially useless, and this problem can only get more widespread as more countries join. NATO may be the most credible international military organisation in existence, but that isn't necessarily saying much.

NEC (Network Enabled Capability): A staff-jargon phrase meant to describe an ideal state one would wish to achieve where all friendly units and headquarters can communicate seamlessly and securely over integrated high-speed data networks. One should note, however, that Network Enabled Capability is not actually new: warships have been digitally networked for decades, and often aircraft too. Moreover, compared to other kinds of military hardware communications networks are not particularly expensive. The attempt by UK Defence Minister Geoffrey Hoon during 2004 to pretend that he was cutting combat units across all three services in order to pay for Network Enabled Capability was not very credible.

Nimrod: A black name from the distant past to the near future of British defence procurement. All Nimrods are military versions of the long-defunct De Havilland Comet airliner, which failed commercially owing to several high-profile disasters. The Nimrod first came into RAF service in 1969 as a maritime-patrol aeroplane, primarily intended to hunt Soviet submarines. In this form it was reasonably effective, although the RAF was compelled to purchase many more Nimrods than it actually required, in order to sustain the British large-aircraft industry, which subsequently perished anyway. In the late 1970s there were thus a dozen very expensive Nimrods sitting unused in storage. At that point, the UK decided to attempt to build its own airborne-radar aircraft, despite the fact that the rest of NATO was adopting the American AWACS. GEC (now part of British Aerospace) undertook to convert several of the unused Nimrods to radar aircraft, in a project usually referred to as Nimrod-AEW. It was a colossal, unmitigated disaster: ten years later, with close to £2bn in today's money spent, the radar Nimrods still didn't work and didn't seem likely to. The project was cancelled and the UK was compelled to purchase AWACS anyway. Yet the curse of the Nimrod had still not been lifted. In 1996, the original anti-submarine Nimrods were becoming obsolete and worn out. Despite the fact that no clear need for anti-submarine patrol planes existed (even the well-funded US Navy has not bothered to renew or replace its similarly aged P-3 Orions) British Aerospace was contracted to completely rebuild the RAF's 21 Nimrods at a cost of £2.2bn, with the planes due in service by 2003. The estimated cost of the project, designated Nimrod MRA4, is now rising through £3.3bn; the RAF is to receive only 12 planes, not 21; and the in-service date will now be 2009 at the earliest.

PAAMS (Principal Anti-Air Missile System): The radar and missile system which is to be fitted to the new Type 45 destroyers of the Royal Navy. A cooperative French–British–Italian project.

Phalanx: An automatic air-defence gun system for ships, similar to Goalkeeper. Phalanx is entirely US-made.

PJHQ (Permanent Joint Headquarters): A UK command structure recently created to prevent squabbling between the three existing single-service command HQs. The PJHQ is tri-service manned and in most circumstances is in charge of any actual military operations that the UK may be conducting. Nonetheless, the three original HQs still exist, and they still get to place representatives of their own within any British Joint command. Establishment of the PJHQ would seem merely to have added a purple tribe (see Joint) to the struggle between the browns, dark blues and light blues.

Pongo: A member of the British Army. It is widely believed in the other services that soldiers do not wash, and therefore 'where the army goes, the pong goes'. Not a term much used in the soldiers' presence, given their unfortunate propensity to violence.

Puma: An old, smallish utility helicopter, still in RAF service though now rather worn out.

Radar: Short for Radio Detection And Ranging. A radar set emits radio waves which travel outwards, bounce off solid objects, and return to the radar to be analysed. This allows correctly-designed radar sets to detect, locate and track aircraft, missiles, surface ships, vehicles, etc, sometimes at ranges of hundreds of miles, regardless of darkness and usually of weather. It is important to remember that radar cannot normally see anything below the horizon: hence it is most effective when high above the earth's surface. Also, any radar which is switched on and emitting radio pulses is easily detected by the enemy. Finally, radar does not work under water: sonar is necessary here.

Rapier: A light SAM used for air defence by the British Army. It is not man portable, but can be carried in light vehicles. It did well in the Falklands, and has been comprehensively updated since then.

RE (Royal Engineers, aka Sappers): The senior of the British Army's various technical and engineering corps. The whole organisation is commonly referred to as the Sappers, although strictly sappers are the enlisted ranks and the officers are engineers. In fact, Sapper officers are not required to qualify academically in any technical discipline, and the corps confines itself to relatively simple civil engineering: bridging, entrenching, demolitions and the like. The Sappers are rated as a combatant corps, as they are often well forward of everybody else, clearing paths though minefields, obstacles etc. This status means that Sapper officers may rise to become big generals in command of all-arms forces, unlike lowly REME or RLC types, and that the Sappers look down on these others. The Royal Engineers are locked in a constant turf war with the RLC regarding bomb disposal. The RLC have gained the upper hand in actually disposing of IEDs, but the Sappers hold several important roles too, particularly on the battlefield and in searching out IEDs before they are dealt with.

Recce: Pronounced 'recky', as in reckless. The usual British abbreviation of 'reconnaissance', a military activity that consists of finding out where the enemy is and what he is doing. Americans would say 'recon'. There are many ways of doing this. One may use aircraft such as the ASTOR, or more conventional ones which can survey ground only visually. UAVs are also very useful, and so are satellites in some situations. Failing such safe, high-tech methods, it may be necessary to send people out to take a look personally: this is a primary mission of the Special Forces and similar organisations. The traditional armoured-warfare means of doing recce is the use of light, fast tanks which will range ahead of the main body, fighting anybody they can beat and leaving the tough nuts for the heavy forces to crack. The British Army has no fewer than five complete light-tank cavalry regiments organised just for this, which would formerly have been judged enough for a much bigger army.

Red Banner Northern Fleet: The main fleet of the old Soviet navy, principally made up of highly dangerous nuclear-powered submarines. It was based in Arctic Russia, threatening the sea lanes of the North Atlantic and thus NATO's ability to reinforce Europe from the USA. The Royal Navy of cold-war days was, at least ostensibly, focused almost entirely on a possible battle with the Red Banner Northern Fleet in the freezing seas between Iceland and the Faeroe Islands. Inertia from those days is one of the reasons that Britain has continued to purchase enormous amounts of expensive anti-submarine equipment ever since. ('Red Banner' was an honorific title often given to Soviet fleets; their Baltic fleet actually received it twice, and was formally known as the 'Twice-Honoured Red Banner Baltic Fleet'.)

REME (Royal Electrical and Mechanical Engineers, Corps of): A relatively junior British Army organisation which is responsible for maintaining most of the army's machinery and electronics. It is consequently large in manpower but small in status. REME officers actually are qualified engineers, unlike those of the Royal Engineers, but on average REME work is less dangerous than that of the Sappers, and so earns less kudos and recognition.

Reservist: A serviceman or woman not in the full-time, regular forces, but still liable for military duty in certain circumstances. All British regulars automatically become reservists when they leave the service, whether they want to or not. The other main source of reservist manpower is volunteer organisations such as the Territorial Army. It has become more normal to turn first to the part-time volunteers of the Territorials and their naval and air force equivalents. Most large British military operations nowadays require the call-up of at least a few reservists: the regular forces never have enough personnel, particularly in certain logistic specialties. So far this has not caused any great difficulty; reservists normally step forward willingly, pleased to have a chance of active service after the long decades when they were hardly ever used. How long this keenness will last is uncertain.

RFA (Royal Fleet Auxiliary): A flotilla of specialist merchant shipping maintained by the Ministry of Defence. The ships are manned by British civilian seamen rather than members of the armed forces, and are much cheaper to buy and run than navy warships. They are also able to remain in operation far from home for much longer, as their personnel, training and leave cycles operate very differently. The downside to this is that an RFA crew is not nearly as cohesive a unit as a navy ship's company. RFA vessels are mostly fuel tankers and supply ships used in support of the navy proper, but they include a number of amphibious assault ships largely indistinguishable from those of the navy. Other RFA vessels occasionally take on duties resembling combat roles. The division of tasks between navy and RFA is unclear and often inconsistent. It often appears that the RFA is simply given those jobs and ships which the navy can't be bothered with, or finds dull, or needs to implement cheaply.

RLC (Royal Logistics Corps): Also known as the Rather Large Corps, as it is the biggest corps in the army. The RLC are the supply and transport arm, formed by amalgamating several older organisations such as the Royal Corps of Transport, the Royal Army Ordnance Corps and others. This brought with it several things which do not seem to an outsider to fall naturally under the logistics banner, such as the disposal of IEDs.

Rock-Ape: A member of the Royal Air Force Regiment, after the barbary apes of Gibraltar. The RAF Regiment provides manpower for the Joint Nuclear, Biological and Chemical Defence Regiment, and has six Field Squadrons, equivalent to light-infantry rifle companies. One of the Field Squadrons specialises in ceremonial, in the same way as the Guards; another, astonishingly, is parachute trained. Rock-ape instructors are attached to most air force units and bases, charged with keeping up institutional expertise in self-defence from chemical weapons and attacking ground forces.

RPG: Rocket Propelled Grenade, or, more correctly, Raketniy Protivotankoviy Granatomet ('Rocket Anti-Tank Grenade Launcher'). Refers to various Soviet-designed shoulder-fired anti-armour rockets. Unlike a western-style LAW, the RPG launching tube is re-used, the firer fitting a fresh projectile to the front for each shot. RPG-pattern weapons are in very widespread use by terrorists, insurgents and military forces all over the world. They lack the power to seriously threaten the heavy AIFVs and Main Battle Tanks of western armies, but they can often damage or destroy lighter vehicles, even when these are fitted with protection. RPGs are also a major threat to any helicopter which hovers or lands nearby.

SAM (Surface to Air Missile): The usual term for anti-aircraft missiles, especially land-based ones. SAM networks are always less powerful and effective than a proper system of jet fighters directed by AWACS or similar airborne-radar platforms. Reliance on SAMs for national air defence is to admit that one is a third-rate country with no realistic hope of controlling one's own airspace against serious opposition – let alone anyone else's. Nonetheless a properly organised national SAM network can be a tough nut for a middle-ranking air force to crack, and may slow down even the US forces briefly. Such heavyweight SAM systems, in addition to big missiles which can intercept aircraft at high altitude, will require a number of radars to detect and track their targets, and a communications network to coordinate themselves. This will mean that enemy bombers and other aircraft can fly over the defended area only at great risk (apart from American Stealth planes). However, the world's more capable air forces will normally be able to locate SAM installations and pick them off fairly safely using various high-tech methods, so gaining control of the skies (see SEAD). Apart from heavyweight SAM networks intended to protect large areas, there are various kinds of lightweight systems, often small enough to be fired from the shoulder. They cannot generally threaten high-flying aircraft, but may well be effective against those at low altitude. This latter SAM threat cannot normally be eliminated except by occupying the area with ground troops (and perhaps not even then). Such man-portable systems are quite a serious problem for the Western powers, especially when employed as terror weapons against civilian airliners. Fortunately they are not in nearly such wide circulation as the RPG, and require more skill to be maintained and used effectively. Examples of shoulder-fired SAMs include the US Stinger (issued in large numbers to Muslim extremists by the CIA during the 1980s) and the ex-Soviet SA-7 series (NATO codename 'GRAIL', also manufactured in China, Pakistan and Egypt).

SAS: The legendary Special Air Service, properly 22 SAS Regiment of the British Army, the major unit of the UK's Special Forces. An SAS trooper always begins as a proven serviceman, usually but not exclusively in the army infantry. SAS selection and training is largely in common with the SBS, and includes extremely arduous route navigation in the Welsh hills to weed out the infirm of purpose, followed by many weeks of jungle work in the Far East and other such joys. After getting through the basic pipeline, which 90 per cent of candidates fail, the recruit is considered to be 'badged' and is then given specialist training in field medicine, demolitions, communications or such like. He will also be trained in one or another exotic method of inserting into his mission area: freefall parachuting, covert underwater swimming, long-range desert ops etc. He may later go on to train in counter-terrorist work, bodyguard duties or almost anything that could be imagined: there is very little that the Special Forces don't consider themselves competent to do.

SA80 Rifle: The normal personal weapon for most UK servicemen and women. It came into service in 1985, produced by the then state-owned Royal Small Arms Factory, who were given the contract because they were being prepared for privatisation. The SA80 rifle was of unbelievable shoddiness when first introduced, and swiftly acquired a dreadful reputation. Its only virtue is its accuracy, oft-mentioned by its defenders, well though they know that there is no requirement for a standard combat rifle to be accurate beyond a few hundred metres. Some of the faults were fixed, but the SA80 continued to be one of the worst and most unpopular rifles in the world right through the 1990s, particularly its light-machine-gun version. After endless complaint and scandal, it was officially admitted in 1997 that the SA80 suffered from issues of reliability in 'extreme temperatures only'. This led to it being upgraded to the A2 mark. The A2 upgrades were done in Germany at a greater cost than buying new weapons. The machine gun versions were also fixed up, but there was no way to make these latter effective without a complete redesign; they have since been replaced by the Minimi, at yet more expense. It is said that the A2-upgraded basic rifle is now at last tolerably serviceable, twenty years after its introduction and having cost double or triple what it should have. Officially, however, there has never been more than a minor problem with the SA80 in desert conditions: no blundering has ever taken place and the mere fact that front-line troops carried defective weapons for decades is not worthy of discussion.

SBS: The Special Boat Service, the rather less-well known, somewhat smaller maritime counterpart of the SAS. The SBS is part of the Royal Marines, and still draws most of its recruits from them although it is now under the Directorate of Special Forces like the SAS. SBS basic training is the same as that of the SAS, but SBS swimmer-canoeists normally focus on maritime special-warfare techniques, learning covert swimming, boating and diving techniques, the use of limpet charges and methods of deploying in and out of submarines. There is a large UK maritime counter-terror (MCT) organisation led by the SBS, paralleling the SAS' dry-land one, all ready for the day when some enterprising baddies seize a ship or oil rig in Hollywood style. Regrettably the world's terror groups seem not to watch the right movies, and the MCT organisation has largely languished in idleness.

Sea Dart: the old and largely useless fleet-air-defence missile system currently fitted in the Royal Navy's aged Type 42 destroyers.

Sea Harrier: See Harrier.

Sea King: A 1970s-vintage naval helicopter, designed in the US but made for the Royal Navy under licence in Britain. It was replaced long ago in the US Navy. The British anti-submarine version is now finally being superseded by the long-awaited Merlin, but the similarly antique utility Sea Kings of the Commando helicopter-lift squadrons (now part of the Joint Helicopter Command) have no replacements in sight. These aged helos have done excellent service in their long active careers, but they are now almost completely worn out. They can no longer fly at all in hot temperatures, even at sea level.

Sea Wolf: A short-range naval air-defence missile manufactured by British Aerospace. It is fitted in British frigates and nowhere else. The frigates are thought to need Phalanx or Goalkeeper gun systems as well, which gives a fairly accurate idea of how good Sea Wolf is. Unlike a longer-ranged fleet air-defence system such as Sea Dart or PAAMS, Sea Wolf only has the reach to protect the ship it is on, and that is all it was designed to do. Given the utter lack of useful tasks for frigates during an air attack (other than soaking up hits which might otherwise sink important vessels) it is occasionally claimed that Sea Wolf has some use in protecting other ships – although it is actually inadequate even to defend the one it is mounted on.

SEAD (Suppression of Enemy Air Defences): An activity whereby hostile ground-based air defences are engaged and destroyed from the air. This may be quite simple, as when an anti-aircraft gun position is bombed, but it is usually a complex, high-tech field of warfare. Generally, SAM targeting radars are stimulated into switching on by probing flights overhead. They are then easily located, and can be taken out by special missiles which home on the radar transmissions. Of course, the operators may switch their radar off if they detect such missiles approaching them; but this is likely to prevent their own missiles from taking effect. Furthermore, now that the missile batteries have been located they can be struck by smart bombs or cruise missiles. A full spectrum of SEAD capabilities is possessed only by the US Air Force, but second-ranking Western military powers can also make a decent effort at it. Aircraft dedicated to SEAD duties were formerly referred to as 'wild weasels'.

Self-Propelled Gun: An artillery piece mounted in a tracked vehicle, for the purpose of keeping up with armoured forces. The British version is called AS90, now being upgraded as Braveheart. SP guns usually have some armour protection, and are the mainstream form of artillery in well-funded armies. They suffer from the same problems of unwieldiness and logistic burden as other components of the armoured juggernaut. Like all artillery systems, they tend to find their targets stolen from them by strike aircraft. The huge trouble and effort required to get them into theatre and supply them is looking less and less worthwhile.

SF (Special Forces, also UKSF): The general term for those form-ations reporting to the Director of Special Forces. Principally this includes the SAS, the SBS and the body formerly known as '14 Int', now a regimental-level command like the other two. The latter group is recruited from the armed services just as the SAS and SBS are, but unlike them it takes women, and it is focused more on surveillance and intelligence-gathering oper-ations than on recce, raiding etc. It had its genesis in Northern Ireland counter-terror operations, but now operates on a wider stage. The whole Directorate is shrouded in secrecy, with the MoD always refusing to comment about any aspect of it to the press. Details of SF operations do not generally become known until years afterwards, if at all. This secrecy is oper-ationally useful, and is also, perhaps, the main reason that Special Forces are usually the first military choice for British politicians, even more than the operators' undoubted compe-tence. The secrecy also permits the special forces to purchase proper foreign or US equipment rather than British or British-European politically-mandated junk. In 2004, the Directorate of Special Forces was also assigned command of a battalion of the Parachute Regiment, elite Airborne infantry, which is intended to form the basis of a 'ranger' unit. If 'ranger' turns out to mean what it does in the US Special-Ops community, the Paras will operate in larger groups than the SAS and SBS do and will tend to play supporting parts rather than lead roles in the special-warfare dramas of the future.

Smart Bomb: An aircraft bomb of either conventional or cluster-bomb pattern which has been fitted with a guidance kit. This will consist of adjustable fins, controlled by a seeker head, which steer the plummeting weapon so as to impact much closer to its target than it would if left to fall freely. The seeker head is aiming to hit a bright dot of light, produced by a laser target designator of some type. Most often this laser will be in a targeting pod such as the British TIALD, mounted in the aircraft which dropped the bomb or one accompanying it. Sometimes the laser mark may be provided by ground forces, especially Special Forces. The latest smart bomb kits use GPS as a backup in case of cloud or smoke or other difficulty with the laser; but this is significantly less accurate. Smart bombs are quite cheap compared to most guided weapons, generally costing only a few thousand pounds on top of the price of the actual bomb. It is not always remembered that they have a failure rate of around 10 per cent. This means that smart bombs will still cause a lot of civilian casualties if dropped into urban areas, no matter how precisely the target may have been located and identified.

SNAF (Soviet Naval Air Forces): the other great threat to the Royal Navy during the cold war, complementing the submarines of the Red Banner Northern Fleet. The SNAF favoured the use of long-range high-altitude bombers which would launch massive, fairly slow, high-trajectory anti-ship missiles against the NATO fleets. This is the threat that the Type 42 destroyer was designed to counter. It might conceivably have worked in that particular case, owing to the old-time Soviets' sportsman-like conduct in approaching and attacking at high altitude, ensuring that even a surface-ship radar would detect them hundreds of miles off.

Sonar: The only effective type of underwater sensor. Contrary to movie convention, it is seldom possible to see more than a few dozen metres through water: scenes in which the whole length of a submarine – or even, two submarines at once! – can be clearly made out are merely artistic licence. Sonar works on a similar principle to radar, using sound waves instead of radio. It is much less reliable and precise than radar and achieves much shorter detection ranges. Sonars are fitted in submarines and surface warships, employed in homing torpedoes, lowered into the sea from hovering anti-submarine helicopters, and are often deployed in sensor buoys dropped from a variety of aircraft. The complex and difficult-to-predict effects of water temperature, currents and salinity mean that the use of sonar is often as much of an art as a science. Just as with radar, a sonar set which is actively 'pinging' sound pulses into the water is easily detected by the enemy. It was formerly common practice to use very sensitive listening-only sonars ('passive' sonars) to detect machinery noise or other sounds emitted from enemy ships or submarines, but modern vessels can often cruise so silently as to render such tactics ineffective. The use of low-frequency active-pinging sets such as the new Sonar 2087 for the Royal Navy's frigates is the latest trend.

Sonar 2087: The current golden-haired child of British defence procurement. Sonar 2087 is intended to replace the present submarine-detecting equipment of the Type 23 anti-submarine frigate, which has never been of any use. Sonar 2087 is seen as a work of genius because it was 'de-risked'. This means that a prototype was actually built and tested before the equipment was put into production. 'De-risking' is portrayed as the very latest in good practice: expensive consultants were hired in order to come up with it. (It had been normal practice in defence procurement not to bother with prototypes and simply to hope that brand-new, cutting edge equipment would work perfectly even if nothing similar had ever been built before.) The big problem with Sonar 2087 is not whether it works, however; it is simply that it isn't actually necessary. With the Soviets out of the picture, there is only a tiny submarine threat in our future wars, and even in the event of encountering submarines it will normally be exceptionally unwise for a frigate captain to take his ship anywhere near them: aircraft and our own subs are the preferred means in such a case.

Staff: a military word of almost mystical significance and various meanings. Properly speaking a staff is a group of officers who do not command units of their own but act as assistants to an important senior commander, helping him to plan and direct his battles and to prepare and maintain his forces when they are not fighting. The term staff is much misused, however, often being applied to almost any activity by uniformed personnel other than service in an operational unit.

Starstreak: A newish light SAM employed by the British Army's cloud-punchers in addition to Rapier. Starstreak is deployed in small vehicles, and there is also a shoulder-launched version.

Storm Shadow: The RAF's latest toy, a short-ranged cruise missile which is released from a Tornado bomber. It reportedly costs around £2 million a pop, despite the fact that Britain has ordered fully 500 and it is being made for the French as well. It is very hard to see why Britain needed the Storm Shadow at all, given that we already had proper Tomahawk cruise missiles, which are much longer ranged and so can be fired from a ship or submarine safely out at sea, rather than requiring a Tornado crew to fly over hostile territory and an airbase somewhere for the Tornado's fifty-odd support personnel, all now targets for local extremists or whoever. Tomahawks, when bought in the hundreds, cost less than a quarter what Storm Shadows do, too. Storm Shadow, it is true, does have a penetrator warhead which is said to be very useful for hitting deep bunkers and the like, but first-hand reports from ordnance-disposal teams in Baghdad suggest that it is highly unreliable, and in any case such targets are rare and the need to strike them dubious. The true reason why Britain has bought hundreds of rubbishy Storm Shadows and only a few dozen vastly more useful Tomahawks is that Storm Shadow is partly British made and Tomahawk is American.

Strike: A popular military word generally referring to the delivery of a large explosive warhead of some kind. Also employed in a wider sense by the RAF: Strike Command is the part of the air force containing all its useable combat aircraft and units, including air-to-air fighters, radar, transports, helicopters, ground infantry and many other things aside from strike planes.

Presumably the RAF considers that the primary purpose of all these other things is to support the delivery of Strikes.

Submarine: A naval vessel with a greater or lesser ability to manoeuvre beneath the sea's surface. These are of two main types, conventional and nuclear-powered. A conventional (or diesel-electric) submarine uses diesel engines, which require large supplies of fresh air and have to be shut down whenever the submarine dives, from which point it must run on battery power. While on batteries, a submarine can only move at a crawl. It can briefly achieve speeds approaching those of surface ships, but this will usually drain the batteries completely in less than half an hour: such a burst of speed must normally be saved for making a getaway after launching torpedoes. These very severe limits on underwater speed and range mean that a diesel submarine must normally run on the surface if it is to get anywhere near an enemy fleet or convoy – such was very much the case with the German U-boats of World War II, which were of this type. Unfortunately for the diesel submariner, the moment he appears on the surface, or even raises his periscope, he will be quite easily detected on radar and promptly destroyed. (This is also the case when using a 'snorkel' air tube to run diesels while just under the surface – and anyway the snorkel limits underwater speed nearly as badly as running on batteries.) A nuclear-powered submarine is much more dangerous: it can stay underwater for months if need be, going as fast as a surface ship – or even faster – the whole time. The present heavy bias of the Royal Navy toward anti-submarine warfare developed in response to the numerous nuclear-powered subs of the Red Banner Northern Fleet. Fortunately, nuclear-propelled submarines are possessed only by the five major world powers: in the post-cold war era they are not a likely threat. Submarines are normally armed with torpedoes, and perhaps ship-killer missiles such as the Harpoon configured for underwater firing. Major powers also use submarines as launch platforms for cruise missiles and ICBMs.

STA (Surveillance and Target Acquisition): A particular type of recce, in which one searches out juicy military targets over a wide area, ranging far beyond one's own forward units. Once these juicy targets are found they will be blown up by one or another long-range weapon system (the army would usually prefer that this be some kind of artillery rather than an air weapon or cruise missile). STA is perhaps best done by Special Forces, ASTOR type aircraft and/or UAVs. However, in the British Army, STA is also seen as justifying the retention of an otherwise disproportionately large number of light-tank cavalry units.

Territorial: The Territorial Army is an organisation of volunteer army reservists, most of whom have not previously served in the full-time, regular forces. There are parallel naval and air force organisations. Such servicemen and women normally have civilian jobs, and carry out military training during evenings and weekends. Formerly the volunteer reserve forces were almost never used: when there was a need for supplementary manpower it was more common to recall regulars who had recently left. It is probably still the case that in general the forces would rather have recent ex-regulars than part-timers, but the call-up of reservists is now so frequent an occurrence that the use of mostly unwilling personnel is not seen as politically acceptable, and during the 1990s the volunteer part-timers became the usual first choice.

TIALD (Thermal Imaging And Laser Designation) Pod: A weapons-targeting pod of this type must normally be fitted to any aircraft wishing to drop smart bombs effectively. The pod's infrared camera will enable the air crew to see through darkness, clouds, smoke, sandstorms etc and pick out enemy tanks, guns, armoured infantry carriers or whatever. These can then be marked with a laser pointer, which allows the smart bomb to home in accurately on the target. Unfortunately, the RAF's TIALD pod doesn't work properly (it was made by GEC, now a division of British Aerospace). In Iraq in 2003, British aircraft could normally only identify their targets in clear visibility, while American planes happily carried on wiping out the Iraqi army regardless of conditions. Another triumph for Defence Procurement.

Tomahawk: the standard American cruise missile, also procured in limited numbers by the British forces. It is fired from a ship or submarine safely out at sea to strike pretty much any target in the world. Only very advanced defences would be able to stop such attacks. AWACS or an equivalent directing modern fighters could do so, but Tomahawk flies too low to be detected by ordinary ground radars except in unusual circumstances. High-tech surface-based systems such as Goalkeeper or various light SAMs might defend specific locations against Tomahawk attack, but not large regions.

Tornado: Yet another great British fiasco. The Tornado fast combat jet was made collaboratively by several western European countries to implement the now-discredited low-level-attack doctrine. The idea was that speedy, low-flying Tornados would slip through below Soviet radar coverage and knock out enemy airbases in the event of the cold war ever turning hot. Fortunately, the occasion never arose, but RAF Tornados did test the concept in 1991. Even against comparatively feeble Iraqi defences, the British fliers were decimated for very little in the way of appreciable results. RAF higher command resolutely refuse to admit any such thing, but they have since quietly discarded the Tornado bomber's low-level weaponry and re-equipped it with systems designed for use from higher altitudes. There is also a Tornado fighter version, made by British Aerospace, widely regarded as one of the worst air-to-air combat aircraft in the world. The RAF was compelled to take it, as it was the only British make available: the Saudis were the only other buyer.

Torpedo: The main underwater weapon, apart from mines. A torpedo is driven at high speed (considering that it is moving through water) by one of several kinds of motive power. Old-fashioned types simply run in a straight line and must be aimed very carefully to achieve a hit, but modern ones seek their target. A torpedo is generally half again or twice as fast as even the speediest ships or submarines, and so will be able to intercept them from various ranges depending on their speed and whether they are approaching or going away. In many cases where the torpedo is older or less capable and the target is moving fast, slow-moving torpedo launch platforms may be unable to get into a position where their torpedoes can reach the target. Furthermore, torpedoes are always limited in range compared to above-surface weapons. (This has led more advanced submarine forces to favour subsurface-launched missiles for use against surface vessels.) Torpedoes are of two main classes: long-range heavyweight ones launched from submarines and short-range lightweight ones which are normally dropped into the sea from aircraft. Lightweight torpedoes are employed exclusively against submarines, and generally activate their own tracking sonar as soon as they enter the water. If they have been dropped close enough to the sub they will swiftly find it and hit it. The lightweight torpedo has supplanted the depth charge, which was simply a warhead with no propulsion at all. As one might expect, it was a rare event indeed to actually cause any damage to a sub using depth charges. This formerly didn't matter very much, as conventionally-powered submarines could not keep up with a surface fleet when underwater and were no threat at all if driven below periscope depth. Nuclear depth charges might have been rather more effective, but have also been phased out.

Type 23 Frigate: The mainstay of the British surface fleet, and the Royal Navy's latest ship. It was designed in the 1970s to hunt the Soviet submarines of that day. These subs were extremely noisy, and could be detected by simply listening for them with passive sonar: this was to be the main purpose of the Type 23, and for this reason it is capable of cruising almost entirely silently itself (which cost a pretty penny). Sadly, the newer Soviet subs of the 1980s were too quiet to be heard, rendering the Type 23 obsolete before it was even built. Then, at the turn of the 90s, the Soviet sub fleet ceased to be a threat altogether, meaning that the Royal Navy now had almost no need to hunt submarines at all. Despite this, expensive Type 23s were delivered, and further batches ordered, all through the 1990s. This was all the more irritating as when they first began to arrive, their combat computer systems didn't work, forcing the crews to work on paper in the style of the 1940s rather than using proper battle displays. By that point the ships were so late that the navy decided to accept them rather than admit to the problem. The computers weren't sorted out for many years, and once that was fixed there was still the problem of the frigates being unable to detect submarines: hence the Sonar 2087 project, currently underway, although this is really a case of throwing good money after bad. The Type 23 is occasionally described as having purposes other than hunting submarines, but in fact it possesses no capability which could justify its substantial cost and sizeable crew.

Type 42 Destroyer: The current British destroyer, intended for the defence of a fleet against attacking aircraft and missiles, specifically against Soviet Naval Air Forces. These vessels are seagoing antiques, long obsolete, never really effective and now mostly unserviceable. Even in the Falklands, over two decades ago when they were fairly new, they proved largely impotent against Argentine air strikes. This is as much because the whole concept of surface-based anti-aircraft systems is severely flawed as it is because the Type 42 is a bad design. Nevertheless, the Royal Navy is pressing ahead with the Type 45, a colossally expensive, brand-new Type 42.

Type 45 Destroyer: The new air-defence destroyers for the Royal Navy, essentially exactly the same as Type 42s but with updated missile and radar technology. It is thought that the concept may work this time, even though it failed comprehensively on the first try. If the Type 45 destroyers function perfectly they will be able to defend future British fleets and convoys from limited numbers of sea-skimming anti-ship missiles and attacking planes, both of which threats are rare and anyway better dealt with by jet fighters and airborne radar aircraft. It is more plausible that the ships' performance will be less than perfect, as their computer software is to be Microsoft Windows based and their weapons (PAAMS) are a collaborative European project like the Merlin, the Eurofighter or the A400M. Each Type 45 is to cost approximately £1 billion, almost enough to buy a carrier whose aircraft could not only do the destroyer's job better but also many other much more likely tasks.

UAV (Unmanned Aerial Vehicle): The usual military term for remote-controlled drone aircraft. These are now in widespread use by better-funded military forces. Their development was initially driven by army artillerymen, who wished to obtain a means of aerial recce under their own control (manned aircraft having a distressing tendency to destroy all the targets found themselves, leaving little for the artillery to do). In the British forces, UAVs remain under artillery control at present, and so are used mainly for STA activities within artillery range. In America, other agencies now employ UAVs. The US Air Force uses them far beyond friendly lines, mainly to find targets for strike aircraft. The CIA has also employed UAVs as weapons platforms in their own right, notably to assassinate specific people in otherwise difficult to reach areas. A UAV can have much more range and endurance than a manned aircraft, normally needs much less in the way of support and basing, and of course does not require an air crew to run risks. It is possible that UAVs will eventually take over most manned aircraft tasks: there will soon be few if any technical obstacles to this. However, such a change would involve huge and painful cultural readjustments within the various military air arms, so it may occur only slowly if at all.

Utility Helicopter: A helicopter intended to carry personnel or materiel, rather than to fight in its own right. By far the most useful type of military helicopter, and always the one most in demand during real operations. Utility lifters are much less popular at procurement time, for reasons of inter-service strife and idiocy: as a result, Britain is currently very short of such aircraft. Many helos of this type were originally developed as sub-hunters or attack helicopters, but were later supplied in a much cheaper utility variant; examples include the Sea King, Merlin and Lynx.

Voyska PVO: The old Soviet air-superiority and air-defence force, which was separate from the main air force. It controlled Soviet fighter aircraft and associated forces. 'Voyska' means 'Troops' or 'Force': PVO stands for Protivo Vozdushnaya Oborona, or Anti-Air Defence.

Warrior: the current British AIFV. It has performed well during the armoured-warfare blitzkriegs in the Gulf, although the bulk of the opposition in those cases had been so cut up by air power that no great trial of armoured strength can be said to have taken place. Perhaps more importantly, Warrior is also extremely popular and effective in the current counter-insurgency struggle being waged in Iraq. British Warriors are frequently plastered with RPGs and occasionally hit by large, powerful IEDs, but so far have almost always preserved their passengers' lives. The severe logistic burdens associated with heavily armoured tracked vehicles would be appear to be conclusively worthwhile in this case.

INDEX

aerial reconnaissance 158–62; *see also* ASTOR; JSTARS
Afghanistan 24, 83, 155, 172
air-air refuelling 107–8
Air Interdiction 134
air superiority 103, 296–98
air support 3, 71, 89, 91–2, 130, 153–8, 167
air-to-ground weapons 255
air transport 168–71, 173–8, 299–300
Airbus Military 175
Airbus UK 176
aircraft: *see also* bombers; fighters; transport aircraft
  A-10 Thunderbolt 154
  armament 70, 105
  attack 130
  comparison with artillery 156
  comparison with helicopters 87–8, 100
  gunships 154–6
  indiscriminate nature of killing 16
  need to operate from ships 296–7
  radar 122–3
  RN loss of control 209–10
  role in anti-submarine warfare 196
  strike jets 156–7, 162
  transport of 179–80
  wild weasel 132, 137
airfield defence 42
airhead seizure 35
Al Qaeda 146
Al Yamamah weapons contract 246–8
Albania 140–41
Allied Command Europe Rapid Reaction Corps 142
ALLIED FORCE, operation 138
ALLIED HARVEST, operation 138
ammunition
  artillery 68, 70, 72–3, 76
  failures 146
  runway denial 135
  tanks 50, 51
  transport 70
amphibious operations 40–41, 90, 172–3, 183–5, 186
anti-aircraft units 76
anti-submarine warfare
  aircraft 196
  continued development of equipment for 275
  depth charges 198
  helicopters 96–8, 198, 199: *see also*

  helicopters; Merlin
  lack of threat 199–200, 327–8
  perceived threat 194–7
  sonar 197, 199, 251–2, 255, 340–41
  Type 23 frigates' uselessness 197–9
anti-surface warfare 200–202
Arbuthnot, James 86, 290
Armed Forces Parliamentary Scheme 291
armoured forces 310–311
armoured infantry fighting vehicles 30–31, 49, 309
arms exports 268–9
arms plot mechanism 30, 37
  Army, the: *see also* artillery; infantry; infantrymen; officers; tanks
  bomb disposal career tracks 221
  career paths 223–4
  ceremonial duties 38, 63, 76–7, 301, 322
  current situation 3
  cut backs and reorganisation 33, 37–40, 78, 282
  deployment 166–73
  establishment 64
  and helicopters 89–92, 98
  lightening 298–99
  MoD doctrine 275
  promotion 231–2
  quality in 1914 2
  ranks 232, 234, 293
  regimental system 28
  role 293–6
  share of defence budget 273–4
  strength 219–20
  support personnel 220
  Territorial 343
  women in 16–17
Army formations
  3 Para 91
  5 Airborne Brigade 34, 35
  7 Parachute Regiment, Royal Horse Artillery 75
  16 Air Assault Brigade 35, 75, 95, 99, 309, 310, 325
  321 Explosive Ordnance Disposal Company, RAOC 294
  Argyll and Sutherland Highlanders 34
  Army Air Corps 89, 114
  Guards 38, 39, 322
  Household Cavalry 49, 63, 63–4, 322

Joint Nuclear, Biological and Chemical
    Defence Regiment 57
the King's Troop, Royal Horse Artillery 76–7
Light Infantry 32
Parachute Regiment 28, 34, 35–7, 38, 39,
    309–10
Royal Armoured Corps 49
Royal Electrical and Mechanical Engineers,
    Corps of (REME) 54–6, 115, 332, 333
Royal Engineers 55, 331–2
Royal Green Jackets 15
Royal Irish Regiment 39
Royal Logistics Corps 166, 332, 334
Royal Regiment of Artillery 66, 69, 78
Royal Regiment of Scotland 38
Royal Tank Regiment 57–8, 314
Staff Corps 238
Third Regiment Royal Horse Artillery 69, 72
artillery 16
    4.5 inch naval guns 212–13
    105mm 75–6, 212–13
    155mm 299
    accuracy 66–7
    air-defence units 76
    AS90 66, 70, 76, 77, 156, 338
    AS90 Bravehearts 72, 314
    battalion 27
    beaten zone 67
    ceremonial duties 76–7
    comparison with aircraft 156
    cost 78
    depth fire 71, 72–3
    destructive power 65
    direct fire 65
    elite spotters 74
    Forward Observer Officers 66, 73–4, 299
    'Horse' 77
    increasing range of 72–3
    indirect fire 65–6
    infantry role 78
    and the invasion of Iraq, 2003 68, 69, 71–2,
        76
    kinetic targeting 71–2
    the King's Troop, Royal Horse Artillery 76–7
    lack of precision 67
    light 75–6
    logistical nightmare 69–70
    organization 68, 69
    parachute 34, 75
    quality, 1914 2
    reorganisation 77
    rocket 67–8, 77
    role 69
    self propelled guns 66, 338
    shells 68, 70, 72–3, 76
    Surveillance and Target Acquisition (STA)
        73–4
    threat of air support to 71
    use of UAVs 74–5
ASTOR (airborne stand off radar) 160–62, 255,
    298, 311
AWACS 122–3, 312

Barrow, General Robert H. 165
Belgrade 139
Bellamy, Professor Christopher 233
Berlin airlift, 1948–49 291
Bett Report, the 232–3, 234
Bett, Sir Michael 232
bio-weapons 257
Blair, Tony 141, 279–80, 287
Bloody Sunday, 1972 39
Blunt, Crispin 274

body armour 58–62, 300, 317–19
Boeing 94–5, 176
bombers
    accuracy 129–30, 134
    B-1 bomber programme 132
    B-52 Stratofortress 131
    casualties 129, 135
    deep bombing 151–3
    development of 127–32
    failure of 129–30
    future developments 162–3
    Jaguar 282, 324–5
    low flying 132–6, 137
    made obsolete by ICBMs 131–2
    Serbia bombing campaign, 1999 137–44, 149
    stealth 132
    Tornado 106–7, 133–6, 150, 161–2, 247, 254,
        344
    V-bombers 131, 134
bombs
    accuracy 129–30, 134, 136–7, 145
    cluster 314–15
    failures 146, 339
    jettisoning 138
    JP233 135, 137
    precision 136–7
    smart 136–7, 144–5, 146, 156, 341
boots, combat 19–20
Borneo 92
Bowman digital comms infrastructure 285–6
British Aerospace (BAe) 312–13
    and the 2004–05 defence budget shortfall
        276
    aerospace industry consolidated into 106
    Al Yamamah revenue 247
    Al Yamamah weapons contract 246–8
    as asset-stripper 244–6, 269
    and civil aircraft production 252–3
    continued existence 124, 125
    domination of British arms manufacture
        249–50
    employees 268
    and the Eurofighter project 119, 120, 248,
        250–1
    failure of 253
    and the FLA project 176, 255
    government responsibility for 271
    involvement in future kit developments 255
    involvement with ASTOR 160–61
    lack of confidence in 160
    MoD working relationship 266
    need for foreign involvement 256
    and the Nimrod upgrade project 264, 265
    opposition to reform 302
    origins 243–4
    political clout 272–3
    ponderousness of 3–4
    Portillo non-executive director of 265
    privatisation 244
    purchase of Royal Ordnance 45
    quality of product 252, 254
    redundancies 245–6
    refusal to release full technical data 260
    and the Sea Wolf 211
    Serious Fraud Office investigation 248
    shipbuilding 249
    software engineers 268
    Sonar 2087 project 251–2, 255
    and Storm Shadow cruise missile 152–3
    subsidies 244
    suspected bribery 247–8
    takeover of Rover Group 245
    Tornado 106–7, 344

turns back on Europe 267
Type 45 destroyer contract 209
British Aircraft Corporation 244
Brown, Gordon 278–81, 282–3
Burridge, Air Marshal Brian 148
buy-British policy 105, 160–61, 174, 176, 253, 256, 262, 267

casualties
  artillery 65
  autopsies 60
  bomber crews 129, 135
  civilian 146–7, 149–50
  Falklands War 179
  friendly fire 60–62, 122
  invasion of Iraq 146, 149–50
  tendency to be low 2
CBI (Confederation of British Industry) 281
Cebrowski, Vice Admiral Arthur K. 8
Challenger II 50–51, 56, 61, 63, 64, 254, 314
chemical weapons 257, 304
chief of defence staff 235
Chief of Joint Operations 235
Chiefs of Staff 303
Clark, General Wesley 140, 143–4
Clinton, Bill 141
close air support, weakness in 3
cluster weapons 67–8, 314–15
Cole, USS, suicide attack on 200
collaborative projects: see also Eurofighter
  project
  Common New Generation Frigate 206
  the F-35 119–20
  FLA project 174–8, 255, 312
  Merlin anti-submarine helicopters 96–7
  PAAMS 207–8, 331
  the Tornado F3 106
combat engineers 27
combat personnel, minority of MoD employees 9
command authority 235–6
command structure 235–7, 241
Commando 21 41
Commons Defence Select Committee 86, 158, 263, 290–92, 315
communications 285
computers 207, 208, 215
Conservative Party, defence policy 287–8
Dartmouth 53–4
Day, Sir John 250
de-risking 251
Defence Aviation Repair Centre 115
defence budget
  2004–05 shortfall 276–84
  2005 election promises 287
  artillery spend 78
  Challenger spend 64
  cuts 280–84
  division between services 273–4
  helicopter spend 100–101
  industry subsidised by 268–70
  majority of workers 4
  potential savings 301–3
  and the survival of BAe 124
  from taxation 11
  wastage 9
Defence Clothing and Textiles Agency (DCTA) 20
defence establishment 4, 12
Defence Export Sales Organisation 268
Defence Logistics Organisation 3–4, 166, 221, 229, 259, 317
defence ministers 272
defence policy

2004 defence cuts 286–7
  lack of 182
  lack of scrutiny 290–2
Defence Procurement Agency 3–4, 162–3, 250, 259, 275
'Delivering Security in a Changing World' white
  paper 284–7
deployment, logistical demands 166–73
dinosaurs 4
Directorate of Special Forces 36, 338–9
divorce 26
Dixon, Dr Norman F. 230
donkeys 1–2, 12
drug busting 213–14
Dutch navy 17

(European Aeronautics, Defence and Space) 267
effects-based operations 284
'effects-based technology' 7
Enfield Lock 244
Enhanced Combat Body Armour (ECBA) 58–62, 317–18
Euro-forces 289
Eurofighter project 119–20, 158, 318
  aircraft order 120–21, 124–6, 250–51
  BAe involvement 119, 120, 248, 250–51
  budget peak 276
  cost 120–21, 123–4
  cost per plane 120–21, 125
  dependence on America 261
  Liberal Democrat plans 288
  need to cancel 297
  quality of 254
  range 120, 202
  root of today's problems 287
European arms industry and market 256–7, 266–7
Evans, Sir Richard 248
expeditionary warfare 295–301
Falklands War, 1982
  air attack and 103
  Argentine pilots 118
  Argentine submarines 96, 196–7
  artillery 75
  Bluff Cove 205
  casualties 179
  Exocet missiles 204–5
  friendly fire cases 61
  lack of air support 180
  landings 41, 173
  lessons 2
  naval gunfire support 213
  sinking of the General Belgrano 201
  sinking of the Atlantic Conveyor 205
Felix Centre, the 294
fighters: see also Eurofighter project
  crews 108–13
  F-15 Eagle 118, 124, 320
  F-16 89
  F-22 Raptor 124, 320
  F-35 119–20, 203, 255, 260, 299, 319, 320–21
  future requirements 118
  Harrier 87, 88, 111, 162, 210, 252, 254, 323–4
  Lightning 105–6
  MiG-25 132
  need for 103–5, 118
  Phantom 105, 107
  Sea Harrier 107, 180, 202–3, 252, 323–4
  Tornado F3 105–8, 116–17, 118, 120, 247, 254, 344
Fiji, recruits from 18

financial retention incentives 112–13
fire storm effect 128
firemen's strike, 2003 228
Fleet Air Arm 92, 114, 181, 193, 209
forced theatre entry 173
foreign purchased equipment, ability to use 258–9
France 46, 90, 175–6, 267
French Foreign Legion 46
FRES (Future Rapid Effects System) 299–300
friendly-fire cases 60–62, 122
Future Offensive Air System project 162–3, 319
Future-Rapid Effects System 168, 319–20
future role for armed forces 293–6

Gardiner, Peter 247
General Electric Corporation (GEC) 122, 246
Germany 46, 142, 175–6, 267
global economy 257–8
Goalkeeper automatic gun system 211, 255, 321
government 271–2, 293
GPS (Global Positioning System) 144–5, 260, 321–2
Gray, James 291–2
Gray, Group Captain Peter 151
Gregory, Brigadier Andrew 68, 71, 75
grenades 20, 21, 24, 67, 255, 334
Gulf War (1991) 22, 32, 68, 87, 108, 134–6, 137, 200–201
Gurkhas, the 18, 38

Hatfield 245
Hawker Siddeley Aviation 244
Hawker Siddeley Dynamics 244
headquarters buildings 145–6
Heckler and Koch 45
helicopters
  the 4000 pound rule 91–2
  advantages 33–6
  aging 93–4
  anti-submarine 96–8, 198, 199: see also helicopters; Merlin
  Apache 85–7, 88, 89, 92, 254, 310
  attack 85–9, 154, 200–201, 313–14, 322
  attempt to reform situation 98–100
  Bell UH-I Iroquois (Huey) 80
  Chinook 81, 94, 94–5, 100, 255, 314
  comparison with aircraft 87–8, 100
  complexity 79–80
  cost of Apaches 85–6
  cost of Merlin anti-submarine project 96–7
  costs 100–101
  counter-thrust 80
  engines 79
  fuel consumption 81
  fuselage 80
  Gazelle 85, 321
  gearbox 79
  gunships 324
  inter-service conflict and 88–99
  lack of troop carrying 34
  Lynx 92, 254, 326
  maintenance 81
  Merlin 94, 96–8, 100, 180–81, 254, 298, 327–8
  mission systems 80–81
  modifications 93
  nap-of-the-earth 87
  numbers 95
  performance and capability 81
  pilots attitudes 92–3
  Puma 93, 94, 254, 331
  radar 203, 209

reconnaissance 85
role 82–5
rotors 79–80
Sea Kings 93, 94, 96, 97–8, 180–81, 254, 337
speed 81
transport 82, 83, 93–5
transporting 81, 82
UH-60L Black Hawk 100
use in the Suez Crisis 90–91
usefulness 100
utility 93, 100, 326, 328, 331, 337, 347
vulnerability 82–3, 87
weakness in 3
high-intensity warfare 59
Hogg, Ian 21
homelessness 125
Hoon, Geoff 33, 61–2, 118, 279, 284
horse riding 53–4
hospital ships 183
Hungary 141–2

IEDs (Improvised Explosive Devices) 324, 332
infantry
  air assault 33–7, 92, 309
  airborne 309–10
  armoured 30–31, 33, 39
  Conservative plans to save 287–8
  cut backs and reorganisation 37–40, 282
  light 32–3
  mechanised 31, 327
  organization 20, 25–9
  tank killing 52
infantrymen
  background 16–18
  clothing 19
  combat boots 19–20
  definition 15
  educational standards 17–18
  encounter interaction options 16
  fire teams 20
  foreign recruits 18, 47
  kit 19–20, 31–2
  loyalties 37–8
  need for more 295
  percentage of Army personnel 15
  quality 46
  recruits 17–18, 47
  role 29–37
  salaries 25–6
  terms of service 46–7
  training 18–19, 21
  waterproofs 20
  weapons 20–25
  webbing 20
  women as 16–17
Insys 255
inter-service conflict 3, 87, 88–99, 150, 157, 178, 181, 302–4
international law 305
IRA 39
Iran 258, 260, 304–6
Iraq 6, 33, 107, 148–9, 150, 172
Iraq, invasion of, 2003
  air strikes 145–50, 151–2, 156
  Al Faw landings 213
  amphibious operations 41
  armoured assault 33
  artillery 68, 69, 71–2, 76
  bombing 156, 157–8
  death of Sergeant Roberts 58–62, 318
  expenses 278
  helicopters 94, 209
  Iraqi military 2

logistics 239
RAF personnel deployed 220
SA80 used in 24
Tornados role 108
use of Apaches 88
use of tanks 50–51
Israel 95, 114–15, 156–7
Italy 117
Jackson, General Sir Mike 37, 38–9, 78, 142, 143–4, 303
Japan 46, 128
John Hopkins University 146, 149
Johnson, Samuel 11
joint authority 303–5
Joint Force Harrier 110, 209–10, 325
Joint Helicopter Command 99, 234, 325–6
JSTARS (joint surveillance and target acquisition radar system) 159–60, 161, 298, 311
'just enough, just in time' stores policy 259
Jutland, battle of, 1916 189

K-FOR (Kosovo Force) 143–4
Keetch, Paul 289
Kipling, Rudyard 188, 293
Kosovo 22, 138–44, 149
Kuwait 172

language, confusing nature of 8
LAW (Light Anti-tank Weapon) 326
Liberal Democrats, defence policy 288–9
lions 1
living costs 26
Lockheed 176
logistics
    air transport 168–71, 173–8, 299–300
    air transport capacity 170–71, 173, 177–8
    artillery 69–70
    civilian personnel 221
    daily supply consumption 169
    and deployment 166–73
    fuel 170
    importance of 165–6
    local supplies 170
    officers 229
    personnel 166
    procurement 229
    sea transport 168, 171–3, 178–86
    sea transport capacity 184–5
    spare parts policy 259
    water supplies 170
low-intensity warfare 33, 59, 294–5
Lygo, Admiral Sir Raymond 249–50

Macedonia 140, 141
machine guns
    7.62mm medium machine guns 22
    general purpose (GPMGs) 26
    light 20
    the Maxim 7
    Minimi 24, 44, 255, 328
    quality, 1914 2
manufacturing industry 268–70
media coverage 5–9
Members of Parliament
    and the buy-British policy 262
    conflicts of interest 290
    constituency protection 262–3
    and defence policy 290–292
    lack of knowledge 291–2
    military experience 291–2
    salaries 292
Memoirs of an Infantry Officer (Sassoon) 231–2
merchant ships 171, 172, 178–9, 196

Microsoft Windows 208, 261, 346
Miles, Sergeant Jamie 24
military forces, need for 4
Milošević, Slobodan 138, 140, 141, 142–3
Min Veterans 272
mines 191–2
Minister of Defence 272, 274
Ministry of Defence
    2004–05 budget shortfall 276–84
    admits SA80 reliability problems 22
    BAe working relationship 266
    'body armour' controversy 58, 60
    and the Chinook HC3 94–5
    civilian payroll 64
    cock-ups 25, 276–84
    contracts 277–8
    desire for JSTARS type system 159
    employees 9
    and the Eurofighter project 120, 121, 124, 125
    'fat cats' 9
    and the FLA project 174–5, 177
    and friendly-fire cases 61
    helicopter project team 99–100
    and the invasion of Iraq, 2003 278
    make do solutions 22
    mandarins 273
    media apparatus 6–7
    and military doctrine 274–5
    need for change 4–5
    permanent bureaucracy 273–5
    politicians and 272–3
    reform 275
    response to mistakes 60
    Roberts investigation 62
    on salaries 25–6
    as source of information 12–13
    space warfare project team 99
    wastage 9
missiles
    air-to-air 118, 255
    ALARM 254
    anti-aircraft 46, 154
    Aster 206–7
    ballistic 315
    counter-missiles 206–8
    criticisms of 103–5
    cruise 73, 152–3, 162, 254, 255, 297–8, 315, 341, 343–4
    Exocet 204–5, 319
    Harpoon 255, 319–21
    ICBMs 131–2, 324
    MILAN 255, 328
    Moskit (Mosquito) 206
    Patriot 313
    Principle Anti-Air Missile System (PAAMS) 207–8, 331
    Rapier 76, 254, 331
    Sea Dart 204, 205, 254, 337
    Sea Wolf 211, 254, 337
    ship-killer 204, 206–7, 319, 322–3
    ship-to-air 204
    Starstreak 76, 254, 341
    Stinger anti-aircraft 46
    Storm Shadow 152–3, 162, 254, 315, 341
    surface to air (SAM) 300, 334–5
    Tomahawk 152–3, 255, 297–8, 315, 341, 343–4
    Vampires 207
Moseley, Lieutenant General T. Michael 74
Multiple Launch Rocket System 67–8, 77, 255, 301, 328–9

National Audit Office 329
national interest 274
national security, as obstruction to public
    knowledge 7–8
NATO 137–44, 149, 329
Naval Air Command 210
naval gunfire support 212–13
network enabled capability 284–7, 329–30
Nimrod project 123, 160, 254, 263–6, 275, 276,
    281–2, 301, 330
9/11 terrorist attacks 146, 147
non-commissioned officers 25–6, 28, 293
Northern Ireland 2, 39, 59, 83–4, 293–4
Northwood 240
Nott, John 198–9
nuclear-biological-chemical defence 57
nuclear weapons 128–9, 131, 257, 304–6

officers
    air commodores 226
    air marshals 110, 226
    base commanders 223
    brigadiers 29, 225
    captains 27
    captains, RN 230–31
    career paths 12–13, 27, 223–5
    cavalry 53–4
    colonels 29, 111, 233–4
    desk jockeys 227–9
    field marshal 29
    flight-lieutenants 110
    frigate/destroyer specialists 192
    front-line experience 223–5
    generals 29, 219–20, 225
    group-captains 226
    half pay 234
    lieutenant-colonels 27, 29, 111, 233–4
    lieutenant-generals 29, 225
    logistics and procurement 229
    major-generals 29, 225
    majors 26
    mess bills 54–6
    naval aviation 110
    promotion 230–32
    proportion of desk jockeys 226–7
    RAF 109–10
    ranks 293
    REME 55
    salaries 9–10, 99, 292
    second-lieutenants 26
    senior naval 192–3, 216, 217–18
    senior RAF 226
    service chiefs 235
    special forces 237
    squadron-leaders 110
    staff 27, 235–40, 341
    tactical and strategic role 238–9
    top heavy with 9
    wing-commanders 110, 226
order of battle, outdated 10
organization
    army corps 29
    artillery 68, 69
    battalion 27–8
    battle groups 28–9
    brigade 29
    divisions 29
    field army 29
    headquarters companies 27
    infantry 20, 25–9
    large-regiment concept 37–40
    manoeuvre support companies 27
    platoons 26

regimental 28, 37
rifle companies 26–7
Royal Marine Commandos 41
sections 25–6
tanks 49, 52, 56–7

parachute operations 34–5, 90–91, 173
paramilitary forces, fighting personnel 15
peacekeeping 293
pensions 277
Pentagon 146, 266
Permanent Joint Headquarters 235–6, 240, 331
Persons Of No Tactical Importance (PONTIs)
    240
Phalanx automatic gun system 211, 255, 331
political consciousness 304
pongoes 140, 331
Portillo, Michael 263–6
pre-emptive invasion 305
prerequisites for reform 5
Prime Minister 274
Priština 143–4
privatisation 44–5, 244
procurement ministers 272
Project Red Dragon 115
Provisional IRA 83–4
public knowledge 5–8
public opinion 4, 5, 7
public scrutiny, lack of 5

radar 104, 105, 107, 122–3, 203, 208–9, 298,
    311, 331
radio 285
radio operators 26
RAF Air Power Review 151
RAF Coltishall 280, 282
ranks 25, 27, 29, 110, 232–4, 293, 301
Raytheon 160–61
reconnaissance units 27, 56–7, 298, 332
recruits 1, 17–18, 47
Red Army 66
Red Banner Northern Fleet 190, 332–3
reform, opposition to 301–4
Reid, Dr John 272
reservists 333
riflemen 15
rifles
    7.62mm SLR 23
    AK47 61, 310
    assault 22, 311
    M16 23, 44
    quality, 1914 2
    SA80; see SA80 (L85A1)
Roberts, Sergeant Steve 58–62, 318
Robertson, George 98
rocket cluster-bomb systems 67, 77
Rolls Royce 253
Rosyth 262–3
Rover Group 245, 268
Royal Air Force: see also officers
    2004 defence cuts 282
    air support shortcomings 157–8
    aircrew 108–13
    career paths 224–5
    contribution 127
    deployment 113
    financial retention incentives 112–13
    future role 302
    gains control of RN aircraft 209–10
    ground personnel 113–16
    Harrier force 111, 210
    and helicopters 89, 91–4, 95, 98–9
    inability to deliver airborne brigade 35

lack of gunships 155
manpower problems 110–13
MoD doctrine 275
Navigators 109, 111, 112
non-flying 'wings' 113–14
overmanning 113–16
personnel-aircraft ratio 113–16
personnel turnover 116
Phantom forced on 106
potential adversaries 117–18
RAF Regiment 16, 41–2, 57, 334
ranks 110, 234, 293
role 127
salaries 109–10, 115
sea service 181
share of defence budget 273–4
support personnel 220–21
terms of service 115–16, 162
training 108–9
transport aircraft 170–171, 316
and UAVs 74–5
women in 109
Royal Fleet Auxiliary 171–2, 178, 184, 185,
  196, 333–4
  Argus 183, 200
Royal Marine Commandos 40–41, 191, 225,
  293
  3 Commando Brigade 75, 184, 315
  Commando Logistic Regiment 166
Royal Navy: *see also* officers; Royal Marine
  Commandos; warships
  2004 defence cuts 282
  admiral factory 216
  attacks on shore targets 150–51
  aviation officers 110
  career paths 224
  conservatism 189, 192, 218
  contribution 218
  current situation 3
  desire for frigates 198–9
  dislike of helicopter assault ships 182–3
  Engineer (Training Management) branch 222
  financial retention incentives 112
  forces the Phantom on the RAF 106
  friendly-fire cases 61
  helicopters 92, 93, 95–8
  hydrological surveying and charting flotilla
    185–6, 317
  infantry forces 16
  lack of sense 181
  loss of control of aircraft 209–10
  love of escorts 215–17
  mismanagement 218
  numbers of uniformed personnel 5
  plan for 2015 192
  principle warfare officers 214–15
  promotion 230–31
  quality, 1914 2
  ranks 234, 293
  sea command by desk jockeys 230
  share of defence budget 273–4
  shore postings 181
  strength 190–91, 192
  support personnel 221
  training 221–2
  Warfare or Executive Branch 224
  women in 17
Royal Ordnance, privatisation 44–5
Royal Small Arms Factory 44, 244, 336
RPGs (Rocket Propelled Grenades) 168–9
rucksacks 20, 31, 313
runway denial 134–6

SA80 (L85A1) 20, 336
  accuracy 21–2
  based on American design 257
  breech locking mechanism 22
  cost of modifications 23–4
  design flaws 21
  L85A2 22–3, 24–5, 336
  L86A1 Light Support Weapon 21, 21–2, 22,
    23
  L86A2 Light Support Weapon 24
  MoD press-briefing 43–5
  modification programme 22–4, 45
  need for endless maintenance 23
  paratroopers refuse to carry 22
  production 244–5
  production guaranteed 45
  quality of 254
  reputation 22
  whitewashes 21–2
salaries 9–10
  infantrymen 25–6
  MPs 292
  RAF 109–10, 115
  senior naval officers 216
  senior officers 99, 292
  X-factor 228
sanctions enforcement operations 213–14
Sandys, Duncan 103, 105
SAS 22, 23, 42–3, 46, 294, 335–6
Sassoon, Siegfried 231–2
Saudi Arabia 117, 124, 246–8
SBS 42–3, 336–7
Scimitar light tanks 56, 63
Scottish Aviation 244
sea transport 168, 171–3, 178–86
Security Studies Institute 233
Serbia bombing campaign, 1999 137–44, 149
shipbuilding 249, 253, 297
'shock and awe' 147
Shorts 161
Sierra Leone 212
Sikorsky, Igor 81
Sir Galahad, loss of 205
Skynet 286
sleeping bags 19, 20
smart procurement 250–51, 265, 276–7
Smith, Sir Roland 245–6
software 260
sonar 197, 199, 251–2, 255, 301, 340–1
Sonar 2087 project 251–2, 255, 301, 340–1
sovereignty 256
Soviet forces 30
Soviet Naval Air Forces 190, 339
Soviet Union, threat of 189–90
spare parts 258–9
special forces 42–6, 94–5, 237, 338–9
Squire, Rachel 262–3, 290
Stalin, Josef 66
Stirrup, Air Chief Marshal Sir Jock 303
strategic bombing 127, 128–30, 131
Strategic Defence Review, 1998 35, 98
submarines 342
  Astute class 255, 276, 311
  crews 217
  diesel 195–7
  lack of threat 199–200, 345
  perceived threat 194–7
  Soviet 190
  surface defence 201
  women excluded from 17
Suez Crisis, 1956 35, 90–91, 239
suicide vessels 200
supplementary incomes 54

support personnel
　administrative 222–3, 227
　Army 220
　career paths 223–5
　civilian 221
　RAF 220–21
　RN 221
　training 221–2
Suppression of Enemy Air Defences (SEAD) 132,
　337–8
Surveillance and Target Acquisition (STA) 73,
　342–3
Swayne, Major Desmond, MP 291

tanks: see also Challenger II
　army faith in 52
　cannon 50, 51
　cavalry officers 53–4
　definition 49
　deployment 51
　drawbacks 51
　formation reconnaissance units 56–7
　future need 299
　light 56–7, 63
　Main Battle Tank 49, 63, 326–7
　mechanics 54–5
　number of soldiers 64
　organization 49, 52, 56–7
　role 50–51
　shells 50, 51
　tank killing 51–2
targeting pods 157–8, 162, 254, 343
taxation 4, 9–10, 11, 24
technological interdependence 257–8
Thales 251–2, 267
torpedoes 254, 344–5
Torpy, Air-Vice-Marshal 157–8
training
　aircrew 108–9
　All Arms Commando Course 23
　cavalry 63
　infantry 18–19, 21
　marines 40
　P Company 36
　parachute 36
　personnel 221–2
　relevance 1
　SAS 337–8
　special forces 43
transport aircraft
　C-5 Galaxy 169–70, 315–6
　C-17 Globemaster 169–70, 173–4, 175, 177,
　　255, 299, 316
　FLA cost per plane 177
　FLA project 174–8, 255, 312
　Hercules 169, 170–171, 175, 177, 255, 291,
　　316
　Transall 175
Treasury, the 278–9, 286
two-power standard 188

UAVs (Unmanned Aerial Vehicles) 74–5, 85, 159,
　298, 346–7
United States of America
　air transport capacity 170–71, 173
　consent for operations 296
　defence cartels 266
　defence spending 257
　divisions 47
　and the global economy 257–8
　high-tech prevention 261
　inter-service conflict 157
　logistics 169–70

Office of Force Transformation 8
refusal to release full technical data 259–60
terms of service 46–7
use of UAVs 74
US Air Force 89
　air support 154–5
　air transport fleet 169–70
　B-1 bomber programme 132
　break away from army 131
　and the F-22 124
　and the Vietnam War 132
US Army 80, 89, 95, 100
US Marine Corps 157, 325
US Navy, strength 188

Vann, John Paul 16, 69, 77–8
vehicles
　Land Rovers 171
　Saxon 31, 167–8
　Stryker 300, 320
　trucks 32
　Viking 41
　Warrior 31, 167–8, 254, 320, 347
Vietnam War 39, 83, 132, 154
Vosper 254

warships
　air defence 200–201, 202–12
　aircraft carriers 106, 130, 185, 203–4,
　　209–10, 255, 296–297, 310, 319
　alternative to destroyers 208–9
　amphibious-warfare ships 183–5, 310
　Common New Generation Frigate 206
　cost per Type 23 frigate 213–14
　cost per Type 45 destroyer 208
　costs 200
　destroyers 194, 204, 205, 208–9, 210–11,
　　211–12, 215, 317
　digital networks 286
　dreadnoughts 2, 187–8
　escorts 194, 200, 201–2, 204, 214–7, 318
　escorts as tactical shields 205, 211
　fighter screen 203–4
　frigates 194, 198–9, 200, 205, 211, 212–13,
　　215, 319
　frigates running costs 216
　guns 212–13
　helicopter assault ships 182–3
　HMS Ardent 205
　HMS Daring 208
　HMS Ocean 182–3, 200
　HMS Sheffield 205
　minehunters 191, 192–3, 215
　MoD doctrine 275
　point defence 211
　quality 2, 254
　through-deck cruisers 179–82
　Type 23 frigate 197–9, 206, 213–14, 215,
　　345–6
　Type 42 destroyer 204–6, 212, 215, 282, 339,
　　346
　Type 45 destroyer 206–8, 209, 212, 255, 261,
　　346
　USS Cole 200
　as venues for cocktail parties 214–15
Wehrmacht, the 144
West, Admiral Sir Alan 205, 216, 217, 218, 303
Westland, Apache production 85–6
women 16–17, 43, 109
World War I 1, 65, 72, 127, 189
World War II 66, 103, 128–30, 179, 212
wounds 59